Cities and Cars

Cities and Cars

A Handbook of Best Practices

Edited by Roger L. Kemp

McFarland & Company, Inc., Publishers

Jefferson, North Carolina, and London

LIBRARY OF CONGRESS CATALOGUING-IN-PUBLICATION DATA

Cities and cars : a handbook of best
practices / edited by Roger L. Kemp
p.   cm.
Includes bibliographical references and index.

ISBN-13: 978-0-7864-2919-6 (softcover : 50# alkaline paper)

1. Traffic flow — Government policy — United States — Case studies.
2. Traffic congestion — Government policy — United States — Case studies.
3. Traffic engineering — Government policy — United States — Case studies.
4. Urban transportation — United States — Case studies.
5. Automobiles — United States — Case studies.   I. Kemp, Roger L.
HE355.C53   2007   388.3'420973 — dc22   2007004866

British Library cataloguing data are available

Cover photograph ©2007 PhotoAlto

Manufactured in the United States of America

*McFarland & Company, Inc., Publishers
Box 611, Jefferson, North Carolina 28640
www.mcfarlandpub.com*

To Eva, my mother,
who has made the world a better place

Acknowledgments

Grateful acknowledgment is made to the following organizations and publishers for granting permission to reprint the material contained in this volume: American Planning Association, Congressional Quarterly Inc., Hanley Wood, Harvard University, International City/County Management Association, Intertec Publishing Corporation, League of California Cities, Local Government Commission, National Association of Regional Councils, PRIMEDIA Business Magazines & Media Inc., Sage Publications, The Atlantic Monthly Company, Urban Land Institute, World Future Society, World Watch Institute.

Contents

Part III: The Future

Preface

Citizens for years have considered the automobile as a form of freedom. People can now live in the country, or suburbia, and work in the city. Conversely, they can live in the city and have a workplace in the country. Because of housing costs, many younger families are now forced to purchase their home many miles away from the city in which they work. Suburbia and shopping malls were both made possible by the automobile. And none of this would have been possible if not for the legal and financial commitments made by all levels of government to expand America's interstate freeway systems, regional highways, expressways, arterials, commercial avenues, and residential streets.

Our society now has a number of significant diseconomies associated with the individual use of the automobile. Traffic congestion and pollution in our inner cities have led to a new wave of policies and practices to improve these conditions. In many of our communities, vast roadways and parking lots have distorted our cityscapes, and sprawling suburbs now occupy the open spaces that once surrounded our cities. Because of these negative circumstances, the focus of public officials and citizens in most large urban centers is on public mass transportation, such as trains, light-rail systems, and the increased use of buses. In the interim, traffic management practices have increased in importance.

Throughout our history, these problems did not exist with other forms of transportation, although none were as effective in moving people as the automobile. Transportation in America began with rivers and canals, and then shifted to private railroads, followed by public streetcars, then personal bicycles, private automobiles, and, finally, commercial airplanes. Typically each form of transportation led to another, more sophisticated and desirable, mode of personal mobility. Automobiles and airplanes now seem to dominate mass transportation systems in our society. Because of the problems associated with the widespread use of automobiles, and our inadequate public mass transit systems, this volume focuses on how governments, and their public officials, are coping with cars to improve the condition of our cities as well as the quality of life for our citizens.

This volume is divided into four sections for ease of reference. The first section, "cities and cars," introduces the reader to this widespread and complicated subject. The second section, and by design the longest, includes numerous case studies, or best practices, on how cities, towns, and communities throughout the nation are using policies and practices, including the latest technologies, to control and manage the unrestricted use of the personal automobile. The next section discusses the future of urban transportation, and examines evolving trends. The several carefully selected appendices included in the last portion of this volume represent important information in this dynamic and rapidly changing field.

Based on this conceptual schema, the

1

four primary sections of this volume are briefly highlighted below.

- Cities and Cars. Chapters in this section describe issues related to cities, streets, and the automobile; traffic and personal safety; and provisions for adequate public parking. The last two chapters examine the evolving role of the states as well as the federal government in the rapidly changing fields of transportation and urban planning.
- The Best Practices. The cities, towns, and communities in this volume, including the states and countries in which they are located, are listed below categorically in alphabetical order.
- Cities: Austin, Beaverton, Bethesda, Boston, Boulder, Chicago, Cincinnati, Denver, Duxbury, Georgetown, Hayward, Houston, Kansas City, London, Los Angeles, Madison, Miami, Minneapolis, Mountain View, Nagano, New Bedford, New York, Oakland, Orlando, Palo Alto, Petaluma, Portland, St. Louis, Salt Lake City, San Carlos, San Diego, San Francisco, Santa Monica, Seattle, Toronto, Trenton, Valencia, Washington DC, and West Palm Beach.
- States: California, Colorado, Florida, Illinois, Maryland, Massachusetts, Minnesota, Missouri, New Jersey, New York, Ohio, Oregon, Texas, Utah, Washington, and Wisconsin. The Provinces of Alberta and Ontario, Canada, are also included.
- Countries: United States, Canada, Japan, and the United Kingdom. Some examples from other countries are included because they represent exemplary and innovative practices to improve the quality of life for their citizens.
- The Future. This section examines the future relative to urban transportation in general, solving problems associated with the automobile, and what the public should expect with respect to roadways and highways in the coming decades. The last chapter discusses the impact that new technologies are having on personal automobiles.
- Appendices. Several appendices are included: a glossary of transit terms, a listing of U.S. periodicals focusing on urban transportation, a listing of U.S. research centers and specialized libraries focusing on urban transportation, a regional resource directory (of all of the cities, towns, and communities included in "The Best Practices" section of this volume), and a national resource directory of major professional associations and research organizations serving public officials, as well as professionals and concerned citizens, on issues related to both public and private transportation.

The case studies contained in this volume reflect state-of-the-art practices on how local governments are working with higher levels of government as well as other public, private, and nonprofit organizations to reduce problems associated with the personal use of the automobile, enhance public mass-transit, as well as other practices to increase the flow of traffic on our public roadways. These case studies represent an important effort to collect a body of knowledge on the best practices available to improve our society's urban transportation problems.

These best practices are designed to achieve certain goals to reduce traffic, enhance the flow of traffic, improve the safety of motorists, and facilitate the development of public mass transit systems. New residential developments are emerging to encourage citizens to live next to public transit stations (such as TODs: Transit Oriented Developments). The evolving field of transportation corridor planning includes the restoration of nature, reducing urban densities, and limiting growth around our major public roadways. Some cities have even reoriented their planning practices to focus on people rather than cars. The management of automobiles, including how they are used and stored, is also a major form of economic development.

The case studies examined in "The Best Practices" section of this volume are typically applied in a piecemeal and incremental fashion throughout America. For the most part, public officials in government agencies, and citizens in nonprofit and private organizations, are busy doing their own thing within their own communities. They do not have the time to find out what their counterparts in other neighboring areas are doing, let alone what other cities are doing in far away places throughout the country. For this reason, the case studies selected for this volume represent an important codification of knowledge on successful ways to improve the condition of our urban transportation systems.

This reference work assembles, for the first time, material based on a national literature search, and makes this information available to citizens and public officials throughout the United States in a single volume. The goal of this work is to help educate citizens and public officials on how best to use these state-of-the-art practices to improve the quality of life for citizens in their own inner city and suburban neighborhoods.

I would like to thank representatives from the following national professional associations, not-for-profit organizations, and publishers for granting me permission to reprint the chapters contained in this volume. Professional associations include the American Planning Association, International City/County Management Association, League of California Cities, National Association of Regional Councils, the Urban Land Institute, and the World Future Society. Not-for-profit organizations include Harvard University, the Local Government Commission, and the World Watch Institute. Publishers include Congressional Quarterly, Inc., Hanley Wood, Intertec Publishing Corporation, PRIMEDIA Business Magazines & Media, Inc., Sage Publications, and the Atlantic Monthly Company.

Roger L. Kemp, Ph.D.
Meriden, Connecticut
Spring 2007

I. Cities and Cars

CHAPTER 1

Cities, Streets, and Cars

Dan Burden

From the narrowest alley to the largest interstate highway, all streets help us get around our towns and cities. From trucks, to cars, to bicycles, to feet, a community's street system accommodates many modes of transportation. Each street within the system has many functions and is designed to carry out these functions as effectively as possible.

Every Street Is Part of a Transportation System

Streets in business districts are designed to accommodate pedestrians, cars, transit, and bicycles, serving a mix of activities. Streets in residential areas are designed to carry people to and from their homes. Interstate highways and many principal arterials are designed to carry large volumes of people and freight over long distances at higher speeds.

Designing streets is complex because each transportation mode may place different demands on the street system. Sometimes these demands conflict. For example, bulb-outs or curb extensions shorten the crossing distance for pedestrians at an intersection. They also reduce the speed at which vehicles can turn at an intersection. For these reasons, bulbouts make intersections safer for pedes-trians. However, on major streets, we need to be careful not to eliminate the space needed for bike lanes.

Street Classifications

Street classifications define the function of each street and the standard to which it should be designed and used. Many factors determine a street's classification, including: travel demand, street right-of-way width, maintenance costs, needs for access to adjacent property, safety, preservation of neighborhood character, distance between major streets known as arterials, adjacent land uses, and connections to the regional transportation system and to major destinations.

Street classifications can limit the types of design or operational changes that can be made to a street. Many of the treatments presented in this guide are appropriate for use only on certain streets.

"Arterial streets" and "residential streets" are designated, in part, by the use of nearby properties. The arterial street system is designed to carry the majority of traffic — generally 1,500 to over 40,000 vehicles per day through and around a community. Residential streets provide access to and from individual homes and generally carry fewer than

Originally published as "Street Wise," *Streets and Sidewalks, People and Cars*, April 2000. Published by the Local Government Commission, Sacramento, CA. Reprinted with permission of the publisher.

Figure 1. Typical Street Classifications					
Classification	*Local Access*	*Number of Lanes*	*Average Daily Traffic*	*Typical Speed Limit*	*Signal or Block Length*
Regional Freeway	restricted	4–12	30,000+	55 mph	no standard
Principal Arterial	limited	2–6	5,000–40,000	30–45 mph	1 mile
Minor Arterial	somewhat limited	2–4	3,000–15,000	30 mph	½ mile intervals
Collector	unlimited	2	1,000–5,000	30 mph	¼ mile intervals
Commercial Street	unlimited	2–4	low	25 mph	1 block intervals
Residential Street	unlimited	2	under 1,500	25 mph *(20 mph in school zones)*	500 feet intervals

1,500 vehicles a day, usually with no trucks or transit vehicles.

The Anatomy of a Street

Streets are used for many activities such as walking, bicycling, parking and driving. Most are designed to balance the demands of different uses and create an atmosphere that is safe, accessible, economically viable and lively.

Like people, each street has an anatomy, and each part has one or more functions. For example, curbs define the edge of the roadway, improve safety by separating pedestrians from vehicles, and channel excess water to storm drains. Street lights increase our ability to see and be seen after dark. Signs orient us to locations, warn us about upcoming obstacles or changing conditions and regulate vehicle movements. Utilities and sewers, though often underground, are important to the smooth functioning of streets.

The street often includes vehicle travel lanes, paved shoulders, parking, bicycle lanes, walking areas, street furniture, bus stops, utility poles, planting areas for landscaping and trees, and signs. The street right-of-way is the publicly owned area adjacent to private property.

The intersection of two streets is one area where pedestrians, bicyclists and drivers meet and must navigate shared space. Crosswalks and curb ramps are used at intersections to define the pedestrian crossing area. Roundabouts control traffic at intersections while maintaining a smooth and steady traffic flow. Sensors known as signal detector loops can be set to change the signal when they detect a car or bicycle waiting for the light.

Sidewalks, walkways, and paved and unpaved shoulders within the street right-of-way are the pedestrian domain. Effective sidewalk width is the area of the walkway clear of obstructions. A sidewalk that is 10' wide may have an effective width that is significantly narrower due to the placement of bus stop shelters, utility poles, newspaper racks, signs and trees. It is important to retain as much effective sidewalk width as possible so that wheelchair users and others have room to navigate. All street furniture or landscaping should be arranged so that pedestrians have adequate space to travel. Neighborhood sidewalks need to be a minimum of five feet wide to accommodate two people walking abreast. When sidewalks are next to the street they must be at least six feet wide.

Transportation and Land Use

Transportation and land use are closely linked. Higher density land uses make it more efficient, easier and cheaper to provide transit service, and encourage people to walk and ride a bike. Mixing land uses provides opportunities for living, shopping, and working in the same area, reducing the need for vehicular travel. In lower density areas, the automobile is the most practical and often only means of transportation.

The street environment is shaped by the location and design of adjacent buildings. These are controlled by land use ordinances, including zoning codes and design guidelines for the neighborhood. Buildings with blank faces on the street are unpleasant to walk by, while those that are built to the sidewalk and have windows and entrances are inviting to pedestrians. Buildings that have signs readable at driving speeds, or buildings that are separated from the sidewalk by driveways or parking lots are designed for drive-by traffic and create an automobile-oriented environment.

Some land uses lend themselves to certain kinds of street activity and transportation choices. For example, a coffee shop with outdoor seating is a magnet for pedestrians. Customers will come by foot, bus and bicycle to enjoy the ambience of the street while they drink their coffee. On the other hand, a car wash or gas station creates an entirely different type of environment: one that is convenient for automobile access, but difficult for pedestrians.

Some types of land uses can be designed to give priority to one type of user over all others. For example, a bank can be designed with a front door and a walk up cash machine that faces directly onto the sidewalk. The same bank can be designed to favor the automobile by locating its front door facing a parking lot. In these examples, the activities are closely tied to the patterns of transportation choice and affect the character of

the streets on which they are located. These various types of land uses have important effects on the street. Consider the impacts of a drive-through restaurant on a neighborhood commercial street. In addition to the noise and smells, there may be cars crossing the sidewalk creating safety concerns for pedestrians, or the cars might line up on the street and block the flow of traffic or reduce access to on-street parking.

Streets Influence a Driver's Behavior

The speed at which most cars travel down a roadway is dictated by several dozen environmental and human factors. When 60–85% of the motorists are driving faster than the posted speed, there are serious problems with the design of that street space. Speed limit signs and the threat of enforcement do little to set the speed of most vehicles.

Physical design influences a driver's behavior more than any other factor. Often we post a local street for the maximum speed the law permits (25 mph in most areas). Roadway designers will try to provide for an additional margin of safety on the road by designing the street to accommodate cars traveling an additional 10 mph over the posted speed limit, or 35 mph. Auto designers have made sure that cars can comfortably be driven at higher end speeds. Thus, many drivers travel as fast as 40–45 mph on streets where we live, walk and bicycle that are posted for 25 mph.

Figure 2. Design Matrix for Healthy Streets

Street Type	Max. Width	Max. Design Speed	Maximum Corner Radius	Max. Ctrline Radius
Trail	8–14'	20 mph	n/a	95'
Alley	10–12'	10 mph	15'	50'
Lane	16–18'	20 mph	15'	90'
Street	26'	20 mph	15'	90'–120'
Avenue	varies	30 mph	15–25'	250'
Main Street	varies	15–25 mph	15–25'	600'
Boulevard	varies	30–35 mph	25'	500'
Parkway	varies	45+ mph	25'	1,000'+

Ideally, streets and neighborhoods should be designed so that after-the-fact retrofits to calm the traffic are not necessary. One key element to designing streets that keep cars from speeding is to keep streets physically or visually narrow. Well-designed streets should also be part of a network that disperses traffic evenly and accommodates bikes and pedestrians, and where the number and width of travel lanes is not excessive for the traffic volume.

Older, traditional narrow streets built in a grid pattern better distribute and naturally calm traffic. As shown in the diagram on the previous page, the traditional design of short blocks set in a grid provides a human-scale environment where there are often stores and offices not far from homes, and multiple routes of travel for vehicles. The conventional design on the right, in contrast, separates stores, homes and schools, requiring us to use a motor vehicle to reach most destinations. In addition, long, spaghetti-like street patterns with few connections require wider travel ways to accommodate higher traffic volumes.

All people — pedestrians, bicyclists and motorists — have a natural desire to stay in motion. Congestion on arterial streets creates delays that frustrate roadway users, sending them looking for other options. Because motorists have the means to travel quickly over longer distances, they can avoid traffic lights or congestion by cutting through neighborhoods. Some motorists, particularly older drivers, may be drawn to residential streets to avoid troublesome intersections and fast-moving traffic.

"Rat Running," as it is called, is the second greatest traffic management problem described by neighbors. Motorists cutting through the neighborhood are usually in a hurry, and drive at speeds unacceptable to residents.

The Preferred Route

Moving the traffic back to the arterial system requires making the arterial street a more desirable option than the residential street.

On neighborhood streets, solutions include eliminating route continuity and slowing motorists with traffic calming features such as bicycle boulevards, partial closures, intersection chokers, intersection medians, and one-way out streets.

On principal roads, solutions include improving intersections and reducing delays through the use of roundabouts, turn pockets, or improved signal timing. Engineers have a choice of which mode of travel and which behaviors they wish to reward.

CHAPTER 2

Cars, People, and Safety

Pam Broviak

"In 2002, there were 42,815 fatalities and over 2.9 million injuries on the nation's highways. Crashes on rural roads — roads in areas with populations less than 5000 — account for over 60% of the deaths nationwide, or about 70 deaths each day. Further, the rate of fatalities per vehicle mile traveled on rural roads was over twice the urban fatality rate."

This quote, from a General Accounting Office (GAO) report issued in May 2004 (*Highway Safety: Federal and State Efforts to Address Rural Road Safety Challenges GAO-04–663*), clearly shows the importance of improving safety along rural roads. Public works employees working in these areas of limited population, however, usually have few resources to deal with the problem.

Fortunately, the federal government realizes that local agencies need help to reduce crashes in their jurisdictions. Through the efforts of the Federal Highway Administration (FHWA), many tools and programs have been developed to provide guidance to local agencies, including the Local Technical Assistance Program (LTAP).

Funded with federal and state dollars, LTAP centers offer assistance to all local agencies and tribal governments across the nation. An LTAP center has been established in each state and is either administered by a university or state DOT. There is also an LTAP center in Puerto Rico serving 78 municipalities and the Virgin Islands department of public works.

During development of the GAO report, LTAP centers were asked to identify the five most important tools they provide to local agencies for improving safety on their roads and streets. Although the responses varied, all fit into the basic categories of training, publications, technical assistance/advice, equipment, newsletters, software, and technology transfer.

Training Opportunities

Most LTAPs offer some form of training. In addition to traditional classroom instruction, a few state LTAPs offer online training materials and course books, classes, and links to training provided by public and private partners. A few LTAPs even extend training opportunities to nongovernmental personnel.

Lindsay Nathanial, training coordinator of Colorado's LTAP said, "Our focus is on local agencies: cities, counties, and towns. However, we do not limit our classes, mailing list, or library rentals to local agencies; private companies are welcome to use our resources."

Originally published as "Tapping into LTAP," *Public Works*, Vol. 136, No. 8, July 2005. Published by Hanley Wood, Washington, DC. Reprinted with permission of the publisher.

In addition to course offerings, the Colorado LTAP Web site has links to several online training opportunities. The most relevant for improving safety along rural roads is the *Roadside Design Guide*, National Highway Institute course #380032C. According to the site, "This Web-based course is approximately 14 hours long and is available anytime, 24 hours, 365 days a year via the Internet. Emphasis is on current highway agency policies and practices." There is no cost to take the course, but participants are required to purchase a copy of the American Association of State Highway and Transportation Officials' *Roadside Design Guide*.

The state of Washington LTAP offers a wide range of training opportunities for both public and private sector employees involved in highway design, construction, and maintenance. Several classes are related to rural road safety such as bridge inspection, gravel road basics, low-cost safety improvements, and troubleshooting roundabout designs.

The site also lists courses provided by the Washington DOT at no cost for in-state local agencies. The Roadside Safety and the Roadway Geometric Design courses could be particularly useful to public works staff responsible for designing rural roads. Registration for these classes, along with others offered by the Washington LTAP, can be done online.

On-the-road training is offered by several LTAPs. Minnesota has established a Circuit Training and Assistance Program, or CTAP. According to their Web site, CTAP uses a fully equipped van to provide onsite technical assistance and training to maintenance personnel throughout Minnesota. Some workshops offered through CTAP include gravel road maintenance, dust control on unpaved roads, and culvert installation and maintenance.

Publication Offerings

LTAP centers distribute publications directly to local agencies upon request, or they lend a limited number of resources for a specific time period. "If we receive multiple copies from our various sources, we distribute the extra copies to interested customers and then retain one copy for our publication library," said Bob Raths, director of the Oregon LTAP. "Items that we maintain in our publication library are listed on our Web site under 'publications.'

"The publications in our library are available for loan to our customers — those

---

What Is LTAP?

The Federal Highway Administration defines the Local Technical Assistance Program (LTAP) as the primary transportation information resource for local and tribal governments. In accomplishing this goal, LTAP provides access to technical assistance, training, and information on new transportation technologies. Technology transfer activities are made available through a variety of projects including services provided by a network of 57 LTAP centers located in each state, Puerto Rico, and six Tribal Technical Assistance Programs (TTAP).

The federal government pays 50% of the annual funding for LTAP centers up to $110,000, and 50% or more matching funds are obtained from state, university, and local funds. Monies also come from contributed resources and services, training funds, statewide planning and research funds, and safety funds. Tribal LTAP centers are 100% federally funded.

Each center's director has the flexibility to tailor the program to local needs. Responsibilities include conducting training, delivering technical assistance, and publishing newsletters. Centers adapt a mix of technology transfer and marketing tools to meet their localities' unique circumstances.

being city, county, tribal governments, and federal agencies that reside in Oregon. We also lend publications and videotapes to other state LTAP programs. If a publication has no copyright, or is 'in the public domain,' we will usually make a copy and send it out rather than providing a loaner copy." Each local agency is advised to access its own state's LTAP to review specific policies for publication distribution.

The Iowa LTAP offers — through the Web site of the Center for Transportation Research and Education (CTRE) at Iowa State University — links to numerous research reports that are either completed or in progress. One report completed for the Minnesota DOT, *Safety Impacts of Street Lighting at Isolated Rural Intersections,* is available for download as a PDF file. According to the Web site, "this study was initiated to evaluate the effectiveness of rural street lighting in reducing nighttime crashes at isolated rural intersections so that Minnesota agencies have more information to make lighting decisions."

Many other resources related to rural road safety can be found at CTRE's Web site under the "Traffic Safety" link. Kentucky's LTAP also has a similar offering on its Web site under the "Focus on Safety" link, which links to the Kentucky Transportation Center at the University of Kentucky. Reports such as *Traffic Control at Stop Sign Approaches* and *Crash Rates at Intersections* can be reviewed and downloaded in PDF format.

Resources also are provided by LTAP centers in the form of videotapes, CD-ROMs, and newsletters. Maryland's LTAP center has an extensive library of 450 videos. Their lending policy is that tapes are loaned free of charge for a period of two weeks. The Center has also obtained permission to duplicate selected videotapes; these may be purchased for $15 each. Videotapes on specific topics can be located through an online search. Orders also can be placed online.

Two examples of videotapes related to rural road safety are:

Traffic Safety Series — Identifies highway safety problems and solutions and provides information on evaluating and selecting the best safety alternatives and evaluating safety program results.

Highway Safety Design — A course on how to use accident information in design decisions. Subjects covered are the appropriate use of accident data, highway cross-section and horizontal curves, pedestrian and bicycle safety, effects of roadway factors on severity and frequency of accidents, conflict types, accident variables and types, and accident reduction factors.

Other options also are available. "We offer free publications provided by the FHWA and other agencies that represent the latest research in transportation issues," said Wendy Schmidt, training operations coordinator for the Washington LTAP. "Our video lending library contains over 500 training videos. The videos are ordered by phone and are borrowed for a two-week period."

Providing Additional Resources

Several LTAP centers provide software applications to local agencies. One such program is the Interactive Highway Safety Design Model, accessed through a link on the Ohio LTAP Web site. This software helps agencies evaluate safety and operational effects of geometric design decisions on two-lane rural highways; it can be downloaded free of charge. Product registration, user manuals, and technical support also are available.

But some public works employees may not have time to visit Web sites, read publications, and watch videotapes. For them, the Maine LTAP provides an alternate solution: onsite assistance and consulting directly to local towns through the services of Phil Curtis, a local consultant hired by LTAP. Maine's "Road Ranger" will visit with the public works department at the garage or on a jobsite. He answers public-works related questions, teaches workshops, and is available to meet with local committees and elected officials.

There are numerous resources available through a network of LTAP centers, and with a center located in each state, local agencies don't need to look far for assistance. "Generally when we get requests for information from out-of-state local agencies we try to refer them to their state's LTAP center; a LTAP center from the same state as the local agency will know best how the requested information relates to the local agency," said Tim Colling, P.E., assistant director for the Michigan LTAP center. "That being said, all of the LTAP centers work together in the end, so if another center needs a resource we have, we will gladly send them the material we have."

Still, chances are that Phil the "Road Ranger" is unlikely to show up at public works garages run by local agencies outside of Maine.

Note: A comprehensive list of Web sites and contact information for each LTAP can be found at www.ltapt2.org. This site also provides additional resources on rural roads through the "Resources" link.

CHAPTER 3

Downtowns, Cars, and Parking

John W. Dorsett

Parking is not just a convenience, it is a necessity — one that many customers and tenants take for granted. There are real costs associated with providing parking, and they can significantly affect real estate projects and even block their development. When shopping centers, office buildings, and hotels do not charge for parking, there is the popular misconception that it is free; however, someone must pay for the parking facility — as well as for the land under it and the lighting, insurance, security, and maintenance needed to keep it functioning — and that money must be recouped. There also are design, testing, and contracting fees, as well as financing costs, developer's costs, and surveying costs. On top of all that, owners of parking facilities often pay property, sales, and parking taxes.

If these costs are not covered by parking fees, they are passed on to the facility owner and ultimately to the facility users. For example, to cover parking costs at a shopping center, the owner charges tenants higher rents and common area maintenance fees. In turn, the tenants charge consumers higher prices for their services and merchandise. Hotels indirectly bill the cost of parking to their guests as part of the cost of overhead. In short, just as there is no such thing as a free lunch, there is no free parking.

Identifying Need and Clients

Many owners do not worry about parking facility finances until they think they need a new facility. Before exploring financing options for new development, however, owners should make sure that existing parking spaces are not going unused because of poor management. Is a new lot or garage really needed? If it is, then the owners should be able to pass on all or part of the project's capital costs and operating expenses to parking patrons, or financing may be difficult to secure.

Owners also must determine what type of parking facility will be most efficient. The cost of construction of a parking garage runs five to ten times higher than the cost of surface parking; however, if a proposed structure is in an urban location where land is at a premium, a multilevel parking facility, which requires less land, should be considered. Other options that could be considered before constructing a garage include the following:

- If it is cost effective, provide shuttle-bus service to transport parking patrons from a remote surface parking lot to their destination.

Originally published as "The Price Tag of Parking," *Urban Land*, Vol. 57, No. 5, May 1998. Published by the Urban Land Institute, Washington, DC. Reprinted with permission of the publisher.

- Restripe existing parking facilities to increase the number of parking spaces, and implement additional parking management strategies (such as shared parking, which minimizes the number of reserved spaces) that allow existing parking resources to be used more efficiently.
- If a loss of green space is acceptable, build a surface lot on existing vacant property.

After choosing either a structure or a surface lot, the question remains: Can the project generate sufficient revenues to offset operating expenses and potential debt service? If not, how can the operation be subsidized? Structured parking facilities that are not profitable often are subsidized by companion office buildings, hotels, or retail shops.

When projecting revenues for a prospective parking facility, it is important to identify user characteristics. Who will use the garage? Considerations that will help identify likely patrons include:

Cost. What are the customary parking rates within the immediate area? What rates could be supported at the proposed parking facility?

Traffic and Pedestrian Circulation. Is the parking facility easy to get to? If it is located on a one-way street that makes access awkward, fewer motorists will use the facility than would if it were located in a more convenient spot.

Ease of Use. Can patrons enter and exit quickly? Can they find their way around the facility easily? Can they easily locate their vehicles?

Cleanliness. Is the parking facility clean? If it is dirty and the one across the street is clean, patrons could be lost to the tidier facility.

Ancillary Services. Does the parking facility operator provide services within the garage such as car washing and/or detailing, vehicle repairs, oil changes, or a dry cleaning pick-up/drop-off facility? Such benefits often can sway patrons toward a facility.

Safety and Security. Is the parking facility perceived by patrons to be safe and secure? Is it well lighted? Is the facility equipped with security features appropriate for its environment?

Site and Market Area Characteristics

The parking facility's site and market area determine, to some extent, its ultimate success or failure. Factors that need to be considered when projecting revenues include:

Parking Space Supply and Demand.

Figure 1. Examples of Parking Space Solutions

Shopping Centers: Instead of employees occupying spaces closest to the stores, create remote parking facilities for employees and establish protocol that discourages employees from parking in "shopper designated" parking areas.

Mixed-Use Parking: Hotels and office buildings can experience a shortage of parking spaces. Hotels have shortages during evening hours, while office buildings have shortages during business hours. Instead of each having exclusive parking privileges, they can negotiate an agreement to share their parking with each other, thereby circumventing the need to develop additional parking.

Remote Parking: To increase the use of remote parking, develop a tiered-pricing scheme that requires higher parking rates for convenient spaces and lower parking rates for spaces in remote locations.

How many parking spaces exist in the market area of the proposed parking facility? Are they now being used? Are there a lot of inexpensive, unused spaces?

Nearby Land Uses. What land uses exist within a block or two of the proposed site? Will those uses generate significant numbers of patrons?

Building Occupancy. What is the building occupancy rate in the market area? Is it expected to increase significantly in the future, thereby creating additional demand for parking?

Future Developments. Are any proposed developments slated for construction in the near future? How will they affect future parking demand?

Competition. Who provides parking in the market area? What rates are charged? Are those rates subsidized? If so, how does that affect the feasibility of a new parking facility?

Measuring demand for a garage involves identifying the number of patrons who will use the garage by hour of day, day of week, and month of year. This includes an estimate of how long patrons will park, how many times each space will be used during a 24-hour period, and when demand will occur. Does the surrounding environment consist primarily of offices in which most employees work 8:00 A.M. to 5:00 P.M. on weekdays? Are there other uses such as retail stores, restaurants, hotels, or entertainment venues that create evening and weekend demand?

Development and Operating Costs

Development and operating costs of parking projects differ widely. Construction costs vary depending on geographic area because of differences in labor rates, materials, and construction methods. Typically, developers can count on construction costs ranging from $6,000 to more than $15,000 per parking space for a garage built below grade.

Figure 2. Distribution of Parking Garage Operating Expenses	
Maintenance	13.5%
Utilities	14.5%
Miscellaneous	19.4%
Cashiering and Management	53.0%

Land costs affect development costs; for that reason, structured parking facilities instead of surface parking lots often are built. Soft costs such as design and testing fees and financing costs also must be considered during the project planning stage.

Since few parking projects are paid for in cash, the cost of financing becomes an important factor. Most parking projects are financed at fixed interest rates with no equity. The interest rate is determined by the debtor's credit history, the amount of collateral, and possibly the amount of insurance purchased to secure the loan. Currently, parking projects are being financed as both tax-exempt and taxable facilities at rates ranging from six percent to more than 10 percent. The customary term for most loans is 20 years.

Operating expenses of parking facilities also vary dramatically. Variations are due to geographical location, size of facility, staffing patterns, method of operation, and local legal requirements. These expenses include the cost of utilities, supplies, daily maintenance, cashiering, management and accounting services, on-site security, structural maintenance, and insurance. Types of insurance coverage include comprehensive liability, garagekeeper's legal liability, fire and extended coverage, worker's compensation, equipment coverage, money and security coverage (theft occurring on the premises), blanket honesty coverage (employed theft), and rent and business interruption coverage (structural damage resulting from natural phenomena). Annual operating expenses for structured parking facilities typically range from $200 to more than $700 per space.

Figure 3. Monthly Revenue Needed to Achieve Breakeven*						
Construction	Annual Operating Expense per Space					
Cost/Space	$200	$300	$400	$500	$600	$700
$1,500	$42	$50	$58	$67	$75	$83
5,000	74	82	91	99	107	116
6,000	85	94	102	110	130	139
7,000	97	105	114	122	130	139
8,000	108	117	125	133	142	150
9,000	120	128	136	145	153	161
10,000	131	140	148	156	165	173
11,000	143	151	159	168	176	184
12,000	154	163	171	179	188	196

Construction cost inflated by 35 percent to include contingency, design, testing, and financing cost; bond financing terms assumed on eight percent annual interest for 20 years (ten years for surface lot).

Development and operating costs together determine the revenue necessary for the project to generate a positive or breakeven cash flow. The monthly revenue needed to reach the break-even point usually ranges from $42 to $196 per parking space, excluding land costs.

Parking facilities frequently are not profitable ventures and therefore must be subsidized. For that reason, parking authorities or city parking departments often become active in their ownership and operation. Public sector involvement typically is motivated by a desire to encourage economic development by keeping parking rates artificially low rather than charging market rates. Parking authorities and city parking departments sometimes have the advantage of not having to pay debt service on older parking facilities. In addition, public entities often supplement off-street parking operations with revenues generated by on-street spaces and through parking violation fines.

While many people believe that parking should be provided free of charge, parking is expensive and the costs must be recouped by the owner, whether by direct or indirect means. Owners should explore less costly options before deciding to build a new parking structure. If a new structure is necessary, the next question is whether or not it is affordable. Determining project affordability can be difficult due to problems in projecting operating revenues and costs. Care should be taken to budget for realistic operating costs and debt service. Because of variations in these factors, some parking facilities provide lucrative investment opportunities while many others must be subsidized.

CHAPTER 4

The States and Transportation Planning

Lawrence D. Frank *and* Robert T. Dunphy

Because traffic congestion is one of the public's major objections to growth and because extending transportation facilities is necessary to support growth, transportation is an integral component of any smart growth strategy. Growth management most often is politically acceptable when a region is perceived as experiencing extreme traffic congestion, which is usually attributable to unplanned growth. Planners need to propose programs that address these conditions. Once adopted, the programs must be able to weather economic downturns as well as changes in the political composition of the legislature. Growth management programs in the states of Washington and New Jersey and in California's Contra Costa County all have had to withstand political pressures resulting, in part, from periods of economic hardship.

Washington State: Sprawl and Environmental Degradation. The state of Washington has witnessed significant population growth in the latter half of this century, with most growth occurring in the Central Puget Sound region — from 1.5 million in 1960 to 2.8 million in 1990, an 87 percent increase.

Employment grew at the even faster rate of 147 percent. More than two-thirds of the growth during the period occurred in the unincorporated areas of the region, while the central cities of Tacoma, Seattle, Renton, and Everett began to show signs of decline. During the 1980s, traffic grew at 6 percent annually, two to three times the rate of population increase; agricultural land and open space was lost; air, water, and land population problems began to appear; and pristine habitats throughout the state began to be degraded, threatening many plant and animal species.

By the late 1980s, the impact of unplanned growth led to elected officials' recognition that growth management had become a popular and in some cases required component of a successful political platform. In 1990, the Washington legislature adopted the Growth Management Act. The unexpected decision was attributable to a political deal: Democrats would support a gas tax increase to fund transportation improvements if Republicans supported a growth management bill, including a transportation concurrency provision implemented at the local level.

Originally published as "Smart Growth and Transportation," *Urban Land*, Vol. 57, No. 5, May 1998. Published by the Urban Land Institute, Washington, DC. Reprinted with permission of the publisher.

Contra Costa County: Growth Management as an Afterthought. One of the San Francisco Bay Area's fastest growing localities, Contra Costa County provides its residents access to jobs in both San Francisco and Silicon Valley in Santa Clara County. A growth management program (GMP) was established in the late 1980s as part of a comprehensive effort to deal with growth and traffic. Bay Area jobs surged and growth boomed in the 1980s, just as the tax-cutting fervor of Proposition 13 and other limits on government spending kicked in. California's resulting cuts in highway investment during this period of economic prosperity, coupled with low-density development patterns, made traffic congestion the region's number-one concern. In response, Contra Costa attempted to replicate nearby Santa Clara County's successful sales-tax initiative to raise money for transportation. A 1986 vote for a one-half percent sales tax increase to pay for $1 billion in transportation improvements in Contra Costa failed, however, causing advocates to reexamine their approach.

Proponents learned that a significant portion of the opposition did not object to the tax or the projects but wanted to ensure that new development did not swallow up the increased capacity resulting from transportation improvements. Industry, environmental, and citizen groups were brought together to devise a two-part plan for a one-half percent sales tax increase coupled with a growth management program that would encourage localities to develop plans that might lead to more coherent regional growth. The revised plan, known as Measure C, passed by a 58 percent vote in 1988, promising an estimated $1 billion over 20 years, of which about 40 percent was earmarked for highways and arterial roads and 30 percent each for transit and transportation management programs.

New Jersey: Combating Urban Decline and Traffic Congestion. In contrast to the state of Washington and Contra Costa County, there has been limited growth to manage in New Jersey and few governmental programs to manage it. New Jersey had a home-rule tradition of highly local control of planning, and the key factors were municipalities and townships, which covered the entire state. New Jersey has no unincorporated areas.

New Jersey is the most urban stare in America. When the state's economic resurgence began in the 1980s, especially along the Route 1 corridor in central New Jersey around Princeton, traffic congestion became an issue. The state needed to do something, given its other pressing problems — the increasing concentration of poverty and minorities in urban areas, crumbling urban infrastructure, spiraling housing costs, loss of farms and open space, and inadequate consideration of spillover effects in local land use decisions.

A state development and redevelopment plan was initiated during Governor Thomas Kean's administration in 1986 and adopted in 1992, under Governor Jim Florio. The current governor, Christine Todd Whitman, who took office in 1994, strongly endorsed the plan, which emphasizes concentrating growth into urban centers — known as "communities of place" — along main transportation corridors, in contrast to the prevailing spread of development to rural areas. The terminology was carefully chosen to avoid more common planning terms such as "urban villages," which were felt to have a negative connotation. The plan is supposed to allow the state to maintain and improve transportation facilities in established urban areas and to avoid expensive and/or underused highways and transit in undeveloped regions.

Organizing to Manage Growth

Washington State. Local control is a cornerstone of Washington's growth management program. The state department of community, trade, and economic development is responsible for implementing growth management. Washington has what is often characterized as a bottom-up growth management program, leaving the balance of power at the local level. Unlike in New Jersey, Oregon, and Florida, there is no state-level plan. The Growth Management Act does, however, provide the state with some review and legal authority. Washington requires *internal* consistency among the elements of the comprehensive plan.

The state's growth management legislation stipulates that a developer must mitigate the effect of a proposed project on transportation along all arterials and transit routes so that within six years they meet a preestablished level of service (LOS). This transportation concurrency requirement is an adaptation of Florida's growth management policies. Each jurisdiction must adopt a concurrency ordinance that establishes an LOS standard on all arterials in its jurisdiction and monitor their performance; transit routes have yet to be addressed. Developers whose projects would bring the LOS below the adopted standard are required to mitigate its impact or improve traffic conditions to comply with the standard. Each jurisdiction also is required to limit transportation plans assumed over a six-year period to projects that are affordable based on current funding levels adjusted for inflation. The intent is to ensure that transportation investments support the land use policies adopted in the jurisdiction's concurrency ordinance and conversely that land use policies support earmarked transportation investments. A Growth Management Hearings Board was established to settle conflicts relating to the implementation of the Growth Management Act.

Contra Costa County. The newly formed Contra Costa Transportation Authority (CCTA) found itself with fresh revenues from Measure C and a mandate to improve transportation and manage growth. The transportation mission was pretty clear, since voters had approved a concise expenditure plan along with funding. The growth management component was less precise. It consisted of a two-page description — which had been on the ballot — that took two years to develop into a five-volume set of codes to make the program operational. The carrot for local governments was the opportunity to share in 18 percent of the revenues from the sales tax, which were reserved for transportation-related projects — from potholes to bike lanes. That incentive became increasingly attractive as the Bay area boom of the 1980s turned into a bust and tax revenues became increasingly scarce. To comply, local governments needed to adopt LOS standards for streets and a five-year capital program for transportation projects and to participate in a multijurisdictional planning process. Measure C projects would be used to pay for the "past sins" of neglect and to improve congestion for current residents.

Paying for new growth — "future sins" — became the responsibility of new residents through development fees. In the sprawling eastern part of the county, 50,000 new homes are expected to be built. At fees of $5,000 per house, this area is expected to contribute $250 million for the expansion of a state highway from four to eight lanes, including high-occupancy vehicle (HOV) lanes, and for a future Bay Area Rapid Transit (BART) line. According to Martin Engelmann, who manages the GMP, "the impact fee program established in the eastern part of the county represents a major commitment on the part of new development to fund a significant regional facility that will serve as the transportation lifeline to that development. The agency never has to tell project proponents that we don't like their project or that they won't get their project — simply, that if they want it, they will have to pay for it themselves."

New Jersey. A major challenge for New Jersey was gaining localities' support for a state development plan. The state office of planning was established as a division of the

---

Figure 1. Washington's Growth Management Goals

Because the state of Washington has strong private property rights, local control, and limited capabilities for public sector intervention in the private development process, goals identified in the growth management program represent a balance of public and private sector concerns. Public sector goals include the:

• Creation of an efficient multimodal transportation network;
• Promotion of sustainable development patterns;
• Preservation of pristine lands;
• Promotion of economic development; and
• Provision of affordable housing to all segments of the population.
   Private sector goals stipulate that:
• Private property shall not be taken for public use without just compensation and private property rights shall be protected from arbitrary and discriminatory actions; and
• Applications for both state and local government permits shall be processed in a timely and fair manner to ensure predictability.

---

state treasury department to oversee the ongoing development and implementation of the state plan; the office is chartered to review and report the progress made toward achieving specific plan goals. Rather than a top-down process such as Florida's, which was recognized as politically unacceptable, or Washington's bottom-up approach, New Jersey chose an informal process called cross-acceptance. Cross-acceptance involves reaching agreements among state, county, and local governments regarding the appropriate level of development for specific land areas. This process is designed to generate a written statement of areas of agreement and disagreement. An update of the state plan, currently underway, is scheduled for adoption next spring.

Influencing Transportation Investment

While the Contra Costa program is focused on raising and spending money on transportation projects, the Washington and New Jersey programs can change state transportation spending priorities to support local growth management plans.

Washington State. Since the implementation of the Growth Management Act in 1994, the Central Puget Sound region has seen rapid growth. A review of the impact of growth management and transportation concurrency ordinances on land use and transportation investment suggests that central cities have been affected less than their suburban counterparts. The city of Redmond, home of Microsoft, is located 15 miles northeast of Seattle. This suburban community, bounded on the east by the adopted urban growth boundary, has nearly met 90 percent of its employment target and 25 percent of its residential growth projected for 2012. Redmond has 42,000 employees, but only approximately one in four resides in Redmond. As a result, a reverse commute has emerged between Seattle and Redmond. Redmond is one of several suburban communities in the area that have experienced significant job growth resulting in complex commute patterns for the region.

As a result of the rapid rate of growth in suburban communities such as Redmond, meeting the concurrency requirement has been a challenge. In many instances, developers in Redmond have to pay the normal impact fees and bankroll projects adopted in the long-range transportation plan for which public funding is not yet available to bring them into compliance with LOS standards. In some instances projects have been delayed and in a few cases even denied, not because their developers were unwilling to pay for additional transportation improvements but because the city felt that the projects were not in keeping with its comprehensive plan. This is a fundamental growth management issue. The types of improvements that the current vehicle-based level of service method would suggest — for instance, double or even triple left-turn lanes — are not compatible with the type of community that Redmond is trying to cultivate.

Contra Costa. In 1991, the CCTA was designated the county's congestion management agency under a new state-mandated program with goals similar to CCTA's. This gave the transportation authority a say in how federal and state dollars would be spent and enhanced the connection between the growth management program and transportation investments. In addition, the agency has managed to expand the multijurisdictional, cooperative planning process to include adjacent counties, allowing them to openly discuss multicounty transportation issues with counties that are not part of the Bay Area. Surprisingly, despite California's reputation as a regulatory hell, there are no state or regionwide growth management programs with any real clout.

The Measure C revenues have had enormous leverage. For example, sales tax revenues paid for the $100 million local match for the BART extension, which cost $500 million. Even the "future sins" money being raised from developer fees is being leveraged. For the three urban portions of the county currently imposing impact fees on new development, it is estimated that a total of $189,000 million in impact fees will be matched by $214 million in federal and other public funds.

New Jersey. In addition to the state development plan, two major transportation initiatives were adopted to further focus development priorities and state investment. An access management code for developments that need driveways along state highways gives the state even greater say over adjacent development than the state plan, requiring consistency with the department of transportation's (DOT's) functional plan. If a development project requires an extra lane on a state highway or intersection improvements nearby, the developer is responsible for paying a fair share. This code also provides incentives for developers by relaxing LOS standards to encourage development in established centers.

Transportation development districts identify areas designated by the county and the DOT commissioner for planned growth and document the transportation infrastructure needed to serve them.

A fee schedule is then developed so that development fees will supplement the funding needed to provide adequate multimodal transportation for the area, allowing development to proceed. A new initiative, the Public/Private Partnership Act, signed into law last year, allows the transportation commissioner to negotiate with the private

---

Figure 2. Robbinsville, New Jersey

Robbinsville, New Jersey, is a small rural village crossroads on a main highway. The town center plan calls for developing the entire area as New Jersey's first pedestrian-oriented, mixed-use community based on neotraditional design principles. It is located in Washington Township, which was an early advocate of the state plan and has developed policies to direct development into compact, mixed-use nodes; preserve open space and farmland; and discourage suburban sprawl. The state DOT has supported plans, which call for on-street parking downtown and reduced traffic speeds on a state highway.

sector to design and/or build transportation projects.

DOT has been the only state agency to dedicate funding to designated centers. In addition, its programs are reinforced by the federal transportation enhancements program, which took effect as part of the 1991 Intermodal Surface Transportation Efficiency Act (ISTEA), just before the state plan was adopted.

With local agreement on key aspects of the state development plan, Governor Whitman directed state agencies to coordinate their efforts, giving the state plan more clout with the DOT. In establishing the state's transportation program, consistency with the state plan now counts for 25 percent of the weight in DOT's rating system, up from a mere 10 percent when the state plan was first adopted. Other factors, including system preservation, safety, congestion mitigation, and political realities, still count, but the state plan is beginning to affect how transportation dollars are spent. Further reinforcement comes from the three metropolitan planning organizations — the North Jersey Transportation Planning Agency, the South Jersey Transportation Planning Organization, and the Delaware Valley Regional Planning Organization — that also select projects that are consistent with the state plan.

Access management plans are beginning to have an influence as well. A planned connection to the Garden State Parkway is finally under design, and it also will facilitate access to expanding retail development in the area. The state was able to develop a comprehensive approach to access permits, rather than reviewing them one at a time as it did in the past. While there has not yet been a thorough cost accounting, John Jennings, supervisory planner for the DOT, feels there has been "more attention to transit and pedestrian projects and greater investments in the older cities, including Camden and Trenton." Despite the state development plan's official support for the older cities, it was not until 1998 that Governor Whitman announced a $400 million program to promote infill development, a strategy that until then only the DOT was backing with its pocketbook.

Results and Lessons

Washington State. While growth management has increased coordination between state and local agencies, it also has met with significant resistance. If the growth management program provides for a timely and predictable permitting process, developers may be strong supporters. Another form of resistance has come from local governments concerned with the impact of development on state-owned highways. They have proven to be very reluctant to include limited-access, state-owned highways in their concurrency ordinances because of the high costs of mitigating that impact and the inability to predict state investment in the roads.

Coordination amongst adjacent jurisdictions has been hampered by the fact that each local government has adopted a unique system to monitor the level of service on its roadways. The ability to receive credit for diverting some of the traffic generated by new development to transit has been limited because the measures do not give credit for transit access. Broadening the transportation measures beyond traditional LOS measures could give planners a wider range of choices to serve the needs of new development, including public transit and pedestrian and bicycle routes rather than road improvements only. This is essential to ensure that the highway system maintains or exceeds a desired capacity. The city of Renton developed a level of service system based on travel time to address system performance from a multimodal perspective. This first, admittedly limited, approach provides the theoretical basis required to compare the benefits of various investments across a variety of transportation modes.

Contra Costa. While Contra Costa's transportation tax is now ten years old, it was not until 1995 that county and local plans were fully operational. Different parts of the county have developed different levels of tolerance for congestion before requiring mitigation. In the more urban western part of the county, it is accepted that there will be extended periods of congestion during both morning and evening rush hours, continued growth in developed areas, higher congestion as the norm in such areas, and transportation investments that emphasize carpooling incentives and transit. The program also has been successful in reducing distrust between upstream jurisdictions undergoing development and established downstream jurisdictions through which the new traffic passes, by creating forums in which all parties have a say. The program has kept a number of confrontations out of the courts and has brought relative harmony to neighboring jurisdictions that historically were in conflict.

Efforts to push the bounds of development densities have been less successful. Urban village concepts repeatedly have encountered significant backlash from residents who live near transit stations. Ironically, at the Pleasant Hill BART station in Walnut Creek, plans for a major transit-supported retail center have been stalled by residents who only a few years earlier had first bought into the village concept. They argue that higher densities will bring only more traffic, noise, and crime.

Now that the economy is back on track, local programs are doing little to stem the tide of new growth, nor were they designed for that purpose. What the growth management programs have accomplished is to ensure that new development will be approved only if the developers can demonstrate that standards for traffic, police, fire, and other services will be met. Martin Engelmann of the Contra Costa Transportation Authority has said that "this has been somewhat of a disappointment to those people who thought our new programs would put a stop to sprawl on the county's suburban fringes."

New Jersey. The implementation of New Jersey's plan dates only from 1992. The plan was conceived under a Republican administration and a Democratic legislature in good times and had to survive shifting party control and a recession. During that time, funding waned. For the time being, there appears to be good support, with Governor Whitman making the state development plan the centerpiece of her second term and the subject of her inaugural address earlier this year. Building consensus among state and local officials proved difficult, however, even in a state that is so highly urbanized.

Adapting to the new business environment is a significant challenge. The vast majority of New Jersey's growth in such key growth industries as telecommunications, pharmaceuticals, and chemicals has come in corporate campuses outside designated centers, and it creates special transportation challenges. Stephen Dragos, president of the Somerset Alliance for the Future, which serves as the transportation management association for Somerset County, points out that in a state that developed along rail corridors, "the trains run the wrong way today, serving the outbound commuters from New Jersey communities to New York and Philadelphia, rather than bringing them in to emerging job centers." Even then, getting commuters from the train station to the office requires a route carefully tailored to the needs of office workers, who may not tolerate long waits and slow speeds.

The Bottom Line

Growth management needs to carefully balance the interests of both the public and private sector to survive. To make a difference in transportation, it needs to alter local development policies to significantly reduce the impact of growth on state roads, which would allow current transportation dollars to go further. State governments can use their control of transportation funds to encourage land use actions that are consistent with adopted growth management policies and, in the process, become consistent with these policies themselves.

On the other hand, political expediency could make smart growth policies an excuse to avoid undertaking important transportation improvements. Contra Costa's billion dollars was considered a shot in the arm compared with the $4 billion needed. In New Jersey, a 1991 study by the Foundation of the New Jersey Alliance for Action, Inc. (just as the state plan was being adopted), estimated infrastructure needs of $10 billion annually, half of which was for transportation, and called for doubling current spending levels. The state of Washington similarly estimated needs for $27 billion over the next 20 years, which represented a $16 billion shortfall from current revenues, or a $9 billion gap assuming historical trends that would imply a gas tax increase.

The Contra Costa County experience, where growth management was an afterthought, illustrates a clear policy on increasing revenues to finance new transportation facilities. Perhaps its lesson, that citizens are willing to pay for new transportation initiatives as long as the increased capacity is not "wasted" on new development, is relevant elsewhere. New Jersey raised additional revenues by a constitutional change dedicating the gas tax to transportation. According to the DOT's John Jennings, "it is easier to make a case for increasing spending to the citizens and the legislature if you can show that it will be spent to support smart growth." Smart transportation will increasingly require that transportation agencies convince the public that new facilities are part of an agreed-upon strategy for managing growth.

CHAPTER 5

The Federal Government and Transportation Planning

Bruce D. McDowell

Governmental regions often are difficult to build and maintain. Resistance to them frequently comes from state and local governments and state agencies that feel threatened by the prospect of having to share power with regional organizations. However, federal initiatives can stimulate and nurture effective regional organizations that are deemed helpful to the proper administration of federal programs which spill across the boundaries of state and local governments that divide natural service areas.

One of the most effective federal initiatives supporting regional organizations in recent years has come from the Intermodal Surface Transportation Efficiency Act of 1991 (ISTEA). This act's innovations have strengthened many regional organizations and led both practitioners and scholars to suggest the ISTEA approach as a model for other functions of government that have regional dimensions. Congress has continued ISTEA's innovations with only modest refinements for another six years by enacting the Transportation Equity Act for the 21st Century (TEA-21). The ISTEA/TEA-21 approach brings well-funded planning together with strong links to implementation decisionmaking processes.

This chapter briefly:

- reviews historic federal roles in supporting regional organizations;
- describes how ISTEA has refined the federal government's role in region building;
- draws some key principles from the ISTEA experience that might be applied to other federal-aid programs; and
- suggests six other federal program areas in which the ISTEA model of regional problem solving could be applied beneficially.

The Federal Role in Supporting Regions

Regions are natural for almost everything but governance. For example, nature has its watersheds, river basins, mountain ranges, ecological regions, wildlife habitats, wetlands areas, estuaries, and outstanding natural features worthy of preserving as parks, wilderness areas, and marine sanctuaries. Economies have their market areas, commuter sheds, labor markets, newspaper

Originally published as "The ISTEA Model of Region Building," *The Regionalist*, Vol. 3, No. 1/2, Fall, 1998. Published by the National Association of Regional Councils, Washington, DC. Reprinted with permission of the publisher.

circulation and broadcast areas of influence, and international trading regions.

But, when it comes to governments, we have the nation, the states, and local governments, all with relatively fixed boundaries and presumed monopolies over the authority to govern within their borders.

For certain special purposes — single functions with demonstrably essential needs not being met by general-purpose governments — limited-purpose units of government have been established. Examples are special districts, school districts, the occasional river basin commission, the Tennessee Valley Authority, and the Appalachian Regional Commission. The latter two organizations are historical anomalies, originally intended to be models for establishing regional organizations to boost economic development in other underdeveloped areas, but they were not replicated after the concepts they represented lost political favor.

In general, however, the boundaries of nature and the boundaries of markets do not match the boundaries of governments. Yet, governments must respond effectively and efficiently to nature and to markets. The concept of governmental regions attempts to bridge this gap between natural, economic, and political realities.

The idea that regional analysis is the only way to "get your arms around" certain types of governance issues makes common sense, and is tolerated by state and local governments as long as the organizations responsible for preparing regional analyses have no governing authority. Therefore, most regional organizations in the U.S. are largely limited to planning responsibilities. Although a few also have some service delivery responsibilities, and one is an elected government, most use only persuasion and the serendipitous confluence of favorable political conditions to lead state and local governments to think regionally and act accordingly.

Relying only on advisory powers, many regional planning bodies have had rather lim-

ited success, leaving many people wondering whether they are worth the money, time, and effort it takes to keep them going. Too often, it is difficult for them to point to tangible benefits they have produced.

The federal government generously supported regional planning organizations with some three-dozen programs in the 1960s and 1970s, and assisted the states in blanketing the nation with metropolitan and non-metropolitan planning regions by the end of the 1970s. Then the federal government lost faith in regions for many of its programs. (ACIR, 1982 and McDowell, 1986)

In the early 1980s, federal support for regional planning declined precipitously. The Environmental Protection Agency, the Office of Management and Budget, and the Departments of Housing and Urban Development, Health and Human Services, Labor, Agriculture, and Justice dropped their regional planning programs. Today, federal aid for regions survives primarily in two programs; one (administered by the Department of Transportation) supports transportation planning for 340 metropolitan areas, and the other (administered by the Department of Commerce, Economic Development Administration) supports economic development planning for 320 small metropolitan and nonmetropolitan regions.

Although three-fourths of the regional planning organizations once supported by the larger array of federal programs have survived, many of them have abandoned most of their planning and regional problem-solving roles. Instead, they now emphasize technical and convener services to local governments. The 1998 directory of regional councils, prepared by the National Association of Regional Councils, lists 501 currently active general-purpose regional councils.

Two lessons emerge from the recent history of regional organizations. First, the federal and state governments can cause the creation of regional organizations and give them areawide problem-solving roles. Second, when the forces supporting regional roles from outside the regions are withdrawn, local support tends to lead them toward technical service roles, and away from contentious interjurisdictional problem-solving and policy-making roles.

In sum, a federal role makes a real difference in how regional organizations are structured, what they do, and how well they do it. The federally-supported metropolitan planning organizations (MPOs) required by ISTEA provide very clear current examples of the effects the federal role can have.

The ISTEA Model of Region Building

The most important thing that ISTEA has done for metropolitan regional organizations has been to give them effective leverage over funding decisions in a group of high-stakes federal-aid programs for surface transportation worth $20–$30 billion per year. Before ISTEA, the states ran the majority of these programs with a pretty free hand. Now, the designated MPO in each metropolitan area over 200,000 population shares in many of those decisions. They do the detailed planning for the metropolitan transportation system, take the lead in setting the priorities for spending the federal funds allocated for use within their areas (consistent with recognized funding constraints), and negotiate with the state department of transportation (SDOT) for the use of statewide funds within the metropolitan area.

Mutual Leverage

The MPO's negotiating leverage for state funding rests on the mutual vetoes that the MPO and SDOT hold over the use of each other's federal funds in the region. In short, ISTEA made the larger MPOs into real decisionmakers that allocate funds in an essential public works program, and put them into a close partnership with the state.

The MPOs are better suited to these detailed planning roles because of their greater ability to involve the citizens, local governments, and other affected parties in the heavily populated portions of the state. Giving these responsibilities to the MPOs frees the state DOTs to concentrate their efforts on statewide issues.

Although some of these state-metropolitan partnerships have been rocky, ISTEA brought the destinies of the nearly 140 larger MPOs and their SDOTs closer together. It is more difficult, now, for one to succeed without the other.

It should be noted, however, that even though the approximately 200 smaller MPOs are required to meet the same planning requirements as the larger ones, they have neither the assured level of planning funds, the regionally allocated program implementation funds, nor the federally enforced decision-making partnership with the SDOT that the larger MPOs have. Thus, the full ISTEA model applies to less than half of the MPOs. Nevertheless, it sets a precedent that the smaller MPOs and many other federal-aid recipients envy.

ISTEA also broadened the scope of transportation decisionmaking. Planning and funding decisions now are supposed to be made on the basis of intermodal analyses that show how people and goods can be moved most effectively and efficiently by the combination of means that will produce the greatest benefits for customers, while minimizing adverse impacts on the environment, energy resources, and social equity. That is far different than the single-minded highway construction goals of the past.

To support this new style of planning, implementation funds from the federal highway and transit programs now can be used flexibly, not just for construction and equipment purchases, but also for operations, maintenance, and demand management, and for such related programs as bicycle and pedestrian facilities, goods movement, and intermodal connections (including port access). And the larger MPOs have a strong voice in determining the use of these funds.

Fortunately, MPOs are funded generously by the federal government to do their required planning using set-asides from the surface transportation programs to a large extent. (The ISTEA/TEA-21 construction, operations, and maintenance funds still go to the state DOTs or the transit authorities, rather than to the MPOs.) These federal planning funds make the MPOs the best funded and most stable regional planning bodies in the country today. For those MPOs that are regional councils, their federal transportation funding helps to strengthen their broader regional planning programs.

However, in return for these new responsibilities, the MPOs are required by the act to pursue a more thorough and more comprehensive planning process, and to more thoroughly involve a much wider range of interested and affected parties than ever before. Although federal law has required transportation planning organizations to exist ever since 1962, they played less important roles in earlier years and received less attention. ISTEA added the following very ambitious new requirements:

- provide a level playing field for involving all the affected parties as they make broad-ranging transportation decisions;
- produce flexible "performance-based plans" that integrate all the transportation modes to move both people and goods more effectively and efficiently;
- use better analytical techniques to study broad sets of alternatives and produce higher quality plans;
- develop "financially constrained" implementation programs that establish priorities among alternative proposals to achieve the greatest performance improvements consistent with available funds; and
- broaden and intensify public involvement in the planning process from beginning to end.

Each of these five far-reaching MPO requirements is described below, based on two recent studies by the U.S. Advisory Commission on Intergovernmental Relations (ACIR, 1995; ACIR, 1997). They offer potential for emulation in other federal-aid programs that use regional organizations.

The Level Playing Field

ISTEA requires the MPOs to provide a decisionmaking process that includes all the affected local government officials in the region, as well as state transportation officials, transportation providers, and state and regional air-quality officials when transportation plans and implementation programs are being developed and approved.

Although ISTEA does not specify exactly how this requirement must be met, the ACIR research has shown that many MPOs have increased the numbers and types of members on their governing bodies and established new intergovernmental agreements to broaden participation in the decisionmaking process. In addition, technical committees and special committees for new topics such as freight planning have been established or expanded to provide a wider range of inputs to transportation decisions. The idea is to get all the key stakeholders involved in the MPO decisionmaking so that the results will be sustained by strong and consistent local, state, and federal support.

ISTEA's ideal of broad and deep involvement frequently is difficult to achieve, however. For example, federal field personnel (especially those from FTA) may not attend MPO meetings regularly because of time and travel constraints. In addition, both federal and state representatives may hold different views than local officials, but not resolve these differences within the MPO process. Such factors may lead to MPO decisions being overturned at a later time by either state or federal action, or both.

It takes great skill and patience by the

MPO to draw the federal and state officials into the decisionmaking process deeply enough to ensure that the MPO decisions can be relied on to be implemented with state and federal support in all but the most unusual circumstances.

Performance Plans

The transportation performance plan is expected to bring all the related programs together to allow the flexible funding mixes needed to get desired results, skirting the arbitrary program barriers that often have stood in the way. ISTEA provides a substantial amount of funding flexibility among separate transportation programs if the planning process supports it.

ISTEA's substitution of flexible performance goals for the mode-specific goals of individual programs may be reinforced by the Government Performance and Results Act of 1993 (GPRA). U.S. DOT has taken the outcome-oriented performance goals supported by both acts to help it move beyond the individual programs in ISTEA and other DOT legislation toward the "One DOT" concept. This means that U.S. DOT now expects all 10 of its major organizational units to work together to achieve the following five performance goals:

- mobility of people to jobs and services (including a new welfare-to-work objective) and access of goods to production sites and markets;
- economic vitality of the nation enhanced by efficient transportation and trade;
- safety and security of transportation in America (to save lives and protect property);
- environmental protection and community livability features of transportation systems in America; and
- national defense capabilities of America's transportation system.

Thus, DOT is taking steps intended to take the integration of Federal Highway Ad-

ministration and Federal Transit Administration programs established by ISTEA even further under GPRA to include railroads, ports, airports, pipelines, and shipping. ISTEA (and now TEA-21) requires each MPO to take into account all the modes relevant to its region, and GPRA provides an extra push to get the additional modes to join the integrated effort.

Obviously, these goals also have a lot in common with goals of other federal departments and agencies, including HHS, Labor, EDA, EPA, and Defense. This suggests that there may be advantages if the MPOs also have relationships with those organizations, and if these federal departments and agencies have relationships with each other regarding these closely-related programs. Many MPOs, indeed, do have such relationships, often continued from the 1960s and 1970s when they were promoted heavily by the federal government. (ACIR, 1973, pp. 226–227)

CPRA requires all federal departments and agencies to promote interagency coordination where it can help to improve the performance of federal programs. DOT has already built such coordination into its programs for such matters as air quality, water quality, wetlands, and welfare-to-work.

Common performance goals and measures, and coordinated reporting of performance, are becoming essential parts of the federal-aid process. (McDowell, 1998) They are the means by which the federal, state, regional, and local partners can support each other's success in meeting broad performance goals. In the past, it often was so difficult for federal agencies (sometimes even in the same department) to coordinate with each other that regional planning organizations were expected to coordinate the federal programs. Although that is an attractive idea, it often is difficult to accomplish because of the separations and incompatibilities built into the individual federal programs. ISTEA bridged some of those difficulties with its flexible funding provisions, and GPRA encourages DOT as well as the other federal departments and agencies to go even further toward program integration.

Enhanced Analytical Techniques

The kinds of outcome-oriented performance goals that are beginning to drive transportation and other federal programs require more powerful analyses that can look into the future and estimate the potential impacts on society of new facilities, better maintenance, more efficient operations, no action, and other program options.

Transportation programs have depended on simulation models for many years, but ISTEA has created the need for even better models requiring still more and better data. DOT has geared up by spending significant money to:

- upgrade transportation simulation models;
- develop better data to support the new models;
- make transportation data more readily available to support new models and powerful geographic information systems (GIS);
- develop realistic performance measures;
- create and support interactive decision-support systems; and
- train MPO and other planners how to use the new data and analytical techniques effectively.

Realistic Implementation Programs

Before ISTEA, transportation implementation programs were largely limited to capital improvements listed in the Transportation Improvement Program (TIP). Now, implementation plans include much more than capital improvements. The new elements are: innovative finance plans; regulatory plans aimed at reducing travel demand or improving air quality; and system man-agement, routine maintenance, and operating plans aimed at squeezing greater service out of the same facilities and equipment.

Noncapital and low-capital alternatives for meeting performance goals stretch public transportation dollars, but they require a different type of planning and analysis than traditional transportation planning programs. ISTEA's "financial constraint" requirement — limiting proposed spending to the revenues demonstrated to be available during the implementation period — put a premium on low-cost alternatives and criteria for systematically assigning priorities to the projects and programs that will produce the greatest amount of performance per dollar.

Enhanced Public Involvement

"Inclusive," "early," and "often" are the watchwords of ISTEA's public involvement requirement. MPOs are required to reach out to all the affected parties, and seek to involve them in the MPO process from beginning to end. This is true particularly for the hard-to-reach sectors of the population such as: persons with disabilities (who may need special means of communicating and special accommodations at meetings); ethnic groups (that may have language and other cultural barriers to overcome); and the poor and disadvantaged (who may be transit-dependent but unable to participate in public forums to make their needs known).

This enhanced involvement is intended to make the transportation programs customer-oriented, to take advantage of the unique insights that come from viewing the programs "from the other end of the telescope," and to help create a body of support for the programs that will best meet the needs of the customers. Successful public involvement programs typically use a wide variety of techniques appropriate to reach the diverse groups found in most communities and to match the different stages of the planning process.

DOT funded a new inventory of these techniques (Howard/Stein-Hudson) and made case studies available to illustrate the benefits that can come from such activities. The time and resources required to pursue sincere and creative public involvement programs may be substantial, but the effort can pay off in plans and projects that have the breadth of support necessary to be implemented.

MPO Capacity Building

FHWA-sponsored studies (ACIR, 1995; ACIR, 1997) found that the MPOs have adapted very significantly to the ISTEA innovations, but they still need to make further improvements, and they are looking for help. One reason they are looking for help is that the larger ones (over 200,000 population) must be certified by the federal government every three years. The certification process assesses the extent to which these MPOs are meeting the federal planning requirements outlined above, and makes recommendations for improvement. A number of conditional approvals have been issued, allowing brief periods to rectify deficiencies. (ACIR, 1997) Although MPO funding and implementation funds in the MPO's region could be cut off, that has not yet happened. Nevertheless, the certification requirement provides a strong incentive for MPOs to meet the federal requirements.

To help all MPOs meet federal requirements, FHWA is funding development of a learning network through the Association of Metropolitan Planning Organizations (AMPO). The primary goal is to share good practices quickly and effectively among the MPOs to help them become high-performance organizations. It is expected that a permanent website will be operating as part of this network in 1999 to help MPOs get up to speed and maintain their high performance well into the future as techniques continue to improve.

The main point to emphasize here is that DOT is making very substantial investments in building MPO capacities to help ensure that they will be the strong partners needed to help implement the national transportation policies spelled out in ISTEA.

Principles for Federal Support of Regional Institutions

The ISTEA experience suggests that the federal government could substantially enhance its support for regional organizations in ways that could significantly improve the performance of other national goals. This could be accomplished by distilling the lessons of ISTEA into a multi-purpose model of region-building and applying it to additional federal-aid programs. Five principles that should be included in such a model follow.

Define Regional Interest

The federal government should carefully delineate the program areas in which it has a regional problem-solving interest. This delineation should include the scope of the federal interest, the existing programs that relate to it, and the federal performance goals established for the program area.

Each program area should incorporate a significant amount of federal funding over which a designated regional organization would have authority to assign spending priorities consistent with an adopted performance plan and realistic financial constraints. Within the program scope, flexibility should be created for transferring funds among related programs to help meet performance goals more effectively and efficiently.

The following areas are suggested for consideration, along with some of the major departments and agencies that might be involved.

Economic Development. Major related programs exist in the Economic Development Administration, the Appalachian Regional Commission, the Small Business Administration, and the Departments of Housing and Urban Development, Defense, Transportation, Agriculture, Education, Interior, and Labor.

Community Development and Housing. Major related programs exist in the Departments of Housing and Urban Development and Agriculture.

Social Opportunity, Health, and Public Safety. Major related programs exist in the Departments of Health and Human Services, Labor, Education, and Justice.

Pollution Control. Major related programs exist in the Environmental Protection Agency, the Departments of Energy and Defense, the Nuclear Regulatory Commission, and the Federal Emergency Management Agency.

Natural Resource Use and Preservation (including water resources). Major related programs exist in the Environmental Protection Agency and the Departments of Interior, Agriculture, Commerce, and Defense.

Disaster Mitigation. Major related programs exist in the Federal Emergency Management Agency and 27 other federal departments and agencies.

Assign Regional Institutions

The federal government should assign a federally-assisted regional planning and coordinating role to appropriate regional institutions for each of the "regional interest" program areas defined above. In general, the choice of institutions should be the general-purpose regional councils already established for other federal and state programs. Multiple programs should be assigned to the same regional organization whenever possible to facilitate coordination and encourage program synergies.

Where regional councils are not the best choice (perhaps because they lack capability and authority, or appropriate geographic scope), some flexibility should be provided to allow conformity with other applicable state laws, interstate compacts, watershed or river basin organizations, or other regional structures that may already exist for other purposes. Combinations of regional councils may be appropriate in some cases. If regional councils are not designated for a particular program area, coordination with those that exist in the geographic area should be required. The federal government should play a special role in helping to support or create interstate regional councils where needed to address areawide concerns that cross state lines.

Opportunities for coordinating related federal programs and agencies should be seized. Regional planning requirements should be as consistent as possible from one program area to another to allow efficiencies in meeting federal planning requirements. Duplicate planning should be avoided by incorporating the relevant elements of related regional, state, and local plans into the designated regional organization's planning reports and policies.

To the extent possible, planning assumptions (such as population growth rates and future development patterns) should be consistent from one program to another. This practice was heavily promoted by the federal government in the 1970s, but was deemphasized until ISTEA renewed the emphasis on coordinating land use, environmental protection, and transportation. TEA-21 increases that emphasis.

The planning funds to support designated regional organizations should be provided as a percentage set-aside from the related implementation programs. This arrangement has worked well in the transportation field, while the use of separately appropriated planning funds has not worked well in other fields.

Require Regional Dialogue

The federal government should establish performance requirements for (a) inclusiveness in the policymaking bodies of the designated regional institutions, (b) a collaborative decisionmaking relationship between the regional institution and the related state agencies, and (c) ISTEA-style public involvement. The designated regional organization should be a partnership mechanism, responsible for bringing the affected and responsible parties together to help broaden consensus. This is not always easy to accomplish, so the federal government may have to assist some regional organizations in getting some of the parties (such as a state agency) to the bargaining table and keeping them there in a constructive relationship. DOT has found this role necessary in a few cases.

Empower Regional Partnership

Federal officials in the field should be active partners in the regional planning and problem-solving process. They should attend regional planning meetings faithfully, participate fully, and abide by the regional decisions made in the collaborative process, except in clear cases when the regional decisions violate federal law.

This role will be a significant culture change for many federal officials who have been accustomed to monitoring compliance with detailed federal-aid regulations. In addition, it will require a greater federal field presence than is available presently in many of these programs. However, this approach would require less time for regional office and headquarters reviews, and would diminish the need for unilateral federal decisions made from afar. Special training for federal field representatives should be provided to facilitate the transition from "compliance officer" to "full partner." A recent report by the National Academy of Public Administration (NAPA) is available to support such training.

Build Regional Capacity

Federal agencies should help to build the capacity of regional councils and other designated regional organizations, and facilitate their operations. Federal research, program evaluations, and training programs are important sources of information for regional organizations about what works.

In addition, the federal government is in a position to sponsor "learning networks" for regional organizations to help them share experiences about good practices. Federal agencies, including DOT and HUD, also are beginning to package data conveniently to assist their grantees in performing required planning analyses and preparing helpful maps and graphic displays for decision-support purposes — a technique that should be applied more fully to regional programs. Finally, federal agencies are beginning to establish nationally comparable regional indicators and automate many aspects of the grant management process — from applications for funds to disbursements and project closeouts.

Precedents for these helpful practices have been cited above, but most are not widespread outside the ISTEA/TEA-21 orbit. Fuller use by federal agencies in a wider range of regional programs could significantly aid the effectiveness and efficiency of regional organizations and enhance the performance of many federal programs.

Conclusion

After nearly two decades of neglect by most federal programs, it is time for renewed initiatives by the federal government to take advantage of the benefits that regions can provide. The partnership model embodied in ISTEA, and continued by TEA-21, is effective and worthy of broader application.

Now is a particularly good time to pursue this regional initiative because of the outcome-oriented performance management requirements of GPRA. Many federal-aid programs have regional dimensions, and it is in the regions that their benefits will be produced. These programs will be delivered by federal-aid recipients, not by the federal government itself. So the partnership idea takes on new meaning; federal program performance will need to be measured largely by the success of the partners. The federal interest in strengthening regional councils, therefore, is the same as its interest in seeing its own programs succeed.

REFERENCES

Howard/Stein-Hudson Associations, Inc., and Parsons, Brinkerhoff, Quade & Douglas. 1996. *Public Involvement Techniques for Transportation Decision-Making*, prepared for the Federal Highway Administration and the Federal Transit Administration. Washington, D.C.: U.S. Department of Transportation.

McDowell, Bruce D. 1986. "Regional Planning Today," Chapter 6 in Frank S. So, Irving Hand, and Bruce D. McDowell, editors, *The Practice of State and Regional Planning*. Chicago: American Planning Association.

McDowell, Bruce D. 1998. "The Results Act: Implications for Managing Federal Grants," *Assistance Management Journal*, Volume 8, No. 4, pp. 1–10.

National Academy of Public Administration 1997. *Principles for Federal Managers of Community-Based Programs.* Washington, D.C.: The Academy.

U.S. Advisory Commission on Intergovernmental Relations. 1973. *Regional Decisionmaking: New Stategies for Substate Districts.* Washington, D.C.: U.S. Government Printing Office.

U.S. Advisory Commission on Intergovernmental Relations. 1982. *State and Local Roles in the Federal System*, Chapter 5, "Areawide Organizations: Metropolitan and Nonmetropolitan." Washington, D.C.: U.S. Government Printing Office.

U.S. Advisory Commission on Intergovernmental Relations. 1995. *MPO Capacity: Improving the Capacity of Metropolitan Planning Organizations to Help Implement National Transportation Policies.* Washington, D.C.: ACIR.

U.S. Advisory Commission on Intergovernmental Relations. 1997. *Planning Progress: Addressing ISTEA Requirements in Metropolitan Planning Areas*, A Staff Report. Washington, D.C.: ACIR.

II. THE BEST PRACTICES

CHAPTER 6

Alberta, Other Urban Areas, Design Highways to Protect Animals

Elaine Robbins

Drive 53 miles east from Seattle, and you'll soon find yourself in the cool elevations of the Cascade Range, in a recreation area called Snoqualmie Pass.

Some 24,000 cars and trucks a day travel through the scenic mountain pass on Interstate 90, Washington's major east-west interstate, on their way to and from Seattle. To accommodate the growing traffic, the Washington Department of Transportation (DOT) plans to expand the highway on the eastern side of the pass from two lanes to four.

They know it will not be a standard-issue road expansion project. That's because Snoqualmie Pass is an important travel corridor not only for humans but also for deer, elk, pine martens, bobcats, coyotes, and other animals that must travel through the bottleneck of the mountain pass to reach larger wilderness areas to the north and south. The expansion of I-90 will create a formidable barrier for these animals.

"We identified this area as one where we wanted to focus on improving habitat connectivity," says Paul Wagner, the biology program manager for the Washington State DOT. "We asked, 'What kind of design-related response do we need?'"

Transportation planners across the country are asking similar questions as they recognize the serious impact of highways on wildlife. About one million animals are killed on U.S. roads each day, according to the Humane Society. Just as worrisome to wildlife biologists are that large animals often avoid roads altogether, making the nation's four million miles of roads a major contributor to the problem of habitat fragmentation.

Harvard landscape ecologist Richard T. T. Forman, author of *Road Ecology*, estimates that while roads cover just one percent of the U.S. landscape, their ecological impact is actually closer to 20 percent. But transportation planners and wildlife biologists in the U.S. and in Europe, Canada, and Australia are sharing what they learn in the search for solutions. Employing a toolkit that includes wildlife crossing structures and statewide habitat connectivity plans, they hope to increase the wildlife "permeability" of highways, particularly in sensitive areas.

"We're out of the era where we were building tons of roads, and we're into a phase

Originally published as "No More Road Kill," *Planning*, Vol. 69, No. 2, February 2003. Reprinted with permission from *Planning*, copyright © February 2003 by the American Planning Association, Suite 1600, 122 South Michigan Avenue, Chicago, IL 60603–6107.

of maintaining and improving existing roads," says Amanda Hardy, wildlife biologist at the Western Transportation Institute at Montana State University. "In the process, we're realizing that maybe we didn't do too well the first time around. We're thinking of how we can improve our existing infrastructure the second time around."

Such activities have increased markedly since 1998, when federal TEA-21 funds became available for wildlife mitigation. Under TEA-21, 10 percent of the $217 billion in funding for surface transportation programs was allocated for 12 "enhancement" categories, among them wildlife crossings on new and existing roads as well as habitat connectivity measures. Transportation departments and conservation groups such as Defenders of Wildlife are lobbying for similar funding levels when TEA-21 comes up for reauthorization in fall 2003.

Wildlife Crossing Here

Although transportation experts use a variety of tools to design "green highways," the primary tool is the wildlife crossing structure. In the past 30 years, an estimated 100 to 200 underpasses and six overpasses have been built on highways in North America. When used in conjunction with roadside fencing, these "critter crossings" have proved effective in significantly reducing roadkill and providing safe passage for wildlife.

Banff National Park in Alberta, Canada, has become an international model of wildlife-crossing design. There, the Trans-Canada Highway, Canada's major east-west thoroughfare, crosses the national park in a place where grizzly bears, black bears, deer, elk, moose, wolves, coyotes, and bighorn sheep travel through the Bow River Valley. As early as the 1970s, animals attempting to cross the highway after dusk often were killed.

"We had an exceptionally high kill rate," says Bruce Leeson, senior environmental assessment scientist for Parks Canada. "We

were getting in excess of 100 large animals a year killed on the highway."

As traffic increased in the late '70s, transportation planners proposed a highway expansion. The proposal provoked a debate. Why, critics asked, should Canada's flagship national park have a highway running through it in the first place? Eventually, the road expansion was approved, but only "with exceptional measures to protect wildlife and to solve the problems that already existed," says Leeson. "So here we were faced with this challenge and duty to solve this problem."

Over a 20-year period starting in the 1980s, Canada spent millions of dollars on 24 crossing structures along a 28-mile stretch of highway. In addition to 22 underpasses, two 164-foot-wide overpasses were built.

Planted with native trees and shrubbery, they provide cover for everything from black bears to chipmunks and an open view that grizzly bears, elk, and deer prefer. To keep wildlife off the highway and direct them to the crossings, engineers installed eight-foot-high fencing along both sides of the highway. In the last section of work, they buried a section of chain-link fence in the ground "to deal with the diggers — primarily wolves and coyotes," says Leeson. "We discovered that these animals would dig under the fence and get between the two fences and become even more vulnerable."

Since the crossings were installed, wildlife roadkill has been reduced by 80 percent — and as much as 96 percent for collisions involving ungulates (hooved animals such as deer and elk). But wildlife structure design is still an evolving science as experts learn what works and what doesn't. Wildlife biologists have found, for example, that black bears and mountain lions prefer underpasses, while grizzly bears, wolves, and ungulates like the openness of overpasses where they can get a wide view. All these animals tend to avoid structures that are too close to human activity such as hiking, biking, and horseback riding.

Bill Ruediger, the ecology program leader for highways and roads for the U.S. Forest Service, has seen the biggest failures on projects where state transportation departments take minimum mitigation steps to save money. "If we put $150,000 into a structure that doesn't work, I don't find that to be a cost-effective approach," he says. "It might cost $300,000 or $400,000 to design a structure for a big animal that is much more effective."

The location of a crossing structure is another factor critical to its success. Before making siting decisions, planners should research where wildlife prefer to cross, the location of wildlife connectivity zones, and future land-use build-out scenarios, say Scott Jackson and Curtice Griffin in *A Strategy for Mitigating Highway Impacts on Wildlife*. The authors suggest a few components of a practical, comprehensive approach:

- Avoid highway fencing and Jersey barriers when not used in association with wildlife passage structures.
- Use small (2' × 2') amphibian and reptile passages wherever roadways pass along the boundary between wetlands and uplands.
- Use oversized culverts and expanded bridges at stream crossings.
- Selectively use viaducts instead of bridges at important stream and river crossings.
- Use landscape-based analyses to identify "connectivity zones" where a variety of mitigation efforts can be concentrated to maintain ecosystem processes.
- Selectively use wildlife overpasses and large wildlife bridges with "connectivity zones."
- Monitor and maintain plans to ensure that mitigation systems continue to function over time and that knowledge gained from these projects can be used to further refine mitigation techniques.

Highways and Habitat

Transportation planners know that highway crossings alone won't help wildlife.

"We need to manage adjacent lands appropriately," says Ruediger. "It means that you don't build a Wal-Mart on the other side of a highway crossing — or a condominium or a high-density bike path."

Habitat connectivity was a major goal of the Washington DOT in planning the Snoqualmie Pass highway project. "We studied where crossings would be most effective, where they would line up with connectivity land-management schemes," says Wagner. The DOT worked with the U.S. Forest Service, which had been consolidating its holdings in the Snoqualmie area by swapping land with Plum Creek Timber Company.

The Forest Service plans to manage this land as linkage areas for wildlife. When construction begins in another year or two, I-90 will include crossings aligned with wildlife corridors, fencing to direct wildlife to the crossings, and stream crossings that both remove barriers to fish passage and allow animals to travel along riparian areas.

"From the standpoint of planning, the issue of the surrounding land use is critical," says Wagner. "We don't want to end up in a place where transportation agencies are doing a lot of careful work and spending a lot of public money on these things when there's not the interest or long-term commitment to protecting corridors. That's why we felt like starting where we did made such sense."

The goal, according to Wagner, is to conduct environmental analyses earlier in the planning process. "Now what we're doing is earlier analysis for the 20-year transportation plan," he says. "Is the project in a wetland area? Is it in an area that's typical habitat for certain species, particularly endangered species? Is it within a buffer area of a stream that will be supporting listed salmon species?"

The Washington DOT plans to develop more partnerships with other government agencies as well as private organizations like land trusts — groups that purchase conservation easements on biologically significant lands. "We could fix a lot of the problems that exist with the highways if we had partnerships," says Wagner. "Ideally, you'd have all these players working off the same habitat connectivity plan."

Florida's Road Less Traveled

Florida is at the forefront of a movement to incorporate wildlife protection earlier in the planning process. With a booming population and a rich diversity of wildlife — including the endangered Florida panther and threatened black bear — Florida faces serious roadkill rates and habitat fragmentation challenges.

By all accounts, the Florida DOT has embraced the challenge. "We thought we needed to better implement the planning of transportation, land use, and environmental issues," says C. Leroy Irwin, the environmental manager in the planning office of the Florida DOT. "So we brought together the federal and state agencies and agreed to basically blow up our process and develop a new process that would work for all of us."

The result was the Efficient Transportation Decision Making (ETDM) process, developed in 2000 and set to be fully implemented in 2004. The new process calls for two screenings of environmental data that will automatically highlight potential wildlife problems before a project shows up on the drawing board. The first screening, known as the planning screen, is conducted every three to five years during the development of the long-range transportation plan. At this stage, the DOT conducts an environmental analysis and sends it to 24 governmental agencies for review.

The second step, known as the programming screen, is run each year by the DOT for Florida's 25 metropolitan planning organizations on priority projects that are being considered for the five-year work program. "The programming screen provides more detailed information about the proj-

ect," says Irwin. "Each agency has a responsibility to respond back to the MPO or the DOT. If the agency handles endangered species or habitat, they have the responsibility to tell us at that stage what the problems are."

Under the ETDM process, potential wildlife problems are resolved before a project can move forward. "If the need is great, then the project will move forward, but we can make a commitment at that time to building a wildlife crossing or do further study," he adds.

The ETDM process, which has been praised by conservation groups, has several advantages for DOTs as well as wildlife, according to Irwin. "Rather than being in a reactive mode, we're in a proactive mode," he says. "We can design the project *for* the environmental issues. It also gives us a much better funding scenario. We know what's got to be done, and what we can put more funding into."

A Road Map for the Future

From an ecological perspective, there is no such thing as a "green highway." That's why the first rule in transportation planning is to avoid building or expanding roads in sensitive ecological areas — and when unavoidable, to minimize their impact.

In an effort to more accurately target the areas worth protecting and predict the impact of road projects on these areas, more DOTs and conservation groups are using a new tool: ecological mapping.

In Florida, the DOT contracted with the University of Florida's Landscape Ecology Program to develop a GIS tool that could be used to identify and set priorities for potential roadkill areas. The model allows them to look at everything from species distribution to land use on existing roads to use as a basis for future road project decisions.

These road maps to the state's ecological resources provide the data that make the development of the new planning process possible.

In California, the Nature Conservancy and other conservation groups have done mapping to identify more than 300 different corridors used by wildlife in the state. The California Nature Conservancy, which shares this information with Caltrans and effected change in the agency's wildlife mitigation policy, lists the general advantages of these eco-maps:

- Avoid or minimize transportation impacts.
- Focus transportation enhancement and mitigation funding on high-priority landscapes.
- Encourage better land use.
- Leverage multi-site outcomes.

There are advantages for the transportation agencies as well:

- Enhanced project delivery and time and money savings.
- Shared biological or other resource data.
- Help with land acquisition.
- More environmentally responsible projects.
- Better environmental image.

Washington State's DOT developed a GIS modeling tool to evaluate multi-species, large-carnivore habitat connectivity in the region (Washington, Idaho, and British Columbia). The model is designed to help planners identify major highway segments that intersect habitat linkage areas — and to calculate landscape permeability ratings for specific areas.

This "big-picture" model includes data on land cover, roads and highways, population density and land ownership, topography, and hydrology. These maps have pro-vided a tool for transportation planners to make better informed, long-range planning decisions.

Defenders of Wildlife, which has a Habitat and Highways campaign, recommends that planners in states that lack extensive mapping resources instead use their state biodiversity conservation plan as a tool for identifying high-priority areas for protection. (States must complete these plans by October 2005 in order to keep receiving state wildlife grants from the U.S. Department of the Interior.)

Another new tool is the "road-effect zone" maps designed by Richard Forman to help transportation planners identify the ecological effects of proposed roads, from the impact of traffic noise on birds to channelization of streams. Forman names several key priorities for transportation planners, including directing rural traffic to existing primary highways and avoiding the conversion of rural, secondary roads to medium- or high-traffic usage.

In Florida, where rural roads are rapidly giving way to suburbanization, State Road 46 is a roadkill hotspot in a state where more than 100 black bears have been killed each year over the last few years. The problem is particularly bad in November, when the bears are on the move around Ocala National Forest at dawn and dusk, searching for food as they build up fat stores for the winter. Residents and travelers head through the forest on their way to Orlando to the south or Daytona Beach to the east.

Salvation lies in a simple, dirt-floor culvert — a mere 24 feet wide and 47 feet long, planted with pines to direct bears to the entrance — where black bears, bobcats, gray foxes, and whitetail deer cross under the road and get to the other side.

CHAPTER 7

Austin Uses Transportation Operations Management to Reduce Traffic Congestion

Zia Burleigh

Most local government transportation agencies routinely conduct activities designed to minimize traffic delay and service interruptions. As congestion and service disruptions in the United States continue to escalate, however, local government managers, now more than ever, are challenged by their communities and elected officials, despite significant decreases in local government budgets, to ensure that transportation agencies meet the objectives of reduced congestion, lowered emissions, and improved systems reliability, safety, and convenience.

Due to increased congestion, combined with higher rates of traffic incidents, and heightened public safety concerns, local government managers are beginning to realize that traditional strategies for managing the transportation infrastructure (building new roads and highways) are no longer effective. Even with the availability of intelligent transportation systems (ITS) such as variable message signs (VMS), roadway weather information systems (RWIS), and the growth of traffic management centers (TMCs), many

transportation agencies are still functioning as "stove-piped" organizations, where responsibilities for varied operational activities are often widely dispersed and segregated. Consequently, different units within some transportation agencies manage specific tasks with separate budgets and staffs, often with little interagency or multi-agency coordination.[1]

During traffic-related incidents law enforcement, fire and rescue, emergency medical services (EMS), and other public safety-related agencies are required to work together with transportation agencies because of their roles in highway incident response, traffic law enforcement, special event management, roadway maintenance, and highway construction work zone safety. Clearly, both entities — public safety and transportation — depend on each other to efficiently and effectively serve their communities, as timely emergency response requires navigable roadways, and efficient traffic operations rely on effective public safety services.

Despite this clear relationship both

Originally published as "Transportation Operations Management: Less Congestion, More Cooperation," *Public Management*, Vol. 85, No. 8, September 2003. Published by the International City/County Management Association, Washington, DC. Reprinted with permission of the publisher.

agencies have traditionally viewed themselves as providing two separate and distinct services that don't require interaction or coordination until on the scene of an incident. While this may have been true in the past, the growth in traffic incidents and congestion has caused them to become more interrelated and, in many ways, reliant upon each other today. The need for early planning and collaboration to improve emergency response and decrease congestion is vital.

Breaking down the barriers that have created these fragmented organizations is indeed a challenge that many city/county managers have already begun to address. With budget constraints taking priority, however, many jurisdictions are still struggling to find alternatives that can be used to assist them in implementing more multi-agency programs. The manager, therefore, as the supervisor of these key government services (e.g., transportation, law enforcement, emergency medical services, and fire and rescue), is in a critical position to initiate changes in the way transportation and public safety agencies function.

By encouraging their staffs to learn more about new approaches for performance that include greater coordination and cooperation, transportation and public safety agencies can perhaps begin to develop and implement policies and procedures that facilitate a more collaborative environment.

A Systems Management Approach

Transportation planners predict that the nation's transportation infrastructure will suffer from unbearable gridlock over the next two decades; however, according to the 2002 Urban Mobility Study conducted by the Texas Transportation Institute (TTI), this prediction has already become a reality for many U.S. cities. The TTI study estimated that, in 2000, the nation's 75 largest metropolitan areas experienced 3.6 billion vehicle-hours of delay, resulting in 21.6 billion liters

(5.7 billion gallons) in wasted fuel and $67.5 billion in lost productivity.

Roughly half of the congestion experienced is caused by recurring demands where road use exceeds existing capacity, while the other half is due to non-recurring congestion caused by temporary disruptions, such as traffic incidents, construction work zones, weather, and special events.[2]

Highway and secondary roadway congestion is more than just a problem of recurring "rush hour" delays. TTI estimates that delay due to non-recurring incidents (disabled vehicles and crashes) are slightly larger than delay due to recurring incidents (peak hour commuting) in more than 68 cities. Under pressure to optimize performance during both types of incidents, many local governments are evolving towards a more integrated, systems-level approach to transportation operations management.[3] Increasingly, transportation and public safety agencies are working toward improvement of institutional relationships to foster more integrated day-to-day operations.

Some jurisdictions have adopted formal policies with states and surrounding jurisdictions to promote and maintain congestion management partnerships that provide regional frameworks for the integrated deployment of ITS, such as traffic conditions monitoring, computerized traffic control systems, traveler information systems, and public transit management systems. Many others are developing and implementing formal traffic incident management programs by reorganizing the priorities of transportation and public safety agencies to make improving coordination to reduce response and clearance times a clear operational objective.[4]

The systems management approach can be implemented to link the various operations oriented activities into a synergistic program through coordinated planning, continuous day-to-day cooperation, information sharing, and the development of common performance measurement data.

By implementing a more integrated transportation management approach, improvements to local government transportation operations are taking place on two levels. First, transportation agencies are beginning to recognize the need to replace traditional strategies focused on building more roads and highways with strategies that promote operations and management of existing systems. Second, local governments are beginning to develop a better understanding of the needs and perspectives of its public agencies to better coordinate functions through the following initiatives:[5]

- Building consensus among public safety and transportation agencies to establish cross-agency commitments that identify roles for operations and management activities on a cooperative regional basis (e.g. memorandum of understanding, cooperative agreements, etc.).
- Facilitating coordination among transportation and public safety agencies through the establishment of recurring planning exercises and meetings.
- Allocating funding and operating resources to sustain a continuing commitment to joint systems operations and management (interagency and multi-agency).
- Coordinating the implementation of new information technologies to achieve interoperable communication systems.

The case study box illustrates how Austin, Texas, is using the systems management approach to integrate transportation, law enforcement, and fire/EMS services to better coordinate emergency response and traffic incident management.

Case Study

Integrated Transportation, Law Enforcement, and Fire/EMS Services in Austin, Texas

The local police, fire, EMS, and transportation agencies in Austin, Texas, have partnered with Travis County, the Texas Department of Transportation, and the regional transit authority to integrate transportation and emergency services to develop a Regional Emergency Communications and Transportation Management Center that will serve the Travis County area. The new center will provide an unprecedented degree of coordination among the region's fire and EMS, law enforcement, and transportation services at the city, county, and state levels. Using an integrated communications system, the center will include wireless radio, telephone, video, fax, and microwave technology combined with countywide geographic information system mapping. Both EMS dispatchers and transportation managers will view real-time maps showing traffic and crime incident locations and the location of emergency responders. This will result in quicker, safer emergency response and traffic incident management.

Bridging the Gap

At the federal level, the emphasis is clearly shifting toward measurable customer service benefits as a strategic priority. On May 13, 2003, Transportation Secretary Norman Mineta unveiled the Bush Administration's six-year $247 billion surface transportation reauthorization proposal. "If enacted by Congress, SAFETEA will help modernize safety programs, reduce congestion and minimize project delays, increase funding flexibility for states and local jurisdictions, improve public transit efficiency, and help protect the environment," said Secretary Mineta.[6]

Calling for a safer, simpler, and smarter transportation system, under this bill, the U.S. DOT will attempt to be more efficient, achieve better results, and increase accountability through the amalgamation of public safety and transportation management and a stronger commitment to measuring progress through performance measures. As a result, it is likely that future eligibility for federal funding will require a stronger focus on measuring and reporting of performance.

The reduction of travel time, increased system reliability, and heightened system safety and security are examples of customer service benefits that can be designated as program goals.[7] Measurement of these performance variables is increasingly feasible using ITS technologies. Because of the crucial role they play in today's incident management and highway operations functions, public safety agencies will also come to inevitably share accountability for measurable improvements in system performance. Therefore, the development of common performance measures can provide local governments with a framework that can be used to evaluate and quantify their overall efficiency and effectiveness.

Overall customer satisfaction relies on local government's ability to provide the traveling public with safe, efficient, and reliable transportation networks. The systems management approach is a first step towards bridging the gaps in many of today's transportation agencies. Extending these concepts across transportation and public safety entities is the next frontier. Shared use of communications infrastructures and other technologies will assist in real-time integration of transportation and public safety operations and establish a foundation for developing and achieving common objectives.

NOTES

[1]Lockwood, Stephen. "A Systems Management Approach to Transportation Operations Management." ITS Public Safety Case Studies. Internet: http://www.itspublicsafety .net.

[2]U.S. Department of Transportation, Federal Highway Administration, Office of Operations. "The Congestion Picture." Internet: http://www.fhw.dot.gov/congestion/congpress.htm (19 November 2002).

[3]U.S. Department of Transportation, Federal Highway Administration, Office of Operations. "Congestion Mitigation." Internet: http://www.fhwa.dot.gov/congestion/congest2.htm (November 2002).

[4]Lockwood.

[5]Lockwood.

[6]U.S. Department of Transportation, Office of Public Affairs. "Secretary Mineta Unveils Bush Administration Surface Transportation Reauthorization Proposal." Internet: http://www.dot.gov/affairs/dot04003. htm (14 May 2003.

[7]Lockwood.

ADDITIONAL RESOURCES

For more information on transportation operations and management strategies, visit http://www.ops.fhwa.dot.gov. For information on the Regional Emergency Communications and Transportation Management Center in Austin, Texas, visit http://www.itspublicsafety.net/docs/austin. htm, or contact David Stone, city of Austin project manager at 512/469-5041.

For more information on SAFETEA, visit http://www.fhwa.dot.gov/reauthorization, and for information and assistance on performance measures, visit the International City/County Management Association Center for Performance Measurement at www.icma.org/performance.

This chapter was made possible through a joint project between the International City/County Management Association (ICMA) and the U.S. Department of Transportation (U.S. DOT). ICMA has partnered with U.S. DOT to provide local governments with relevant tools and resources that can be used to assist them in meeting the challenges of implementing and managing safe and effective transportation systems.

For more information about ICMA's transportation program or to request additional information on this subject, visit www.icma.org or e-mail Zia Burleigh at burleigh@ icma.org.

CHAPTER 8

Beaverton, Other Cities, Design Residential Growth Around Public Transit Stations

Terry J. Lassar

The view from many of the station stops on Portland's eastside light-rail line is of the same dreary warehouses that were standing when the line opened 12 years ago. Although light rail helped boost the vitality of the downtown and was a big factor in the rejuvenation of the city's Lloyd District, now home to the Trail Blazers Rose Garden arena complex, the amount of suburban development generated by the first segment of the Metropolitan Area Express (MAX) line was disappointing. Because the Eastside line was built next to a highway, with established neighborhoods on the other side, development opportunities were limited.

Tri-Met, the city's transit operator, was determined to get it right the second time around when it drew up plans to extend the line another 15 miles to the western suburbs. While the Eastside line accommodated existing low-density housing patterns, the Westside line was designed to generate development of large-scale urban villages next to the stations.

When it was planned a decade ago, the Westside line ran through vast tracts of va-

cant green fields owned by big businesses and major landowners that had the deep pockets necessary to take on large development projects. The Westside corridor — a haven for semi-conductor makers and high-tech companies including Tektronix Inc., Sequent Computer Systems, and Intel — has become Portland's "Silicon Forest."

Tri-Met's gamble of using the line to encourage new development patterns rather than following existing ones is paying off. Although the line will not open until this September, development activity on the Westside corridor has been intensive. Between 1990 and 1997, residential and other development projects worth $371 million — including some 6,000 dwellings — have been built or proposed within one-half mile of the 20 Westside MAX stations.

Almost every greenfield site is being developed. The first of these is Beaverton Creek, a 124-acre parcel in the suburb of Beaverton just west of Portland. To maximize development potential and give each of the major landowners equal access to the rail line, Tri-Met placed the station platform in

Originally published as "Portland's On-Track Development," *Urban Land*, Vol. 57, No. 3, March 1998. Published by the Urban Land Institute, Washington, DC. Reprinted with permission of the publisher.

the center of the site. When Trammell Crow Residential (TCR) first considered purchasing 38 acres from U.S. Bank, a primary draw was the rail stop next to the property. Of course, an added benefit was that Nike's world headquarters, immediately north of the station, and Tektronix to the east offered a ready-made market for the more than 800 rental units TCR planned to build.

Making an Impact in No-Man's Land

Development of TCR's holdings south of Millikan Way required straightforward rezoning from campus industrial to high-density residential. Development of the north parcel, however, was more complicated because it was part of the city of Beaverton's "transit overlay district," which called for a greater development mix. So TCR decided to develop the south parcel first, which carried less political baggage.

The main challenge of the first phase — Centerpointe garden apartments — was to establish a residential identity and sense of place in an area surrounded on two sides by concrete tilt-up campus industrial buildings and a large undeveloped tract to the north. TCR wanted a distinctive architectural design that would create an instant address in this no-man's land. It also wanted a "hip, clean, urban look," says TCR's West Coast group managing partner Clyde Holland, to appeal to the market of young but sophisticated employees working at Nike and the many technology-based companies nearby.

The contemporary look created by Seattle-based architects GGLO departs significantly from the typical suburban apartment design. Centerpointe's clubhouse entrance features bold columns wrapped in shiny steel and an asymmetrical barrel-vaulted metal roof. The finishes are sleek and polished. In contrast to the English library style — dark wood, carpets, heavy draperies, and wingback chairs — that TCR uses for many of its clubhouse interiors, here the interior spaces are airy and simple, like those in an art gallery. A neutral palette of white walls and pale maple floors forms a backdrop for colorful abstract paintings and sculptural furniture pieces.

The design for the garden apartments was equally adventuresome. Inspired by contemporary European multifamily housing, the architects emphasized crisp geometric forms that were sympathetic to the industrial character of the Nike campus buildings. Rounded parapets pop out from the building facades. The two- and three-story walkups, painted an industrial taupe, are accented with vivid purple and olive-green highlights.

At first, TCR was nervous about the minimalist design. Its fears that the suburban apartment market might not yet be ready for galvanized metal chimneys and asymmetrical rooflines were assuaged, however, by the project's strong leaseup. The apartments filled within seven months after opening in April 1996. When questioned why they selected Centerpointe, many residents said they were drawn by the bold, contemporary design. The development won a 1997 award of merit from the Pacific Coast Builders Conference Western Building Show and from *Builder* magazine.

Meanwhile, TCR had been participating in a master-planning process organized by Tri-Met to create a transit village for the 124 acres encircling the Beaverton Creek light-rail platform. The area included TCR's holdings north of Millikan Way, where it would build LaSalle, its second development phase; however, the plan focused primarily on the heavily forested land immediately north of the rail platform called "Tek Woods," owned by Tektronix. The master plan — a mix of commercial, retail, and residential development — called for mostly residential development on TCR's land.

Twelve months into the process, the plan unraveled when Nike unexpectedly swooped in and purchased the option for Tek

Woods, immediately south of Nike's headquarters. Nike wanted no part of the transit village. Instead it planned to use the 75-acre parcel for future expansion of its campus. When the master planning stalled, TCR quickly sought approvals for its second development phase, LaSalle, which would include 554 apartments in garden flats, townhomes, and a mid-rise building.

When Holland first asked Tri-Met what it envisioned for the site, Henry Markus, Tri-Met station area development coordinator, said it wanted a dense, mixed-use community with a strong pedestrian environment that would serve as a flagship example of transit-oriented development (TOD). One reason Tri-Met is championing the development of TODs next to its rail line is to boost ridership. "If you get the right mix of development and it is easy to walk to," notes Markus, "the transportation analysts say you can reduce the number of external auto trips by as much as 30 percent, half of which would be replaced by train trips and the other half by walking and bicycling inside the development."

"Both Tri-Met and the city of Beaverton wanted much more density than we could realistically develop," says Holland. "At that time, the rent structures didn't support the extensive mid-rise construction needed to achieve high-density thresholds." After further discussion, Markus said he would be satisfied with a density pattern that focused on the light-rail station. "I wanted a wedding cake," says Markus, "with densities increasing the closer one gets to the station." The densest part of TCR's LaSalle development is the mixed-use, mid-rise building across the tracks from the station platform. The four-story frame structure, above a concrete parking platform, achieves a density of 53 units per acre. Within a quarter-mile radius of the platform, the 554 townhomes and garden apartments are built at 35 units per acre. Density is reduced to 24 units an acre for the Centerpointe apartments, located about one-half mile south of the station.

The densities achieved at LaSalle are the highest of any suburban development on the Westside corridor. Home to some 2,000 residents, LaSalle/Centerpointe has a population that is greater than that of nearly 60 percent of the cities in Oregon. To achieve that density, TCR used a residential product mix and compact site plan that is decidedly more urban than suburban.

Refining the Townhome Design

Best known for its vast portfolio of suburban garden apartments across the nation, TCR has been favoring more intensive urban-style products — townhomes, home/offices, and mixed-use podium mid rises — in its recent Portland and Seattle developments. Townhomes offer many advantages: direct garage access, self-parking design, and no neighbors above or below — not to mention the greater densities that can be achieved without having to include expensive elevator systems. As TCR Northwest caters increasingly to the growing market of "lifestyle choice renters" — affluent individuals who want luxury, comfort, and zero maintenance — "townhomes," says Holland, "are the ideal product. They offer a for-sale living experience for rent."

TCR built its first Portland townhomes four years ago at RiverPlace, a downtown residential community on the Willamette River. A main challenge was meeting the high-density requirement of the city's redevelopment agency, which originally owned the site. TCR's architect GGLO designed a plan consisting mostly of townhomes that were based loosely on mews, the back-of-alley housing built above stables that was popular in 19th-century London. The project leased up within a record six weeks. TCR next explored the market for townhomes in suburban Portland and built 264 townhomes at its Colonnade development in Tanasbourne, several miles west of LaSalle/Centerpointe. They, too, leased up quickly.

The 211 townhomes at LaSalle reflect some of the refinements TCR has made to its unit design over the years. First, it found that the 14-foot wide chassis at RiverPlace was too tight for the suburban market. Many townhome residents, who tend to be older than the average apartment dweller, had moved from single-family homes and owned large pieces of furniture. They needed more space. So TCR added an extra foot and a half to the width. In several new projects, TCR will be building townhomes with a 20-foot-wide chassis that can accommodate two-car garages instead of tandem parking. TCR also learned that residents preferred units with end-kitchens, so that the living and dining areas can be joined into one large space that seems more like a single-family home. Anticipating that they might eventually sell the townhomes, TCR set up separate development parcels for the townhomes and garden units.

Part of TCR's strategy for creating a more compact, walkable development involved reducing the amount of land for parking. Holland's experience with another TCR development, Treat Commons — 510 units built close to the Pleasant Hill BART stop in Contra Costa County, California — suggested that parking should be provided at 1.1 spaces per unit because many residents (about 40 percent) in this development took the train to work. Holland used this same reasoning to convince the city of Beaverton to grant a parking variance at LaSalle of from two to 1.6 spaces; however, an adjacent property owner objected that the lower ratio would prompt overflow parking on his lots. A compromise was reached at 1.8 spaces per unit.

Making Connections

The site plan is described as more pedestrian friendly than many suburban schemes. "The typical garden apartment complex is designed like a donut," says architect Alan Grainger, "where the buildings are placed in the middle and parking on the outside. So one of the biggest challenges of site planning for garden apartments is creating a building edge to the public streets, instead of a parking edge. This motivated us to cluster the garden apartments at Centerpointe and LaSalle around grassy courtyards instead of parking lots."

In contrast to many suburban subdivisions with serpentine roads and cul-de-sacs that are easy to get lost in, the buildings here are organized in a more straightforward grid pattern with interconnecting streets and a comprehensive pedestrian network. Special attention was paid to creating what planners call "connectivity." Alternative walking paths connect directly to the station. The main connection is the north/south pedestrian spine, which was first envisioned in the master plan. It starts at the Centerpointe clubhouse, crosses Millikan Way, then runs north through LaSalle, past the retail shops below the townhouses next to the park-and-ride lot and through the mid-rise building. It finally ends at the landscaped plaza across the road from the light-rail platform. Beaverton required public access on the path.

The ten-foot-wide pedestrian spine, defined with a row of red maples and urban-style street lamps, is the principal unifying element for the development. Although Centerpointe and LaSalle were designed as two distinct projects and are marketed separately, they are physically joined by this central promenade.

The public realm of the development focuses on this promenade. Each of the three community center/leasing offices is placed in a strong axial relationship to the spine. "We looked to traditional town design where the city hall, post office, and other public buildings are sited in prominent locations," says Grainger. "The clubhouses are meant to function as quasi-civic buildings," adds Holland, "and as landmarks for each of the three neighborhoods within the larger development." Besides the leasing office, each clubhouse also contains a business center with computers, printers, and fax machines; a conference room specially set up for business meetings; and an entertainment room with kitchen facilities. An adjacent building with weights and aerobic equipment is designed with large picture windows so that people working out can look directly onto the pedestrian spine. At the same time, walkers have something interesting to view as they pass the building.

The promenade takes on a more urban character as it moves north past the row of LaSalle townhomes with first-floor offices that open directly onto the path, then past the row of retail shops near the station. This type of public space, where one is likely to bump into neighbors, promotes a sense of ownership. Once the rail line opens, the path will be actively used by residents walking to the train. "Activity," says Holland, "is our best security."

Partnering with Tri-Met

While TCR was planning LaSalle/Centerpointe, Tri-Met was finalizing plans for its park-and-ride lot and main access road to the train platform. Wanting to see its development located closer to the platform, TCR asked Tri-Met to move the park-and-ride lot 300 feet farther east. Tom Walsh, Tri-Met's general manager, participated in the negotiations. "It was in our self-interest," says Walsh, "to work with the real estate community to facilitate the kind of development that TCR subsequently built here." The result: hundreds of engineering drawings were tossed and Tri-Met redesigned the lot.

TCR next asked whether Tri-Met would convert some of the commuter spaces to short-term, parallel parking to support the neighborhood retail shops on the west edge of the park-and-ride lot. This would make the retail more convenient; people could park next to the shops and dash in for a latte without having to cross the entire lot. Although this was the first short-term parking to be

built at a Portland park-and-ride lot, Walsh notes that "if the short-term spaces help anchor the retail, which makes the whole neighborhood work, then clearly it works for us."

Tri-Met also supported the idea of creating a neighborhood street on the west edge of the park-and-ride lot with sidewalks, curbs, and street trees fronting the retail shops. Tri-Met and TCR entered into a joint development agreement whereby Tri-Met paid TCR to construct the street and sidewalk finishings. "What was important here," says Grainger, "was laying the foundation blocks to accommodate future changes. When the park-and-ride lot eventually is redeveloped, buildings will edge both sides of the street. So we will have a village street close to the rail stop that might well become a focal point for this neighborhood."

This collaborative redesign of the park-and-ride lot to create an amenity for the adjacent development "happened because both the developer and the transit agency were willing to take risks and try something new," says Henry Markus. Instead of the more typical suburban solution — shielding the development behind a berm and fence — "we married the two uses," says Markus. "We also think that having residents live above the adjacent retail space is a wonderful security measure for the park-and-ride."

Park-and-ride lots also offer valuable land banking opportunities. "They're great redevelopment sites," says Walsh. "Although it won't happen overnight, we eventually expect to see patterns of intense, urban development continuously along the alignment. When the trains are filled by people who have taken feeder buses or have walked to the platforms, the park-and-rides will be obsolete. Meanwhile, they're useful interim uses."

TOD Poster Child

Markus predicts that when the trains start running in September, LaSalle will be *The Oregonian* poster child for transit-oriented development. From the Beaverton Creek stop, train passengers will look out at the landscaped plaza and the signature clock-tower building. They will see early-morning commuters hurrying to drop off their laundry or fortify themselves with a tall latte at one of the neighborhood shops. Tri-Met is working to bring in a daycare operator on the small parcel it owns next to the park-and-ride lot. TCR hopes to draw community-serving tenants such as a deli, coffee shop, and dry cleaners. The Beaverton police department is eyeing one space for a precinct office with meeting facilities. TCR will lower rents, in some cases, to attract the best tenants. "We view the commercial space as an important community amenity," says Holland. The nearly 10,000 square feet of retail space is concentrated in the base of the four-story building across from the MAX station and on the first-floor space of the town-homes next to the park-and-ride lot.

Although LaSalle/Centerpointe meets Tri-Met's aspiration for a transit-supportive development, plans for a more comprehensive transit village were derailed when Nike purchased most of the land north of the tracks. The master-planning process was vulnerable because the property could always change hands. "To get what it wants," says Markus, "a public agency needs to have more control over the process, and the best way to get control is to own the land."

"What creates value for our residents? That's a question I ask with every development decision I make," says Holland, who is bullish about the value-enhancing benefit of the rail connection. Depending on where they work, he notes, a couple living at LaSalle/Centerpointe can easily get by with one car instead of two. Will living in a TOD residence that potentially could save thou-sands of dollars a year prompt residents to spend more on rent? Holland thinks so. Rents at Centerpointe/LaSalle, which now are only about 3 percent higher than those in the area, "will most likely increase as soon as the rail opens and demand for this community escalates," he predicts. A 1994 study by the University of California at Berkeley showed that apartments near the Pleasant Hill BART station rented for around $34 more per month than comparable projects in the area. Another 1995 overview report by Economics Research Associates, which examined numerous studies of nationwide transit-oriented projects, showed strong evidence that apartments located close to transit stations frequently have higher rental rates and higher occupancy rates.

Meanwhile, TCR is working with some of the area's major employers on setting up a private electric shuttle bus service to transport residents to their jobs. Employees commuting to Tektronix and Nike will be able to ride the train to the Beaverton Creek station, then catch the shuttle bus to work. TCR also is working with Tri-Met on a subsidized rail-pass program for LaSalle/Centerpointe residents.

TCR's market research shows that apartment dwellers prefer living in TOD communities with strong pedestrian environments, where they are less dependent on their cars. TCR has taken this concept one step further in its latest Northwest developments at Issaquah Highlands outside Seattle and at Tanasbourne outside Portland. These town-center developments blend major elements of retail, office, and residential space into highly walkable, new urbanist communities where residents can live, work, and play in the same place.

CHAPTER 9

Bethseda, Other Areas, Use Public Transit Stations for Neighborhood Renewal

Alvin R. McNeal *and*
Rosalyn P. Doggett

The Washington Metropolitan Area Transit Authority's (WMATA's) chief mission is to provide safe, clean, and reliable public transportation for the nearly 4 million people in its service region. However, WMATA recognized from the outset that it could recoup part of its public transportation investment by sharing in the value added to land by transit. WMATA has aggressively sought private partners to develop the real property it purchased to accommodate transit stations and related facilities. The authority's public/private land development program has spurred high-density private office, retail, and residential concentrations in many station areas. These improvements, in turn, enhance the quality of life for transit patrons as well as for persons who live, work, and shop in nearby neighborhoods. WMATA's development program is attracting new riders to the transit system, rejuvenating and creating neighborhoods, and augmenting federal, state, and local tax revenues. And it is bringing WMATA significant income,

which the authority pours back into the transit system's operating and capital programs.

WMATA was organized in 1968 by the Washington Metropolitan Area Transit Authority Compact among the states of Maryland and Virginia and the District of Columbia. The authority's governing board comprises six voting members and six alternates representing all members of the compact. One of only a few Washington regional agencies with the authority to implement programs, WMATA is charged with providing metropolitanwide public transportation service. The authority operates a rail system that will encompass 103 miles and 84 stations, when current projects are completed, and a bus system with more than 1,300 vehicles. Approximately 6.5 rail miles and five rail stations are under construction and scheduled for completion by 2001. WMATA's combined rail and bus system carries nearly 1 million riders per day and is the fourth-largest system in the United States; its rail service is the second busiest in the country.

Originally published as "Metro Makes Its Mark," *Urban Land*, Vol. 58, No. 9, September 1999. Published by the Urban Land Institute, Washington, D.C. Reprinted with permission of the publisher.

In 1997, Metrobus operated 73 percent of the total bus service in the Washington region. With increasing pressure to become more consumer oriented and cost efficient, WMATA is energizing its resources to compete with the private sector. To date, it has won contracts to furnish bus and related services in the region's outlying jurisdictions.

Long before the rail system became operational, WMATA's board adopted policies and procedures that formed the basis of the authority's public/private land development program. The first private development project, Rosslyn (Virginia) Metro Center, was initiated in 1973, three years before the Metrorail system opened. To date, WMATA has approved 29 projects; 24 have been completed, providing the authority with nearly $6 million in annual revenue from 4 million square feet of office space, 0.5 million square feet of retail space, 1,000 hotel rooms, and 300 residences. Since the inception of the land development program, WMATA has realized more than $60 million in real estate income. The yield has also included more than 1 million new rail trips per year, more than $20 million in annual taxes to localities, and 25,000 primary jobs.

WMATA receives program revenue from two types of projects: private development on property owned by the authority and private development on non–WMATA-owned sites with direct connections into Metrorail stations. On WMATA-owned land, the authority generally executes a long-term, unsubordinated ground lease with private developers. In a few cases, it makes fee simple sales. Ground leases not only provide for a base rent but also for a percentage rent that allows WMATA participation in the success of a project. In several cases, the authority has participated in the refinance or sale proceeds of improvements. Connection agreements usually provide for a simple annual rental fee with periodic escalations.

Success Stories

Situated in the heart of Washington's central business district, McPherson Square had been a deteriorating section of downtown, notorious for its concentration of adult bookstores and entertainment. Today, the immediate area over the station is home to a first-class, 153,000-square-foot, 12-story office building and 11,000 square feet of quality retail space — all on a WMATA-owned 18,000-square-foot site. The project generates $450,000 annually for WMATA and has had a remarkable impact on the immediate surrounding area, which is now home to some of the most prestigious office buildings in the Washington region. The area has come a long way since the McPherson Square Metrorail station opened in 1977.

Constructed on 18,000 square feet in downtown Washington on upscale Connecticut Avenue, Farragut North embraces 144,000 square feet of office space and 42,000 square feet of retail space both at grade and in a below-grade food court. The food court has a direct connection to the Metrorail station and is an early example of this now-popular food service concept. Constructed in 1978, the development provides more than $600,000 in base ground rent and an annual percentage rent after revenues reach a certain level. In 2000, as part of an adjustment every decade, the project also will pay $1 million to the authority in premium rent. Though Connecticut Avenue has reemerged as a sought-after address, the avenue was losing ground to trendier parts of downtown at the time the station opened.

Bethesda Metro Center is one of a number of examples in metropolitan Washington of how the introduction of rail transit has helped revive a decaying inner-suburban retail district. Situated in Montgomery County, Maryland, at the center of the commercial spine of Bethesda, Bethesda Metro Center contains 378,000 square feet of office space, a 380-room Hyatt Hotel, 60,000 square feet of retail space, and more than 1,140 parking spaces. WMATA receives an annual rent of $1.6 million. In addition to its enormous success, Bethesda Metro Center has spurred a host of major private office, retail, and residential developments — all within immediate walking distance of the Metrorail station. Today, downtown Bethesda has more than tripled the development of its pre–Metrorail days. Montgomery County is home to several major corporations and is recognized nationally for the quality of its land use planning.

WMATA's public/private project at the Ballston Metrorail station encompasses 283,000 square feet of office space, 6,200 square feet of retail space, a health club, a Hilton Hotel, and more than 200 residential condominiums. Situated in Arlington County, Virginia, at the terminus of the Rosslyn/Ballston corridor, the project generates a yearly rent of more than $600,000 for WMATA. An outstanding example of how a community can use transit for economic development purposes, the Rosslyn/Ballston corridor, located along an older commercial boulevard, is punctuated by five Metrorail stations. Arlington County targeted the corridor and its station areas for intensive, transit-oriented growth and, to that end, provided planning incentives such as density/height bonuses. Rosslyn/Ballston is probably the most successful public/private development corridor in the United States. Since Ballston station opened in late 1978, the corridor has seen more than 12 million square feet of new office development in addition to the development of significant multifamily residential, university, and hotel facilities.

Even after all its successes, WMATA still controls more than 1,000 acres of land that are deemed to have development potential. Much of the acreage is used for surface parking that can be incorporated into parking structures as land values increase around stations, thus freeing up the remainder of the authority's property for development.

Efforts to attract development have required a combination of vigorous entrepreneurship and an improving business climate. During the late 1980s and early 1990s, a regional real estate recession caused development to languish. Recognizing that intensive station-area development was pivotal to greater transit ridership in a time of reduced local and national subsidies, the WMATA board of directors reevaluated its non-fare-box revenue programs — such as advertising, parking, and joint use of rights-of-way for fiber-optic cables — and decided to enhance its public/private redevelopment program to make it more active, credible, responsive, and reliable.

The New and Improved WMATA

More Educational Outreach. The purpose of WMATA's educational outreach program is to inform both developers and communities of the advantages of transit-oriented development. Activities have included a highly successful two-day, transit-oriented development conference cosponsored by the Urban Land Institute (ULI), the Federal Transportation Administration, and other organizations. The conference attracted more than 400 participants. Outreach also extends to frequent presentations to real estate industry and civic organizations.

Active Site Marketing. The authority widely disseminated and advertised a comprehensive solicitation for 33 sites in 1996 and two solicitations for 25 sites in 1999. Each year, WMATA markets remaining sites that become available upon completion of portions of the rail system. It also makes consistent use of an upgraded WMATA Web site and other advertising.

A Clear Procurement Process. To encourage the participation of private entrepreneurs, WMATA has clarified its proposal requirements. In particular, it streamlined its procurement process by reducing the number of review and approval steps to ensure a rapid and flexible response to proposals submitted by the development community. The authority also has spelled out each step so that developers can readily envision the full process. And it has incorporated standard commercial tools, such as business term sheets, into its negotiations.

Local Involvement. Local development officials now play a greater role in the selection of WMATA sites to be marketed for development. Officials help market the sites and provide advice during the developer selection process. Consequently, they are inclined to support developer proposals as well as requests for density bonuses at Metrorail station sites.

Clear Selection Criteria. Criteria for selecting projects take the form of project impacts on ridership, fare-box receipts, rental income to help operate the transit system, and local tax revenues. The viability of the proposed development team is also subjected to scrutiny.

WMATA now operates the most active public/private transit program in the United States. As a result of solicitations issued since 1996, the authority has received 31 proposals for 20 sites and is in varying stages of evaluation and negotiation. In all, the proposals include plans for more than 10 million square feet of office space, more than 3 million square feet of retail space, and more than 8,000 residences. Six of the projects, for which preferred developers have already been approved by the WMATA board of directors, would generate $88 million in sales and rental revenue over their first ten years. In terms of rental revenue alone, both old and new projects are expected to generate the equivalent of $12 to $15 million of income per year. WMATA also projects the addition of 105,000 new daily trips with the concomitant increases in annual fare-box revenue.

On Tap for the Future

In the heart of downtown Washington, the proposed Gallery Place project will occupy 1.71 acres that abut the city's new 20,000-seat MCI Center and H Street, which is the retail spine of Washington's Chinatown. The project calls for a 22-screen movie theater, 300,000 square feet of retail space, 180 residences, and 900 parking spaces. WMATA's board recently approved the $26 million sale of the property; construction will begin in fall 1999.

The office/retail/residential project at White Flint will locate on 32 open acres in one of Washington's most prosperous suburbs — Montgomery County, Maryland. The site is the county's last large developable parcel at a well-established commercial destination. Though business terms are still under negotiation, it is likely that WMATA will receive substantial rental payment as the White Flint site is developed in stages over the next ten years. Payments will far exceed those from existing public/private development projects. A Montgomery County conference center on an additional 13 acres of WMATA-owned land is also slated for White Flint.

Located within the city of Greenbelt, a Roosevelt-era town in Prince George's County, Maryland, the Greenbelt project would reconfigure station facilities and a 3,600-space surface parking lot within 78 acres at the Greenbelt Metrorail station. The required WMATA parking will be relocated to a structure pursuant to WMATA's policy that the developer must replace at cost any WMATA facilities that need to be moved. The authority will, however, adjust rental/sales rates in accordance with the facility replacement requirement. The newly proposed suburban development will combine WMATA property and an adjacent, privately owned parcel. Project plans include a 1.8 million-square-foot upscale shopping mall, two 200-room hotels, 1.5 million square feet of office space, more than 2,000 apartments, and 300,000 square feet of entertainment retail space. Greenbelt is the largest WMATA project approved to date.

WMATA's development activity is the product of a renewed interest in both suburban infill locations and previously unmarketable inner-city sites. The authority is moving expeditiously to capitalize on a healthy real estate market and to adopt creative approaches, which will likely include special financial incentives that will spur development on certain remaining sites. Without doubt, suburban traffic problems (Washington is second only to the Los Angeles area in traffic congestion) have helped spark an interest in concentrating development near Metrorail stations.

Getting Results

The benefit to WMATA of an additional $15 million in annual real estate rental income cannot be underestimated. Each year, WMATA Compact members must subsidize WMATA transit system operations by approximately $300 million. The equivalent of 5 percent of that amount earned from real estate revenues is a boon to WMATA operations. Indeed, real estate revenues, including parking and fiber-optic fees, are the single largest source of non-fare-box revenue for WMATA. Further, development earnings can be used at the board's discretion to provide incentives for additional real estate development on sites that are not as readily marketable as those already developed. In fact, WMATA has established a Transit Infrastructure Investment Fund for less promising sites.

Public/private land development revenue will most certainly pay back the estimated $400 million invested since 1968 by the federal, state, and local governments in WMATA rail system property acquisition. Of that amount, state and local government provided 20 percent, or $80 million. By 2003, WMATA's receipts from the public/private land development program will total almost double that amount, a nearly 200 percent return on local investment.

Metrorail's role as a catalyst for transit-oriented development goes beyond Metro-owned station sites. The Urban Land Institute estimates that Metrorail has generated $15 billion in additional development within the Washington region, and that figure is expected to grow to $20 billion with completion of the 103-mile system. The international accounting firm of KPMG Peat Marwick has estimated that the state of Virginia is receiving a 19 percent annual rate of return on its investment in Metrorail as a result of additional development attracted by the rail transit system.

WMATA's proactive management of its real estate assets has produced the desired results for all parties — the authority, developers, the public, and local jurisdictions — showing that transit agencies can be creative asset managers as well as outstanding mobility managers and that, in fact, the two activities are mutually reinforcing.

CHAPTER 10

Boston Uses Public Transit Lines to Stimulate Inner-City Development

Jim Miara

Transit-oriented development (TOD) is a concept that today's urban planners bandy about as gleefully as if they had invented it. But communities have always developed along transportation routes, and savvy real estate developers have always been there to lead or participate in their growth.

The earliest settlements were established at river bends and coastal harbors. Waterways offered a ready supply of fish, but equally important, they provided the fastest and safest routes between villages. In the American westward migration, settlements clustered at convenient stopping points along the dusty trail, and later beside railroad stations. The 20th century's interstate highway system and urban beltways spurred development that quickly sprawled out from the highway's interchanges.

"Today, good development sites around transit are like the highway exits used to be in the 1960s," explains Tony Pangaro, a principal with Millennium Partners–Boston, a development company that is building a $500 million mixed-use complex in downtown Boston within easy reach of three subway lines. "Back then, if you knew where the highway exit was going to be, you bought and built. Much the same is happening today with transit systems."

The idea that people will settle and commerce will develop near transportation systems, which afford easy mobility, is beyond dispute. What is new about the current TOD movement is that urban planners now are using the proven allure of transit systems—commuter rail, light rail, monorail, and buses—to reverse the chaotic development patterns that the automobile has imposed on metropolitan areas over the past 40 years.

Proponents of TOD see it as an integral part of the smart growth movement, which takes a multifaceted approach to controlling growth and preserving a community's quality of life. Smart growth proponents advocate concentrating development in areas where the infrastructure to support it already exists. Public funds and attention, smart growth advocates insist, should be directed away from building new highways and toward installing mass transit systems con-

Originally published as "On Route," *Urban Land*, Vol. 60, No. 5, May 2001. Published by the Urban Land Institute, Washington, D.C. Reprinted with permission of the publisher.

nected to the central city. Planning for these transit systems should include development strategies to revive moribund neighborhoods and to create "transit villages" oriented toward pedestrians.

Transit villages are tightly clustered, mixed-use developments within a half-mile radius of a transit station. They include densely developed housing, stores, commercial buildings, entertainment facilities, social services offices, and public open spaces. Ideally, people who live in these villages can get to everything they need by foot. Those who come to the villages for work — preferably by mass transit — will be encouraged to use the surrounding amenities. Those who live in the village but work outside of it can use the transit system to travel to their jobs.

"Transit systems, particularly rail transit, really do act as a catalyst to economic development," points out Tim Rood, a principal with Berkeley, California–based Calthorpe, Inc., who is working on a light-rail transit (LRT) line in the Twin Cities (Minneapolis/St. Paul). "And transit-oriented development, if planned wisely, is an important component of a strategy to keep our regions livable as they continue to grow."

The impetus behind TOD is not hard to find. Without question, the motivating force is the automobile and the threat it poses to the quality of life. Traffic congestion has increased so much in virtually every metropolitan area that two-hour commutes now are routine. Attempts to alleviate the problem by constructing more highways almost always have led to more sprawl and, eventually, more congestion. And the new highways that run through rural areas spur development in once-cherished open spaces. The rate at which green space is lost to development now exceeds the rate of population growth. In some areas, development is accelerating while the population is declining. And as homes are built farther from the central cities, commuting distances increase, which means more hours in the car, more pollution, and more frustration.

Statistics confirm what every commuter knows intuitively: More cars than ever are on the road. The one-car household is a thing of the past; most have two or three. More people are joining the workforce; they are traveling farther to reach their jobs; and they often choose, or are forced, to drive by themselves. All of which compounds traffic woes. A disproportionately fast growth in travel demand compared with population growth was found by Robert Dunphy, senior resident fellow for transportation at ULI. He attributes the phenomenon to "the three Ds: demographics, dependence, and distance."

According to Dunphy, changing demographics accounted for 36 percent of the travel increase in the 1980s. Between 1983 and 1990, the workforce grew almost 250 percent faster than the population did, mostly because women began flocking to the workplace. At the same time, dependency on the automobile increased, as demonstrated by a decline in the use of transit and carpools. Disaffection with alternative travel modes fueled the growth of automobile travel by as much as 25 percent. Finally, the longer distance traveled per trip, including the commute, boosted travel growth by 38 percent.

"The severity of peak-hour congestion in urban areas became significantly worse during the first half of the 1990s, especially in the nation's 33 urban areas with over 1 million population," Dunphy explained. "These areas account for fully two-thirds of the urban congestion, even though they account for only half of the urban travel."

Frustration caused by traffic jams and air pollution has sparked a search for alternatives to car travel. The traditional approach of building new highways and widening older ones usually resulted in temporary relief, but in the long run simply added to the problem. The pattern has become so obvious even to casual observers, that calls for new highway construction to alleviate traffic congestion often are ridiculed. When Georgia's governor Roy Barnes recommended the construction of a new multilane highway 20 miles north of Interstate 285 near Atlanta, an *Atlanta Constitution* editorial complained that a new highway would simply aggravate the area's already exaggerated urban sprawl. "The plan almost appears sensible," the editorial asserts, "until you pause to examine how such highways actually work. And then it sounds, well ... dumb."

It is apparent, says Ken Kruckemeyer, a research associate at the Center for Transportation Studies at Massachusetts Institute of Technology (MIT), "that people who said we need more highways were proven wrong. We are overwhelming the roadway network, which means we have to find ways to make movement more efficient. Public transit systems are part of the answer. We have to see how people can live closer together and be happy about it. That means building communities." If automobiles are the source of the problem, urban planners say, why not take a look at conditions in American cities before the automobile was so dominant? During the first two decades of the 20th century, travel in and out of metropolitan areas was primarily by railroad or electric streetcars. By 1920, half of the U.S. population lived in metropolitan areas, and the use of mass transit was at its peak. That year, more than 15 billion transit trips were made. Studies of the period found that about 25 percent of the population lived in communities that grew up around streetcar stations.

Not surprisingly, this pattern caught the attention of developers. In their 1996 book *Transit Villages in the 21st Century*, Michael Bernick and Robert Cervero noted that many of America's early electric streetcar lines were built by real estate syndicates. "Trolleys and real estate projects were often bundled together," the authors pointed out. "Transit itself was usually a loss leader that allowed huge windfall profits from land sales."

But after 1920, the growing popularity of the automobile created a different real estate dynamic. The increased mobility that automobiles made possible stimulated visions of get-away-from-it-all single-family homes in the suburbs. As the real estate action moved from the metropolitan centers to their peripheries, the streetcar lines became expendable and the extension of highways imperative. "While in 1910 no one dared advertise a home that wasn't within an easy walk of a train depot, by the 1920s no one dared offer one that didn't have a garage and easy road access," note Bernick and Cervero.

After World War II, the use of mass transit declined dramatically. At its peak in 1945, more than 24 billion passengers boarded mass transit vehicles. Ten years later, the number of riders was down to 11 billion. By the early 1960s, ridership had plummeted so low that many transit lines were on the verge of collapse. In 1964, the federal government stepped in to rescue transit systems, which until then were mainly in private hands. Over the next ten years, the government disbursed $3.3 billion in grants for the acquisition and repair of metropolitan transit lines.

Government support for mass transit systems combined with such federal legislation as the 1990 Clean Air Act Amendments, which set specific air pollution standards, boosted the prospects of mass transit and, in several cases, influenced decisions not to build new highways through central cities. The Intermodal Surface Transportation Efficiency Act (ISTEA) of 1991 set aside $6 billion in congestion management and air-quality funds for transit improvements.

Today, as the efficiency of transit systems improves and the frustration with commuting twice a day grows, the popularity of mass transit is ever so slightly yet discernibly returning. And once again, real estate developers are on top of the trend.

Boston has the oldest and one of the most used transit systems in America. The subway stations are dark and dreary, but the trains run frequently and usually are reliable. The electric trolley lines are slower than the subways, but they provide widespread service that extends well into the city's western suburbs. Like other cities, Boston joined the highway-building craze during the 1950s and early 1960s and neglected its mass transit systems. The popular song of the 1950s about a guy named Charlie getting lost on the Massachusetts Transit Authority (MTA) had the ring of truth to it for most Bostonians.

Also during this period, Boston's central city was losing population to the suburban exodus. Downtown districts that once bustled with theaters and restaurants became dark and empty and home to seedy establishments. But beginning in the late 1970s and escalating in the booming 1990s, Boston's downtown experienced a revival. Young adults and empty-nesters left their suburban homes for apartments or condominiums in the central city, and even the folks who kept their homes in the suburbs traveled downtown to restaurants and entertainment events more often than before. As part of this movement, the transit systems were rediscovered. Over the past decade, service improved and ridership increased.

All of these trends factored in to Millennium Partner's decision in 1999 to develop a glitzy $500 million mixed-use project in a dense, former adult-entertainment district in downtown Boston known as the "Combat Zone." The 1.8 million-square-foot Ritz Carlton Towers project, which will open this summer, includes 309 luxury condominiums (ranging in price from $500,000 to $3.5 million), 191 hotel rooms, 63 rental and extended-stay apartments, a 19-screen cinema, a fitness center, and a full-service restaurant. The complex also includes 1,100 parking spaces, the bare minimum for a project of this size.

"The project could not have been built without the availability of the three transit lines, nor would you want to have built it," explains Millennium's Pangaro. The traffic impact on the neighborhood would have been overwhelming without the transit sys-

tems, he says, but with them, studies showed that 80 percent of trips to the complex would not involve private cars. And because fewer cars were expected, the developers could scale back the number of parking spaces in their plan. If the transit systems were not in place and 80 percent of the trips were by private car, Pangaro notes, it would have been necessary to build a parking garage at an extra cost of about $60 million. "You never get that money back," he says. "Transportation is a large consideration for developers. It's a pocketbook issue. Plus, there's a changing culture regarding transit systems. It is logical, if you think it through, to develop around transportation."

A sign of just how far the interest in mass transit systems has evolved is that it has reached Dallas, where the automobile is deeply interwoven into the image of Texas rugged individualism. Marlboro men do not share a seat on a light-rail vehicle — or at least they did not until 1996, when the first LRT line was opened by the Dallas Area Rapid Transit (DART) agency.

After initial wariness, the system captured the public's imagination. In 1999, more than three-quarters of the voters in 13 Dallas-area cities and towns approved funds to double the size of the LRT system. Last year, DART carried more than 40,000 passengers on its 20 miles of track. Moreover, DART officials say the transit line has increased retail business in downtown neighborhoods by 30 percent. They also estimate that approximately $1 billion in private funds have been, or soon will be, invested in transit-oriented development. The new Dallas subway station, Cityplace, just north of downtown, attracted the developers who built the West Village shopping center and apartment complex.

Dallas officials began thinking of transit systems because traffic conditions grew steadily worse, air quality suffered, and they could find few alternatives. Between 1995 and 1999, traffic delays in the Dallas area increased by 37 percent. During the same period, the population of north Texas grew by 10 percent and the number of miles traveled by vehicle increased by 18 percent. Meanwhile, the Dallas central business district was dying.

"Dallas is a car city; it is not a 24-hour city," says Steven Hamwey, architect and urban planner with the Watertown, Massachusetts–based architecture firm Sasaki Associates, who helped design the DART system. He says a major objective of the design was to revitalize downtown districts. "We placed four stations downtown, all of them in areas we thought would stimulate development. We put one beside an office building that was underused and a hotel that had closed. Today, a new hotel chain is operating the hotel and the office building is doing well," Hamwey says.

This year, more than a dozen cities and towns in the Dallas metropolitan area that previously showed little interest in transit systems have asked DART to extend commuter rail and bus services to their jurisdictions. "We're grappling with how to be fair," DART board member Linda Koop told the *Dallas Morning News* last February. "There's no question that as we get more crowded, it's becoming more important to provide mass transit to the entire region."

More than 2.5 million people — 60 percent of Minnesota's total population — live in the metropolitan area surrounding the Twin Cities, Minneapolis/St. Paul. Over the next 25 years, the population is expected to grow by another 650,000 and bring with it 400,000 new jobs and 350,000 new households. The Twin Cities Metropolitan Council, a regional planning agency, was charged with preparing the area for the onslaught.

Among the council's earliest products was a "transit redesign" document that established guidelines for transit-oriented development. Sprawl development would stop while new growth would be channeled to infill areas and long-neglected neighborhoods. A more recent Met Council document describes the configuration that planning officials want transit-oriented development to take. "The shape of the TOD should be configured such that all areas have easy pedestrian connection to the transit stop and the central area of mixed uses. Impediments to pedestrian movement such as busy arterial roadways, large parking lots, and rugged terrain should not break up the walkable environment of a TOD."

In January, ground was broken for the Hiawatha LRT Corridor, an 11-mile-long line that will connect downtown Minneapolis, the International Airport, and the Mall of America, as well as a number of neighborhoods and activity centers. "Our LRT is right in the heart of a bad area," says Caren Dewar, community development director at the Metropolitan Council. "The challenge is to find out how transit can guide a market. In the Midwest, there are few places where you can live without a car. We chose to locate the Hiawatha line where it is because it is a place where you could live without owning a car."

Dewar favors LRT systems over buses because, she says, "LRTs change lifestyles and development patterns in a way that buses do not. And the tracks signal to the investment community that there is a serious commitment to the route." Dewar points out that the Metropolitan Council is considering other LRT lines along traditional transportation corridors, including the "Greenway," a path that American Indians took to get to the river.

Transit-oriented development as an approach to combat traffic congestion and protect the environment has caught on all across the country. Transit villages are popping up not only in expected places like northern California, but also in unexpected areas such as automobile-dominated southern California. In Hollywood, a $385 million entertainment and shopping center was built around a metro rail station. And the Village Green housing development in Sylmar was designed so that residents have to walk only a few hundred yards to the metro rail station.

In Illinois, three legislative advisory panels recently delivered reports on ways Chicago and other Illinois cities can grow without sprawl. One proposal, the Live Near Work Act, obligates the state to reimburse employers who help their workers with rent or down-payments for homes located closer to the workplace. Another proposal involves incentives to conserve farmland. Under its provisions, developers will be encouraged to contribute to the purchase of "conservation easements" — pledges from farmers never to let their land be developed — in exchange for the right to build elsewhere at higher densities than otherwise permitted. A final proposal calls for creating an executive-level planning office to coordinate smart growth concepts.

Some national mortgage lenders are offering "transportation-efficient loans" for properties located within walking distance of transit stations. The reasoning is that the money a homeowner saves by taking public transportation rather than driving a car can be added to monthly mortgage payments. Thus, higher loan amounts are possible.

We are entering "transit decades," claims Antonio DiMambro, a Boston-based architect and urban designer who has studied urban transportation issues in a number of cities, including Dallas. "The federal government has said, 'enough with building new highways,'" he explains. "There is evidence that when transit lines are built, people use them. People say, 'I don't mind going to work without a car.' In Dallas, car owners pay an average of $8,000 per year to operate a vehicle. If they sold their cars and took mass transit to work, they could rent a car 52 weekends a year for a quarter of that amount," says DiMambro.

In addition, the evidence clearly shows that transit lines stimulate development. "In almost every case," observes DiMambro, "the value of real estate beside a new transit line has skyrocketed." While transit-oriented development may be a concept as old as the hills (or the rivers), the trick for real estate developers has always been identifying the hot transit system. Today, highways are out; urban transit systems are in.

CHAPTER 11

Boulder Redesigns Residential Streets to Focus on People Rather than Cars

John Fernandez

Boulder, Colorado, has a problem shared by cities across the country. Too many of its streets divide rather than integrate. They are single-purpose arteries, emphasizing cars over people. They despoil the environment with their expansive impervious surfaces. They encourage speeding. And they support faceless suburban development patterns guaranteed to worsen traffic congestion.

Residential streets are key determinants of neighborhood quality. They offer a place to walk, to play — and of course to park. Yet ever since the start of the post–World War II housing boom, residential streets have become increasingly devoted to traffic movement. The wide lanes required by today's codes lead to higher speeds, more accidents, and greater urban fragmentation.

In recent years, many planners — and even some traffic engineers — have begun to question whether wider streets are as functional as their advocates claim. Increasingly, designers, public officials, and developers — often spurred by neighborhood activists — are considering the virtues of a hierarchical street classification that would provide for a variety of residential street types, each reflecting different traffic conditions.

Local History

Like many western cities, Boulder was laid out, in 1859, on a grid based on a 400-foot block and 25-foot lots, a pattern admirably suited to speculation. It should be noted, however, that the Boulder City Town Company set high rates for town lots, up to $1,000 for a 50-by-140-foot building site. Even then, it appears, Boulder favored slower growth.

The post–World War II subdivisions disrupted the grid pattern, with larger lots and blocks set along curvilinear streets, and no alleys. In the 1960s and 1970s, more cul-de-sacs appeared, with fewer connections to adjacent development. Today, the city is characterized by a high rate of car ownership (two vehicles for every three people) and a significant jobs-to-housing imbalance. Boulder's employment-to-population ratio is

Originally published as "Boulder Brings Back the Neighborhood Street," *Planning*, Vol. 60, No. 6, June 1994. Reprinted with permission from *Planning*, copyright © June 1994 by the American Planning Association, Suite 1600, 122 South Michigan Avenue, Chicago, IL 60603.

0.83, more than 40 percent higher than the figure for the eight-county Denver metropolitan region. If current trends continue, total employment will exceed population by 2010.

Boulder also has several recent examples of more sensitive residential planning. In 1983, a local developer built the Cottages, a 37-unit affordable housing project, on a woonerf-style street. The 5.3-acre site abuts city-owned open space on the north side. And in 1990, another local developer, William Coburn, built Walnut Hollow, a high-end infill project consisting of nine Victorian-style houses — with detached garages — arrayed along an 18-foot-wide street just east of downtown.

But these projects, both planned unit developments, resulted largely from individual initiatives and not from a community-wide vision of what constitutes better urban development. Moreover, neither would be allowed under the current regulations. In the past, the city's planning department used the PUD ordinance to vary street standards. But as concerns grew over liability, policy makers were unwilling to grant individual waivers in the absence of new citywide street standards.

For the most part, recent new subdivisions have complied absolutely with the letter of the Boulder rules, laid down in the zoning code and subdivision regulations adopted in 1971. The result: three-car garagescape uniformity, the "loops and lollipops" pattern exhibited so well in the city's expanding northeast quadrant.

In 1992, the planning department, aware of the community's growing unhappiness with the look and operation of the new subdivisions, decided to take a more aggressive role in neighborhood design. The staff noted that the city's 1989 transportation master plan called for new residential street guidelines to enhance neighborhood safety and livability.

As it happened, a large new project had just been proposed for the northeast edge of the city — the 140-acre Four Mile Creek. The planning department hired Peter Brown, AICP, an urban designer in Houston, to conduct a design charette before the project entered the development review phase. Brown toured the site and interviewed the developers, a consortium of local builders. Then, working with other team members, he compared construction costs for both a conventional subdivision and a neotraditional design, complete with narrow streets and pedestrian paths, and drew sketch plan alternatives.

The plan that resulted was then presented to the developers, and they used many of the neotraditional design elements in their annexation application. (The annexation ordinance was the legal device used to vary the city's street standards.) The 309-unit project is now under construction. Its gridded street plan includes both boulevards and narrow streets. It also features short blocks; motor courts (oblong cul-de-sacs with central landscaping and parking); a raised intersection (road surface matches elevation of crosswalk); traffic circles; and an alley. There is also an extensive bicycle and pedestrian path network.

The Four Mile Creek exercise was considered a success in that it convinced the city to move beyond simply responding to proposals to assuming a leadership role in defining a vision for development. Under the leadership of its new planning director, Will Fleissig, Boulder is now attempting to relate its street design standards to an overall community planning and urban design program.

Complete Overhaul

The vehicle for this new approach is the Residential Access Project (RAP), which was initiated jointly in the spring of 1992 by the city's planning and public works departments. The impetus was the increasing restiveness of neighborhood residents concerned about traffic congestion. At that point, the planning staff proposed to broaden the residential street guidelines to include the entire movement network in residential areas and to create urban design guidelines.

The entire project is being carried out in house, with no special funding except for a small graphics budget. Both the public works staff member — a transportation planner — and I devote about a fifth of our time to RAP. We report to an interdepartmental steering committee.

The first part of the two-phase project was aimed at devising a statement of purpose and a richer menu of street standards. The project staff has spent the last two years researching standards in other cities and involving residents in a collaborative planning process. A spinoff effort, the neighborhood traffic mitigation program, will encourage the use of traffic calming measures.

In March of this year, the planning board endorsed the staff's recommendation that the city's one-size-fits-all street standard be replaced. The current standard requires 12-foot travel lanes, six-foot parking lanes, curb, gutter, and sidewalk in a 48-foot right-of-way. The new standards would offer four classifications, all of them narrower than the current requirement.

The two lowest classifications would be low-speed (15–20 m.p.h.) "queuing" streets. They could be as narrow as 20 feet, and they would allow on-street parking. To mollify fire officials, the standards provide for fire set-up areas (pads long and wide enough to accommodate fire trucks and close enough together so fire hoses can reach the back of all dwellings).

The standards would also allow alleys, which are officially discouraged in the current subdivision regulations. The planners noted that Boulder residents consistently rate traditional neighborhoods with alleys as most livable.

The planning board also endorsed the staff's recommended street purposes statement. A clear definition of intent is expected

to guide all those involved in administering the new regulations.

The final proposal for phase one is to be presented to the planning board this month. The next step is to translate the proposal into an ordinance for consideration by the city council. That's expected to be done this summer.

Phase two of RAP will address the broader topic of residential-area design, including the building-street relationship, network standards, and "shared" streets (such as the Dutch woonerf). A set of performance-based standards will parallel the new prescriptive standards.

The planning department is putting the draft standards to the test in a subcommunity plan now being prepared for north Boulder. With 9,200 residents spread over 2,300 acres, "NoBo" is the least developed of the city's nine subcommunities. It was annexed four years ago, and its many vacant and underutilized parcels are considered ripe for redevelopment.

At a five-day public charette held the first week of May in the National Guard Armory, more than 300 citizens suggested ways of intensifying the movement grid and reconnecting streets. Their recommendations included both boulevards and skinny streets. A Miami-based urban design consulting firm, Dover, Kohl & Partners, is incorporating their recommendations and many of the RAP concepts into the plan being prepared for city council consideration in July.

Searching Out Models

There seemed to be few models when Boulder started this project two summers ago. Most jurisdictions still use some variation of the highway-oriented street standards that arose in the late 1930s with the creation of the Federal Highway Administration and the "Green Book" published by AASHTO, the American Association of State Highway and Transportation Officials.

Recently, designers associated with the movement coming to be known as "the new urbanism"—Andres Duany, Anton Nelessen, AICP, Peter Calthorpe, and others—have received considerable media attention. But most of their work has been on large tracts of raw land, not the infill projects that are typical of places like Boulder.

There are other models with broader applicability to the situations in which most planners find themselves: infill, redevelopment, and fringe-area development.

One such example is an early one, the "performance streets" standard adopted by Bucks County, Pennsylvania, in 1980. It provides a model ordinance that includes a rich hierarchy of street types, although its use as a model is limited by the emphasis on cul-de-sacs and loop streets, and its lack of attention to alternative modes of travel.

The performance streets concept is also the basis of a new set of supplemental standards for residential neighborhoods now being considered by the city of Houston and surrounding Harris County. The city currently has only two types of residential streets: a 28-foot pavement section with a 50-foot or 60-foot right-of-way. The new standards would create eight street types and allow narrower streets in new subdivisions, with such design elements as "chicanes" (jogs to slow traffic) and flare-outs. The standards were prepared by Peter Brown in collaboration with Patricia D. Knudson & Associates and Terra Associates, both of Houston.

Portland, Oregon's 1991 "skinny streets" ordinance applies to residential blocks where lots are over 5,000 square feet. It allows 20-foot-wide streets with parking on one side, or 26-foot-wide streets with parking on both sides—thus overturning the long-entrenched idea that all streets must provide at least two through lanes of traffic. City engineer Terry Bray reports that 30 blocks of skinny streets were built in the first two construction seasons.

Olympia, Washington's state capital,

has approved transportation policies that prohibit new cul-de-sacs. The policies, adopted in 1992, are an outgrowth of a visual preference survey and urban design plan undertaken with the help of New Jersey consultant Anton Nelessen.

Nelessen also prepared the urban design guidelines now being reviewed in Santa Fe, New Mexico. The guidelines offer 16 distinct land-use and circulation prototypes. Widths range downward to 18 feet, sometimes with no building setback requirement, and curb radiuses as tight as four feet. Frank Diluzio, the city's newly appointed fire chief, says he supports the standards provided that new streets "pretty much keep a 20-foot clear zone," meaning that no parking rules must be strictly enforced.

In Squim, Washington, a retirement community on the Olympic Peninsula, a "block standard" includes a 12-foot alley in a 20-foot easement. Public works director Richard Parker says the alleys work well for utility placement and the city's automated garbage collection system.

Another model is the west end of Vancouver, British Columbia, where traffic calming measures have proven to be an important adjunct to street standards. Street closures and diverters have created a pleasant walking environment in a high-rise district flanked by busy shopping streets.

But the most promising model is an Australian one: the code for residential development prepared in 1992 by the planning and housing department in the state of Victoria. This exemplary document covers the entire residential environment, from lot orientation to regional street networks, and it defines a broad hierarchy of local streets.

The Victoria code includes both performance-based and prescriptive standards, and is specific about details like deflection angles (for speed control). It also requires that all dwellings be located no more than 700 meters (about 2,300 feet) and three "junctions," or intersections, from a major street to balance the amount of time motorists are forced to spend in low-speed environments.

Most important, the code requires development planners to plot out pedestrian and bicycle lanes as well as the usual environmental constraints and opportunities — before the street system is laid out. In this, the Australian planners echo the advice of California architect Christopher Alexander, who says that in urban design, pedestrian spaces should be designed first, then the buildings, then the roads.

Wendy Morris, the senior urban designer in the department's Melbourne offices, described the code in Alexandria, Virginia, last October at the first Congress on the New Urbanism. She said a key to making it effective has been interdisciplinary workshops: "We found that to make real change in building patterns, those who make design, permitting, and development decisions must be involved and retrained."

Ready for Change

Back in the U.S., the Florida Department of Community Affairs has undertaken an ambitious project to develop "community design guidelines" for everything from energy conservation to affordable housing to streets. The project's principal researcher, Reid Ewing, of the Joint Center for Environmental and Urban Problems at Florida Atlantic University/Florida International University in Fort Lauderdale, says the "overriding rationale is to make the street more livable, less energy-consumptive, and environmentally sound." His team has proposed a 20-foot wide standard for all local streets.

Ben Starrett, the director of strategic planning and policy coordination for the community affairs department, says he expects the guidelines to be published soon.

Even the Institute for Transportation Engineers, long a holdout against alternative street standards, is becoming part of the solution. In February, the institute's technical committee on neotraditional town design issued an "informational report" entitled *Traffic Engineering for Neotraditional Neighborhoods.* Frank Spielberg, a traffic engineering consultant in Annandale, Virginia, who chairs the committee, says members hope that ITE will endorse the "recommended practices," which include narrower streets in some cases, within the next year.

As to liability, the bugaboo of city officials, one member of the ITE committee, Walter Kulash — a traffic engineer in Orlando — contends that "legal obstacles to narrow streets are a red herring." He notes that a 1993 study he coauthored for the National Conference on Tort Liability and Risk Management for Surface Transportation concluded that tort cases "invariably have to do with high speed," not street width.

Finally, for those ready to change, a few basic reminders:

The public interest requires safe, livable, and attractive streets that contribute to the urban fabric.

Streets should be designed to suit their function. Many streets, especially local ones, have purposes other than vehicular traffic. Some local residential streets should be designed for speeds of less than 20 m.p.h. Remember that the general population is aging, with the cohort over 85 growing fastest of all.

A hierarchical street network should have a rich variety of types, including bicycle, pedestrian, and transit routes.

Reid Ewing believes the "overall system design has fallen into the cracks between the planning and engineering professions." The entire movement network should be considered, with connectivity given prominence.

Standards should be developed to enhance local streets' contributions to urban design. That means paying attention to "sense of enclosure" ratios (on residential streets, the distance between houses should be no more than 80 to 100 feet), landscaping, parking, setbacks, lot width to depth ratios, block length and perimeter maximums, materials, street furniture, and signs.

A useful guide might be the "performance street" concept, which matches street types with adjacent land uses. Creating a street plan based on this model might seem a daunting task, but be assured that controlling scale (what's called "morphological zoning") can go a long way to ensuring the proper mix of urban elements.

Make the new standards available for infill and redevelopment, not just for new development. Where densification is a concern, maintain existing rights-of-way but narrow roadway width.

Streets should be designed in a collaborative, interdisciplinary process. Do a visual preference survey. Try workshops and charettes. Include your legal counsel. After construction, set up what Kulash calls a "robust, simple, and executable monitoring system."

Don't let cost stop you. We estimate that it will take $1.3 million to reconfigure Norwood Avenue, a 6,000-foot-long residential subcollector in north Boulder, as a 20-foot-wide street incorporating such traffic-calming measures as raised intersections, berms, a multipurpose path, and neckdowns (flared curbs constricting a street entrance). It would take $2.3 million to build a typical 32-foot-wide street. The reconfiguration design has been approved by the city council and is now going through the capital improvements programming process.

Ideally, putting these ideas into effect will lead to a revival of street-centered small communities. Vaclav Havel, president of the Czech Republic, put it best in his 1992 book, *Summer Meditations*. "Villages and towns," he wrote, "will once again begin to have their own distinctive appearance, ... and the environment will become a source of quiet everyday pleasure for us all."

By planning our residential areas at a human scale, considering the needs of the most vulnerable among us, and relegating the automobile to its proper role, we can regain what we have lost.

CHAPTER 12

Chicago Area Officials Explore Suburb-to-Suburb Public Transit Links

Rob Gurwitt

Sometime in the next 10 years, if all goes according to plan, you'll be able to board a train in a far western Chicago suburb and ride all the way to ... well ... another far western suburb. You'll be able to get to Chicago too, but that's not really the point. The so-called STAR Line, to be run by the regional rail agency known as Metra, is designed to let a transit rider go directly from one of the region's fast-growing western or northwestern suburbs to another, without first having to travel into the city. This makes it, oddly enough, one of the bolder transportation experiments in the country.

Transit options exist in the suburbs, of course. There are buses, van pools, paratransit — all the alternatives that transit advocates wish commuters would use more often. None of them has made a serious dent in automobile use, however, and none really gets at the toughest issue in transit planning: developing a viable public transit "beltway"— or circumferential — system. Transit in this country, and rail transit in particular, follows a hub-and-spoke pattern, with the central city at the core and lines radiating out from there.

In this, it lags well behind our living patterns. During the 1990s, for instance, the Chicago metropolitan area grew by 11.6 percent, adding 860,000 people, and although Chicago enjoyed a portion of that growth, most of it went to the suburbs. Moreover, much of the region's job growth has taken place beyond city limits as well. Towns such as Schaumburg and neighboring Hoffman Estates have become major employment centers, with Motorola headquartered in the former and Sears in the latter. Nationally, the patterns are similar: In the largest metropolitan areas, suburbs in the 1990s grew at a rate twice that of central cities and emerged as shopping and work destinations in their own right. For most people, though, the only way to get from one to the next remains the car.

Naperville, Illinois, for instance, sits about 30 miles from downtown Chicago, and every workday morning, says Mayor George Pradel, "we pour cars out of our city into the next one." He adds, "Getting from point A to point B takes a while. It's not gridlock, but so many people are using the highways.

Originally published as "Connecting the Suburban Dots," *Governing*, Vol. 17, No. 1, October 2003. Published by Congressional Quarterly Inc., Washington, D.C. Reprinted with permission of the publisher.

Transportation is our number one problem, with the growth we have."

You can understand, then, why Pradel and other mayors whose towns lie along the proposed STAR Line have so enthusiastically embraced the idea. "We really want this to happen," Pradel says.

And it's likely it will. The STAR Line enjoys strong support from local governments — including the city of Chicago, since it would help connect city residents with the rich suburban job markets — and from regional government councils. Suburban employers like the idea, as well. And perhaps most important, a major portion of the proposed line runs through the district of U.S. House Speaker Dennis Hastert, who has announced his backing for the project in this fall's federal transportation bill.

Yet the truth is, no one knows for certain whether the line will prove to be a huge success or a bust. If riders materialize in the numbers that backers anticipate, its estimated $1.2 billion cost might seem a bargain as the line spurs new development, relieves congestion and helps employers attract workers. Or it could turn out to be a very expensive way of demonstrating, once again, that it's almost impossible to persuade significant numbers of American suburbanites to leave their cars behind when they head off for work or shopping.

Dumbbell-Shaped Trips

There is a reason that transportation professionals tend to be dubious about big suburb-to-suburb transit projects. It's known as the "many-to-many" problem: Commuters traveling from one suburb to another start their trips in many different places and end them in many different places, although for a portion of their commute they may be forced to share the same stretch of roadway with everyone else. "You end up with dumbbell-shaped trips," says Dave Schulz, director of Northwestern University's

Infrastructure Technology Institute and a former county executive in Milwaukee.

Moreover, in a society whose building patterns revolve around the automobile, it's pretty difficult to create a transit system that competes with the car for convenience. "It's not a good thing that we've condemned ourselves through development patterns to almost total auto dependency," says Schulz. "But in fact, the automobile is the most comfortable, convenient form of transportation devised by the mind of man, and it's getting better all the time. With climate control, stereos and all that, it makes the drive relatively painless."

The dynamics are different, of course, when it's a matter of getting between the suburbs and the central city. For one thing, the headaches involved in driving into the city — in particular, the risk of gridlock and the certainty of paying for parking — make using transit more attractive. For another, even if a large portion of the commuting population still drives, the numbers of commuters willing to use transit to get to the same central destinations are such that they can undergird the expense of, say, a rail line. And finally, the politics of transit are more clear-cut when it involves the central city. "When you're talking radial transit to downtown, you get a lot of support from the central-city players," comments Alan Pisarski, a transportation consultant based near Washington, D.C. "When you talk suburb to suburb, it's much harder to generate that political support, because there aren't the powerful proponents to make it happen." Not surprisingly, the more expensive a transit option, the more fraught the politics become.

A case in point might be the so-called "Purple Line" — currently referred to by the state of Maryland as the "Bi-County Transitway" — that has long been proposed for linking several suburbs of Washington, D.C. For years, Montgomery County, Maryland's master plan has called for a rail line running between two of its communities, Bethesda and

Silver Spring; in recent decades, both have seen enormous residential, commercial and employment growth. In 1998, County Executive Douglas M. Duncan and then–Governor Parris N. Glendening floated the idea of a subway "beltway" that would ring the capital region; the notion went nowhere, but Montgomery County pressed ahead with planning for its own circumferential section, with the state promoting an additional segment through neighboring Prince George's County.

"The Washington rail system is a series of spokes designed to take people from the suburbs into the center city, which made sense when the subway system was built," says David Weaver, spokesman for Montgomery County's executive. "But commuting patterns have changed. These days, 65 percent of the people who live in Montgomery County also work here. The bottom line is, in order to better use the transit system, we have to change direction both literally and figuratively in terms of where the subway goes."

Until recently, the chief debates had to do with exactly where the rail line would run and whether it would be part of the Metro subway system or a separate light-rail line. Meanwhile, Glendening, a Democrat, was replaced after the 2002 elections by Robert L. Ehrlich Jr., a Republican. In March, Ehrlich's transportation secretary, Robert Flanagan, confounded local officials by announcing he wanted to explore another option — "bus rapid transit," or BRT, which uses dedicated lanes on existing roadways to allow buses to move faster than automobile traffic.

"We need a project that meets the travel demands in this corridor but is done in the least expensive way possible," says Henry Kay, director of planning at the Maryland Transit Administration. "The ratio of cost and ridership on a [rail] project that relies heavily on tunneling and exclusive rights of way was just getting out of sight. We're re-

opening the draft environmental impact statement [done by the state when it was considering a rail line] to examine more robust bus-based alternatives." Dedicated suburb-to-suburb transit routes are relatively unexplored ground, so reliable cost-benefit models are hard to come by. Still, says Kay, "I can promise BRT will be cheaper than light rail, but I can't promise how much."

Meanwhile, officials in Montgomery County have made no effort to hide their dismay. "Rail, heavy or light, is the preferred mode," says Weaver. "When you go from hard rail to bus, it's a real letdown. And we already have significant bus options along that corridor. It's not much to go from what we have currently to bus rapid transit. We would argue, there's no reason you shouldn't consider both."

The problem Weaver and others foresee is that buses, no matter how rapid, will have a much harder time competing for commuters' allegiance than trains. Maryland's Henry Kay argues that this is not necessarily so. "That may or may not be true," he says. "I think it depends on the quality of the bus service and rail service." But the widespread perception among suburban politicians is that there's no contest.

"It could be argued that the more cost-effective way to do suburb-to-suburb is buses and bus rapid transit," says Al Larson, the mayor of Schaumburg, Illinois, and a prime mover behind the STAR Line. "The difficulty is getting people out of their cars and into buses. You can get people to ride trains."

Existing Tracks

And as transit planners are discovering, you can mitigate the costs of rail if you can find existing tracks that will meet your needs. In the Washington County suburbs of Portland, Oregon, for instance, the regional transit agency, TriMet, is making steady progress on a five-station, suburb-to-suburb line using existing freight tracks. The line would run between the booming communities of Wilsonville and Beaverton, using self-propelled diesel cars, and connect with the regional light-rail system in Beaverton. "Washington County is one of the fastest growing areas in the region," says Mary Fetsch, TriMet's communications director, "and this is our heaviest-traveled corridor. We've had a lot of success with our transit system as we've expanded — every rail project we've built has been on time and budget and has exceeded ridership projections — so there's a strong belief this will work." The $124 million project has already gotten several federal planning grants and is expected to open in 2006.

A more ambitious effort is underway in the Minneapolis-St. Paul region, where a proposal will go before the legislature next session to fund the "Northstar Corridor," a commuter rail line that would run along existing Burlington Northern-Santa Fe freight tracks. The line is not circumferential — it would run between St. Cloud, Minnesota, and the Twin Cities — but it would cover 82 miles of the most rapidly growing segment of the metropolitan area. With major Twin Cities employers starting to locate along the corridor, it would help both suburbanites and city-dwellers commute to suburban jobs, in addition to bringing suburbanites into the central city.

Its strength, backers believe, is that it is both cheaper than a BRT system — because the rails are in place, whereas new busway lanes would have to be built — and more attractive to commuters. "If you add together capital costs and operating costs over 15 years," says Tim Yantos, project director for the Northstar Corridor Development Authority, "Northstar is $515 million and a busway would be $769 million. The truth is, we wouldn't be looking at rail unless the railway was in place and you could go 80 miles an hour to downtown Minneapolis. Rail makes sense because the tracks are in place."

The project has had federal support but in 2002 was turned down for bonding by the state legislature; its backers failed to get any new funding this year, and Republican Governor Tim Pawlenty has put off deciding whether to back it until a new legislative report on the project comes out next year.

Regional Cooperation

By far the boldest proposal for suburb-to-suburb rail, however, is the 65-mile-long STAR Line. It is, in a sense, a hybrid: One portion, running northwest from O'Hare Airport along I-90, would require new construction; the rest, running south from Hoffman Estates to Joliet, would run along rails owned by the Elgin, Joliet & Eastern freight line.

The idea is an offshoot of an eight-year-long effort by the mayors of five communities along the I-90 corridor — including Schaumburg, Hoffman Estates and Elk Grove Village — to find a way of relieving congestion. These towns, once typical pillars of residential suburbia, have urbanized at a rapid pace over the past 15 years or so — they now host over 600,000 jobs, with 100,000 of those in Elk Grove Village Industrial Park alone. "The Northwest Tollway is the main route through there," says Larry Bury, transportation director for the Northwest Municipal Conference, which has helped coordinate the transit effort, "and it's choked with traffic — it's over capacity eight hours a day. So it's very difficult to get people in and out of the area in an efficient manner."

As logical as some sort of transit effort might have seemed, when the group of mayors tried to get the idea included in the region's 2020 transportation plan, they were turned down. "We were promised it would be included for future study," says Schaumburg's Al Larson, "so we asked, 'Who's going to study it?' There was no answer, so we said we'd engage a consultant and pay for a study." At that point, the Regional Transportation

Authority agreed to step in and fund the effort, and the planning group expanded to include five more communities, including Chicago. Meanwhile, a separate effort had been underway among the communities lying along the EJ&E tracks; last spring, the two groups agreed to join forces and create one task force to push ahead with planning. "There's a suburban legend that suburban communities are always at each other's throats," says Larson. "But it's wrong. There's been real cooperation over the years."

Given the level of growth they've seen in recent years, any one of the mayors along the proposed line can make a case for it. They cite not just the current levels of congestion but the hope that rail transit between suburbs would allow that growth to continue without over-burdening their communities. "It used to be that you'd get a job and 25 years later you'd get your watch," says Arlene Mulder, the mayor of the village of Arlington Heights, which lies a few miles west of O'Hare. "Now, people change jobs, and companies upsize and downsize. You used to move to live where you worked, but these days, you can't be moving every two or three years. You can't uproot your children. So if we give people more options for commuting, corporations realize it's an asset for attracting employees. Those who need to drive will still do that, but the roads will be less congested, because many will choose the faster route of transit."

Density Debates

For the STAR Line to work, though, several things will have to happen. The first is that communities will have to plan for a lot of parking at train stations; as Northwestern's Dave Schulz puts it, "If you don't have a guaranteed or almost guaranteed parking place, it really affects your mode-choice decision."

But providing ample parking must vie with another goal of the STAR Line's suburban supporters: increasing densities near their train stations, and encouraging "transit-oriented development" where it seems appropriate. The problem is that in older suburbs such as Arlington Heights, which already has begun to host high-rise condominium developments, new retail venues, restaurants and theaters, finding the space to provide parking for commuters is growing more difficult. And in the more traditionally suburban communities farther west, increasing densities significantly — which would enable some portion of the commuting population to live within walking distance of the train station — is a contentious issue. "People in the suburbs don't want that kind of development, because they view it as threatening; anytime you use the word 'density,' their eyes glaze over and they think, 'Cabrini Green,'" says Schulz, referring to Chicago's infamous high-rise public housing project.

Still, it is also true that the reason the STAR Line project has built up so much momentum is that suburbanites are putting enormous political pressure on their leaders to find a solution to congestion. Metra's radial rail lines have seen heavy ridership, and the circumferential line's backers are certain that the demand will be there. "I think it's a safe bet out here in the Chicago region," says Larry Bury, "that if you build it, they will come." Given the political backing that the STAR Line has developed, it seems only a matter of time until we'll find out whether he's right.

CHAPTER 13

Cincinnati, Other Cities, Transform Their Old Train Stations into Museums

Janet Ward

Nothing evokes the American past like a train. That is true despite the fact that Americans, for whom cars are convenient and air travel is inexpensive, have never been on a train.

Still, there is something almost painfully nostalgic about the sound of a distant train whistle. It is no accident that Americans feel a pang when they hear that yet another line has ceased operation, just as it is no accident that Gladys Knight was able to make a hit out of a midnight train to Georgia that no one rides anymore. Indeed, it was the 1960s demolition of a train station — New York's Pennsylvania Station — that is credited with launching the historic preservation movement.

That nostalgia explains, at least in part, the reluctance to part with the train stations that dot the American landscape like so many town squares. "Trains are a link with our past," says Gary Wolf, president of Rail Sciences, an Atlanta-based railroad consultant. "Railroad stations anchored every city. Development moved away from the train stations. When I'm working in a city I've never been in, I have no trouble finding the train station. I just go to the center of town."

Because train stations are centrally located, it makes perfect sense for cities seeking to revitalize their downtowns to tap the grand old buildings that once housed the railroad lines. Some, like St. Louis and Scranton, Pa., have turned their stations into prosperous hotels. Some stations, like those in Omaha, Neb., and Cincinnati, have become museums.

Jacksonville, Fla., transformed its old station into a convention center. Stations in Pueblo, Colo., and Collierville, Tenn., now house municipal offices. Still others, like those in Anchorage, Alaska, and Fargo, N.D., have been converted into microbreweries. "That makes perfect sense," Wolf says. "The old stations had big baggage rooms that were perfect for brewing tanks."

Imagination — and Money

In fact, the number of uses for train stations — the massive ones and the little depots — seems limited only by a city's imag-

Originally published as "Cities Engineer Train Station Revivals," *American City & County*, Vol. 114, No. 6, June 1999. Published by Intertec Publishing Corp., Atlanta, GA. Reprinted with permission of the publisher.

ination and money. Lack of either can doom the grandest train station to decrepitude. Stations in Detroit and Buffalo, N.Y., as well as countless tiny architecturally interesting depots, have fallen victim to neglect or to ownership battles between railroads and cities.

In Decatur, Ga., for example, a battle between the city and CSX Railroad has meant a slow death for the little building that once was a thriving restaurant. (The railroad wants the city to buy its depot; the city wants the railroad's taxes.) Sacramento, Calif.'s station currently is the focus of a fight between Amtrak, which wants to continue to use it as a train station, and the city, which wants it for virtually anything else.

Because of their size — and the quality of materials used to construct them — aging train stations are outrageously expensive to renovate. For the same reasons, they are nearly as expensive to demolish, according to Rob McGonigal, an associate editor with Waukesha, Wis.-based *Trains* magazine. "These are massive structures with a lot of heavily built portions to support the tracks," McGonigal says.

However, cities willing to do a little legwork can find the financial wherewithal to protect their stations. Federal grants for urban revitalization, state money and local bonds proceeds all have contributed to the renovation of stations nationwide.

Finding the Money Train

In Kansas City, Mo., which is nearly finished with a project that will convert its French Renaissance station into a science museum, voters turned down several referenda that would have jump-started the renovation project. Then, three nonprofit groups — the Kansas City Museum, the Union Station Assistance Corp. (USAC), and Kansas City Consensus — went to work finding the funding. (All had different interests but the same goal: the museum group wanted to build a world-class science mu-

seum; Kansas City Consensus was working on a bi-state cultural district; and USAC just wanted the station restored.)

Two local charitable foundations kicked in upwards of $40 million, and Westwood, Kan.-based telecommunications giant Sprint added another $9 million. "That money made the project real and allowed us to take planning quite far," says Science City Museum Director Dave Ucko.

Meanwhile, USAC worked the federal government for grant money, and Kansas City Consensus began lobbying for a local sales tax. That ⅛ cent sales tax, the first bi-state sales tax ever passed in the area, was approved in November 1996 in three Missouri counties and one Kansas county.

"We had to get identical enabling legislation passed in both states," Ucko says. "Then, each of the counties had to agree to put it on the ballot." Proceeds from that tax eventually will fund half the project's $250 million cost.

Despite their initial reluctance to fund the renovation, Kansas Citians never considered demolishing Union Station. The building was intricately woven into their history and, even when it fell into disuse and underwent unsuccessful attempts at modernization, it retained its caché. (According to an article in *Trains*, Kansas Citians gathered at Union Station to celebrate the end of World War II.)

Over the years, a number of reuse plans faltered, and a Canadian firm with redevelopment notions bought the station in 1974. When nothing — except construction of an office building that split the station in half — came of the firm's efforts, the city sued for possession of the station. Under a settlement, the company conveyed the station to USAC. With renovation nearly complete, the science museum is scheduled to open in the fall.

All Aboard

Local voters also helped save Cincinnati's Union Terminal, a beautiful Art Deco station that had been unsuccessfully converted into a shopping center. The architecturally significant station was dying when a Save the Terminal campaign resurrected it with the idea that its half-million square feet of space would be ideal for a museum.

In May 1986, Hamilton County voters approved issuance of $33 million worth of general obligation bonds specifically for the renovation of the terminal. State and city grants, individual contributions and money from private companies and foundations filled financing gaps.

In 1990, the Museum Center at Union Terminal opened. Home to the Cincinnati Historical Society Museum and Library, the Cincinnati Museum of Natural History, the Cinergy Children's Museum, and the Robert D. Lindner Family Omnimax Theater, the center was named one of the top 10 new tourist attractions in the United States by the Austin, Texas–based Weissmann Travel Reports in 1991. Currently, it attracts more than 1 million visitors each year.

It took Cincinnati and their train restoration projects off the ground. However, in Omaha, Neb., there was little question about the rebirth of the city's Union Station.

A classic Art Deco building, the station closed to passenger travel in 1972. Its builder, Union Pacific Railroad, donated the station to the city, and the landmark re-opened in 1975 as the Western Heritage Museum. ("Durham" was added to the name later to honor a locally prominent family that had provided significant financing for the renovation.) The museum features a railroad exhibit that includes everything from rail cars to a 70-foot-long model train layout that portrays the trip from Omaha to Deadwood, S.D.

Pulling in the Private Sector

As in Omaha, private funding was key to the successful restoration of Union Station in Albany, N.Y., which now serves as "the most expensive building per square foot in the Fleet Bank empire," according to Fleet spokesperson Karl Felsen. (It is difficult to transform train stations into commercial space because of the tremendous amount of open area, which in the business world is considered dead space.)

The station, which opened in 1900 and closed 68 years later, was failing fast, according to Felsen. Trees were growing in the roof, which had been stripped of its copper overlay, when local banker Peter Kiernan rescued it.

The Peter D. Kiernan Plaza, as the station is now called, suffered the failure of countless reuse proposals. Despite the best efforts of the late Albany mayor, Erastus Corning, Union Station looked doomed.

Then, in 1984, a plan to convert the facility into a bank was floated. The station re-opened in 1986 after a meticulous renovation, during which contractors raised the building's marble floor to install a technology center beneath it. "Technology and history can be wedded together if you're ambitious and clever enough," Felsen notes.

Local and private money also figured significantly in the renovation of St. Louis' Union Station, perhaps one of the best examples of reuse in the country, according to Mc-Gonigal. The Romanesque station, which opened in 1894 as the largest single-level passenger rail terminal in the world and closed in 1978, is now a mixed-use development that includes a mall and the Hyatt Regency at Union Station.

Restoration of St. Louis' train station was headed up by The Rouse Co., a Columbia, Md.–based urban renovation specialist. When it was completed in 1985, the $150 million project was the largest adaptive reuse project in the United States.

Building Works of Art

Naturally, the price tag for station renovation dwarfs the original construction costs. However, those were not insignificant. The $6.5 million construction cost for St. Louis' station was considered astronomical for its day. And it was the rule, rather than the exception.

Built largely by the railroads — the most lucrative businesses of the late 1880s — the stations were not designed to be merely functional. They were looked on as the public face of the railroads; thus, the railroad magnates determined that they would be works of art.

"These buildings are magnificent architectural landmarks," says Rail Sciences' Wolf. "They would bring in the best craftsmen from Europe. The railroads commissioned incredible works of art for their stations. It was almost a competition to see who could build the most beautiful train station."

Omaha's Union Station, for instance, features the largest half-dome rotunda in the Western Hemisphere, 105-foot-by-20-foot mosaic murals by German artist Winold Reiss, and beautiful fountains. In St. Louis, the locally based Terminal Railroad Association, which financed the station's original construction, commissioned "Allegorical Window," a stained glass work that is framed by the station's "Whispering Arch." (The arch is so named because of a distinct architectural design that allows a person to stand on one side of the arch, talk into the wall and be heard by someone standing at the arch's other end.)

Most renovators attempt to keep stations' architectural details intact. The St. Louis Hyatt, for example, features not only Allegorical Window and Whispering Arch, but also Union Station's Grand Hall, a 65-foot barrel-vaulted ceiling decorated with gold leaf that spans the building's lobby and lounge. Because of its structural beauty, most of the station's original interior has been carefully preserved. For instance, the hotel's restaurant, the Station Grille, was once a Fred Harvey restaurant.

(A digression: According to the book, "The History of the Atchison, Topeka and Santa Fe," Harvey, a genteel Englishman, made his fortune creating nice restaurants at train stations and alongside depots. Prior to Harvey's efforts, passengers had no choice but to make do with trackside greasy spoons. Those roadside diners, the story goes, would serve the passengers, and moments later, the "All aboard" would sound. The passengers would leave half-eaten meals that the diners then tossed back into pots for the later enjoyment of the passengers on the next train. For their cooperation, engineers would get a nickel a meal from the diners.)

From Sleepers to Hotel

Train stations can be converted to a number of uses, but hotels seem to be particularly popular ones. That is partly because the huge open spaces that are anathema to most commercial owners are favored for hotel lobbies and ballrooms. In fact, the Chattanooga Choo Choo, a hotel in Chattanooga, Tenn., represents one of the nation's first adaptive reuse projects.

The centerpiece of a 1970s revitalization campaign, the Choo Choo features shopping, restaurants and Pullman sleeper cars that guests can rent for the night. It is one of the South's most popular tourist destinations.

Scranton, Pa., also transformed its French Renaissance Lackawanna Station into a hotel. The station, now the Radisson Lackawanna Station Hotel, was the linchpin of Scranton's downtown revitalization program.

Opened in 1908 and closed in 1970, the station was purchased by MetroAction, a Chamber of Commerce corporation that concentrated on downtown development.

Using the financial theories that helped convert Scranton's mining-based economy to a manufacturing-based one, MetroAction began looking into reuse alternatives. Ultimately, the Erie-Lackawanna Restoration Associates, a group of private investors, began the restoration with the support of a financial package involving federal, state and local funds, as well private money donated by businesses and local banks. The station/hotel, renovated for $13 million, reopened on New Year's Eve in 1983.

Like St. Louis' station, the Lackawanna Station was notable for its artwork and its design. The two-and-a-half story waiting room featured a barrel-vaulted, leaded glass ceiling, Sienna marble walls and washboards of Alpine green marble. A series of faience panels modeled after the paintings of American artist Clark Greenwood Voorhees, depicts scenes along the railroad's Hoboken-to-Buffalo route.

Other Uses

Hotels, museums, malls and banks are fine examples of reuse, but train stations also provide some of the nation's most impressive municipal office space. Pueblo, Colo.'s once-derelict station, renowned for its beautiful woodwork, now houses the city administration. So does Collierville, Tenn.'s old station, which still features dining cars that locals can rent for special functions.

Louisville, Ky., won a Design for Transportation award from the U.S. Department of Transportation and the National Endowment for the Arts for the transformation of its station into offices for the Transit Authority of River City. At a cost that was about three-quarters that of a new facility, the authority restored the station, meticulously matching the missing pieces of marble wainscot panels, cleaning stained glass and ceramic tile, and restoring red oak staircases and paneled walls. Most of those aesthetically appealing details would be unaffordable in modern construction.

Renovation and restoration projects involving train stations are as varied as the stations themselves. Cities are capitalizing on the old buildings not just for their intrinsic value but for the boost they provide their communities. "These places are deeply rooted in the American experience," McGonigal says. "That's why there is so much support for saving them."

CHAPTER 14

Denver Uses Public Transit System to Enhance Citizen Access to Its Downtown

Sam Newberg

It was a long time coming, but downtown Denver has realized a transformation in the past ten years that is matched by few other American cities. Restored warehouses with swanky restaurants and upscale urban lofts, light-rail transit with ridership above projections, an office vacancy rate of less than 5 percent, recreation paths along the waterfront, new stadiums for professional sports teams, one of the few successful pedestrian malls in the United States — and a new, international airport that makes getting there that much easier — all in the shadow of the Rocky Mountains.

Downtown Denver as it exists today is a combination of public and private cooperation, successes of the past, a plan enacted in 1986, and a prosperity in the 1990s that increased the population of Colorado by 30 percent. What is known today as the Downtown Denver Partnership, a nonprofit business organization that works to keep downtown healthy, was formed in the 1950s. One of the first steps taken was Dana Crawford's historic renovation of Larimer Square in the 1960s, and the 1982 dedication of the 16th

Street pedestrian mall. The oil crash of the 1980s put Denver's back to the wall. The private sector had its hands tied, and the public sector stepped in. In 1984, Mayor Frederico Pena appointed a steering committee to oversee the creation of the downtown area plan. The plan, issued in 1986, set forth a visionary course for the city. Four overall goals were established for downtown Denver: to be economically healthy; to be the social and cultural center of the region; to be beautiful and full of people and activity; and to be a good neighbor to the city's other neighborhoods.

Thanks to a good economy, coupled with good transportation into downtown and a large number of residents, downtown Denver currently is economically healthy. With a performing arts complex, several sports complexes, the Denver Art Museum, a convention center, and many galleries and restaurants, downtown Denver is the cultural and social center of the region. Organized street sweeping of the 16th Street mall and other efforts have beautified downtown Denver and filled it with activity. The Downtown Den-

Originally published as "Denver's Center," *Urban Land*, Vol. 60, No. 5, May 2001. Published by the Urban Land Institute, Washington, D.C. Reprinted with permission of the publisher.

ver Partnership works with surrounding neighborhoods to organize acceptable growth and development that are compatible with its surroundings and that are beneficial for the city overall.

Five critical needs were outlined in the plan: maintaining a vital retail center in downtown; developing people connections among downtown's activity centers; improving access into downtown; enhancing distinct districts in downtown; and providing housing downtown.

Due to the marketing efforts of the Downtown Denver Partnership and good property management in retail projects, the retail market in downtown Denver currently is both distinct and vibrant. The 16th Street mall, the spine of downtown, offers free shuttle-bus service that provides easy access to most of downtown. The planned expansion of both 16th Street and the light-rail system will improve connections among downtown's activity centers. The light-rail system, a streamlined bus service, and improved road access and parking have made the downtown area more accessible. Thousands of housing units are proposed or under construction in and around downtown.

The Birthplace of Denver

Lower Downtown (LoDo), the birthplace of Denver, is considered the most distinctive area in the city. The downtown area plan emphasized the importance of enhancing districts such as LoDo. Today, it is home to many restored warehouse buildings, which are used as office, retail, hotel, and residential space.

LoDo, which was rezoned from industrial to mixed use in 1981, was declared a local historic district in 1988. The Downtown Denver Partnership created a Lower Downtown Business Support Office that, with financial support from preservation groups and the state of Colorado, encouraged renovations. More than 20 buildings in LoDo

have been renovated since 1991, and there are nearly 1,400 housing units in the area.

Preservation has been a successful venture throughout downtown, not just in LoDo. A selective preservation overlay district for downtown Denver covers historic buildings. Only older buildings are required to be reviewed for preservation purposes. Buildings throughout downtown have been restored or converted into office and retail space that competes in rental rates with the newest skyscrapers.

There has been new development as well, such as Denver Pavilions, a 350,000-square-foot entertainment center anchored by Nike-town, Hard Rock Café, a Virgin Records megastore, and a 15-screen United Artists theater, with 50 other local and national retailers. Denver Pavilions borders on the 16th Street mall shuttle bus route, making it readily accessible from anywhere in downtown. The project's completion in the late 1990s signaled the true revival of retail in downtown Denver.

With regard to the office market, Integra Realty Resources ranked downtown Denver the number one city for investment in 2001. Downtown Denver has more than 25 million square feet of rentable space, and Class A space has a vacancy rate of under 5 percent, down from 20 percent in 1990. A new mixed-use project located on the 16th Street mall called 16 Market Square provides a transition between LoDo and downtown proper, combining 183,000 square feet of office space with 23,000 square feet of first-floor retail space and 25 for-sale penthouse condominiums. In addition to 16 Market Square, which opens this year, a new 40-story office tower is due for completion next year. These two projects are the first new office construction downtown has seen since 1985.

Downtown Denver has 5,000-plus rooms in 16 hotels, six of which were built or renovated in the 1990s. Hotel occupancy rates for downtown are over 70 percent, which is higher than the national average.

Just beyond LoDo and Union Station lies the Central Platte Valley neighborhood, which consists mostly of vacant land and the new Commons Park along the South Platte River. The integration of this neighborhood with downtown was envisioned in the downtown area plan. Residential development is already occurring. Over time, the street grid of downtown and LoDo will be extended into the Central Platte Valley. Later this year, the 16th Street shuttle bus will be extended to serve this neighborhood.

Along the course of Commons Park are the Children's Museum, Colorado's Ocean Journey, Six Flags Elitch Gardens amusement park, the Pepsi Center, and the new Denver Broncos stadium. More than 2,000 housing units also are planned for this area. Commons Park is an amenity for the emerging neighborhood and for visitors.

Packing Them In

Stadium development is as popular in Denver as anywhere in the United States, and the past ten years has seen three new stadiums built. Beginning in 1995 with Coors Field in LoDo, home of the Colorado Rockies baseball team, each of these stadiums has been built in or immediately adjacent to downtown. The Pepsi Center, which opened in 1999, is home to the Denver Nuggets basketball and Colorado Avalanche hockey teams. The new Broncos football stadium, located next to the team's old Mile High Stadium, is due to open later this year.

Coors Field is considered the most impressive of the new stadiums. Awarded an expansion baseball team in 1991, Denver chose not to build a stadium along an interstate surrounded by parking lots, but instead to put it on the edge of LoDo, with a brick exterior that evokes the architecture of the surrounding old warehouses. Because downtown's historic preservation legislation was in place, property owners were discouraged from tearing down historic buildings for sta-

dium parking. Instead, the baseball stadium stimulated adaptive uses throughout the area and attracted people to downtown restaurants and galleries. Visitors regularly use the free shuttle bus on the 16th Street mall as part of a day spent downtown at a baseball game, art museum, or other attractions in between.

At the opposite end of the 16th Street mall from LoDo, the State Capitol building sits across Civic Center Park from Denver's city hall. The park is host to summertime concerts and other events, and is also flanked by the Denver Public Library and the Denver Art Museum.

Also located within two blocks of the 16th Street mall are the Denver Performing Arts Complex and the Colorado Convention Center. The arts complex includes seven theaters and one concert hall, and is the second-largest performing arts complex in the United States. In November 1999, voters approved a $289 million expansion to the convention center, including a 1,100-room convention hotel, scheduled to open in 2003.

At Home and on the Move

Approximately 25 percent of the office workers in downtown use some form of public transportation to get to work. Denver's public transportation system has been improved greatly in the past ten years with the opening of a light-rail transit line that bisects the 16th Street mall. All buses into downtown are routed to a station at the end of the 16th Street mall, from where riders can make easy connections to the free shuttle.

A light-rail spur is planned to connect the existing light-rail line with Union Station, and to serve along the way the Auraria Higher Education Center campus (located on the southern edge of downtown), the Pepsi Center, the new Broncos football stadium, and Six Flags Elitch Gardens. The extended 16th Street mall will also reach Union Station. Additional train service from Union Station is planned, including possible service to Denver International Airport and Boulder.

A substantial goal of the downtown area plan was to add housing. The core population in LoDo and the central business district is approximately 3,700 residents, up from 2,700 in 1990. The Downtown Denver Partnership is surveying the 115,000 downtown employees to assess housing needs. Its goal is to construct more housing that serves the needs of downtown workers first, which not only helps reduce commuting traffic into the city, but also makes the area more vibrant.

The success of the downtown Denver renaissance is leading to redevelopment in surrounding neighborhoods, which are growing. Their population stands at 65,000, up from 58,000 in 1990. Thousands of new housing units are planned or are under construction.

Post Properties is constructing 949 rental units in a three-phase new urban project located in the Uptown neighborhood, which is just east of downtown. When completed, the development will have approximately 30,000 square feet of retail and live/work space.

Two blocks southeast of the State Capitol, in the Capitol Hill neighborhood, a 145-unit apartment building recently has been completed. Named Capitol Heights, the project incorporates ground-level retail with residential units above. The Capitol Hill and Uptown neighborhoods also contain some of Denver's oldest housing, much of it Victorian in style.

New housing projects in the Central Platte Valley include the Flour Mill Lofts (in a former flour mill) and Commons Park West, a 340 unit rental project.

With thousands of new housing units, three new stadiums, an enhanced public realm, a new light-rail system, and historic restored warehouses, Denver has an amenities advantage unmatched by most cities.

The collective imagination and a city-led, consensus-driven downtown area plan have helped Denver recover from its hard times in the 1980s and solidify downtown's position as the true center of the region.

CHAPTER 15

Duxbury, Other Cities, Embrace Multi-Purpose Vehicle Corridor Planning

Pamela Freese

Corridor planning is a familiar tool for transportation infrastructure planning. The concept has also successfully been redefined as a comprehensive tool for a range of planning applications, including economic development, environment, and historic or heritage-related efforts. As the applications continue to diversify and the land-use implications increase, it is important for planners and zoning professionals to be familiar with corridor planning as an effective planning tool.

Corridor Planning Basics

All corridor planning processes share four general characteristics: clearly delineated spatial boundaries, stakeholder participation, a need for authorizing legislation and intergovernmental agreements, and a comprehensive planning process. These characteristics interact differently based on the scope and objectives of each individual corridor planning application.

Spatial Boundaries. Corridor planning efforts have a linear designation, either connecting two points or preserving a large area to maintain unrestrained movement or development within specified boundaries. For example, the Heritage Corridor Planning Council was established in Illinois to consider a highway corridor connecting Interstates 55 and 80. Alternatively, river corridors often prioritize preservation of the aesthetic and ecological elements of waterways, in addition to maintaining healthy waterway linkages.

Stakeholder Participation. Regardless of whether a corridor crosses jurisdictional boundaries, a wide array of stakeholders is often involved, including planners, mayors, developers, environmentalists, property owners, and forest preserve districts. Section 1 of the Indiana Code mandates the creation of a corridor planning board to ensure broad-based representation of the parties. The board must consist of a commissioner, director, representatives from the agricultural and railroad industries, local government representatives, and two other individuals, one of whom must own corridor property. All par-

Originally published as "The Evolution of Corridor Planning," *Zoning News*, December 1998. Published by the American Planning Association, Suite 1600, 122 South Michigan Avenue, Chicago, IL 60603–6107. Reprinted with permission of the publisher.

ties are appointed by the governor, and not more than five members of the board may belong to the same political party. Public participation requirements also attract developers, taxpayers, environmentalists, and other interested stakeholders.

Authorizing Legislation. State legislation can authorize zoning controls helpful in corridor preservation, such as overlay zones, planned unit developments, site plan review, and interim uses employed primarily for transportation corridors. Other planning and zoning tools include discretionary review power, land-use intensity review, comprehensive plan review, density transfers, and development agreements.

Authorizing legislation can also establish a corridor, such as the Mississippi River National Heritage Corridor, created in recognition of the unique and nationally significant resources associated with the Mississippi River. The corridor's planning commission calls for the boundaries to coincide with existing political and administrative boundaries, and that they include the regions of concern or interest to the organizations and individuals involved in the Mississippi River. The recommendation welcomes stakeholder involvement and strives to limit intergovernmental disputes.

Planning Process. Corridor planning traditionally includes identifying the proposed corridor, securing necessary authorizing legislation and intergovernmental agreements, seeking public input, refining corridor goals, identifying funding, and implementation.

The planning process is perhaps most clearly defined in the Transportation Equity Act for the 21st Century (TEA-21) as it applies to transportation planning. TEA-21 calls for all transportation planning efforts requiring federal funding to undergo a Major Investment Study (MIS). The MIS requires that the project area be well-defined, that the planning process consider all feasible alternatives, and ample opportunities for input be allowed for by all interested parties, including the public. Only when the process has met the designated planning requirements for scope, participation, and evaluation, will funding be approved for the "preferred alternative."

The Northeastern Illinois Planning Commission (NIPC) has defined a corridor planning process encompassing projects that may not require federal funding, but can benefit from the cooperative analysis process. The NIPC approach creates a local corridor planning council representing a diverse range of environmental, municipal, local, and pro- and anti-development perspectives to ensure the best solution.

In Oregon, transportation corridors are defined as broad geographic areas served by various transportation systems that provide important connections between regions of the state for passengers, goods, and services. In Phase 1 of Oregon's corridor planning program, strategies are established to address the goals and policies of the state transportation plan and statewide mode plans. Phase 2 focuses on developing corridor improvement and management elements, and city and county transportation planning. Phase 3 calls for the refinement of all particular land-use, access management, or related issues that demand more in-depth analyses than typically required to prepare a corridor improvement and management plan.

Technology. Advancements in geographic information systems (GIS) allow for faster evaluation, analysis, and presentation of planning elements. Sophisticated technology makes it possible to consider the implications of a proposed project on a wider scale through modeling and illustrative techniques. In Duxbury, Massachusetts, the Metropolitan Area Planning Council implemented GIS technology to better serve its 101 member communities. One of the first applications of the new technology involved defining a one-eighth mile corridor or "buffer" around major transportation networks to guide business location and help in rezoning decisions. The technology improved the speed and quality of analyses while reducing long-term costs.

Corridor Planning Adaptations

Corridor initiatives have evolved into the areas of economic development, tourism, industrial retention, environmental conservation, and historic and heritage preservation. Transportation-related corridor planning projects remain the most common adaptations.

Corridors for Tomorrow, a grassroots environmental organization in Illinois, advocates using highway rights-of-way to provide much needed habitat for native plants, birds, mammals, and insects. Proposed revegetation buffers potentially soak up pollution, capture and store carbon dioxide, filter and dilute dust and exhaust pollution, retard erosion and loss of top soil, prevent siltation of streams, rivers, and lakes, and reduce maintenance practices, including mowing and herbicide application.

Multi purpose public paths created from abandoned railroad corridors, called Rail-Trails, also build upon obsolete transportation facilities. To date, more than 900 Rail-Trails (totaling almost 10,000 miles) have been created across the country. RailTrails also serve as historic and wildlife conservation corridors, linking isolated parks and creating greenways through developed areas. According to the Rails-to-Trails Conservancy, many corridors also stimulate local economies by increasing tourism and promoting local business.

Economic Development Corridors

Corridor planning is sometimes used to foster or increase economic development. Integral to each effort is a common thread — often a linear path — that holds the corridor together. The Central North American Trade Corridor Association has as its mission statement "promoting and developing tourism, trade, and commerce throughout the North-South corridor from Alaska and the Port of Churchill through Canada, the United States, and Mexico, with a focus on rural revitalization."

Washington State's 10-mile Technology Corridor caters to master-planned business campuses and advanced technology employers. Developed originally as a marketing tool, the corridor's business parks have attracted more than 200 companies in the last five years, encouraging software, electronics, biotechnology, communications, and computer equipment companies to locate in Snohomish County. The Technology Corridor includes 1,600 acres zoned for research and development, light manufacturing, and technology facilities. Landscaped lots and boulevards, jogging trails, and open space grace the corridor. Employers include well-known firms such as Microsoft and Motorola. Exploiting the region's transportation links, businesses located in the corridor can access shipping ports in Seattle and Everett in less than 30 minutes. Two interstate freeways and five state highways network the corridor to the rest of the state.

Central to the development of the Technology Corridor was cooperation between public planning entities, private developers, and the Snohomish County Economic Development Council, which now markets and promotes the corridor. According to George Sherwin, former Snohomish County planning director, planning and zoning officials worked closely with private sector developers to create a business park ordinance. The ordinance allows for business/industrial uses capable of being constructed, maintained, and operated in a manner uniquely designed to be compatible with adjoining residential, retail, commercial, and other less intensive land uses. The business park ordinance was adopted into the zoning code for Snohomish County. Nearby Bothell, Washington, and

Snohomish County amended their comprehensive plans to reflect the new business park classification. Developer involvement pushed the plan forward quickly, making the Technology Corridor an excellent marketing tool and allowing the area to target high-tech companies worldwide.

Seven industrial parks currently share the corridor. Aesthetic standards help to create cohesiveness while retaining individual park identity. The parks have comparable ingress and egress design, access points, a three-story height limit, building material restrictions, and centralized parking and park-and-ride features. According to Michael Cade of the Economic Development Council, open communication between the public and private entities, especially zoning and planning officials, has been the biggest asset in ensuring the corridor's success.

Chicago's 22 industrial corridors are part of a comprehensive economic development initiative to link predefined industrial areas. Retaining Chicago's ability to meet the needs of industrial interests while allowing for neighborhood growth and development was considered essential in the corridor development plans.

Industrial corridors are a zoning overlay that allows for greater flexibility to meet industry's changing needs. To assure stable land use within the corridors, proposals for non-industrial development in the corridors are required to undergo full review through the planned development process. City planners are given full consideration of the operational needs of existing industries when reviewing proposals to rezone property near industrial corridors and when updating the existing zoning standards for manufacturing districts.

According to Donna Ducharme, former deputy commissioner for the city's Department of Planning and Development, each industrial corridor plan has five objectives: to

---

What Planning and Zoning Professionals Need to Know

Planning and zoning professionals can use corridor planning as a tool to inform decision-making on a range of land-use, environmental, and economic development issues. Planners interviewed for this issue of *Zoning News* offer the following six suggestions on what other planners should know about corridors and whom they should be in touch with on this issue:

- Find out if authorizing legislation for establishing corridors exists and what attributes it has. If none exists, explore the option of creating one, using examples from other states.
- Become familiar with the details of other zoning controls, including zoning overlays, interim uses, density transfers, and development agreements. These tools are beneficial for other planning purposes as well.
- Be familiar with projects underway in your planning department and related departments. Is there potential for using corridor planning techniques to meet a broader range of stakeholder needs and land-use planning objectives?
- Be involved with organizations for developers, planners, and land-use groups to become familiar with relevant stakeholders and their positions and objectives.
- Become familiar with intergovernmental agreements and how they can position the planning organization. Determining each stakeholder's role at the outset of a project can help streamline the planning process and expedite planning and implementation of effective strategies.
- Become familiar with corridor planning terminology and concepts from various applications, such as "functional connectivity."

ensure safety, accessibility and function, competitiveness and marketability, manageability, and attractiveness. Designated improvements to the Ravenswood Model Corridor project improvements include viaduct enhancements, park-and-ride facilities, decorative lighting, an external building improvements program, landscaping, security initiatives, and traffic and public transit studies. A preliminary budget of $1.25 million was proposed for the project.

Species, Environment, and River Conservation Corridors

Conservation-related corridors are defined by the Ninth U.S. Circuit Court of Appeals (1990) as "avenues along which wide-ranging animals can travel, plants can propagate, genetic interchange can occur, populations can move in response to environmental changes and natural disasters, and threatened species can be replenished from other areas."

Protecting core reserves and landscape connectivity for species conservation is the goal of the Sky Island/Greater Gila environmental corridor, spanning from Arizona and New Mexico south to Mexico. An acknowledgment of mating needs and migration patterns of area species prompted a coalition of environmental organizations to support a corridor preservation plan. Plan proponent Andy Holdsworth, Sky Island Alliance's Arizona field coordinator, recognizes the importance of working cooperatively with other stakeholders, including county planning departments in both states and Mexico.

Holdsworth says a critical element in biological corridor development is the need to maintain or restore functional connectivity, or provide flexible corridor boundaries to accommodate species' changing needs. If adopted into actual corridor planning efforts, the concept will require zoning solutions such as overlays and interim uses.

Historic and Heritage Corridors

Also evolving out of corridor planning are historic or heritage linkages. The Royal Missionary Road of the Californias corridor stretches from the Los Cabos region in Mexico north to Sonoma, California. The historical significance of the corridor dates back to the establishment of the Mission Nuestra Senorade Loreto in 1697. Mission and archaeological sites, ancient structures, and important ecological zones add to the corridor's unique heritage. Preservation efforts are being led by a diverse team of stakeholders in Mexico together with a group that represents wide-ranging American interests, including California's parks and recreation department.

In the East, corridor planning was presented in numerous bills to link historic locations such as revolutionary war sites so tourists can more easily follow the history of the region. American heritage corridors would be a "museum without walls," says Connecticut State Representative Sherwood Boehlert (R–New Hartford). The legislation recommended a partnership between the federal and local governments to coordinate corridor improvements such as road signs and better preservation of historic sites.

Corridor Planning Challenges

Achieving broad participation and stakeholder cooperation is a major challenge of corridor planning. In 1992, the Oregon Department of Transportation (ODOT) adopted the Oregon Transportation Plan to address corridor planning. A case study tracked the experience of ODOT in its efforts to develop a corridor plan, parts of which would have to be adopted and/or implemented by 34 local jurisdictions and four other state and federal agencies. A key element of the process was the creation of several groups to maximize stakeholder participation. The groups included an intergovernmental policy and coordination committee comprised of an elected official and a key staff member from each of the participating 27 cities and seven counties, a management-level staff person from each of the four other key states, and federal agencies. Over the next two years, each participating jurisdiction's commitment to the planning process and outcome deepened. ODOT came to recognize the benefits of broad public involvement in decision-making and land-use planning.

Unanticipated outcomes are another common challenge with corridor planning efforts. Recent developments in transportation planning suggest that capturing the true implications of corridor development requires a broader geographic analysis. A 1998 *ITE Journal* report by Decorla-Souza notes "the only way to ensure that all benefits are accounted for is to perform the analysis at the region-wide level." Others argue in defense of corridor planning, noting that regional planning misses many important local considerations, such as neighborhood density and character.

In a June 1998 *Urban Land* article, William Hudnut III, former mayor of Indianapolis and senior fellow at the Urban Land Institute, says "Building relationships across boundary lines that traditionally have divided and diminished a community is more important than constructing new systems of government. The emphasis now is on collaboration, networking, engaging, participating and sharing, not on empire building." As an intermediary between regional planning and local planning efforts, corridor planning provides an important perspective to an increasing range of land-use issues.

CHAPTER 16

Georgetown, Other Area Schools, Plan to Accommodate the Growth of Automobiles

Steven Kleinrock *and*
Roger Courtenay

Buildings are renovated to accommodate new technologies and teaching methods. New buildings are proposed when long-standing facilities become inadequate for new or long-standing programs. Universities in Washington, D.C., must not only justify proposed construction to their respective boards of trustees, they must also justify the need to various regulatory agencies and to adjacent communities. A complex legal and regulatory process ensues — one that can involve significant time and resources from the institution and the community — when a university decides to renovate or build a new facility.

The city requires each university to update its campus master plan about every 10 years. This is intended to ensure coherent and planned institutional growth, in keeping with the city's comprehensive plan for the neighborhoods in which the universities are located, and to provide communities with a way to influence change. An effective campus master plan is meant to anticipate and justify enrollment growth projections (or declines); propose new facilities, modifications, and enhancements to open space and landscape plans; and address changes in parking requirements, access, and traffic management. An additional requirement calls for the involvement of adjacent communities through community meetings and formal hearings.

Over the past few decades, universities in the Washington metropolitan area have dealt with a broad range of complicated issues. Faced with a need to expand, the universities often find themselves at odds with established neighborhoods whose goal is to maintain stability. This is of particular concern in urban areas, where campuses established many years ago — 108 years ago in the case of American University and 212 years ago at Georgetown University — have limited growth potential within campus borders.

The issues are the same for Montgomery College, established 50 years ago and located near the Washington city line, but its regu-

Originally published as "Washington Copes with Campus Growth," *Planning*, Vol. 69, No. 9, October 2003. Published by the American Planning Association, Suite 1600, 122 South Michigan Avenue, Chicago, IL. Reprinted with permission of the authors.

latory environment is governed by state as well as local requirements.

The challenge, then, is for universities and institutions to find positive ways to rework relationships with their adjacent neighborhoods in order to satisfy the needs and objectives of both. A successful relationship, from the university perspective, results in neighbors viewing the university as an asset and a vital component and contributor to urban life. There are benefits to working together:

- Achieving consensus is a less painful, more positive framework for change.
- Acceleration of the approvals process saves valuable time.
- Joint sponsorship improves the likelihood of a positive reception from the city's oversight, regulatory, valuation, and taxation systems.
- Both parties can pay a significant price for non-cooperation, not just financially and emotionally (in terms of investment in the planning and approvals process), but more significantly, in terms of poorly or insufficiently informed decision making.
- Academic institutions are permanent. They can be a positive force for thoughtful development in city neighborhoods, where demographic and business changes can be more cyclical and pervasive.

Despite ever-increasing tensions, it is possible for universities and communities to work together. Community leaders must be willing to make reasonable compromises and seek long-term solutions that can serve the interests of both the university and community. Universities must reach out to the community before potential issues cloud relationships.

Overall, the discussions should be based on this assumption: There are fundamental and often conflicting forces shaping urban life. For example, institutions must renew facilities and adapt to changes in technology

and programs, and to the needs of faculty, staff, and students. Expansion, renovation, and replacement of existing facilities are the typical outcomes.

Neighborhoods often resist change, not recognizing that urban areas are always in the process of change. Some of those changes reflect shifts in regional and national demographics and economics. Others reflect a shifting real estate market that responds to citywide planning and transportation decisions. Neighborhoods and institutions can find common ground in addressing issues of real estate valuation.

Strategies for Community Engagement

Universities are often challenged to find creative ways to work with their neighbors and to guide projects through the regulatory process. Several Washington-area institutions have learned from their successes and miscues. These include the following:

- Help with housing and parking. Communities get especially upset when they perceive that adjacent universities allow their students to park on neighborhood streets and to live in group homes off campus. The new Southwest Quad at Georgetown University, to be completed this month, addresses both of these issues by creating new undergraduate housing, a new dining facility, a residence for the Jesuit community center, and underground parking for about 800 cars, thus helping to alleviate neighborhood strains.
  In addition, Georgetown University and American University each provide shuttle bus transportation to Metro train stations to help reduce traffic and congestion both on campus and off campus.
- Control light pollution. In an effort to acknowledge community concerns, the design for the new Katzen Arts Center at American University placed most larger, public

spaces away from residential properties. This involved major concessions from the users and resulted in painting and art studios facing south (instead of the more favorable north) on the public side of the building. Smaller windows along the residential property, and an extensive landscaped buffer zone, help to cut down the amount of light spilling into the neighborhood.

• Forge an agreement between the university and nearby residents to help mitigate noise during evening and weekend hours. Careful selection and placement of building mechanical equipment for the Katzen Arts Center was a major factor in the planning of the new facility. Discussions with neighbors resulted in the placement of chillers in the basement, and an agreement to select rooftop equipment, to be located in an enclosed, screened penthouse with favorable noise ratings.

All loading dock facilities and garage entrances were located away from the neighbors to create a more pleasant environment. Student's outdoor activities now take place within a system of open quadrangles at the campus core. Landscape buffers and scheduling sports events during the daylight hours both help to mitigate noise during the evenings and weekends.

• Be sensitive to surrounding buildings. Building massing that is compatible with the scale of neighboring residential buildings has greatly helped in the campus planning process. Many campuses try to build taller, denser facilities at the campus core, away from neighborhood streets.

At Montgomery College in Takoma Park, Maryland, formal meetings and presentations with the community helped to establish a dialogue that turned potential community opposition into support for a new student services building. These community presentations resulted in lower massing and the use of details such as bay windows on the side of the building facing nearby residences. A double row of street trees not only added to the quality of the neighborhood, but helped to screen the new building.

• Make change palatable. Most communities resist development, whether positive or negative. Often, though, development can have a major positive impact on both the institution and the community. Nowhere is this more striking than at Georgetown University. The new Southwest Quad creates a memorable addition to the city skyline and adds to the historic context of the campus as seen along the Potomac River.

At the Takoma Park campus of Montgomery College, the addition of the new Health Sciences building, proposed to contain both academic and public health uses, extended the campus to a more visible location along a key thoroughfare and became a catalyst for urban redevelopment.

Careful planning and open communication between neighbors and an institution often result in long-term decisions that are mutually beneficial and support the needs of the campus and the public.

CHAPTER 17

Hayward Uses Public Transit Villages to Stimulate Urban Redevelopment

Ruth E. Knack

In its first two decades, the San Francisco Bay Area Rapid Transit District concentrated on building up its heavy rail system — now 72 miles — and providing riders with parking. As a result, most of the 34 stations are surrounded by acres of surface parking lots.

Now, says Michael Bernick, one of BART's nine elected directors, BART should be moving in a different direction, creating high-density mixed-use "transit villages" around its stations. The idea got a boost last fall when the California legislature passed a bill that allows local governments to designate station-area redevelopment districts. Although the law, which Bernick helped write, doesn't include all the redevelopment powers he had hoped for, it does introduce the concept of transit districts, and that's a major step forward, he says.

In its early years, BART, which began operations in 1972, made several stabs at "joint development," seeking to attract office developers to build on agency-owned property. Little was accomplished, however. Then, about four years ago, the agency's property development department initiated a series of market studies and community assessments, which suggested that, at least for some stations, mixed-use development had a good chance of success.

Thinking Big

Of several plans now under way, the one for Oakland's Fruitvale station is the most ambitious. The station is important because it's a transfer point for the city of Alameda and its naval air base. But the surrounding, predominantly Hispanic commercial area is raggedy, and a huge parking lot separates the station from the shops on East 14th Street. A transit village plan spearheaded by the Spanish Speaking Unity Council, a local community development corporation, calls for new housing, a community medical center, and a revitalized retail strip.

The plan is a response to an earlier BART proposal for a new parking structure. "We opposed it," says Arabella Martinez, the council's executive director, "because

Originally published as "BART's Village Vision," *Planning*, Vol. 61, No. 1, January 1995. Reprinted with permission from *Planning*, copyright © January 1995 by the American Planning Association, Suite 1600, 122 South Michigan Avenue, Chicago, IL 60603–6107.

it would have further separated the BART station from the neighborhood." Instead, the council pushed for a comprehensive neighborhood plan, lobbying to get about $300,000 in planning grants from the city.

U.S. Transportation Secretary Federico Peña gave the plan a boost when he visited Fruitvale in 1992. "He asked us what our vision was," says Martinez. "We explained that instead of having a vast sea of parking, we wanted housing and a pedestrian plaza linking the station to 14th Street." Over the next year, Martinez's group, working with BART and the city, received $475,000 in federal ISTEA funds to produce planning studies of the area. A financial feasibility and market assessment report, by Keyser Marston Associates of San Francisco, is due out this month.

In July 1993, BART learned that it would receive $750,000 in ISTEA enhancement funds to build the pedestrian plaza, and the council won $5.4 million on HUD's Section 202 funds for new senior housing. The city also agreed to locate a senior center on the site, and Martinez has applied to the U.S. Department of Health and Human Services for funding for a Head Start center.

The council is also talking with private housing developers and with a supermarket chain interested in opening a store on 14th Street. The city is now studying the area's zoning, with higher residential density a likely result, Martinez says. Meanwhile, the council is about to issue an RFP for a final site plan.

"There's not many times in life you're doing something you truly believe in," says John Rennels, Jr., senior real estate officer in BART's property development division. "For me, this is one of those times. Fruitvale is a classic example of a project that maximizes the value of the public infrastructure. By providing a mixed-use development that has a sense of community, you bring life and activity back to the station — and you put tax dollars back into the community."

Edge City Remake

The high-rise offices and hotel around the Pleasant Hill BART station make it a classic edge city. Forty percent of this unincorporated area just off the Interstate 680 ramp in Contra Costa County is built out. According to Robert Cervero, codirector of the University of California transit center, about 40 percent of the residents and 10 percent of the employees commute by BART.

In the late 1970s, says Bernick, the San Francisco planning firm of Sedway Cooke prepared a specific plan for Pleasant Hill calling for a wider range of development. Then came the market slowdown. Now BART is picking up pieces of that plan, focusing on the potential of shared parking. According to Bernick, a major movie theater chain is interested in the site for just that reason. "Their needs dovetail with ours," he says. "They need parking nights and weekends; we need it during the day."

An outlying station with even more potential — if the jurisdictional problems that surround it ever get resolved — is the East Dublin-Pleasanton station. It's part of the 7.5-mile BART extension being built in the median strip of Interstate 580. Some 20 acres of largely vacant land are adjacent to the station, which is in an unincorporated part of Alameda County adjacent to the Hacienda Business Park, and Camp Park, an Army reserve training facility.

Parking First

Parking is a major issue in every BART project. In Castro Valley, the nonprofit Bridge Housing Corporation of San Francisco cut its proposed development by a third to ensure adequate parking for BART commuters. The location is also in an unincorporated part of Alameda County.

"In the beginning, we hoped to do a project with 300 units," says Bridge senior project manager James Buckley. "But BART was concerned about parking, so we are now focused on a project of about 100 rental units, including some for seniors." The design, by Treffinger, Walz, MacLeod of San Rafael, calls for townhouses and apartments on a podium above the parking structure. It includes a police substation — a feature of several BART projects.

"At the moment, units in the $10.3 million development are contemplated to be below market rate," Buckley says. "We are working on getting low-income tax credits, and we will also ask the county for housing development funds." Bridge, the nation's largest nonprofit housing developer, built a similar complex in Richmond, near another BART station but on privately owned land.

At El Cerrito Plaza, the Koll Company of San Diego is using funds from a transit-related bond measure to build a parking structure. BART's John Rennels says the agency is now seeking financing as well for the project's housing component, to be built by the nonprofit San Jose Housing Corporation.

El Cerrito, a Contra Costa County bedroom community with many senior residents, already has one BART-related development, the two-year-old, 135-unit Del Norte Place. Now plans are under way for a similar project on a vacant site a block south. But El Cerrito's redevelopment program manager, Gerald Raycraft, says finding a mixed-use developer has not been easy. The current proposal, by Charles Oewel of Mill Valley, calls for 216 apartments in a three-story building atop a parking structure, 20,000 square feet of retail space — and a 20-screen movie theater.

The attraction for the movie theater, says Oewel, is BART's willingness to enter a shared parking arrangement with its 2,000 parking spaces.

Raycraft says the El Cerrito city council has gone on record as wanting to intensify development around the stations. A bal-lot measure narrowly passed by local voters in November amends the city's redevelopment plan to allow the redevelopment agency to incur new indebtedness — a substantial boost for additional transit-related projects, Raycraft says.

Retrofits

At several stations, BART's plans fall into the retrofitting category. Fruitvale is an example, as is Hayward, farther out in Alameda County.

John Rennels describes Hayward as a station "development has passed by." Located in a compact downtown characterized by its Art Deco facades, the station is viewed as a potential catalyst for renewal, particularly if a proposed pedestrian promenade connects it to the small shops of the four-block-long B Street Plaza.

As at the other stations, BART hopes to include housing, and Rennels says the city has recently acquired an appropriate site. Financing remains the sticking point for potential mixed-use developers, but Rennels says the California Housing Finance Agency is a possibility for the housing component.

Not in My Backyard

Not everybody thinks BART's transit villages are a good idea. Castro Valley's recently adopted specific plan calls for joint development around the BART station. But some local residents are skeptical of any proposals that include "affordable" apartments. "They're afraid of what mass transit could bring to their community," says one planner.

In Oakland a few years ago, the opposition of neighborhood residents helped kill a plan to rezone the area around the Rockridge station for higher density apartment development. Some neighbors also opposed the Rockridge Market Hall, the upscale shops that occupy the corner across the street from the station. But the market hall, which has offices above, was approved and has turned out to be a marketing — and design — success.

According to Rennels, the agency has learned from the Rockridge experience. "BART came in with a development plan without doing its constituency building," he says. "Now our philosophy is that we won't go into a community to promote development if it is not the wish of the community."

Last year, the agency hired the San Francisco planning and design firm of Kaplan, Diaz, McLaughlin to work with a citizen group in the neighborhood around the MacArthur Station in North Oakland. The busy station at the crossing of two BART lines has long seemed a likely spot for transit village development.

Kaplan, Diaz planner Morton Jensen says the firm is "seeking to develop consensus on what some alternatives might be not only for BART-owned property but for property surrounding the station." The process has taken time, he adds, "because it is a community with lots of opinions."

Three transit village alternatives will be described in the final report, Jensen says. All call for housing. The difference is the number and type of commercial uses.

The most ambitious of the three alternatives includes a large supermarket, which Jensen says has drawn some objections because it is likely to attract more automobile and truck traffic to the neighborhood.

Driving Force

Michael Bernick, the new chairman of BART's board of directors, has been on a mission ever since his election to the board in 1988. "I intend to continue to push along the transit village plans," says Bernick, an attorney with a San Francisco firm.

Bernick has a history of public interest work. For eight years, until 1986, he directed San Francisco Renaissance, a job training organization. Several years ago, he helped establish the National Transit Access Center, a research center that is part of the Institute of Urban and Regional Development at the University of California in Berkeley. He now codirects the center with planning professor and transit expert Robert Cervero.

Last year, Bernick and Cervero drafted the state's Transit Village Development Act, which was signed into law by Gov. Pete Wilson September 30. The act allows cities to designate quarter-mile-radius transit redevelopment districts around stations, and to grant density bonuses and tax breaks to developers in those areas. "We originally drafted it to give the districts redevelopment powers," including land assembly and tax increment financing, Bernick says. Political opposition killed those provisions, considerably weakening the incentives available to entice developers for transit-related projects.

But Bernick remains optimistic, even after the November elections, which have left funding for many public projects questionable. "I don't think transit investment is going to change much," he says. "I think rail transit is one of the few areas where you really have bipartisan support."

CHAPTER 18

Houston, Other Cities, Regulate the Automobile to Control Urban Sprawl

Jonathan Barnett

American cities have a choice. They can take control of their present and their future by following the example of thriving Portland, Oregon, or they can let events take their course, which may well put many of them in the position of cities like Detroit, whose prospects look far bleaker.

Downtown Portland's landscaped streets, light rail system, innovative parks, and meticulously designed new buildings have transformed what was once a mediocre business district into a thriving regional center. While there are areas of poverty in the city, there are also many strong neighborhoods.

The whole three-county metropolitan area has been growing rapidly, and it has the usual commercial strips, big subdivisions, suburban malls, and office centers. But, since 1973, Oregon has also had a comprehensive land planning law, which requires growth boundaries that limit urban sprawl. The Metropolitan Service District was established in 1979 to harmonize the Portland region's growth plans and design its transportation systems.

In 1992, Metro was transformed into an elected regional government. One of its major achievements was the adoption last December of the Region 2040 Growth Concept, which demonstrates that new buildings can be kept almost entirely within growth limits by completing the regional rapid transit system and focusing new development around the stations. The public has recently backed this plan by adopting bond issues to construct the next increment of the light rail system and to fund open space acquisition and park improvements.

Rigid Boundaries Hurt

By contrast, the Detroit metropolitan region is rapidly splitting apart. The central city is more and more irrelevant to the cities and counties that surround it, and there are no viable plans to put city and region back together again.

One reason for Detroit's plight was offered by David Rusk, the former mayor of Albuquerque, in his 1993 book, *Cities with-*

Originally published as "Shaping Our Cities: It's Your Call," *Planning*, Vol. 61, No. 12, December 1995. Published by the American Planning Association, Suite 1600, 122 South Michigan Avenue, Chicago, IL 60603–6107. Reprinted with permission of the author.

out Suburbs. Rusk argues that cities like Albuquerque that can annex new suburban development are more likely to prosper than cities that are confined within limits set decades ago. To prove his point, he pairs statistics for different metropolitan areas.

He notes, for example, that both Houston and Detroit occupied roughly the same area in 1950. But Houston's land area has grown by 237 percent since then, while Detroit has not expanded at all. Detroit's 1950 population was about 1.6 million, which is roughly what Houston's population is today. Detroit's current population is just over a million — 44 percent less than it was in 1950.

Another telling statistic: 43 percent of the 2.4 million new home buyers in the Houston metropolitan area settled within the city's expanded boundaries. The "capture rate" of the city of Detroit was *minus* 42 percent. Houston's average per capita income is 89 percent of the average per capita income of its metropolitan area. Detroit's average per capita income is only 53 percent of the area's. And so on.

Of course, annexation can provide statistics that mask serious problems. Houston has areas of poverty that are just as devastated as any in Detroit. But city finances and the business climate are going to be more favorable in Houston.

Rusk's analysis is discouraging for cities like Detroit, or St. Louis, or Camden that are not likely to annex their suburbs or become part of a consolidated city-county like Indianapolis. But even in such places decay is not inevitable. Portland's metropolitan plans, we should note, do not depend on annexation.

Regional Assets

Even the most landlocked cities have the potential for major redevelopment. The same underused streets and utilities, boarded-up schools, shuttered factories, and abandoned railyards that are seen as municipal burdens also represent a tremendous opportunity. Despite the cleanup costs associated with industrial pollution, the values of existing land, buildings, and infrastructure are immense, particularly when the cost of replicating them at the urban fringe is figured in. The real estate market may not see these values right now, but the taxpayer ought to.

One city that is actively pursuing the redevelopment of bypassed areas is Denver. An ambitious plan for Stapleton airport, replaced this year by the new international airport, calls for residential neighborhoods, office centers, and industrial development on the eight-square-mile site, which lies within the Denver city limits.

In addition, Denver has for several years been pushing a plan to redevelop strips of largely vacant land in a 10-mile stretch of the South Platte Valley adjacent to downtown. The plan identifies several big parcels for residences, industry, and offices that are comparable to those available in suburban locations. It also provides new locations for major regional attractions: the Elitch Gardens amusement park — now under construction — and a new arena for Denver's hockey and basketball franchises.

In Pennsylvania, the state legislature has created a "regional assets district" for Pittsburgh and Allegheny County, backed by a one percent increase in the sales tax. Half of the tax revenue is to be used to support facilities like the airport, the zoo, large parks, and libraries. The other half goes to the county's municipalities to reduce their property taxes.

The assets fund has allowed Pittsburgh to reduce its operating budget from other sources by $7.5 million. The city has reallocated this money to pay the debt service on a $60 million bond issue, which creates a revolving fund to support new investment. The county has a comparable development fund, and the nonprofit Allegheny Conference for Community Development is establishing a foundation with another $50 million.

The purpose of all these initiatives is to provide low-interest loans and other bridging measures to help the private market redevelop disused industrial sites and vacant sites downtown — any locations where new investment could have a spinoff effect in building up the local economy.

Danger Signals

Big-city problems are also spilling over into the primarily residential older suburbs that don't have a strong downtown or regional assets to support social services.

Myron Orfield is a Minnesota state legislator who has been tracking these problems. When the poverty rate goes above about 10 percent, he says, crime statistics rise sharply. During the 1980s, for example, the serious crime rate of the close-in suburbs north of Minneapolis and south of St. Paul was 20 percent higher than in the suburbs slightly farther from the cities. Poverty was increasing at the same time, as measured by the fact that by 1994, nine of the area's 11 inner-ring suburban school districts were serving free lunches to over 20 percent of their children.

Another danger signal is a shrinking school-age population. In the Twin Cities region, Orfield notes, 170 schools in older suburbs have closed. At the same time, 50 schools have been built in newly developing communities on the metropolitan fringe.

It is disconcerting that Orfield finds evidence of deteriorating suburban economic health in the Twin Cities region — an area whose revenue-sharing policies are frequently cited as an example for the rest of the nation. The situation may be even worse elsewhere. In the Chicago area, Orfield spotted deterioration as far as six suburbs out from the Chicago boundary to the south and five suburbs out to the west.

As for a cure, Orfield offers three prescriptions: regional fair housing policies to take the pressure off the inner suburbs and central cities; property tax-base sharing; and directing infrastructure investment away from the urban fringe to take advantage of underused land in older suburbs. He believes that the inner suburbs may have the political strength to bring these changes about because their swing voters hold the balance of power between the Democratic central cities and the Republican outer suburbs.

Development Spiral

At the same time that many older cities and suburbs are declining, other suburbs — and rural counties as well — are choking on new development. Communities that initially welcome new investment are often disillusioned by overburdened school districts, traffic congestion, and the loss of familiar landscapes. Their response is to tighten development regulations, which causes builders to look for sites even farther out.

This leapfrog process places corporate offices so far from the original downtown that they are out of commuting range for inner-city residents — but not for suburbanites. Often, the employees at these exurban locations move still farther out to once-rural towns where housing is affordable. Soon shops and offices follow, and the urbanized area is extended yet again.

A series of perfectly reasonable decisions by companies and individuals becomes an immensely destructive mechanism, ripping up the landscape to produce scattered, inefficient development, and splitting the metropolitan area into a declining old city and a self-sufficient, but fragmented, new city.

The best way to stop this process is to draw an urban growth boundary like Portland's, coupled with fiscal policies that equalize all the communities within a region. The problem is that the idea of limiting growth is not politically feasible in most of the states that need such boundaries the most. Without the growth boundary, the urban future is going to look a lot more like Detroit than like Portland.

Up for Grabs

We are already seeing less demand for office space, which until now has driven both downtown and suburban development. "Hoteling" permits employers to dispense with permanent offices for sales people and others who don't come in to work every day. Voice mail and computers mean less space is needed for secretaries and other support staff. The paperless office isn't here yet, but, when it comes, it will reduce space needs even more.

Another result of the new information technology is that business location decisions now depend less on access to big labor markets. Sites can be chosen for the way of life they offer. This means more bad news for older areas since businesses can now walk away from places that need high taxes to support social services.

Now that many urban occupations can be carried out just about anywhere, small towns — particularly those within a few hours driving distance of a university and other regional attractions, and less than an hour from a well-served airport — are increasingly attractive to entrepreneurs, consultants, and small companies. There is already statistical evidence that some small towns outside major metro areas are gaining back population.

But for those who don't have the opportunity to do big city work in a rural village — most of us — the choice is clear. We could live in a well-balanced region of cities and towns like the one Portland projects for the year 2040. Or we could find ourselves in a region with an ever more fragmented and gridlocked urban perimeter, surrounding a dangerously decaying central city and its even more devastated inner suburbs.

CHAPTER 19

London Fights Traffic Gridlock by Charging Motorists to Drive in Central City

Jay H. Walder

On the morning of February 17, 2003, London began a radical experiment designed to counter crippling traffic gridlock: it started charging motorists £5 (about $9) to drive into the central city on weekdays. Although this charge applied to just 5 percent of the city's roadways, the payment zone included the financial district, the West End theatres, the Oxford Street shopping district, and national landmarks such as Buckingham Palace and the Houses of Parliament.

Before the congestion charge began, London drivers and passengers were spending up to half their time on the road stalled in traffic, averaging 2.3 minutes of delay for every kilometer they traveled. Road congestion was costing the local economy nearly $4 billion a year in lost productivity.

Of course, traffic is a serious problem in many cities, but governments have been reluctant to impose congestion charges (with Singapore a notable exception). Yet Ken Livingstone, London's first elected mayor, ran on a platform explicitly promoting the groundbreaking policy. Even after his elec-

tion, pessimistic media emphasized concerns that the scheme would fail technologically or — perhaps even worse — exert no impact on drivers' entrenched behavior.

Typical of the media comments was one that appeared approximately a month before the start of charging: "The scheme will be condemned as a failure within days, perhaps hours, of it starting. The senior officials in Transport for London will be named and shamed. Livingstone will be told he must resign." (*The Guardian*, January 8, 2003)

But despite predictions that Londoners would run Livingstone out of town, the system proceeded virtually without a hitch. Of course, a few rough edges and minor "teething problems" did occur with the administration and processing of the charge. Simple mistakes, such as human error mistaking O's for 0's and 1's for I's, were troublesome. Also, the number of vehicles entering the zone without a permit was much higher than expected, which in turn highlighted a lengthy and cumbersome penalty process. Experience gained in the first months

Originally published as "London's Bold Experiment with Congestion Pricing," *The Taubman Center Report*, 2005. Published by the A. Alfred Taubman Center for State and Local Government, John F. Kennedy School of Government, Harvard University, Cambridge, MA. Reprinted with permission of the author.

of running the scheme has led to improvements, and the system now runs more smoothly.

Most important, the impact on traffic was immediate, and compliance and support for the scheme's effectiveness remarkably quick. Even Prime Minister Tony Blair attested, "Yes, I think that it was an experiment that a lot of people were dubious about frankly, including me, and I think [Livingstone] deserves credit for having carried that through ... people were predicting a disaster and it wasn't." (*Financial Times*, April 27, 2003)

Has It Made a Difference?

Two years later, some 18 percent fewer vehicles now enter the center of London, and congestion has dropped 30 percent. Bus delays within central London owing to traffic congestion are down 60 percent, and bus ridership in and around central London has risen nearly 38 percent. Long derided as a mode of transport only for people without cars, buses have become a reliable and cost-effective alternative for all: many new riders come from the upper end of the income spectrum. Air quality has improved, with emissions of key pollutants — nitrogen oxides (NOx) and particulate matter (PM10) — dropping 12 percent. Roads have also become safer, with fewer accidents occurring within the zone (the number of traffic accidents has also fallen throughout London). Meanwhile, the system has raised over $300 million to invest in London's transport system.

Although cities around the world have sought to understand why congestion pricing works in London, none are close to introducing a similar system. Two-thirds of voters opposed a recent referendum that would have imposed congestion charges in Edinburgh, for example, and other areas of the UK now seem likely to delay attempts to replicate London's success.

Why were proponents able to introduce such a scheme in London, and why did it work so well? I believe the answer lies in three broad areas: relatively simple technology, a well-developed public transport system, and the emergence of devolved local government within the highly centralized British political system.

Why It Worked

An oft-stated trap for an innovative project is reliance on promising but unproven technology. Though London did not erect the traditional payment mechanisms of tollbooths, the congestion payment system is, nonetheless, far from cutting edge. A network of fixed and mobile cameras reads license plates as drivers enter or navigate within the charge zone. The system then checks the database of cars whose owners have purchased permits for that day. (Drivers may use various methods to pay the £5 charge. Text messaging has proved the most popular, but drivers can also pay online, through a call center, and at retail outlets, car parks, and gasoline stations throughout London.) Once the database has linked a vehicle's registration number with a payment, it automatically deletes the photographic image of that vehicle, leaving only vehicles whose owners failed to pay the charge, who are penalized £50 (approximately $95).

Tests show that the system "captures" more than 90 percent of vehicles within the payment zone — well above the rate needed to ensure compliance. While the system relies on the cameras to identify potential evaders, there is a manual check to avoid mistaken charges. More sophisticated systems would have improved the capture rate, but would have also cost more, taken longer to implement, and required emerging and unproven technologies.

Success also depended on a sober assessment of London's public transport system. Even before the congestion charge took effect, nearly 85 percent of travelers within central London relied on public transport — enabling the city to start from an enviable position. But the London Underground has suffered from decades of disinvestment, limiting the potential for rapid improvement. Recognizing this, Transport for London concentrated on augmenting the surface transport network, which carries nearly twice as many people as the Underground on a typical weekday. As part of the strategic plan to improve transportation across London, the agency concentrated on bus routes in and around the Congestion Charging zone. Hundreds of new buses were added, providing more than 10,000 extra seats during peak hours. Before imposing the congestion charge, local government also extensively analyzed the potential for unintended traffic impacts, such as surplus traffic on the zone's boundary. It also recognized that neighboring areas would be unhappy if drivers avoided major roadways and took to using local residential streets to avoid the charge or parked their cars on residential streets just outside the charging zone. Thirty-five million dollars was invested to reconfigure local streets, set up permitted resident-parking areas, and implement traffic calming (e.g., speed humps) as a deterrent to cutting through residential areas.

Finally, a recent move by the national government to devolve powers to the new Greater London Authority allowed a risk-averse central government to distance itself from a controversial decision. Who better to take the risk than a firebrand mayor who had been kicked out of the Labor Party when he challenged its hand-picked mayoral candidate? With no direct party pressure and a longstanding willingness to buck the status quo, Ken Livingstone took responsibility for the success or failure of the congestion charge. In the process he did more to solidify local government than Parliament could possibly have anticipated when it decided to devolve much of London's governance. (The central government still retains many respon-sibilities typically associated with U.S. state and local government, such as education, policing, and the ability to tax business and property.)

What Next?

Meanwhile, many of London's roadways are still choked with congestion — projected to worsen as a result of projected population growth. In response, the city is considering, in consultation with stakeholders, extending the payment zone from the center, where the focus is on radial trips, to the west, where trips are more neighborhood based. In thinking about an extension, planners must ensure that the new boundaries facilitate efficient movement and take into account the road network capacity; but they do not want to segment communities by disregarding the accompanying land uses. A poorly drawn boundary can create an invisible barrier bisecting neighborhoods in much the same way that interstate highways — such as the Southeast Expressway in Boston, recently torn down as part of the Big Dig — resulted in divided communities with depressed property values and loss of social cohesion.

The city sees the western extension as the first step in a much broader plan to surmount a cordon approach and impose distance-based charges city-wide. As a flat daily fee, the London charge is a relatively blunt instrument — one that is not easily scalable. There is an upper limit for expanding the current camera-based congestion charging system to a broader area — expand to too large a geographic area and the system becomes logistically unworkable. There are charging options currently being studied that would both work for a large geographic area and more precisely capture the true economic cost of a driver entering the road network, where a charge could potentially vary based on time of day, level of existing congestion on the road network, and distance traveled.

An option that could handle variable

charging is a "tag and beacon" microwave or infrared system, whereby vehicles would be fitted with transponders. Such a system is familiar to many drivers today who travel on the U.S. East Coast with the E-Z Pass System or use new toll roads such as SR91 in California. Nevertheless, existing systems require that drivers pass through either a tollbooth or electronic gantry so that the proper toll can be deducted. Such a system works well for a multilane interstate highway, but would be incompatible with local streets in an urban area. This is particularly so for a historic city such as London. City officials, rightly so, would find installing gantries in local neighborhoods incongruous with preserving the city's architectural heritage. Transport for London will soon test less obtrusive equipment that could be mounted on posts that resemble cantilevered light fixtures. If successful, this will open the way for the implementation of a road pricing system that covers much or all of London and offers sophisticated options to tailor prices to the levels of congestion.

Long term, congestion charging could move towards a Global Navigation Satellite System, such as the Global Positioning Satellite system (GPS) or the European version Galileo. This step seems a logical one, particularly for those who already use satellite technology in their cars to help them find their way from point A to point B. There are some technical refinements to be made — ensuring that the margin of error is small enough that we properly charge vehicles close to the boundary and correcting for interference from tall buildings — and the price of on-board equipment must be much less prohibitive (currently over $500). Of course, the political process is no less important than the development of technology. Public debate, consultation, and planning approvals can take several years even after the technology issues are resolved.

Drawing on London's experience, the central government is now considering a national system of road pricing in congested areas. A key issue is whether the revenues raised in a national system would be additional to existing motor vehicle taxes and fees (perhaps allowing greater investment in public transport, as currently happens in London), or would replace existing vehicle taxes or local council taxes (similar to property taxes), which exert less influence on driving behavior. While London might be able to implement road pricing in five to seven years, a national distance-based scheme could take twice as long.

A little more than a century ago, London built the world's first underground railway — an innovation that provided a dramatic increase in transport speed and capacity that other major cities quickly replicated. However, today neither the political will nor the financial resources are available to promote a new program on a similar scale. Congestion charges provide another way forward — one that may prove as important as the construction of the London Underground or the U.S. interstate highway system.

For too many years we have treated urban roads as a free public good, despite overwhelming evidence to the contrary. Fortunately, we now have an alternative that encourages us to value roads as a scarce and costly resource.

CHAPTER 20

Los Angeles, Other Cities, Use Toll Roads as a Congestion-Management Tool

Patrick DeCorla-Souza

Federal, state, and local governments' interest in road pricing as a congestion-management tool has grown during the past few years. The Bush administration's Safe, Accountable, Flexible, and Efficient Transportation Equity Act of 2003 (SAFETEA) proposes the tolling of any federal network component — existing or new — given a goal to manage congestion or improve air quality. Additionally, SAFETEA would permit conversion of high-occupancy vehicle (HOV) lanes to *high occupancy toll* lanes, or HOT lanes, that allow single-occupant vehicles (SOVs) to access the limited-use facilities as long as they pay a toll. Tolls are required to vary by time of day to ensure maintenance of free-flowing traffic conditions, and excess revenues are to be used for Title 23 purposes. This allows use of revenues for transit capital projects but not for transit operations. A required agreement identifies congestion or air quality problems, goals, and performance measures.

The House reauthorization bill, House Resolution (HR) 3550, under the Value Pricing Pilot Program, eliminates states' current opportunities to use variable pricing to reduce congestion. It limits use of tolls to new highway capacity only. It requires dedication of toll revenues to pay for new capacity costs and removal of tolls after paying for these costs. Senate Bill (S) 1072 is similar to the administration's proposals but broadens permissible uses of excess revenues to include Title 49 purposes, allowing use of revenues for transit operations. The Senate provisions give states and local governments broad flexibility to implement variable pricing on the interstate highway system to manage congestion or to improve air quality. State and local governments are generally more responsive to the local citizenry than is the federal government.

Road Pricing as a Congestion-Management Tool

Freeway bottlenecks are the prime source of recurring congestion on freeway networks in major metropolitan areas. Freeway bottlenecks include mainline capacity shortfalls, interchange bottlenecks, and weave-and-merge friction at freeway entrance and exit ramps (Lockwood, 2003). Recent research suggests that eliminating these bottlenecks can result in eliminating recurring congestion as well as increasing vehicle throughput by as much as 50%.

Chen and Varaiya (2002), in their article

Originally published as "Fair Highway Networks: A New Approach to Eliminate Congestion on Metropolitan Freeways," *Public Works Management & Policy*, Vol. 9, No. 3, January 2005, pp. 196–205. Copyright © 2005 by Sage Publications. Published by Sage Publications, Thousand Oaks, CA. Reprinted with permission of Sage Publications, Inc.

titled "The Freeway Congestion Paradox," demonstrated that once freeway vehicle density (measured in vehicles per mile) exceeds a certain critical number, both vehicle speed and vehicle flow (measured in vehicles per hour) drop precipitously. They have demonstrated the phenomenon with actual data from a section of westbound I-10 in Los Angeles. Until 5:10 A.M., a flow of 2,100 vehicles per lane per hour is maintained, at a speed of 58 miles per hour (mph). As density increases after 5:10 A.M., speed steadily drops, until at 7:00 A.M. speed is a stop-and-go 15 mph, and flow decreases to 1,300 vehicles per lane per hour. Even though demand on I-10 starts to decrease after 8:00 A.M., the freeway does not recover its full efficiency until 11:30 A.M. because queued vehicles from previous hours keep vehicle density high. At these high densities, the freeway stays in "breakdown" flow condition throughout the morning hours. Flow randomly fluctuates between 1,300 vehicles per lane per hour and 2,000 vehicles per lane per hour. Speeds randomly fluctuate between 15 mph and 30 mph.

Varaiya (2003) evaluated ramp metering as a way to maintain freeway throughput and free-flowing travel speeds. Ramp metering keeps excess vehicles from entering the freeway when critical vehicle densities are being approached. In an analysis of the Los Angeles freeway system, Varaiya estimated that a systemwide ramp-metering strategy could reduce annual congestion delay from 75 million vehicle hours to 25 million vehicle hours. The analysis assumed that no motorist would choose alternate routes to avoid ramp delays and thus exacerbate existing arterial congestion; also, the analysis did not account for possible delays to motorists on arterial streets resulting from queuing backups at freeway entrance ramps. Varaiya's analysis shows that although ramp metering accomplishes much, at least a third of freeway delay remains, even if additional delays to arterial motorists are ignored.

Road pricing, on the other hand, accomplishes the objective of freeway efficiency *without* ramp delays, that is, eliminates all freeway delay. Essentially, a price, in the form of a vari-

able toll, dissuades motorists from queuing up to use a freeway approaching critical density and induces them to shift to carpooling and transit use. They may also shift their route or time of travel, or choose to forego the trip entirely. Solo drivers who arrive when demand is high pay for the guaranteed congestion-free service electronically. A ramp-metering strategy, on the other hand, would have motorists pay for freeway access with ramp-delay time. Time wasted at ramp meters cannot be regained — it is gone forever, an utter waste of a scarce resource. Road pricing has no waste of either time or money, because toll revenue can be "recycled" to provide other public benefits, such as transit fare subsidies or a return to taxpayers in the form of tax reductions.

FAIR Highway Networks Concept

Potential changes in federal legislation and the freeway congestion paradox are increasing the interest of state and local governments in innovative road-pricing concepts. One such strategy is the FAIR (fast and intertwined regular) highway network concept (DeCorla-Souza, 2004a), an innovative and relatively low-cost pricing strategy that has been developed to eliminate existing congestion on freeway networks in metropolitan areas. The concept evolved from the FAIR *lanes* concept, which would involve separating congested freeway lanes into two sections — fast lanes and regular lanes. Under the FAIR lanes concept, fast lanes normally would include two lanes in each direction and would be tolled electronically, with tolls set in real time to ensure that demand is kept at a level that allows traffic to move at the maximum allowable free-flow speed. Users of regular lanes still would face congested conditions but would be eligible to receive credits if their vehicles have electronic transponders. The credits would be a form of compensation for giving up the right to use the existing lanes converted to fast lanes.

The FAIR highway network concept is more ambitious than the FAIR lanes concept and entails three key features:

(a) Conversion of *all lanes* of the existing freeway network *during peak periods only* into a premium-service, free-flowing freeway network that provides new fast, frequent, and inexpensive bus service, free premium service for carpools, and premium service for SOVs paying a charge that varies to manage demand and keep the freeway congestion free;

(b) An intertwined network of improved free arterial routes, including management and operations improvements; and

(c) Credits or refunds of peak charges for low-income commuters to address equity impacts and reduce the incentive for them to divert to an alternative free route.

A FAIR highway network does not necessarily entail construction of new lanes on the freeway mainline. It generally needs only existing physical freeway rights-of-way and infrastructure. Some new construction will be needed to mount new electronic equipment for toll collection and for management and operations of the freeway and arterial networks that includes traveler information, new parking facilities, and direct access ramps to and from these facilities on behalf of those choosing to park and ride in a carpool or an express bus. Due to the limited amount of new construction, an entire metropolitan FAIR highway network may be put in place in a relatively short time, without the need for time-consuming and lengthy environmental review processes. A FAIR highway network may also be self-financing. It generates surplus revenue that helps pay for expansion of the transportation network, which in turn addresses capacity needs at the most severe bottlenecks and thereby accommodates growth in population, jobs, and travel. In fact, the magnitude of the motorist's willingness to pay, expressed through the market-clearing peak period charges on various freeway segments, would provide a clear indication of the locations of the most pressing expansion needs.

FAIR highway networks would operate in peak periods only. There would be no change in freeway operating policy outside the peak periods. Free service would be provided to all vehicles outside the peak periods, just as it is currently. The freeway network would operate in peak periods as if it were a system reserved for free premium service to carpool vehicles and transit, somewhat like the existing peak period operation of I-66 inside the Capital Beltway in Washington, D.C. However, in addition (unlike I-66), solo drivers would be permitted to use the system with payment of a variable peak service charge. Solo drivers who wish to travel when demand is high may choose to pay for the improved service. They may shift to other travel modes (i.e., enhanced transit or carpooling), to other times of the day, or to other (free) arterial routes.

Low-income commuters are the ones most likely to divert to arterial routes to avoid paying the peak charges. Although their value of time is likely to be high relative to their wage rates, it is likely to be lower than the peak charges more often than it is for higher income commuters. To reduce the inducement for traffic diversion, as well as to address concerns about equity toward these commuters, they would be offered credits (or refunds) to help them pay for out-of-pocket costs they may incur for peak period charges. Many local governments already have such means-tested programs for school lunches and property tax relief.

Relatively few vehicles need be removed from the traffic stream to have a substantial impact on congestion. For example, Wachs (2003) observes that traffic in Boston is surprisingly free flowing on a Jewish holiday; the same phenomenon occurs in California when only California state employees have a state holiday. These occurrences suggest a need to induce only a few motorists to change their peak-period travel behavior to substantially reduce congestion. To keep these or new motorists from returning to the highways in order to take advantage of the improved travel times after congestion is relieved, we need a variable pricing mechanism to prevent demand from rising due to the reduced travel time "price."

FAIR Highway Networks induce a shift from solo driving by providing inexpensive, high quality transit service, or incentives to share the ride with someone else. To maximize the potential for change in travel behavior, complementary strategies may also be used, such as requirements for employers to provide their employees with an option to "cash out" parking that is currently given to them for free, tax incentives for businesses to locate at high-density employment sites, and incentives for developers to invest in transit-oriented development in residential areas.

Due to the significant travel-time savings from the avoidance of traffic-flow breakdowns, the value of time saved would exceed by far the peak service charges, and the overall time-plus-money cost (i.e., the generalized cost) of solo driving would fall. However, an inducement to shift from solo driving is also provided because inexpensive express transit service and carpooling are made even more attractive with features such as convenient park-and-ride facilities. David Lewis (2003) posits that an improvement in transit service reduces congestion on *all* modes in a congested corridor. New, improved, and reliable transit service is like a scanner line in a grocery store that guarantees service in 5 minutes. If the other human service lines exceed 5 minutes, shoppers will gravitate toward the guaranteed-5-minute line, so that the other lines also never exceed by very much the service time of 5 minutes. According to Lewis, with reliable transit service, automobile travel times will likewise be kept down to the service times provided by transit. This phenomenon is known as Mogridge-Lewis convergence because it was originally posited by the late Martin Mogridge, a U.K. operations analyst. By introducing new, reliable transit service on a systemwide basis, FAIR highway networks will keep travel times down for the auto mode across the entire freeway and arterial networks.

FAIR Highway Network Operations

The example of I-10 in Los Angeles, discussed above, may best explain operation of a FAIR highway network. Given a FAIR highway network in place, westbound motorists after 5:10 A.M. would see a variable message sign saying:

> PEAK CHARGES IN EFFECT
> 10 CENTS PER MILE, HOV 2 + FREE
> SLUG LINE, TRANSIT, PARKING
> AT NEXT EXIT

HOV2+ is the shorthand term commonly used to refer to HOVs with two or more persons. A "slug" is an informal carpooler who waits to be picked up at a designated location by a solo driver who wishes to make free use of HOV lanes by giving a free ride to the required number of passengers. This form of carpooling, called "casual carpooling" or "dynamic ride sharing," is practiced in the Washington, D.C., San Francisco, and Houston metropolitan areas. A solo driver would understand from the sign that he or she has several options:

(a) *Stay on the freeway and pay the designated toll* at highway speed using a previously acquired transponder. Transponders are currently available in the form of vehicle stickers for as little as $5.00 and can be dispensed from automated teller machine (ATM)–like vending machines. There would be no need to stop or even slow down. Open-road tolling would be employed. Even vehicles without a compatible transponder would not need to stop. License plate recognition technology would identify the vehicle owner, who would be sent a bill in the mail. An administrative charge would be added to the bill to cover expenses. Highway 407 toll road in Toronto, Canada currently employs this system (Samuel, 1997).

(b) *Park and use express transit service or get a free ride in a carpool* by joining a slug line at the next exit. Special park-and-ride lots with direct access to the freeway would include express bus stations so that solo drivers could park and take the bus or join an informal carpool as a slug.

(c) *Drive on the freeway for free by picking up a passenger from the slug line.* Of course, regular commuters could form a conventional carpool, so that stopping to pick up a passenger, or waiting to be picked up by a solo driver, would be necessary only on those days that a conventional carpool was missing a passenger for any reason (e.g., vacation).

(d) *Exit the freeway and take an alternate toll-free arterial route.* In travel corridors with good transit service or carpool incentives, the number of commuters making this choice can be kept to the minimum. Low-income commuters are discouraged from using this alternative to save money by providing them with credits or refunds based on income level. Investments in advanced arterial signal systems will permit accommodation of traffic diversions (if any) without exacerbating arterial congestion. Of course, due to Mogridge-Lewis convergence, diversions from arterials to the freeway are likely to exceed any diversions from the freeway to arterials.

A motorist with a passenger (i.e., in a two-person carpool) would simply continue to drive on the freeway. Special HOV access lanes would be provided near freeway entrance ramps, in association with park-and-ride facilities. Carpools going through these lanes would have their vehicle transponder identification numbers recorded, so that zero charges would apply to them at all charging points on the freeway. Video surveillance technology, supplemented by police enforcement, if necessary, would be used at HOV access ramps to ensure against use of HOV access lanes by solo drivers. To avoid the need for expensive new gantries, the transponder readers and video surveillance cameras on the freeway would be hung from existing overpasses or from overhead sign gantries wherever possible. The charges would vary dynamically, such as on the I-15 express lanes in San Diego (U.S. Department of Transportation, 2000). To avoid traffic flow breakdowns, the charge during any 6-minute interval would be no higher than that necessary to create the right balance between demand for freeway use and critical vehicle density.

Economic Efficiency and Financial Feasibility

Costs for a typical regional FAIR highway network have been estimated based on the freeway network in the Washington, D.C. metropolitan area (DeCorla-Souza, 2004a). The freeway network would employ open-road tolling, with toll charging points located at approximately 3-mile intervals. New express bus service would be introduced during peak periods. Fares would be $1.00 per trip, and free parking would be provided at transit stations. Each park-and-ride lot would provide for HOV identification for vehicles with two or more occupants so that they would not be billed when their transponders were identified on the freeway. For this purpose, transponder readers and surveillance equipment would be provided in HOV identification zones. Adaptive signal control with advanced signal systems would be implemented regionwide. Total estimated annualized costs to transportation agencies for all key components of a typical FAIR highway network were estimated as follows (DeCorla-Souza, 2004a):

Toll/credit operations	$100.0 million
Express bus service	115.5 million
Park-and-ride facilities	46.4 million
Arterial network	10.0 million
Total system cost	$271.9 million

Benefits from a FAIR highway network include benefits to travelers (such as travel time and vehicle operation cost savings) as well as reductions in external costs, including reductions in air pollution, noise, and crash costs borne by society as a whole. Table 1 provides a summary of estimated annualized systemwide costs, revenues, and benefits from a typical FAIR highway network (DeCorla-Souza, 2004a). The "low" scenario assumes an average base case travel speed on congested freeway segments of 30 mph. The "high" scenario reflects a more severely congested metropolitan area where travel speed on congested freeway segments averages 20 mph. The comparison of systemwide benefits and costs suggests that a cost-benefit ratio in excess of 2.0 will be achieved even in less congested metropolitan areas, whereas more severely congested metropolitan areas, such as Washington, D.C., may see benefit-cost ratios as high as 5.0.

A comparison of systemwide revenues, after accounting for low-income credits, with systemwide costs suggests that annual revenues will exceed annualized costs by about $18 million in modestly congested areas and by more than $300 million in severely congested areas. A $300 million annual surplus could support a $3 billion bond program and allow construction of as many as 375 new lane miles at an average cost of $8 million per lane mile (*Highway Economic Requirements System*, 2000).

Gaining Public and Stakeholder Acceptance

Introducing a FAIR highway network strategy to the public will be challenging. Gaining public acceptance of road-pricing strategies requires many years of effort in public education and debate. For example, London's congestion-charging scheme implemented in February 2003 was first proposed in the Smeed Report in the early 1960s. In the United States, HOT lanes are only now beginning to experience public and political acceptance in a few states, even though pilot projects have been operational in southern California since late 1995 and in Houston since 1998. Explaining the benefits of FAIR highway networks to the public and to stakeholder groups will require considerably more effort than explaining the benefits of HOT lanes. However, in some respects, the case for FAIR highway networks may be more compelling. The marketing strategy will need to focus on a *package* of benefits to the traveling public that will increase their transportation choices. Benefits that could be highlighted include

New and better transportation options:
- New fast, frequent, and inexpensive bus service that will not be stuck in traffic, unlike the existing services familiar to the public;

- A new HOV 2+ system providing guaranteed premium service across the whole freeway network, not just on a few freeway segments, with supporting park-and-ride facilities and slug lines;
- Guaranteed premium service freeway lanes for a larger number of motorists than with HOT lanes, and for a much more affordable price because supply (i.e., number of available lanes) is much greater.

New user-based funding for transportation improvements:
- *Improved transportation system operations.* Revenues from peak charges will ensure stable funding for advanced system operations throughout the network, including arterial signal optimization, traveler information, emergency services, and other intelligent transportation system strategies to keep arterial systems flowing efficiently.

Table 1. Summary of Costs, Benefits, and Revenues (in millions of dollars annually)

	Low	High
Annualized costs	271.9	271.9
Annual social benefits	703.8	1,383.5
Net annual benefits	431.6	1,111.3
Annual revenues	290.3	580.6
Benefit-cost ratio	2.6	5.1
Excess of revenues over costs	18.4	308.7

- *Increased investment in transportation infrastructure.* Revenues from peak charges will ensure stable funding for transportation capacity improvements, including not only freeway improvements but also arterial intersection improvements, bikeways, and pedestrian facilities.

Safeguards to ensure social equity:
- Low-income motorists will have equal access to premium freeway services and will have more and better transportation choices.
- Those who share the ride will pay nothing.
- Solo drivers will get time savings and travel-time reliability benefits whose value exceeds the cost of the charges they pay. A guarantee will be provided to solo drivers that *no* charges will be made to their

accounts if they do not get premium service at free-flow travel speeds. Should they incur any delays on the freeway, their accounts will be credited with the estimated gas taxes paid on the trip.

A diverse range of transportation advocacy groups may potentially provide support for the concept and assist in outreach to the public. Interest groups with a potential stake in the outcomes from FAIR highway networks are discussed below.

Transit interests: With FAIR highway networks, bus rapid transit (BRT) network development will get a jump start. A FAIR highway network would allow a BRT network to be implemented much sooner and at lower cost. A network of the type proposed by Poole and Orski (2003) could take as many as 20 years to complete and generate full benefits for BRT, and would cost much more due to the added costs for construction of direct-access ramps that would be needed. Moreover, capital and operating costs for buses in the Poole-Orski proposal are unfunded, whereas a FAIR highway network will provide a funding source for both capital and operating costs.

Trucking interests: Unlike HOT networks, financial feasibility of FAIR highway networks does not depend on keeping congestion levels high on the regular lanes. Service charges are only applied in peak periods, and are relatively low because "supply" of premium-service road space is larger. That trucks are not excluded from the free-flowing lanes is an advantage that FAIR highway networks have over HOV and HOT networks. Fuel consumption per minute of delay on a freeway designed for 65 mph speeds amounts to 0.328 gallons for two-axle single-unit trucks, 0.447 gallons for three-axle single unit trucks, and 0.578 gallons for combination vehicles (ECONorthwest, Kittelson & Parsons Brinckerhoff, Quade, & Douglas, 2003). On a severely congested freeway, with speeds averaging 20 mph, delays amount to about 2 minutes per mile. Assuming a fuel

cost of $1.50 per gallon, fuel cost savings per mile on a FAIR highway network in the three categories of trucks amount to $0.98, $1.34, and $1.73, respectively. However, peak charges per mile are estimated to be $0.14 per vehicle (DeCorla-Souza, 2004a). Thus, trucks that have to travel during peak periods would see huge monetary savings and an increase in profits. Trucks that travel during off peak would not be charged tolls and would see no change in their operation costs.

Auto interests: Success of HOV and HOT lanes *depends* on continued congestion in the remaining lanes. A commuter's motivation to carpool in HOV lanes or a driver's willingness to pay on HOT lanes depends on amount of delay in the regular lanes. Thus, HOV and HOT networks must "ensure" that congestion continues on the regular freeway network if they are to be successful. FAIR highway networks, on the other hand, will eliminate *all* congestion on the freeway and reduce the drain on motorists' time, vehicle operating costs, and pollution from stop-and-go traffic. Moreover, because of network equilibration and the Mogridge-Lewis convergence phenomenon, reliable transit service supported by FAIR highway network revenues will lead to reduced auto travel times in all congested corridors, on the freeway as well as on arterials. The value of travel time saved by peak period solo drivers will far exceed the relatively small peak service charges that they will pay. Off-peak drivers, previously subjected to the after effects of traffic flow breakdowns during peak hours, will receive travel-time savings for free.

Some highway user groups have expressed a concern that toll revenues should not be diverted from what the driver is paying for — new road capacity. However, new road capacity becomes available to a motorist in peak periods each time another driver is diverted from solo driving and into a carpool or a transit vehicle. In many cases, it can be less expensive and more cost-efficient to provide public support for peak-period ride sharing and transit service than to provide highway service for solo drivers. For example, at a public cost of 32 cents per mile for a new peak-period vehicle trip (DeCorla-Souza, 2004b), the public cost for a new 10-mile solo-driver commute trip is $3.20. Carpooling and transit use can reduce these public costs by dividing them among more commuters. Auto clubs in the New York metropolitan area understand these benefits and support the use of highway user fees for transit.

Taxpayer interests: FAIR highway networks will not need public subsidies and may, in fact, provide new funds to expand multimodal transportation capacity where demand or market clearing price suggests it is needed. Unlike the Poole-Orski HOT networks proposal, tax dollars will not be needed, and private sector provision of services will be facilitated, making service delivery more efficient and more effective. FAIR highway networks can increase private sector participation in provision of traditional government services.

Transportation industry interests: Transportation builders are likely to appreciate the new funding that will flow from peak charges, which will allow expansion of transportation capacity where needed. Initially, builders will benefit from projects for construction of park-and-ride facilities and access ramps. After revenues start coming in, surpluses will be available to accommodate growth in population, employment, and travel and maintain high levels of mobility and access for all. The intelligent transportation systems industry and tolling industry will benefit from contracts for technology services and electronic toll collection equipment installation and operations.

Environmental interests: FAIR highway networks will increase travel choices. Revenue will be generated to pay for new transportation choices, such as new express bus services, park-and-ride lots for carpoolers, and other improvements to benefit pedestrian and bicycle modes. Also, unlike the HOT networks proposed by Poole and Orski (2003), two-person carpools will be able to use the

premium service on the freeway for free, preserving and enhancing a privilege now available to carpoolers in many metropolitan areas, and increasing equity and travel choices. Due to enhancement of transit opportunities, a FAIR highway network will promote livability and accessibility and reduce auto dependence. Jonathan Levine (2003) posits that simply investing in highway improvements may discourage transit use, due to relocation of activities to more distant locations to take advantage of lower land costs. Although the highway improvement may increase mobility, that is, result in shorter travel time per mile, it may end up reducing accessibility, that is, result in more time to get to a more distant destination. On the other hand, improved or new transit service, as proposed with FAIR highway networks, encourages business and residential activity to locate near transit stations at higher densities. When destinations are brought close to one another, *mobility* may be reduced; that is, it may take more time *per mile* to access them by transit or walking, but *accessibility* will be higher; that is, less total time will be needed to get to a destination, due to proximity.

Demonstration of the Concept

Despite the potential appeal of a FAIR highway network, it may be difficult to get public acceptance due to the complexity of the scheme, public mistrust of government, and the difficulty in explaining concepts such as the freeway congestion paradox to the public. Public trust, understanding, and acceptance of the strategy may be facilitated with a small-scale pilot project to demonstrate the concept.

The concept may be demonstrated on I-66 inside the Capital Beltway in Washington, D.C. The facility is currently restricted to HOV2+ vehicles in peak hours. HOV occupancy requirements could be raised to the original HOV3+ requirement, and HOV2 and SOV use could be permitted with payment of a peak service charge set high enough to ensure free flow of traffic. Revenues may be dedicated to improve or further subsidize transit service in the corridor.

When the public realizes, through a pilot implementation project, how much difference FAIR highway networks can make to congestion, mobility, transportation choices, air quality, and livability, it may be easier to expand the concept to the entire metropolitan network. Expansion to the network may be executed in stages, although this might reduce the viability of the transit system. The most congested corridors would be the prime candidates. The FAIR highway network concept does not have to be implemented in *every* existing congested corridor in order to be effective. For example, if the Capital Beltway in northern Virginia between the Woodrow Wilson Bridge and Tyson's Corner to the west is priced in peak periods, this is likely to reduce traffic volumes and congestion on the bridge itself, as well as on freeway segments to the east in Maryland.

Summary and Conclusions

A FAIR highway network may provide significant net social benefits and also generate sufficient new revenues to pay for arterial network and freeway network management and operations (including toll collection) as well as the new express bus service and ancillary park-and-ride facilities. Surpluses may also be available to address needs of new transportation capacity in growing areas. Although public acceptability is a major hurdle, it is conceivable that FAIR highway networks can gain support from stakeholders and political leaders if its benefits are carefully explained and if a pilot project is implemented to demonstrate its effectiveness and operational feasibility.

NOTES

Chen, C., & Varaiya, P. (2002, spring). The freeway-congestion paradox. *Access*, 20, 40–41.

DeCorla-Souza, P. (2004a, January). *Clearing existing freeway bottlenecks with FAIR networks: Issues and impacts* (Paper No. 04-3993) [CD-ROM]. Presented at the annual meeting of the Transportation Research Board, Washington, D.C.

DeCorla-Souza, P. (2004b, June). Implementing priced freeway networks in metropolitan areas: Benefits and prospects. *ITE Journal on the Web.* Washington, D.C.: Institute of Transportation Engineers. Retrieved from http://www.ite.org/itejournal/webarticles.asp

ECONorthwest, Kittelson & Associates & Parsons, Brinckerhoff, Quade & Douglas. (2003). *A manual of user benefits analysis for highways.* Washington, D.C.: American Association of State Highway and Transportation Officials.

Highway economic requirements system: Vol. IV. Technical report (Report No. DOT-VNTSC-FHWA-99-6). (2000). Washington, D.C.: U.S. Department of Transportation.

Levine, J. (2003, June). Transit and transit-oriented development for metropolitan accessibility. In G. C. Sciara & P. Brinckerhoff (eds.), *Traffic congestion: Issues and options* (pp. 19–20). University of California, Los Angeles, Extension Public Policy Program. Retrieved from http://www.uclaextension.org/unex/departmentalPages/public policy/report.pdf

Lewis, D. (2003, June). The case for increasing transit capacity to mitigate congestion. In G. C. Sciara & P. Brinckerhoff (eds.), *Traffic congestion: Issues and options* (p. 9). University of California, Los Angeles, Extension Public Policy Program. Retrieved from http://www.uclaextension.org/unex/departmentalPages/publicpolicy/report.pdf

Lockwood, S. (2003, June). Mainstreaming management and operations into transportation program development. In G.-C. Sciara & P. Brinckerhoff (eds.), *Traffic congestion: Issues and options* (pp. 16–17). University of California, Los Angeles, Extension Public Policy Program. Retrieved from http://www.uclaextension.org/unex/departmentalPages/publicpolicy/report.pdf

Poole, R., & Orski, C. K. (2003). *HOT networks: A new plan for congestion relief and better transit* (Policy Study No. 305). Los Angeles: Reason Public Policy Institute.

Samuel, P. (1997, May 15). The 407 revolution. *Toll Roads Newsletter*, No. 15, p. 1.

U.S. Department of Transportation. (2000, July). *2000 report on the value pricing pilot program* (No. FHWA-PL-00-026). Washington, D.C.: Federal Highway Administration.

Varaiya, P. (2003, June). Reducing delays using ITS to manage traffic and incidents. In G. C. Sciara & P. Brinckerhoff (eds.), *Traffic congestion: Issues and options* (pp. 15–16). University of California, Los Angeles, Extension Public Policy Program. Retrieved from http://www.uclaextension.org/unex/departmentalPages/publicpolicy/report.pdf

Wachs, M. (2003). Congestion in cities — Where, when, what kind, how much. In G. C. Sciara & P. Brinckerhoff (eds.), *Traffic congestion: Issues and options* (pp. 4–5). University of California, Los Angeles, Extension Public Policy Program. Retrieved from http://www.uclaextension.org/unex/departmentalPages/publicpolicy/report.pdf

Author's Note: The views expressed in this chapter are those of the author, and not necessarily those of the U.S. Federal Highway Administration or the U.S. Department of Transportation. The chapter presents the status of Federal legislation as of October 2004 as this chapter went to press.

CHAPTER 21

Madison Uses Transportation Planning to Accommodate Traffic and Residential Growth

Ruth E. Knack

On May 22, the Dane County Regional Planning Commission in Madison, Wisconsin, is expected to vote on a controversial new land-use and transportation plan. Three months ago, the commissioners told state officials that they needed more time to review the "Vision 2020" plan, which had drawn criticism from both rural township supervisors, who complained that it was too much centered on Madison, and Madison residents who contended it was too automobile-oriented.

Both sides agree on one thing: that Madison is a special place. Last summer *Money* magazine put it at the top of its list of "best places to live," and a recent *American Health* story said its low crime rate and good schools help make it the "healthiest" city for women. It doesn't hurt that Madison occupies a splendid site. "No other city of the world, so far as I know, has naturally such a unique situation on a series of lakes," planner John Nolen wrote in 1908.

Madison is at the center of one of the "urban constellations" identified by retired University of Wisconsin landscape architect professor Philip Lewis. Within this four-state, upper Midwest "Circle City" constellation, Lewis has written, live 17 million people. They threaten to fill in the relatively undeveloped "driftless" area at the middle, part of the landscape that was spared by the glaciers thousands of years ago.

The city's twin anchors are the 40,000-student University of Wisconsin campus and the elegant state capitol. Both are major population draws, helping the population of Dane County grow from 292,000 in 1970 to 390,000 in 1994. By 2020, according to the new plan, another 100,000 newcomers will bring the total to about 490,000.

During the same period, the plan estimates that 57,000 new jobs will be added — in state government, the university, and the high-tech businesses that are increasingly moving into the area. To house the newcomers, the plan estimates that 40,000 new dwelling units will be needed.

To planners in New York or California, those figures, based on projections by the

Originally published as "Go Badgers, Fight That Sprawl," *Planning*, Vol. 63, No. 5, May 1997. Reprinted with permission from *Planning*, copyright © 1997 by the American Planning Association, Suite 1600, 122 South Michigan Avenue, Chicago, IL 60603–6107.

Wisconsin administration department, may not seem like a big deal. But to rural Wisconsin residents, they evoke Chicago-like images of high-density development, traffic congestion, and social problems.

Madison has already seen some rather large demographic changes, including a growing homeless population. University of Wisconsin planning professor Jerry Kaufman, AICP, describes Madison as a "threshold" city because of the changes that have taken place in the last 15 years. Minority peoples — Hispanics, African Americans, and Asians (including a large Hmong population) — represented 10.5 percent of Madison's population in 1990, "probably more today." That's enough, says Kaufman, to have significantly altered the perceptions of longtime residents.

Hot Issues

"We are suggesting some things in the Vision 2020 plan that are very controversial for some people, both from a land-use and transportation standpoint," says Robert McDonald, AICP, director of transportation planning and a 22-year veteran of the Dane County Regional Planning Commission staff.

Among the red flag issues are the plan's recommendations for higher residential densities throughout the county (five dwelling units per acre rather than the current average of three to four), that the countywide balance of singe- and multi-family housing approach 50–50, and that outlying communities provide a broader range of housing types (e.g., affordable housing).

"Some people interpreted that to mean rent subsidies, although that's not what we're saying," McDonald says.

The plan's transportation section includes a recommendation for a new transit corridor running from Middleton west of Madison through the central Isthmus area to the eastern suburbs. But the plan also lays out $373 million in road capacity improvements — including new west and north beltways — that are likely to be needed by 2020, based on the plan's projected congestion levels.

The result, according to a recent opinion piece in *Isthmus*, the area's weekly newspaper, will be to make Dane County look like the "concrete tangle around O'Hare Airport" in Chicago.

"There's a strong contingent that doesn't want to see any road improvements," McDonald says. But even with new rail and bus lines, he adds, "many of the trips will be suburb to suburb, and 97 percent of them will be made by auto. So we need to add capacity."

Tricky Part

According to consultant Charles Causier, AICP, it wasn't hard to get area residents to agree on goals for the new plan. Causier, who is director of planning services for HNTB in Milwaukee, initially shared consulting tasks with Lane Kendig, AICP, of Mundelein, Illinois, in effect becoming project manager when Kendig's role ended rather abruptly.

"There was a consensus," Causier says, "that you want to protect farmland, and have balanced communities with different types of land use so people can work and live in the same place. There was also an overwhelming sense that this is a wonderful area and that we want to keep it that way."

The tricky part, says Causier, was when the planners started saying where growth should go. There was tension from the beginning between the county's 26 incorporated cities and villages, including the city of Madison, and the unincorporated townships.

The RPC staff and consultants began by presenting 10 alternative growth scenarios, ranging from continuing current growth trends — in other words, sprawl — to encouraging traditional neighborhood development like Middleton Hills, the 150-acre Duany-designed project west of Madison.

Two computer models were used to narrow the alternatives: One was the SAVES model (strategic analysis vision evaluation system), designed by Kendig to evaluate land-use development patterns. Those results were then fed into the transportation model, TRANPLAN. "We used it to figure out what sort of transportation system would be needed to serve each of the alternatives — as well as potential ridership and costs of light rail and busways," McDonald says.

The land-use and transportation connection was key to this process, McDonald says. "ISTEA [the federal Intermodal Surface Transportation Efficiency Act] requires all metropolitan planning organizations to update their transportation plans — and to consider land use. We did more than just consider it. Our new plan will actually merge our existing land-use and transportation documents. We wanted people to know the consequences of moving one way or another."

Don't Tread on Me

Not everyone wants to hear about the consequences. Vision 2020 strongly recommends that new housing and new jobs be directed to existing communities that are served by public water and sewer services.

To Robert Bowman, a retired University of Wisconsin professor on the board of supervisors in Cross Plains, an unincorporated town of 1,340 west of Madison, that's an example of the county's bias toward its largest city.

In 1964, Bowman bought a 30-acre tract in Cross Plains. Then in 1981 Wisconsin passed a farmland preservation act and Bowman's land became part of an agriculture preservation zone that allowed only one house per 35 acres. "A few years ago," he says, "our daughter wanted to build a house on our land, and we applied for a permit to split off five acres. But even though our land is

rocky and hilly, unsuited for farming, the county would not grant a variance."

Bowman sued and eventually got his zoning. But the affair soured him on the county's regulatory process and led to his decision to run for supervisor, he says.

In Bowman's view, "the Vision 2020 process was designed to come out with a certain result. Under all 10 of the scenarios, Madison was free to grow," he says. "I took exception to the idea that there should be virtually no development in the countryside."

In a book called *Cities Without Suburbs*, David Rusk, former mayor of Albuquerque, takes a different view of Madison's efforts to annex. Rusk's thesis is that cities that annex aggressively — as Madison did between 1950 and 1990 when its land area grew by 275 percent — do far better economically than cities that don't. He notes that Harrisburg, Pennsylvania, another state capital, grew by only 29 percent during the same period and is in a poorer position because of it.

"Annexation is not a dirty word," says former Madison mayor Paul Soglin, who did not run for reelection last month. The outspoken Soglin, who served as mayor from 1973 to 1979 and again since 1989, is used to attacks on this issue. Soglin says he sees Dane County being remade into something like the collar counties around Chicago, defined by a desire to convert farmland into subdivisions and shopping centers.

"When Madison annexes," he says, "it develops at eight times the density the towns do. And we provide housing, not just strip commercial. Meanwhile, the towns get to be part of the Madison community without having to pay for services."

Madison's Take

To ensure that the city's interests — particularly those of the central area, the Isthmus — were taken into account, Soglin appointed the Isthmus 2020 citizens task force, which is chaired by Richard Wagner, former chairman of the county board of supervisors.

"We frankly were not happy with all the consultants' projections," which allocated some of the new growth to outlying areas, says Wagner. "The land-use model seemed to emphasize trends that showed suburban growth. Our data showed that the Isthmus could accommodate a lot of that growth."

With the help of Todd Violante of the city's planning staff, the committee sponsored several events designed to show Madison residents what that growth could look like. In one exercise, flash cards were used to demonstrate concepts like "medium high density"; in another, participants were asked to move transparent rings on an aerial photo to find the best locations for new rail stops in a proposed transit corridor.

At the conclusion of this process, the committee decided that the Isthmus could handle another 4,500 housing units and, with adequate transit, another 14,000 jobs. Those figures were accepted by the regional planning agency for incorporation into the plan, Wagner says.

Like other Isthmus 2020 members, Anne Monks, longtime assistant to Mayor Soglin and a former city council member, believes that the larger Vision 2020 process failed in terms of public participation. "There was never an adequate plan for involving the public, and they never came up with anything that all those Dane County villages and towns could identify with as a statement of where they wanted the county to be going," Monks says.

Consultant Lane Kendig says the problem was an inadequate budget that included only four public hearings over three years. "You have to do more if you're really interested in citizen participation," Kendig says.

Money is also a factor in carrying out the Isthmus 2020 plan. Monks notes that many of the recommendations for more compact residential development and a "Main Street" approach to commercial areas would require new zoning.

"A lot of changes that the committee is asking for will lead to more work on the part of the city planning staff," she says.

What's Next

It won't be Paul Soglin who worries about finding the money for the staff needed to carry out those changes, however. The April 1 election gave Madison a new mayor and Dane County a new executive. Susan Bauman won the mayor's race over a fellow city council member, Wayne Bigelow.

In the county executive race, Karen Falk, who has a strong reputation as an environmentalist, won over the more conservative Michael Blaska, who had been chairman of the county board, where he was seen as a representative of the Dane County Towns Association.

Meanwhile, the regional planning commission staff is preparing for that May 22 vote on the new plan. "We're looking more closely at some of those roadway improvements in response to some of the criticism," says Bob McDonald. After a decision on the draft plan was postponed, a subcommittee was formed to attempt to balance some of the concerns voiced by area residents, he says.

According to McDonald, the commission's staff of about 12 planners did not grow for this project. "The ISTEA money did not filter down this far," he says.

After the commission acts, the plan goes to the state Department of Transportation, the Madison city council, and the Dane County board. If they approve, and if the plan is also approved by the other local governments within the county, it will replace the present regional development guide and transportation plan as the county's governing documents.

How likely is implementation?

Bob McDonald is hopeful because the Vision 2020 plan does something that has never been done before in integrating land-use and transportation decisions.

But Lane Kendig says he's skeptical. "People talk about the Madison area becoming the Portland of the Midwest, filled with nice new neotraditional developments. But unless they're willing to change the basic zoning structure, they won't be able to do it. They're zoned for auto-oriented development."

"I think most people in this region want the things the plan calls for," says Jerry Kaufman. "They'd like to see more compact development and more transit. The question is whether we have the mechanisms to accomplish these things." Kaufman is talking about more than new zoning. "We lack metrowide institutions that could equalize the disparities between rich and poor communities," he says. "As a result, Madison tends to suffer from growth rather than benefit from it."

But the biggest deterrent to change seems to be the state. In 1909, Wisconsin became the first state to authorize cities to form planning commissions. But since that time, its planning record, with some exceptions such as the agricultural preservation act, has been negligible.

"We don't have a state legislative framework," says George Austin, Madison's planning director since 1983. In 1994, Gov. Tommy Thompson appointed a strategic growth task force to "develop a land-use vision for Wisconsin." The task force was charged with dealing with such issues as annexation and consistency of town and county plans and zoning codes. Its recommendations will eventually go to the legislature, but Austin says he's not hopeful that new laws will emerge any time soon.

Paul Soglin views Vision 2020 as "a modest beginning," but says he's not very hopeful about the future in a state with such timid politicians. "We lost the opportunity 20 years ago when we could have emulated the state of Oregon," he says.

There are bright spots, though, including the recent formation of 1000 Friends of Wisconsin, modeled after 1000 Friends of Oregon. And both the city of Madison and Dane County have been buying land to create some of the corridors and greenways called for by Philip Lewis.

At a 1995 symposium to commemorate John Nolen's landmark 1908 plan for Madison, neotraditional guru Andres Duany said of the Madison area: "This is one of the few places that is growing now that can still do it right." The Vision 2020 plan and the local efforts in support of it are a start.

CHAPTER 22

Miami Agency Purchases Hybrid Vehicles to Reduce Fuel Costs and Emissions

Sean Kilcarr

Although it can be tricky to save fuel using hybrid technology, government fleet managers are finding other ways the vehicles can contribute to the bottom line. Utilities and transit agencies are using hybrids to reduce emissions, noise and maintenance costs.

Hybrid vehicles are designed to reduce the fuel consumption of cars, trucks and buses by mating a gasoline or diesel engine to an electric motor and battery pack. However, hybrids only save fuel in stop-and-go driving, when the electric motor powers the vehicle at a low speed and then helps with acceleration.

"The critical focus is on this technology's economic viability," says George Survant, director of fleet services for Miami-based Florida Power & Light (FP&L). The utility is purchasing 20 hybrid utility boom trucks — diesel-electric hybrid vehicles combining a six-cylinder diesel engine — from Warrenville, Ill.–based International Truck & Engine with a hybrid-electric drivetrain developed by Cleveland-based Eaton.

Fuel economy was the rationale when FP&L first considered purchasing hybrids, but the utility saw other advantages in reducing vehicle noise and emissions. "Most emission solutions add cost, whereas the hybrid option can reduce cost by burning less fuel, benefiting our shareholders and customers alike," Survant says. "The wear-and-tear savings are going to be one of the pleasant surprises from hybrid technology, right up there with noise reduction. We get a real good reception in residential neighborhoods when we arrive to restore power — and they're going to be even more delighted when we do that without waking the babies."

Allen Schaeffer, executive director of the Frederick, Md.–based Diesel Forum, sees advantages beyond fuel economy. "There's a real sea change going on where diesels are concerned," he says. "A typical diesel-only city bus averages a road call every 1,700 to 2,000 miles of operation. With these diesel-hybrids, the average jumps to 7,000 miles."

Hybrid Buses

Transit buses are one area where hybrid technology is taking off, even though the an-

Originally published as "Driving Forces," *American City & County*, Vol. 120, No. 8, July 2005. Published by PRIMEDIA Business Magazines & Media Inc., Overland Park, KS. Reprinted with permission of the publisher.

Hybrid Truck Systems:
Who Makes What

There are several different kinds of hybrid truck systems, covering everything from sport utility vehicles (SUV) to transit buses. Following is a sample of the different chassis, systems and manufacturing companies.

Oshkosh, Wis.-based **Oshkosh Truck** is producing a 66,000-pound, heavy diesel-electric hybrid chassis designed for refuse applications, powered by a 300 horsepower (hp) Cummins ISB engine connected to the company's ProPulse electric drivetrain.

Detroit-based **Ford Motor** plans to produce a diesel-electric hybrid version of its super-size SUV, the Excursion. The company currently builds a hybrid version of its Escape mid-sized SUV, which operates in electric-only mode when the vehicles travel at low speeds or are idling at a stop.

Warrenville Ill.-based **International Truck & Engine** is building two medium-duty diesel-hybrid trucks: a four-door crew cab 4700 model truck equipped with a dry van freight body for pickup and delivery operations, and a utility boom truck. The Class 6 crew cab truck uses a 175-hp three-liter inline four cylinder married to a parallel hybrid drivetrain. International's 4000 Series also provides the base platform for its diesel-electric hybrid utility truck, which couples a DT 466 in-line six-cylinder diesel engine with an Eaton hybrid-electric drivetrain — comprised of a transmission, batteries and permanent magnet motor. The system recovers kinetic energy during braking, charging the batteries while the truck is slowing down and also provides additional power for acceleration.

Detroit-based **General Motors** is building a 40-foot hybrid transit bus combining a diesel engine with an Electric Drives EP System, developed by its **Allison Transmission** subsidiary, designed to produce lower hydrocarbon and carbon monoxide emissions. GM also is building hybrid pickups and plans to roll out hybrid versions of its Chevy Tahoe SUV in 2007 using a new dual mode system developed with Stuttgart, Germany-based **DaimlerChrysler**, which plans to roll out a gasoline-electric hybrid version of its Dodge Durango SUV in 2008.

Toyota is offering a diesel-electric hybrid truck chassis through its **Hino Motors** subsidiary — the Hino 165 conventional Class 4, a chassis rated at 16,000 pound gross vehicle weight powered by the company's standard four-cylinder, five-liter diesel. The system includes a proprietary flywheel generator/starter that captures braking force when the vehicle slows, storing it as electrical power in a battery array. The electrical power is then used to augment the diesel on startup, as well as cruising.

Winnepeg, Canada–based **New Flyer Industries** is building gasoline-electric hybrid 40-foot urban transit buses based on a propulsion system designed by **ISE Corporation** of San Diego. ISE offers a gasoline-fueled variant of the ThunderVolt drive system, which combines a Ford ultra-low emission V10 gasoline engine, **Siemens** drive motors and generator, batteries and other hybrid-electric drive components. Benefits include the reduction of nitrous oxides and particulate matter emissions.

Mississauga, Canada–based **Orion Bus Industries**, a division of Greensboro, N.C.–based **DaimlerChrysler Commercial Buses North America**, offers a hybrid version of its Orion VII 40-foot bus that uses the HybriDrive diesel-electric propulsion system developed by British aerospace engineering firm **BAE Systems** to reduce particulate emissions, NOx and greenhouse gases.

DaimlerChrysler also is testing a plug-in hybrid version of its Dodge Sprinter vans that can be connected to an electric outlet at night to recharge the vehicle's battery pack in addition to the recharging that occurs when the vehicle runs its gasoline or diesel engine. One diesel-electric and two gasoline-electric Sprinters are being tested this year.

ticipated fuel savings do not always materialize. For example, King County Metro has purchased 235 buses from Winnepeg, Canada–based New Flyer Industries to serve routes in the Seattle area. The buses' diesel-hybrid system was expected to improve fuel economy by 60 percent, saving the county an estimated 750,000 gallons of fuel per year.

The Seattle Post Intelligencer reported slightly poorer fuel economy — 3.6 miles per gallon (mpg) versus 4 mpg from diesel-only units. That is largely because the hybrids were placed on longer-haul suburban express routes that are the antithesis of the stop-and-go environment where hybrid technology saves the most fuel, according to Jim Boon, Metro vehicle maintenance manager.

At a cost of $645,000 each — approximately $200,000 more than a new diesel bus — hybrids might not seem like a wise investment. However, Michael Voris, the agency's procurement supervisor, notes that the electric engine is especially valuable during acceleration from zero to 12 miles per hour, when a diesel engine would otherwise be burning the most fuel and getting the most wear and tear on its components.

Boon says that Metro's hybrid fleet is saving $3 million a year in maintenance cost over the older diesel-only buses they are replacing. He also says they produce far less noise than diesel buses and accelerate much better on hills and highways because of the electric motor power.

Houston Metro Transit is adopting hybrids by buying four 40-foot hybrid diesel-electric buses from Detroit-based General Motors (GM) with a grant from the federal government's Clean Cities/Clean Vehicles program. The city is a non-attainment area, meaning that its air quality is extremely poor, so the agency will use the buses to help reduce emissions. GM's hybrid bus produces much lower hydrocarbon and carbon monoxide emissions than conventional buses, lowering particulates, hydrocarbon and carbon monoxide emissions by up to 90 percent and

nitrogen oxides by up to 50 percent, the agency says.

The Capital Metropolitan Transportation Authority of Austin, Texas, also is testing GM's hybrid buses. "The key is that these [hybrid] buses are quieter, more efficient and have much lower emissions than their diesel counterparts, without losing any performance," says Fred Gilliam, president and CEO of Capital Metro.

The diesel engine on Capital Metro's hybrid buses powers an electrical generator, which, in turn, charges a battery pack on the roof. The batteries then power an electric motor that turns the wheels with the bus switching automatically between battery power and diesel power depending on speed and torque. The vehicle moves on battery power alone from zero to 20 miles per hour, and the batteries recharge when the vehicle is not accelerating.

"The hybrid's clean diesel engine is significantly smaller than traditional buses, closer to the size of a large pickup truck," Gilliam says. "Any vehicle emits the most pollution when it accelerates from a stop or goes up hill. The hybrid bus uses electric power from its batteries when it accelerates, eliminating the excessive dark cloud that an accelerating vehicle typically emits."

Saving Fuel

Cutting fuel costs are a top priority for New York City Transit, which recently ordered 325 hybrid buses from Mississauga, Canada-based Orion Bus Industries. The buses are equipped with a HybriDrive propulsion system from United Kingdom-based BAE Systems. The fleet operates 4,373 buses traveling more than 107 million miles using 38 million gallons of gasoline per year.

A New York City Transit hybrid bus study determined that the vehicles would help cut fuel costs. In the study, diesel buses averaged 2.42 mpg, while the hybrid buses averaged 2.65 mpg. That translates into 45 cents worth of diesel per mile for regular buses, while the hybrid buses used 39 cents of diesel per mile, for a savings of about $6.4 million dollars per year. Hybrid buses are expected to consume slightly higher amounts of oil — between 0.72 and 0.22 quarts per thousand miles — adding about $15,000 to $50,000 more per year in oil costs.

The buses feature a regenerative braking system, which uses the drive motor to slow the bus, effectively turning the motor into a generator to help recharge the energy storage system. That feature saves energy and also lessens brake wear — thus reducing the frequency and cost of brake maintenance.

Indeed, as the cost of crude oil reaches new highs, fuel savings may once again become the main reason for purchasing hybrids. But unlike fluctuating fuel prices, lowering emissions, decreasing maintenance cost and quieter operation provide buyers all the reasons they need to consider hybrids for the long run.

CHAPTER 23

Minneapolis Uses New Technologies to Facilitate the Movement of Traffic

Christopher Swope

Ken Livingstone, the one-time socialist rabble-rouser and current mayor of London, isn't your typical free-market disciple. But when Livingstone, who still goes by the nickname "Red Ken" in some circles, talks about how cities can tackle traffic congestion, he sounds like a conservative economist.

When Livingstone took office in 2000, traffic in central London was perpetually gridlocked. The streets were so clogged with cars and trucks, as well as the city's famous double-decker buses and black taxi cabs, that they all poked along at an average speed of 8 mph. In 2003, Livingstone devised a plan, which combined market principles with new technology, to get London moving again. He drew a ring around the 8 square miles of central London, and set up cameras alongside all roads into town. Whenever a car passes into the "congestion charging zone" on a weekday between 7 A.M. and 6:30 P.M., its license plate is photographed and entered into a database. Drivers are assessed a toll of about $9.50, and have a choice of paying online, by phone, at kiosks, stores or gas stations. Anyone who hasn't paid up by midnight on the day of

travel receives a $190 ticket by mail. "I nicked the idea off Milton Friedman," Livingstone once said.

Livingstone's critics predicted that congestion pricing would prove a spectacular disaster. The technology would overload, they said. Even if it did work, the scheme wouldn't put a dent in congestion anyway — and it might just spark a commuter rebellion. "CONGESTION CHAOS IN STORE," predicted the *London Evening Standard*.

None of the doomsday scenarios came to pass. Rather than revolting, drivers did one of two things: They either paid up, as 100,000 a day now choose to do, or they changed their commuting behavior. Many people who used to drive to work switched to mass transit, which became a more attractive option because Livingstone pumped toll revenues into expanded bus service. Other commuters bought scooters or bikes, either of which they can ride downtown for free. All in all, 60,000 fewer automobile trips are made into central London today than before the charge. Traffic moves more quickly, there are fewer accidents, and taxis and buses are

Originally published as "The Fast Lane," *Governing*, Vol. 18, No. 8, May 2005. Published by Congressional Quarterly Inc., Washington, D.C. Reprinted with permission of the publisher.

more plentiful. Livingstone got re-elected handily last June, some say because of— not in spite of— his congestion-charging scheme.

London's experiment with road pricing has sparked a lot of discussion in the United States. The reason is not because lots of American cities will want to copy London. With the exceptions of Manhattan, San Francisco, Chicago or Washington, D.C., traffic congestion in this sprawling country is much more a highway phenomenon than a matter for the downtown street grid. Rather, people are talking about London because Livingstone showed that voters might agree to putting a price tag on driving — so long as they get a better ride in return.

Could the same principle apply in the car-crazy United States? Conventional wisdom says no: Americans are accustomed to their freeways being free. But a dramatic shift in thinking is going on among highway planners and the politicians who give them orders. More and more, it seems, American policy makers are coming around to the idea of charging rush-hour commuters. That's because three important trends are converging all at once: Congestion in many metro areas is getting palpably worse; states are running out of money to build new roads; and "smart" tolling technology is making it possible to charge drivers according to when, where or how often they use the roads.

Minnesota's HOT Climate

One version of that future will be unveiled this month in Minnesota. Starting May 16, congestion pricing is coming to Interstate 394, west of Minneapolis. The highway's carpool lanes will open up to solo drivers, who may buy their way into the lanes using a transponder attached to their windshield. Sensors in the pavement will monitor traffic volume, feeding data into a central computer every 30 seconds. The price will fluctuate as often as every three minutes, depending on how heavy the traffic is, and will

be determined based on an algorithm intended to keep traffic moving in the toll lanes at 55 mph. During rush hour, the total price for an 11-mile trip could rise as high as $8. Late at night, when fewer drivers are on the road, it will cost a flat 50 cents to use the toll lanes (the price will be posted on electronic highway signs). Carpoolers and buses can still use the lanes for free.

Minnesota's approach isn't entirely new. A similar system has been operating on a patch of Interstate 15 in San Diego since 1996. Other congestion pricing experiments are running in Orange County, California, and in Houston. But Minnesota's variable pricing plan, called MnPass, is significant in two ways.

First, Minnesota is leading a new wave of these so-called "high occupancy toll" or "HOT" lane projects. Colorado, Washington State, Georgia and Virginia all have HOT lane projects under construction or under review, while Maryland, the Bay Area of California and San Diego are looking at creating regional networks of toll lanes. "For about the cost of a good cup of coffee, drivers have another option to get to where they need to go on time," says Federal Highway Administrator Mary E. Peters. "And advances in technology mean drivers aren't inconvenienced by having to stop at toll booths."

Minnesota's HOT project also proves that the politics of road pricing have changed. The early experiments with congestion charging in California were continually dogged by a social-justice critique that said only rich people could afford to buy into toll lanes. Critics called these projects "Lexus lanes," invoking an image of luxury cars breezing past lower-income drivers, stuck in their Chevys and Hondas amid the red glow of brake lights. Today, however, the Lexus lane argument seems to be fading. For one thing, California's experience is proving it wrong. It isn't just rich people using the fast lane. But there also is a new consensus on road pricing, between many on the political right and the left, that didn't exist just a few years ago.

Historically, it was free-market conservatives who gravitated to the idea of using tolls to manage congestion. Economists have been talking about it since the 1950s; Friedman himself once co-authored an essay on the topic. Through the 1990s, the conservative Reason Foundation made congestion pricing one of its most celebrated causes, promoting it as a market-oriented tool for dealing with traffic. Lately, however, the idea is catching on with the political left — not just in the United Kingdom but in the United States, too. Environmentalists have come to see congestion pricing as a way to improve air quality by keeping traffic moving. Transit supporters see toll revenues as a source of funding for public transit systems. And advocates of "smart growth" see any movement to put a price tag on driving as a good thing — hopefully inspiring more people to use transit or to buy homes located closer to where they work. "Road pricing 15 years ago was a bit of a gleam in an economist's eye," says Michael Replogle, a transportation specialist with Environmental Defense. "Today, we see that it works, it's efficient and it can produce a lot of winners."

To see how much the political equation has changed in Minnesota, you only have to go back eight years. In 1997, the state legislature approved a toll plan for I-394 that is almost exactly like the one in motion now. But a public backlash, which revolved largely around the Lexus-lanes argument, forced the state Transportation Department to cancel the project. At the time, Curt Johnson was head of the Metropolitan Council, a regional planning agency in the Twin Cities area. It was his job to run a public hearing on the proposal. "It was the one time in my four years as chairman that I knew if the fire marshal saw how many people were packed in the council chambers, he would have ordered an evacuation," Johnson says. "It was packed, wall to wall with people. It was an angry group. Everyone who wanted to talk was emotional, they were dead set against it. And the few people who said maybe this is a good thing for us to experiment with were drowned out by boos and hisses."

Since then, however, traffic congestion in the Twin Cities area has gotten much worse. According to the Texas Transportation Institute, which measures congestion nationwide, rush-hour delays due to traffic backups in Minneapolis have doubled in the past decade. Meanwhile, an anti-tax mood that has prevented Minnesota from raising its gas tax since 1988 makes financing new roads or expansions difficult. So it was desperation, more than anything else, that turned Minnesota back to HOT lanes. When the legislature debated the issue again in 2003, nobody seemed too concerned about the prospect of turning I-394 into an autobahn for the rich. The plan passed with broad bipartisan support. "There is now a much clearer recognition that the pricing tool is the most powerful way to manage congestion," Johnson says. "We'd be absolutely silly not to give this a try."

Public opinion seems to have shifted, too. In March, the University of Minnesota released a survey of 1,000 people who drive I-394 frequently. Sixty-four percent thought the toll plan was a good idea. Most tellingly, support is just as strong among people whose household incomes fall below $50,000 as it is among those above $150,000. Minnesota's data tracks with surveys from San Diego, where focus groups show that lower-income drivers use the HOT lanes, too, especially when they're in a pinch. "Even for the less well-off, it's affordable, and probably smart, to use the lanes on days when their value of time is higher," says Ken Buckeye, the program manager for MnDOT. If the choice is between paying $1-per-minute late fees at the day care center or a $4 toll, for example, people of all income levels are likely to pay the toll.

Part of the political support for congestion pricing in Minnesota came from transit advocates. One reason is because some of the toll revenues — half of whatever is left after paying to administer the system — will support expanded bus service along the corridor. A second factor is that transit advocates like the idea of sending drivers another price signal, in addition to the cost of a gallon of gasoline, which might induce them to consider alternative modes of transportation. Ann Rest, a Democrat and transit supporter, sponsored the HOT lane bill in the Senate. "I hope that when people begin to see the actual price of driving their single-occupant car, that they will realize the savings they could get from carpooling, vanpooling or taking the bus," Rest says.

Evidence from San Diego suggests that those price signals make a big difference. After I-15 switched over to variable tolling, the number of carpoolers on the road doubled. This is very exciting stuff for transportation planners, because it means that the existing highway capacity is being used more efficiently. "When you've got a finite resource like highway lanes, you've got to manage it in a way that provides you with the greatest return on your investment," Buckeye says. "The variable fee is just a very logical step to manage demand."

Looking to London

While a political consensus is emerging around HOT lanes, other ideas for pricing the commute remain controversial. Mayor Livingstone's scheme in London, for example, has been discussed in several big U.S. cities, but none yet seem willing to copy it. New York Mayor Michael Bloomberg proposed putting tolls on the Brooklyn Bridge and other East River bridges, a plan that he called congestion pricing. But Bloomberg yanked the idea under political pressure. "New York City is an obvious place to do congestion pricing," says Robert Dunphy, a transportation analyst with the Urban Land Institute. "The problem is that New York City politics says you can't get elected mayor by ticking off people in Queens and Brooklyn."

Dunphy, who works in Washington, D.C., says that a London-style system could help the nation's capital relieve its downtown congestion problems. Only 39 percent of Washington commuters take transit to work — a high figure compared with other U.S. cities but relatively low for a dense place with such an extensive subway and bus system. According to Dunphy's back-of-the-envelope analysis, transit's share would rise 5 percent if Washington used a downtown car charge. The problem, though, is that downtown might also lose businesses to suburban office districts where the roads are free.

San Francisco is the one U.S. city that is seriously studying the London plan. In fact, Livingstone will visit local leaders there in June to discuss his system and changes he's making to it, including raising the toll to $15 and possibly expanding the toll zone. The San Francisco County Transportation Authority is looking at what boundaries would make sense for a potential toll zone, how much money a charge might raise and what the impact on traffic would be. "Clearly Mayor Livingstone has done a successful job with it," says San Francisco Mayor Gavin Newsom. "It's worth exploring."

CHAPTER 24

Mountain View Approves Residential Development Around Public Transit Stations

Laura Thompson

Located 10 miles north of San Jose, Mountain View has a resident population of 76,000 and grows to more than 100,000 during the workday.

A successful grassroots effort in 1991 secured extension of the Tasman light rail line from San Jose to downtown Mountain View with a connection to the existing Caltrain commuter rail line to San Francisco. The city committed $15 million to the project and began a 10-year effort to plan and construct dense neighborhoods around the stations.

Mountain View officials recognized the growing imbalance between housing and jobs, and updated the general plan. "Our 1992 general plan established the basic objective of creating land-use densities that would maximize utilization of transit facilities," says principal planner Michael Percy.

To implement the general plan, the city adopted four precise plans and a transit overlay zone. The zoning changes resulted in construction of high-density residential neighborhoods adjacent to three major transit stations and a pedestrian-oriented office area

near a fourth. For these achievements, the city of Mountain View receives the 2002 outstanding planning award for implementation.

Essential Tools

Mountain View used two key planning tools to implement successful TOD — the precise plan and the transit overlay zone. Both contain model standards for dense mixed-use development linked to transit that can be transferred to other communities.

Precise plans replace traditional zoning with customized standards for a designated area. The plans establish broad goals and objectives with detailed development standards. Through flexible design approaches, such plans can encourage a variety of housing types, higher densities, narrow streets, public open space, reduced setbacks, and compatibility with the surrounding area.

"The precise plan is a cross between a planned unit development and a larger specific plan," says Linda Lauzze, neighbor-

Originally published as "Integrated Transit-Oriented Development: Mountain View," *Planning*, Vol. 68, No. 3, March 2002. Reprinted with permission from *Planning*, copyright © 2002 by the American Planning Association, Suite 1600, 122 South Michigan Avenue, Chicago, IL 60603–6107.

hood services manager. "It allows for flexibility, innovation, and public involvement."

In Mountain View's experience, creation of a precise plan takes one or two years. The environmental planning commission approves community-defined goals and development standards established to meet the plan objectives. The architectural review board and the zoning administrator later review and approve the project. Both plan and project are ultimately approved by city council. Since 1998, more than 1,000 housing units have been constructed as part of precise plan visions.

The transit overlay zone was adopted by city council in 1995 and applied to office and industrial uses within 2,000 feet of the Middlefield light rail station. Designated properties are allowed a higher floor area ratio of 0.50 rather than the standard 0.35 in exchange for on- and off-size improvements encouraging transit ridership.

So far, more than 500,000 square feet of bonus office and industrial space have been approved. Companies such as Netscape and Veritas have made improvements on site, including walkways to the rail station and bicycle parking. New buildings are required to orient the entrance to face the rail station, rather than a parking lot.

Companies located in the transit zone also must fund alternative transportation — such as transit shuttles and subsidized transit passes — for employees. In addition, the city levies a fee of $3 per square foot of new building area. The nearly $5 million collected so far has paid for a comprehensive bicycle and pedestrian system near the station.

Creative Infill

Completion of The Crossings TOD in early 2000 transformed an 18-acre former shopping mall site into a high-quality residential community and captured the interest of planners nationwide. The pedestrian-oriented neighborhood combines housing and transit in close proximity to offices and shopping areas.

Designed by Peter Calthorpe, the site incorporates a mix of 359 housing units across the street from or next to a Caltrain rail station. "One of our philosophies is to create a diversity of housing opportunities in each project," says Calthorpe. "We were able to achieve a healthy set of housing types, including small-lot single-family homes, townhomes, and condominiums. This range of housing in a single neighborhood is one of its greatest accomplishments."

The overall density is 21 units per acre; all buildings are oriented to the street and compact townhouses and neighborhood stores face the station.

The vehicle for implementing this development was the San Antonio Station Precise Plan, adopted by city council in 1991. The plan encourages a variety of housing types, coordinated with the transit station, and a strong sense of neighborhood. The design encourages interaction among residents through the placement of sidewalks, pedestrian paths, common open spaces, and front porches.

Once a Factory, Now Homes

Adopted in 1996, the Whisman Station Precise Plan set the stage for a 500-unit residential community on a 40-acre industrial site formerly operated by GTE. Extension of the light rail line through the property gave the city an opportunity to create a mixed-use neighborhood in an office and light industrial area with links to transit.

Because two separate developers owned the land on either side of the railroad, the city required that a master planner develop the site plan for both properties. City planners worked closely with the developers to ensure the goals of the plan were met in a consistent manner.

The result is a walkable and diverse community of small-lot single-family and row houses integrated with public parks and the light rail station. Consistent design standards, landscaping, and pedestrian paths link the two development projects. The houses sold quickly; 42 more units will be built on adjacent land.

Principal planner Michael Percy stresses the importance of working with developers to ensure that objectives are achieved in a project that can actually be built. "In conjunction with absolute standards, such as requiring the highest density in close proximity to the transit station, precise plans also offer flexibility," Percy says.

Whisman Station is a case in point. With an average density requirement of 12 to 14.5 units per acre, but no minimum or maximum, flexibility is built into the plan, allowing for a productive mix of housing types.

A New Downtown

The Downtown Precise Plan encouraged a mix of land uses within walking distance of the downtown train station. When the plan was adopted in 1988, the transit station served only Caltrain commuter rail. At the time of the 1999 update, which established standards for higher residential densities, the station was the center for Caltrain, light rail, and bus services.

The plan provided the framework for stimulating public and private investment in the city's main street and adjacent transition blocks. It led to rebuilding downtown with a new city hall, library, performing arts center, and two parks for outdoor concerts and other events.

Private developments followed with 40,000 square feet of new retail, 260,000 square feet of office space, and 220 new housing units within the last year. Several companies that moved to downtown Mountain View were motivated by proximity to transit, retail, and other services. A large mixed-use project with public-private partnership is now undergoing development review.

Across the street from the downtown multi-modal transit station, the Evelyn Avenue Corridor Precise Plan guides development along a major street and community gateway. In response to plans for light rail extension, city planners and residents developed the precise plan in 1994 to maximize housing opportunities close to the station and maintain the character of one of the city's most established neighborhoods.

Commercial property was rezoned residential, and two vacant parcels were developed with 67 new housing units. Extensive public input guided the new housing design to incorporate what Michael Percy describes as a "layer cake development effect." Slight increases in housing density were allowed at the boundary with the existing neighborhood, gradually increasing to higher densities near the transit station.

CHAPTER 25

Nagano, Other Cities, Use Intelligent Transportation Systems for Traffic Management

Committee on Intelligent Transport

Modern life demands growing mobility. This mobility is increasingly provided by private cars, but the very freedom that cars offer is severely reduced by chronic traffic congestion. Our cities have responded to this crisis with policies that try to reconcile our insatiable demand for increased mobility with the need to reduce traffic jams, protect the environment, and ensure safety. But further efforts are clearly needed.

Intelligent transportation systems (ITS) can help by applying communications and information technology to the problem. Whether offering real-time information about traffic conditions, online information for journey planning, or even cars that drive themselves, these systems increase safety and reduce travel times.

The following is an overview of current types of intelligent transportation systems and some suggestions for what they might achieve in the future.

Keeping Things Moving: Traffic Management Systems

Advanced traffic management systems ensure that networks of roadways are used to their maximum capacity. These computerized systems, commonplace all over the world, coordinate traffic signals to minimize delays, control the rate of traffic merging onto expressways, and detect accidents and vehicle breakdowns.

Such systems can be combined to solve complex traffic problems, as was done in Nagano, Japan, during the 1998 Olympic Games. Nagano's infrastructure was underdeveloped. Congestion already occurred daily and was expected to worsen with the influx of visitors. Snowy conditions were also likely.

Sensors were installed along Nagano's main arteries. The system collected and processed information about congestion, travel times, and traffic regulations. This information was provided to drivers via information boards posted along roads, telephones, faxes, and the Internet.

Originally published as "Fighting Traffic with Technology," *The Futurist*, Vol. 34, No. 5, September–October 2000. Published by the World Future Society, Bethesda, MD. Reprinted with permission of the publisher.

Infrared beacons were installed in the vehicles carrying athletes and officials. Optimum routes and travel times were calculated for official vehicles, based on their positions as broadcast by the infrared beacons, and supplied to the drivers. In addition, traffic signals were programmed to give official cars priority. The system succeeded, ensuring safe and efficient operation of official vehicles and providing accurate traffic information to other drivers.

Knowledge Is Power: Traveler Information Systems

Uncertainty is one of the major problems that drivers face. Smart travelers use information to make better decisions about their travel plans. Transportation authorities have been collecting traffic data for many years, but they have seldom shared it with the public. Advanced traveler information systems aim to plug this gap. When more information is available to travelers, they will adjust their time, route, or mode of travel to their own advantage, improving conditions overall.

Simple traveler information systems include radio traffic reports and "localcasts" in the vicinity of special locations such as congested airports. More advanced applications include traffic congestion maps and information accessible over the Internet; in-vehicle navigation systems that provide maps, traffic flow information, and directions; and traffic information broadcast to personal communication devices (pagers, smart watches, cellular telephones, etc.).

More-detailed information that could be regularly broadcast in the future includes predicted journey times, weather conditions, Yellow Page services, parking, and park-and-ride information. Such information could encourage drivers to leave their cars at a park-and-ride site and continue the trip by public transport.

Electronic variable message signs, electronic kiosks, and cable television broadcasts are already deployed in many metropolitan areas and will soon appear in dozens more. A radio channel is being launched in Europe to provide traffic information in the user's own language. Personal information services, such as Trafficmaster (United Kingdom) or Visionaute (France) already enable subscribers to avoid unnecessary delays by avoiding congestion.

Automatic systems that detect accidents or traffic jams and broadcast warnings to variable roadside signs or in-vehicle devices can greatly improve safety. For example, Los Angeles's "Smart Corridor" project uses an array of cameras and other devices to monitor traffic flow on the Santa Monica Freeway. When an accident or heavy congestion occurs, controllers in the traffic center steer motorists off the freeway onto alternate routes by means of variable message signs. Detoured drivers are guided through parallel city routes and back to the freeway with the help of special "trailblazer" signs.

High-Tech Directions

Finding your way in an unfamiliar city using only a printed map is becoming more and more difficult because of traffic congestion. Vehicle navigation systems using the satellite-based Global Positioning System and CD-ROM digital maps are intelligent answers to this problem, but these systems don't take the real-time traffic situation into account.

In a number of cities, especially in Japan, travelers are able to routinely enter a destination into a system that will then calculate the optimum route based on current traffic conditions. The system gives the driver directions either through visual diagrams on a screen or by synthetic voice. In some cases, drivers also have the option of seeing the current picture of traffic congestion displayed on an electronic map and choosing their own routes accordingly.

Figure 1. U.S. Motor Vehicle Deaths	
Year	**Number of Deaths**
1988	47,087
1989	45,582
1990	44,599
1991	41,508
1992	39,250
1993	40,150
1994	40,716
1995	41,817
1996	42,065
1997	42,013
1998	41,471

Source: National Highway Traffic Safety Administration

Roadway Deaths: Motor vehicle accidents have decreased over the last decade because of tougher drunk-driving and seatbelt laws, but these accidents still killed over 40,000 people in 1998.

Such advanced systems will require enough traffic sensors in the road to collect and distribute reliable and timely traffic information. They will also need better wireless connections to quickly handle the data moving between the car's computer and the system's central computer.

When the Car Becomes the Driver

Advanced vehicle control systems actively aid the driver in the task of driving. Vehicle manufacturers and suppliers see a large potential market for these products. Governments encourage these technologies because they improve safety and enhance road capacity.

Technologies already available include antilock brakes, traction control, and skid control. Emerging technologies include adaptive cruise control, driver drowsiness detectors, infrared night vision systems, and lane warning sensors.

Further in the future are automatic collision avoidance systems, which will relieve the driver of some or all control of the vehicle. These will be similar to autopilot systems in airplanes. Fully automated highways will require not only in-vehicle controls, but also in-highway equipment that will guide vehicles to their destinations.

Much work has been done on systems that enhance the vision of drivers in poor weather. This can be done through infrared or other video techniques to provide an image of the road ahead, shown to the driver in a display superimposed over the normal view through the windshield.

Driver assistance such as intelligent cruise controls are beginning to arrive on the market. These detect when the driver's vehicle is following another vehicle too closely and either warn the driver or automatically slow the vehicle to maintain a safe distance. Other systems can detect vehicles straying out of their lane and again warn the driver or guide the vehicle automatically back into the middle of the lane.

Some accidents result from drivers falling asleep at the wheel. Systems are now available to detect drowsiness and sound an alert to wake the driver. Similar systems can detect an imminent collision and deploy crash restraints such as air bags. Other devices actively under development will detect potential collisions and warn the driver or possible take action automatically.

Collision avoidance systems are intermediate steps toward the more distant goal of complete vehicle automation, a concept that has been successfully demonstrated in Japan, Europe, and the United States in recent years.

Managing Emergencies

Travelers want to feel that they are in secure environments where help is immediately at hand when needed. In the case of serious injury or accident, the speed with which skilled first aid can be rendered to victims has a major impact on the medical outcome. Thus, any system that shortens the time before help arrives will save lives.

Trend Analysis: Intelligent Transportation Systems

As more and more governments turn to intelligent transportation systems (ITS) to alleviate traffic problems, we can be sure this technology will have important effects on our lives. Here is an attempt to identify some of those effects.

Economics

The cost of wasted fuel and time caused by traffic congestion exceeds $72 billion per year in the United States, according to the Texas Transportation Institute. Proponents of ITS say the technology will save much of this money by making transport more efficient. While the money saved by individuals may be relatively small, the money to be saved by commercial transportation fleets could be considerable. Lowering the cost of transport could mean lower prices to consumers in the end, especially for difficult-to-transport products such as fresh meats and produce.

In addition, if ITS reduces accidents, it could save part of the economic cost of those accidents, estimated at over $150 billion in 1994 by the National Highway Traffic Safety Administration.

However, implementing ITS in a metropolitan area will cost hundreds of millions of dollars, though bond issues could spread out the burden into future years.

Society

While the gas money individuals save because of ITS may be small, reducing the travel time and stress levels of our daily commute may have important social effects. As many observers have noted, we become less civil toward one another when we get behind the wheels of our cars, seeing other motorists not as citizens but as competitors, or, worse, as obstacles. If ITS works as it is supposed to, we may see a rise in civility on the roadway. In addition, the extra leisure time gained could improve quality of life.

Finally, automobile accidents are a leading cause of death for people 5 to 29 years old, killing over 40,000 people in 1998, according to the latest statistics from the National Highway Traffic Safety Administration. If ITS delivers on its promise to reduce accidents, the social benefits of saved lives could be immeasurable.

Government

Government leaders tend to favor ITS because of its promise to reduce traffic jams and improve safety — two politically popular ideas. A large ITS project may also boost local economies by providing jobs. However, such projects come with huge price tags: Installing ITS infrastructure in a large metropolitan area would cost $420 million, according to the World Road Association. The obvious solution is to raise taxes (gasoline taxes seem a likely target) or to create new ones, perhaps a "driving tax" based on your odometer reading or a "car tax" similar to taxes on homes.

Governments may choose to privatize ITS projects, but here, too, the cost of investment will be recouped by the private company from roadway users in the form of tolls or fees.

Such systems are being implemented by private organizations or consortia in Europe and the United States. They require the combination of vehicle location, as with a Global Positioning System, and wireless communication. Emergency notification can be initiated manually — by the driver pushing a panic button — or automatically —

Expect new legislation as governments negotiate the legal twists and turns of intelligent roadways. For example, who might be responsible for an accident on an automated highway — one of the drivers, the highway operators, or the company that designed the automated car?

Environment

Proponents of ITS say the improved efficiency will reduce vehicle emissions, thereby improving air quality. For example, widely used interactive navigation systems in the United States could reduce vehicle emissions by 5%–16%, according to one assessment reported by the World Road Association. The increased use of vehicles powered by fuel cells, whose only waste emission is water, will likely increase this effect.

However, some environmental groups may oppose ITS projects that involve building new highways or widening existing highways, citing possible disruption of local ecosystems and adverse effects on the plants and animals that live nearby.

Demography

ITS could reduce automobile injuries and fatalities in the demographic groups most likely to have accidents — teens, the elderly, and males.

To the extent that ITS makes commuting easier, it is likely to increase the trend toward suburbanization and exurbanization. People will live farther and farther from the city and their workplaces. Cities will mushroom across the countryside.

If automated cars and highways become common, it could benefit the elderly whose mobility is restricted when they can no longer drive. Formerly homebound seniors could return to work or take a more active part in community life. In addition, the burden on parents, who must spend large amounts of time driving their children to soccer games and other activities, could be reduced.

Technology

Intelligent transportation systems will rely on quick wireless communication and computing power. ITS research will likely spur advances in these fields, if only by providing a proving ground for new technology. Wireless communication with a bandwidth broad enough to accommodate real-time video will likely become an essential part of on-board navigation systems, showing drivers backups and accidents ahead. Computers sophisticated enough to recognize traffic incidents from camera images and powerful enough to calculate alternative routes for thousands of drivers will be an essential part of traffic control systems.

ITS will make cars increasingly sophisticated — and complicated. Initially, this may make the task of driving more difficult: Drivers will not only have to watch the road but keep one eye on a video screen and one ear tuned to the latest traffic bulletins. However, as cars themselves take over more and more of the driver's tasks, the new technology should make driving easier, to the point where a car's occupant could sit back and watch the scenery, read, or even nap.

—Jeff Minerd

through the air bag triggering mechanism, for example. The automatic notification of emergencies, sometimes known as May-day services, is very important in remote rural areas outside the reach of cellular telephones.

Pay As You Go

Electronic toll collection systems are installed at many toll plazas, enabling drivers to pay tolls automatically without cash and without stopping at a toll station. These systems reduce delays and prevent fraud and toll avoidance.

Simple systems are now commonplace around the world. These systems use an electronic tag, which is detected each time the vehicle passes a toll plaza. The driver is then sent a bill, or the toll can be automatically deducted from a prepaid account.

More-advanced systems, which allow transactions at expressway speeds, are used in Toronto on Highway 407. The Melbourne city link road in Australia uses a similar system. Both of these roads offer only electronic toll facilities.

Electronic tolling has worked well in Oslo, Norway. Threatened with chronic congestion, the city asked drivers to use an electronic tolling system. Since 1990, drivers must pay a toll to enter Oslo's beltway. Drivers can stop to pay with cash at a conventional toll booth, or — in the case of the 73% who hold a prepaid ticket — enter the beltway without stopping if their car is equipped with an electronic tag. The windshield-mounted tag contains a driver ID and account information and sends this information via two-way radio communication to a roadside beacon. The tag is checked against a database, and, if the account is not valid, the vehicle is photographed and the driver fined.

Electronic tolling improves driver convenience and reduces labor costs to road operators. Even the non-equipped vehicles benefit, since the lines in the manually operated lanes at the toll plaza also get shorter, reducing the time delay in toll payment.

Improving Public Transport

More-efficient public transportation is crucial to reducing congestion, and intelligent systems can be applied here as well.

For example, the "5T" system helps buses run on time in Turin, Italy. On board each bus is a location system that identifies its position (to the nearest five meters) and reports automatically to a central control room. If the bus is behind schedule, the control center changes the timing of traffic signals ahead of the vehicle. This public transport priority system has improved bus travel time by 14% with no adverse effect on private traffic.

In Paris, a smart card makes the buses and Metro easier to use. The card is prepaid and can be reloaded at vending points at bus and Metro stations. The card communicates with the on-vehicle ticket machine or the ticket gate just by its proximity; it does not have to be placed in a slot, making it very convenient.

Putting It All Together

Transportation professionals need to be aware of the benefits offered by this new technology and the challenges in making it work. Governments around the world are implementing intelligent transportation systems, and they are finding that their efforts require considerable cooperation among many agencies and organizations.

Many different stakeholders are involved. Transportation professionals need to build alliances with public transport operators, private sector information service providers, city planning authorities, banks, electronic payment system providers, and, not least, the general traveling public.

The overriding purpose of intelligent transportation systems is to save cost, time, and lives, and this objective is common to all regions of the world.

Notes

This chapter draws upon the *ITS Handbook 2000: Recommendations from the World Road Association (PIARC)* by the PIARC Committee on Intelligent Transport, edited by Kan Chen and John C. Miles.

The World Road Association (PIARC) is a worldwide association for exchanging knowledge and techniques about roads and transportation. Copies of the book can be obtained by contacting Artech House, 685 Canton Street, Norwood, Massachusetts 02062. Telephone 1–800–225–9977; Web site www.artechhouse.com. (Or order online from www.wfs.org/specials.htm.)

A French version of the book can be obtained by contacting PIARC at La Grande Arche, paroi Nord, Niveau 8, 92055 LA DEFENSE, Cedex, France. Telephone 33-1479–68121; Web site www.piarc.org; e-mail piarc@ wanadoo.fr.

CHAPTER 26

New York Region Thrives on Complex Public Mass-Transit Options

Emanuel Tobier

It is not easy to characterize the recent economic performance of the New York metropolitan region, much less speculate about its future. After all, it has changed course rather dramatically several times over the past three decades or so. The expansion of the global economy since the 1970s certainly has provided the region with new opportunities but also has exposed it to a good deal more instability than it faced in the past.

The region is huge, complex, and affluent. As defined by the Regional Plan Association, it has a population of 20 million and sprawls across parts of three states. With a per-capita income one-third above that of the United States as a whole — and accounting for 10 percent of the nation's gross domestic product — it is not a market to be ignored.

The region's complex economy is a product of nature, policy, and history. From its origin in the 17th century as a trading post at the tip of Manhattan Island, the region always has been influenced by the shifting fortunes of the global economy — inevitable, perhaps, when for three centuries its economic life pivoted on its deepwater harbor.

Well into this century, the region's massive, sprawling waterfronts contained busy piers, warehouses, bulk storage and processing facilities, and railroads that received and shipped manufactured goods and commodities to and from all parts of the world. Many products that passed through the port were produced outside the region, but by the late 19th century the region had a considerable manufacturing sector that owed a great deal to the skills, stamina, and entrepreneurial energy of the vast numbers of immigrants who arrived during the 19th and early 20th centuries. The region's manufacturing sector, which was dominated by production of nondurable goods such as apparel, underwent vast expansion between the 1870s and the period just after World War II, when it reached its apogee.

Originally based on the production and distribution of manufactured goods and commodities, the region's economy slowly shifted to management and finance — in other words, to the provision of services, which was on the whole a more lucrative line of business. The region's physical infrastruc-

Originally published as "New York Revs Its Economic Engines," *Urban Land*, Vol. 56, No. 10, October 1997. Published by the Urban Land Institute, Washington, D.C. Reprinted with permission of the publisher.

ture thus shifted from what were by then extensively developed waterfront and factory districts to central business districts. Of the latter, the most spectacular were skyscraper-dominated midtown and lower Manhattan. By the 1930s, these two districts contained the world's leading concentrations of office space, and they still do today.

Recent Trends

The region's vital signs are encouragingly good. Although its population fell by 3 percent in the 1970s, it regained that much and a bit more in the 1980s. It has added several hundred thousand more residents during the current decade, putting it over the 20 million mark.

This overall stability, however, gives little hint of the significant changes that have taken place in the composition of the population, among them the replacement of a significant portion of the native-born population by persons born outside the United States. The region (and New York City in particular) continues to be a magnet for newcomers to America. With just 7.5 percent of the nation's population, the region has steadily drawn 20 to 25 percent of all legally admitted immigrants over the past 15 years. In 1970, foreign-born persons accounted for 13 percent of the region's population; by 1996, the figure was 22 percent and rising. (For the nation as a whole, proportions of foreign-born persons were 5 percent in 1970 and 9 percent in 1996.) Accommodating so many newcomers can be difficult, especially for the region's hard-pressed public sector, but the overwhelming consensus is that the latest round of young, energetic immigrants has made a significant contribution to the region's service sector and rejuvenated many fading inner-city neighborhoods.

While the region's population remained virtually unchanged between 1970 and 1995, its labor force — those working or looking for work — grew a great deal more, by 20 percent. The job deficit was greatest in the 1970s, when employment grew by a modest 4 percent. In the 1980s, by contrast, employment growth of 17 percent outpaced the 14 percent growth in the labor force. Thus far in the 1990s, employment has contracted at twice the rate of the labor force. The result is that the region's unemployment rate, currently about 6 percent, has been running steadily at between 1.0 to 1.5 percent above that of the United States as a whole.

Employment in the region fell by 7 percent between 1989 and 1992, amounting to three-quarters of a million lost jobs. Through 1996, the region appears to have recaptured about 400,000 of those jobs. A decline of this magnitude is a first for the region in the post–World War II period. The feebleness of its economic recovery, particularly in the context of a national economy that currently is in the midst of a seven-year-long expansion, is disconcerting.

However, the region's performance in the 1990s does have some strong points. Between 1989 and 1994 (the latest year for which data are available), inflation-adjusted average earnings advanced by 6 percent. (Nationally, the figure was under 1 percent.) In the 1980s, the difference in gains in average earnings was even more striking: up 9 percent in the region, down 4 percent for the nation. These longstanding discrepancies imply that the region has been replacing low-wage with high-wage jobs. This process seems to have taken place across industry lines, but it has proceeded furthest in the financial services industry, in which the region's wage premium rose from 43 percent to 88 percent over a 25-year period. With an economic mix dominated by high-value-added activities, the region's firms can afford to pay above-average wages and still earn above-average profits.

The Challenge of the Global Economy

Will the region's economy lift off in the reasonably near future and climb again as rapidly as it did in the 1980s, when it added 1.6 million jobs? A repetition of those heady days is too much to hope for and certainly unwise to count on. But if caution is in order, pessimism is unwarranted; the signs pointing to further expansion and prosperity are impossible to miss. Tourism, entertainment and leisure activities, financial and information services, upscale retailing, telecommunications, and the media (new, old, and multi-) are big growth industries in the global economy and have a natural affinity for places like New York City.

While the ability of its entrepreneurs to navigate the global economy successfully always has been crucial to the region's economic success, the stakes have been raised considerably during the last few decades. For one thing, there has been an enormous expansion in the scale and relative importance of the global economy. In addition, the global industries that are growing most rapidly and offer the greatest rewards are those that involve the production and exchange of ideas, knowledge, information, and images. The region's movers and shakers need to maintain a significant edge over the competition in that area if the economy is to flourish.

And they had better be keen competitors. This is no longer a largely uncontested market to be divided up among a handful of global economy old boys like New York, London, and Tokyo. Dramatic changes in information and communications technology have made it possible for a host of new competitors to vie for a piece of the global economic pie. Top prizes will go to those city-regions that offer key participants the kinds of microenvironments they need.

What those might be will depend on the part of the global economy in which they happen to be operating: in other words, different microenvironments for different folks. Purveyors of newly created financial instruments are likely to need a different mix of supporting services and facilities than such

global economy denizens as cutting-edge fashion designers or the diverse cast of characters populating the fast-merging worlds of media, culture (high and low), and entertainment.

While each part of the global economy has distinctive requirements, they share the need for many kinds of support facilities and services — libraries, museums, universities, and hospitals are leading examples. But they also need hotels, restaurants, and entertainment options that appeal to a wide range of tastes, interests, and pocketbooks. The winning global city-region will provide them all.

The Importance of the Manhattan CBD

Manhattan's only significant — but still distant — U.S. competitors for global city-region status are Chicago, Boston, San Francisco, and Washington, D.C. In competing for global industries, the region has one outstanding asset: the Manhattan central business district, defined as the area south of 72nd Street to the Battery. The part of the regional economy that matters most — the export sector — is located there. While many of the region's export firms always have operated outside the CBD and while there has been a steady dispersal of the city's export base to other parts of the region, the Manhattan CBD still represents its chief drawing card.

As of the mid 1990s, Manhattan had about 2.5 million jobs, of which the lion's share was located in the CBD. Close to one of four of the region's jobs are in Manhattan. The importance of Manhattan to the region's economy shows up even more vividly with respect to its contributions to overall earnings. In 1994, Manhattan-based earnings represented one-third of the region's total, slightly higher than its 1979 level and just a bit below its 1969 showing. The average earnings figure for Manhattan was 43 percent above the regional figure as of 1994; a quarter of a century earlier, the Manhattan earnings premium was only 17 percent.

The big question for Manhattan's future and, by implication, for that of the region, is how much agglomeration is economically productive. Does it really make sense to have more than 2 million people beavering away in a nine-square-mile area? Or will digitized global television and computer networks soon overthrow the ancient tyrannies of time and space, thus making such artifacts as the Manhattan CBD redundant? No one really knows. In the global economy, more and more business will be conducted by electronic means. But the need for face-to-face dealings will continue to grow, and it will make economic and social sense for them to continue to occur in a handful of world-class central business districts.

The Public Sector Role

In a market economy, the identification and provision of inputs needed by global firms to produce and distribute whatever it is they are engaged in can, generally speaking, best be left to those firms. But in the New York metropolitan region, the public sector's role in providing transportation services — subways, buses, suburban transit, air travel, long-distance rail — represents a special case. Given the scale and density of Manhattan, the destination of so many of the region's trips, its economic viability depends on keeping its immensely complicated transportation system in reasonably good working order.

The responsibility for this task is divided among three states, numerous localities, and the federal government. This division of responsibility, implemented through myriad subsidies and regulations, is a sure recipe for conflict and missed opportunities; it is a wonder that it works as well as it does. The negative implications for important sectors of the global economy such as tourism and business travel can best be glimpsed in the still unresolved, long-running dispute

over how to link Manhattan directly to the region's major airports through high-quality transit services.

Implications for Development

Predictably, the region's construction activity swooned along with its economy in the early 1990s. While construction has rebounded somewhat, it is still far below its late 1980s' peak. The modest economic gains of the last few years plus the expectation of, at best, comparably modest gains going forward have dampened the spirits of developers, not to mention those of their bankers. But in a region of this size and complexity, opportunities for new construction always will present themselves, and there always will be substantial activity in the capital maintenance and upgrading of the existing building stock.

The area's office sector took the hardest hit as far as new construction is concerned. The contraction in white-collar employment in the early 1990s followed what proved to be an unsustainable surge in new building during the 1980s. By the end of the 1980s, office vacancy rates had reached high double-digit levels in Manhattan as well as in the surrounding suburbs; more recently, they have fallen to the low double-digit levels. But combined with inflation-adjusted asking rents that are half their level a decade earlier, this is unlikely to lead to much new building. Indeed, when white-collar employment heats up in the future, its impact on demand for office space is likely to be less than in the past, as office managers are under constant pressure to use space more efficiently.

Where the region's building stock portfolio is most overweight is in the industrial sector. Manufacturing employment has fallen continuously since the 1950s, and over the last quarter of a century the region's manufacturing jobs have been reduced by half. Many redundant buildings have been put to, or are awaiting, the wrecking ball, but a surprising number, along with office buildings that have seen better days, are finding new uses as residential lofts or hotels.

Last, vast expansion in the leisure and entertainment industries, as reflected in the enormous growth in tourism, has stimulated hotel building in all price ranges. This phenomenon has benefited Manhattan most of all, but it also has spread to nearby areas.

Back to the Future

The region's origins and its economic livelihood for much of its history revolved around the comings and goings at the Port of New York. The considerable decline of the port for shipping, passenger travel, and industrial use throughout the 20th century has, by default, created a major opportunity for the century to come.

In the years ahead, the region has a chance to reorient itself to its waterfronts and waterways by introducing new uses, including those that can be incorporated in old buildings and landscapes. This process is, in fact, already under way. Announcements of major projects in the port are made on an almost monthly basis. While the port of yesteryear was a place of industry and the physical movement of goods, the port of the future will focus on amenities, leisure, and recreation — and on how to attract residents of the surrounding region. Making this happen is a major challenge for a city-region that remains a top contender in the global economy.

CHAPTER 27

Oakland Revives Aging Neighborhood Using New Public Transit Station

Ernesto M. Vasquez

In the Fruitvale District of Oakland, California, plans are afoot to transform the worn-out, overlooked neighborhood into a vibrant, bustling, mixed-use multicultural center. Now underway and set for completion next year, the revitalization of Fruitvale is being spearheaded by Arabella Martinez, CEO of the Unity Council, a local community development corporation. "I want to infuse Fruitvale's established ethnic identity with a new social and economic vitality," she says. "I envision a complete connection among transportation and land use strategies and economic development for this community." To that end, the private/public partnership formed to revitalize Fruitvale has developed a plan that celebrates Fruitvale's ethnic diversity in a contemporary setting that connects community, retail, commercial, residential, and transit uses — despite the many obstacles.

At first glance, the Fruitvale neighborhood seems riddled with near-empty streets, vacant and ruined buildings, and dark, uninviting sidewalks that connect the community to the Bay Area Rapid Transit system

(BART). It is surprising to note that more than 30,000 commuters a day travel on BART to and from work at the Fruitvale station; however, they do not stroll into the uninviting neighborhood for a bite to eat or to pick up last-minute groceries from the market.

Almost a century ago, the Fruitvale District, considered Oakland's second downtown, was renowned for its extensive orchards, mansions, and convenient streetcar transportation. The business sector thrived in Fruitvale, even attracting retail giant Montgomery Ward in 1923. During World War II, thousands of jobs were created in the district, attracting an influx of African American and Hispanic workers, but when the war ended, the factories shut down and local businesses suffered. At the same time, new freeways and subsidized mortgages encouraged more affluent residents to move out of Fruitvale into the suburbs.

By the 1960s, the district's malaise was undeniable. What few residents remained lived in deteriorating houses or apartments while community parks and facilities went

Originally published as "Bearing Fruit," *Urban Land*, Vol. 59, No. 7, July 2000. Published by the Urban Land Institute, Washington, D.C. Reprinted with permission of the publisher.

unattended. Concerned residents wanted change. In 1989, Martinez began to explore ways to revitalize Fruitvale in an effort to regain some of its past luster.

In 1993, a team of graduate students from the University of California at Berkeley's Oakland Metropolitan Forum performed a study of water use in Fruitvale. The students also devised various ideas for improvements in Fruitvale, including creating a pedestrian link from the BART station to the area's primary shopping/business district on International Boulevard, implementing a building improvement program, increasing signage, and replacing store awnings. Martinez credits the students' report with being the initial template for Fruitvale's redevelopment strategy.

Although funding to complete the changes was not available at the time, the Unity Council began to devise a strategy for forming a new neighborhood. When BART proposed building a stand-alone parking structure on a ten-acre site in Fruitvale that, as proposed, would further separate commuters from the district, the Unity Council took action. Many residents were already dissatisfied because the BART station produced so little pedestrian traffic in the neighborhood, and the community did not want another parking lot. The Unity Council quickly informed local residents of BART's plan, encouraging them to work together to propose other options. Community discussions prompted a number of alternative ideas for the ten-acre parcel, and recognizing the need for community-friendly transportation, BART joined in the efforts. According to Manuela Silva, executive director of Fruitvale Transit Corporation, the implementation arm of the Unity Council, the Unity Council, in partnership with BART, began to develop a plan that included a community center, a shopping area, and a public plaza, linking pedestrians and commuters to the surrounding shopping and business district.

The Benefits of Smart Growth

Fruitvale's redevelopment plan includes 33,000 square feet of retail/restaurant space, 40,000 square feet for a health clinic, 40,000 square feet for offices, a 12,000-square-foot community resource center, a 5,550-square-foot library, and 47 residential lofts. A number of smart growth design and land use concepts have been adopted in designing the project, including infill, mixed-use, and high-density development; concentration of development along rail transit corridors; and pedestrian-oriented retail development. Reducing pollution, traffic congestion, and reliance on automobiles while elaborating on those elements of the city grid that are applicable to development is central to these concepts. Redeveloping an urban infill location will effectively increase density within the neighborhood. The challenge is to use the underused and undervalued land in an adequate and cost-effective manner.

While the project is planned to include commercial, residential, and retail uses, it also will include community facilities such as a health care center, a child-care center, a seniors' center, and a library. The placement of these community facilities within the main plaza should encourage residents of all ages to interact while providing much-needed services. Buildings will house retail stores on the first level, community facilities on the second level, and loft housing on the third level. A central element of the project is a seniors' housing facility called Las Bougainvilleas. Located on land donated by the City of Oakland, the 68-unit housing complex funded by the U.S. Department of Housing and Urban Development (HUD) provides much-needed seniors' and affordable housing in Oakland. The three- and four-story buildings surrounded by fountains, benches, gardens, and landscaping are a welcome addition to the neighborhood. Underground parking and balconies, not generally seen in low-income facilities, optimize use of space. Another key component of Fruitvale will be La Clinica de la Raza's new headquarters, a 40,000-square-foot, state-of-the-art health facility. Serving more than 70,000 patients a year, the facility will have the space to serve a growing public, and it will benefit from its proximity to the BART station and nine bus lines. Fruitvale also will feature 47 live/work loft units. The affordable units are subsidized by a below-market-rate loan from the City of Oakland and will rent for $750 to $950. Market units will rent for approximately $1,150 to $1,550.

One of the early steps in reinventing Fruitvale's image was changing the area's name to Fruitvale Transit Village. According to Silva, the transit village moniker denotes opportunities to link transit to communities and to promote integrated neighborhoods that meet consumer needs for retail stores, housing, and child care. If clusters are designed to complement one another, residents and commuters can benefit from the convenience of Fruitvale's multiple services.

Initially, however, not even the new name convinced shopowners on International Boulevard — most of whom perceived the redevelopment as a hindrance to their businesses — of the project's advantages. Several community forums ensued with the Unity Council, architects, builders, and other members of the redevelopment team to discuss proposed plans and to incorporate the community's recommendations. The forums were crucial in delivering the message to residents and shopowners that their input was important to the planning of Fruitvale Transit Village and that the project needed their participation to be successful.

"When you bring people together, they start taking about their dreams and fears," notes Silva. "We started forming neighborhood associations, offering leadership training, and just getting people involved. Residents started coming out of their homes and shopping on International Boulevard and investing in their community," she explains.

"Both the residents and the shopowners felt included and considered themselves stakeholders in the project. They now have a sense of belonging and a sense of place. And they can't wait for the work to be completed."

Investor Support

Today, Fruitvale has raised nearly $50 million in federal grants and private investments toward its $100 million goal; however, raising the money has not been easy. Private investors initially feared the Fruitvale redevelopment project because there was no money in Fruitvale to support it. Martinez has used her political muscle to secure more than $43 million in federal grants to date. "It takes a tremendous amount of time to make these inner-city redevelopment projects economically feasible and to receive the funding," Martinez notes. "After we secured the first $7.65 million grant, private investors began to support us. When they began to see improvements to the streets, even the shopowners on International Boulevard started to support the project, and they have invested $2.3 million in their own community for redevelopment."

One of Fruitvale's biggest supporters is the City of Oakland. According to Ignacio de la Fuente, president of Oakland's city council, "Our role has been to aid in financially supporting Fruitvale's improvement and facilitating the Unity Council's efforts, especially with land use." With federal and private dollars being raised for Fruitvale, Martinez felt a weight lifted off her shoulders. "The private sector finally appreciated Fruitvale's unique vision," she says. The Unity Council's money-raising efforts are not over yet, however. It currently is trying to fund a bike station at BART.

One of the greatest challenges for a public/private partnership project is the amount of time the development process can take. "Public agencies have their own internal processes, which inevitably take longer than those of a private developer who just wants to get the job done," notes Silva. "On the other hand, one of the great achievements of this project has been that each public agency — knowing its constraints — has assigned a team to facilitate the process and move forward, while the development teams have met to discuss issues and come up with solutions to get the job done. Will this ultimately speed things up? Probably not, but at least we are all working together," she adds.

Another unforeseen obstacle is the economic prosperity the nation is experiencing. The Bay Area, especially Oakland, is pro union, and labor costs have been increasing with the duration of the project. Alternative ways to reduce costs are being researched. Even though some costs are increasing, Martinez praises the builder and the architect for their efficiency and cost-containment efforts.

Mingling Cultures

The inspiration for redesigning Fruitvale came from the idea of increasing interaction between younger and older generations. By intermingling jurisdictions and public agencies, no particular side has full control of the development, and land and facility usage is maximized. Fruitvale's mixed-use design, reminiscent of old town centers where communities gathered and met, is intended to create environments for socializing. Since Fruitvale is a highly multicultural area with Latino, Cambodian, Vietnamese, and African American residents, it was important to represent this ethnic mix in the redesign, and Fruitvale has created its own identity — a contemporary expression of the character of Oakland, with its blend of nationalities and colors and its history — in the urban landscape theme. Everything in Fruitvale will

have its own character — down to the signage. "By capitalizing on the area's strong past and incorporating expectations for the future, the design will capture what makes us feel good about Fruitvale," explains Martinez. In turn, it was important to focus on creating an international theme, through paving patterns, graphics, and signage, to encourage residents and BART commuters to come to the community.

According to Martinez, since redevelopment started, Fruitvale has blossomed. Ten years ago there was a 50 percent vacancy rate on International Boulevard, a high rate of crime and violence, and dirty streets. Today there is less than a 1 percent vacancy rate, less crime, less graffiti, cleaner streets, more than 110 new jobs, and a premium for property. With the area looking better because of the façade improvement program, shopowners continue to invest in upgrading their properties. The results of the long-awaited improvements can be seen in residents' and shopowners' attitudes: there is a sense of pride within the neighborhood.

"To me Fruitvale is already a success," comments Martinez. "With the obstacles we've had to go through, I am satisfied with the positive community involvement and the main street enhancements." Besides the number of Class A tenants signed to a building, the success of Fruitvale can be measured by the level of public acceptance. The hope is that the 30,000 BART commuters will feel safe and comfortable enough to pause in Fruitvale's new shopping and dining district before they travel on to their final destination and that Fruitvale residents will be encouraged to explore the area's heritage. With community stakeholders expressing trust and pride in the Fruitvale redevelopment project, notes Martinez, a special feeling of achievement already is present.

CHAPTER 28

Orlando Uses Free Rapid Transit System to Reduce Downtown Traffic

Craig Amundsen

Bus Rapid Transit (BRT) is growing more popular as a mode of public transportation. Pittsburgh and Orlando, Fla., are successfully operating what could be considered forerunners of today's more complex BRT systems, which are in various stages of development in Cleveland; St. Paul, Minn.; Charlotte, N.C.; Eugene, Ore.; and Boston.

BRT systems are as distinct from conventional bus transit as heavy rail is from light rail. BRT is, at a minimum, faster than conventional local bus service and, at a maximum, includes grade-separated bus operations. The essential features of a BRT system are bus priority, fast passenger boarding and fare collection, and an image that is unique from other locally available modes of public transportation. For local governments that want to increase bus ridership and public transportation passenger satisfaction, BRT offers an alternative to traditional bus and light rail transit in the form of electronically guided, rubber-tired vehicles that operate on exclusive transitways with the same quality of ride, safety and reliability as rail-guided vehicles.

The Components

BRT systems can range from the simple to the complex. A simple system could be totally on-street with reserved lanes marked with painted diamonds and signs, "super" bus stops and limited stop/express service during peak hours. Over time, a simple system could be improved incrementally be permanently separating BRT lanes with a rumble strip and special pavement; constructing larger, more elaborate stations with interactive information kiosks; purchasing low-floor buses of a special color/livery; using an honor fare system to allow for multi-door boarding; and increasing vehicle stop frequencies to permit random passenger arrivals.

A complex system could have a dedicated BRT facility in the median of a boulevard or on an abandoned or underused railroad right-of-way. The system could have stations equipped with a full complement of mode-change facilities, information resources and high-platform boarding for single- or double-articulated, hybrid vehicles. Addi-

Originally published as "Bus Rapid Transit: Everything Old Is New Again," *American City & County*, Vol. 116, No. 6, June 2001. Republished here with permission of PRIMEDIA Business Magazines & Media Inc. Copyright © 2001, PRIMEDIA Business Magazines & Media Inc. All rights reserved.

tionally, a dedicated right-of-way, all-stops service could be operated all day on a 10-minute-or-better headway, with fares collected off-board with smart cards. A complex BRT service could be complemented by market-driven peak express and combined collection/distribution services.

Either system could be implemented with the capital costs of purchasing buses and constructing roadways. Operating costs — dictated by speed of operation and work rules — are relatively low. BRT costs much less than rail transit because it uses multiple vehicles, which is more efficient than using a few rail cars, and the system costs less to operate and maintain than a rail system.

The ingredients of a successful BRT system are:

- **Modern, rail-like vehicles**. The vehicles must offer an attractive exterior and modern interior with large windows.
- **Exclusive rights-of-way**. Signal priority helps, but it is usually not sufficient to achieve the speeds needed to attract riders. The exclusive rights-of-way can be underground, elevated or grade-separated.
- **Attractive infrastructure**. To a large extent, the aesthetic quality of the system's environment, including landscaping, public art and stations, should distinguish BRT from traditional busways.
- **Streamlined fare collection**. Fare collection can be via free-fare zones, self-serve media at stations or even on board vehicles. Pay-as-you-go fare collection inhibits the rapid pace needed for BRT to compete with other forms of transportation.
- **Strong "brand identity."** BRT must be marketed as a fixed guideway line to gain acceptance among residents. The same marketing message will interest real estate developers who are drawn to investing near traditional rail systems.
- **Fast "dwell" times.** Guidance technologies speed docking times and help BRT compete with light-rail transit. Level

boarding is essential, whether accomplished with low-floor vehicles or high platforms.

Orlando's Head Start

Orlando's no-fare BRT system, named Lymmo, has been operating downtown since 1996, and it has been gaining popularity among residents and city leaders. Lymmo is a free bus in the central business district that runs on exclusive lanes for its entire 2.3-mile, circular route.

The lanes are identified with distinctive pavers and are separated from general traffic lanes either with a raised median or with a double row of raised, reflective ceramic pavement markers embedded in the asphalt. In the middle of the route, which has loop sections at each end, the two directions of Lymmo service are on the same street, with one running opposite the flow of traffic.

Because Lymmo operates in places and directions that are counter to other traffic, all bus movements at intersections are controlled by special bus signals. To prevent confusion with regular traffic signals, the bus signals use lines instead of standard red, yellow and green lights. When a bus approaches an intersection, a loop detector in the bus lane triggers the signal in the intersection to allow the bus to proceed.

In addition to dedicated lanes and signal pre-emption, Lymmo includes stations with large shelters and route information; automatic vehicle location; next-bus arrival information at kiosks; low-floor compressed natural gas buses; and a unique brand, which is communicated with vehicle graphics, advertisements and business tie-ins. The Lymmo route replaced an earlier downtown loop circulator, Freebee, and was a substitute for the proposed use of historic trolleys.

In its first year of operation, Lymmo averaged about twice the ridership of Freebee. Its total capital cost, $21 million, was at least half the cost of the trolley proposal. The design of Lymmo's facilities and the quality of the system have made the BRT competitive with other modes of transportation.

Going a Step Further

While Orlando's Lymmo represents a forerunner of the true BRT system, other cities are taking the concept quite a bit further. Cleveland, for example, is designing one of the most sophisticated BRT systems in the country.

The Cleveland BRT is part of a broad redevelopment program for the Euclid Avenue corridor, one of the city's oldest areas. The redevelopment includes a building-to-building reconstruction of Euclid Avenue with enhanced pedestrian zones, sidewalk and center median landscaping, new street and sidewalk lighting, new center median platform stations with distinctive shelter architecture, and exclusive bus and auto lanes. Designated the Euclid Corridor Transportation Project, the construction of the BRT line will connect the region's largest employment center (the central business district) with the second largest employment center (the University Circle area) approximately 4.5 miles away.

The goal of the project is to improve the operational constraints of the existing downtown street network and increase the flow of bus service during peak periods. Motorcoach bus traffic will be directed into and out of the corridor on two north-south streets with auto traffic directed to a third north-south street. The main east-west street of the corridor will have exclusive curbside bus lanes, which will allow better distribution of bus riders to destinations within the central business district.

The project includes construction of an intermodal transfer facility at Public Square in downtown to integrate Euclid Avenue bus service and other suburban bus routes with the rail rapid transit line, which connects to the central business district and, from there,

to the airport. A significant percentage of the new ridership in the corridor is expected to come from the bus/rail transfers at that facility.

The system will consist of an exclusive center median busway on Euclid Avenue and median lanes and center platform stations along most of the length of the street. The city plans to purchase 24 hybrid-electric trolley buses and six spares for the system. The buses are low-floor, 60-foot-long articulated, rubber-tired vehicles with left- and right-side doors. Fare collection will occur onboard the transit vehicles. Reduced-fare and free-fare zones are being considered to encourage ridership.

The project also includes the creation of a new radio communications system to incorporate wide-area coverage, automatic vehicle location (AVL) and emergency alerting. Thirteen of 16 channels will be dedicated to voice communication, and the other three will be data channels, which will provide automated passenger count information and fare collection monitoring. In addition to onboard emergency alerting, the AVL system will include a traffic signal/bus priority system, passenger on-board schedule information, bus stop passenger information displays and a passenger transfer management system.

The city is installing new traffic control striping to conform to the busway design and a new traffic signal system to give priority to buses on Euclid Avenue. A two-foot utility chase will be constructed on both sides of the avenue for traffic signal wiring, street lighting, pedestrian lighting, signs and spare conduit for future growth.

The project involves removing the Euclid Avenue roadway and reconstructing it with a busway and landscaped median, bus stop platforms and a rumble strip to separate the bus and automobile lanes. Sidewalks will be replaced with upgraded treatments, including backfilling and/or reconstruction of underground vaults. Construction of the $220 million Cleveland BRT is expected to start in 2003, with completion scheduled for 2005 or 2006.

Getting on Board

When considering BRT, cities must weigh all the benefits and challenges of rapid transit. Besides costing less than constructing a rail system, BRT is easier to expand than rail. A BRT system can be constructed in successive phases, adding scope and features, such as additional stations, grade separations and electric power, when conditions warrant.

However, changing the image of bus transit to one that lures people out of their cars the way light-rail transit has over the past 20 years is not easy. Opposition to BRT comes from many sources. The public often perceives anything associated with buses as being second-rate — a transportation option to be used only when no other option exists. As a result, municipal officials sometimes discourage consideration of bus options for fear of losing public support for a rail transit investment. Also, many planners do not know the capabilities of BRT and incorrectly attribute the high performance and customer acceptance of rail rapid transit to rail characteristics, such as tracks. In reality, exclusive guideways, stations and service quality are the features of rail rapid transit that attract most riders, and those features are offered by BRT. As BRT systems increase in number and sophistication, they will continue to gain wider acceptance as an effective mode of public transportation.

Note: The Lymmo bus rapid transit system in Orlando is operated by the Central Florida Regional Transportation Authority, which is listed in the *Regional Resource Directory*, at the end of this volume.

CHAPTER 29

Palo Alto, Other Cities, Favor Transit-Oriented Development to Reduce Traffic and Improve the Quality of Life

Jeffrey Tumlin *and*
Adam Millard–Ball

Even a cursory glance around the country suggests that transit-oriented development is hot; new TODs are on the drawing boards everywhere, from Alaska to Florida. Its advocates tout benefits ranging from more compact development and less automobile dependence to new retail opportunities and improved quality of life.

But the same quick survey raises some basic questions about just how fundamentally different many TODs are from their auto-oriented counterparts. We now have "transit-oriented" big box stores and single-story office parks, set in seas of parking. In many cases, developments with just six housing units to the acre are being advertised as TODs.

"The amount of hype around TOD far exceeds the progress to date, with many transit proponents selling new transit investments on the basis of land-use changes yet to come,"

writes Hank Dittmar, president of the Great American Station Foundation, in a forward to a discussion paper prepared for the foundation and the Brookings Institution Center on Urban and Metropolitan Policy.

Most often, he continues, "TODs have conventional suburban single use development patterns, with conventional parking requirements, so that the development is actually transit-*adjacent*, not transit-*oriented*."

Instead of branding anything that is built near transit a successful TOD, Dena Belzer and Gerald Autler of Strategic Economics, the principal authors of the paper, suggest that projects should be judged against specific desired outcomes:

Those outcomes include choice (for example, diverse housing and transportation); livability (less pollution per capita); and financial return (for instance, to developers and transit agencies).

Originally published as "How to Make Transit-Oriented Development Work," *Planning*, Vol. 69, No. 5, May 2003. Reprinted with permission from *Planning*, copyright © 2003 by the American Planning Association, Suite 1600, 122 South Michigan Avenue, Chicago, IL 60603–6107.

First on the List

What can planners do to ensure that TODs actually achieve these outcomes? Robert Cervero, a professor of city planning at the University of California, Berkeley, talks about what he calls the 3Ds, or three dimensions (density, design, and diversity) that are needed for a TOD to work. Of these, says Tom Margro, general manager of the San Francisco Bay Area's BART system, the first is most important. "From the point of view of a transit agency, density is paramount," he says.

In fact, density is a key criterion in the new BART system expansion policy, which was adopted last December. "We're being courted by cities that want BART extensions," says Margro. "The policy helps us reward those communities that make the zoning and land-use changes that we're looking for."

Density is partly a matter of geometry. All else being equal, the more housing and jobs within a short walk of a transit station, the greater the ridership. Nationally, a 10 percent increase in population density has been shown to correspond to a five percent increase in boardings, while doubling density can reduce vehicle travel by 20 percent, according to a 1996 report published by the Transit Cooperative Research Program.

Density has even farther reaching implications. Residents of denser communities are more likely to be able to walk to shops and services and thus to be able to live with just one car — or with none. According to research conducted for Fannie Mae's Location Efficient Mortgage program, vehicle ownership falls rapidly as density increases, reaching an average of just one car per household when density climbs to 20 to 30 housing units per acre.

Many of the best-performing TODs — such as those around Metro stations in Arlington County, Virginia — focus high density immediately around the station. Building height drops rapidly and housing forms change from attached to detached as they approach the existing single-family neighborhoods that surround many of these stations.

The same pattern is seen at the newly built King Farm development in Maryland, close to the Shade Grove Metro station. "We have a gradient away from the village center and a potential future light rail stop," says Neal Payton, director of town planning at Torti Gallas & Partners in Silver Spring, the architecture firm responsible for the King Farm town plan.

"At the center, we have the greatest mix of uses and the highest densities, with town houses and single-family houses appearing as one moves away from the center," he says.

Mixing It Up

Not all land uses are equal when it comes to generating transit ridership. Office or retail development tends to employ more workers and thus to produce more riders than industrial uses, for instance.

A less obvious example is affordable housing. Since low-income households tend to own fewer cars and are more likely to use transit, an affordable housing component of a transit-oriented development can add more riders, as well as furthering other public policy objectives.

A case in point is Alma Place in Palo Alto, California, where peak-hour parking demand has been measured at just four-tenths of a parking space per unit, even though parking is free. The location of this affordable housing development, just two blocks from the Caltrain commuter rail station in downtown Palo Alto, allowed many residents to sell their cars altogether.

It is mixed use ("diversity" on Robert Cervero's 3D list), however, that has demonstrated some of the highest ridership gains. Dennis Leach, a consultant with the firm of TransManagement, is currently researching the performance of TODs in the Washington, D.C., region. "Mixed use is where you get the real payoff in reduced vehicle trips," he says. "It allows residents to walk to shops and services, and it allows employees to take transit to work, since they can do without a car during the day."

In addition, says Leach, mandating or encouraging mixed use helps to avoid a dull monoculture. "Very high land costs tend to push a single use, such as offices," he notes. "That makes for a dead downtown" at night and on the weekends.

Managing Demand

Even the densest mixed-use developments will have only a limited impact if financial incentives discourage residents and employees from taking transit. To achieve the greatest success in reducing vehicle trips, projects need to encompass TOD + TDM, that is, both transit-oriented development and transportation-demand management.

Perhaps the most critical element of a TDM package is parking management. After all, unlimited free (to the user, but not the transit agency) parking is one of the biggest incentives to drive, and also encourages people to own a vehicle in the first place. Conversely, research by UCLA urban planning professor Donald Shoup has shown that ending parking subsidies is an effective way to get people out of their cars, reducing vehicle trips by an average of 25 percent.

Another demand management strategy, used to great effect in Portland, Oregon; Boulder, Colorado; and Santa Clara County, California, is to provide free or discounted transit passes for residents and employees. In 1997, Shoup reported on a survey of Silicon Valley companies that gave their employees Eco-Passes, good for unlimited rides on the Santa Clara Valley buses and light rail. Employee parking demand at these work sites declined by about 19 percent as transit ridership swelled.

Increasingly, parking management strat-

egies are being incorporated into TOD plans from the outset. At San Francisco's Balboa Park BART station, for example, the city's draft neighborhood plan proposes that new development on city-owned land be required to "unbundle" the cost of parking from rents.

"Currently most new ownership housing and some new rental housing has parking included in the base price of a unit," the plan says. "Individuals and families who do not own or may not need a car must pay for the space anyway, needlessly driving up the cost of their housing."

Considering TDM, and particularly parking management, in the earliest stage of planning lets its benefits affect a development's design and allows less parking to be provided. Moreover, if fewer vehicle trips are expected, streets can be designed for lower traffic volume, helping to improve the pedestrian environment.

"TDM is often used as a mitigation strategy," notes Peter Albert, station-area planning manager for BART. "Neighbors and others always use parking as a reason to kill a project. TDM can give local planning commissioners the elbow room to approve a project with less parking."

"Don't Even Think of Parking Here"

In the end, TOD and parking are inextricably entwined. "If the parking requirement doesn't reflect the transit resource, it's not TOD," says Albert. "It's just development close to a transit station." Most conventional development, after all, uses parking ratios derived from suburbs that have little or no transit and where everyone is assumed to have a car.

Building projects with reduced parking is another matter. Larger projects are often constrained by the attitudes of developers and lenders. Nevertheless, an increasing number of small-scale developments are selling well with little or no parking. Examples include the 91-unit Gaia Building in Berkeley, California, and the Seaboard Building, where offices have been converted to apartments in Seattle's Westlake Mall.

"In almost every case, parking requirements aren't an issue with local jurisdictions," says architect Neal Payton. "They're willing to provide less parking." Developers are more hesitant. "They don't want to risk not being able to rent a unit because there isn't enough parking."

Transit agencies themselves are often a source of pressure to provide more parking, in the form of heavily subsidized commuter parking for their riders. The surface parking lots owned or leased by these agencies are often a source of conflict. On the one hand, they're prime sites for transit-oriented development. However, the transit agencies often insist that any spaces lost must be fully replaced as part of the project.

"The ability of the market to support development that includes 100 percent replacement parking, with no revenue to support that parking, has been a huge hurdle to TOD," says Peter Albert. BART is now beginning to charge for reserved spaces at many stations, where before virtually all parking was free. The new revenue may be helpful in supporting the construction of parking structures to replace the lots, he suggests.

In other parts of the country, agencies are moving away from a strict one-to-one replacement policy. In the D.C. region, WMATA's Joint Development Policies and Guidelines, revised last year, now allow projects to be approved with less than full replacement parking. In some cases, the agency is even authorized to cover part of the cost of parking garages.

Such a policy makes sense from the point of view of increasing ridership and revenue for transit agencies, as well as promoting TOD. After all, an acre of dense, mixed-use development is likely to generate more transit trips than an acre of surface parking.

More important, TOD helps to spread ridership more evenly throughout the day, compared to peak-oriented park-and-ride lots. That's a major concern for agencies facing crushing peak-hour loads.

Looking Good

Even better is a transportation-demand policy that invests in alternatives. Pedestrian improvements, bicycle paths, and feeder transit often provide more bang-for-the-buck than parking.

Even with the best of management, however, most TODs still require huge amounts of parking, either in lots or structures. The question then becomes, how can planners reduce its impact?

Neal Payton sees ground-floor uses as key to reducing the impact of parking structures. At Harrison Commons, a planned TOD in Harrison, New Jersey, Payton's firm designed a 2,500-space garage that will accommodate commuters on the PATH commuter rail line. The development will include 3,000 apartments and 100,000 square feet of retail.

The garage will be wrapped on three sides with narrow "liner buildings" containing loft apartments above convenience retail. "You won't be able to see the garage from the street," he says.

In California, liner buildings will wrap around both existing and new garages at Bay Area Rapid Transit's Pleasant Hill station. The garages are part of a transit-oriented development designed by Lennertz, Coyle & Associates of Portland, Oregon.

The location of the parking facility is also important. At Harrison Commons, the mass of the largest garage will serve as a soundwall to buffer neighboring residences from the railroad. Payton warns, however, that this strategy may not be applicable everywhere. "In the New York area, people are used to having their car some distance from their apartment, which gives you a lot of flexibility in the design," he says. "This isn't true in most other places."

Design Solutions

Even the third of Cervero's 3Ds — design — comes back to parking. "Reduced parking allows a finer grain of development," says Payton. "With smaller garages, you can achieve smaller block sizes. And small blocks create variety and interest," he says, encouraging walking.

Dennis Leach says the street pattern and other design factors help to explain why some of the most walkable developments are often in established urban areas. He cites Washington's Dupont circle as an example. "The framework of the street and building pattern is extremely strong," he says.

That's less true in suburban neighborhoods like Bethesda, Silver Spring, and Arlington County, where wide arterials, surface parking, and the lack of a fine-grained street grid make walking a challenge. "The framework for urban development isn't really there," he says. "It has to be retrofitted."

All else being equal, walkability is maximized when streets are designed to accommodate lower traffic volumes in the first place. The key, then, is to factor the reduced trip-making benefits of TOD back into the street design — avoiding the error of widening roads for traffic that never arrives, or worse still, arrives only *because* of the widening.

Many agencies grant generic trip generation credits for transit-oriented development. The Los Angeles Metropolitan Transportation Authority, for example, offers a 15 percent credit for residentially oriented, mixed-use projects that have at least 24 units per acre and that are within a quarter-mile of a light rail station.

An important tool for creating a framework for walkable streets is likely to be the street hierarchy and design standards currently being written by the Congress for the New Urbanism, together with the Institute for Transportation Engineers and the U.S. Environmental Protection Agency. These standards envisage a new hierarchy of streets — from mews and lanes up to main streets and boulevards, rather than local, collector and arterial.

While many of these techniques have been used by new urbanist designers, engineers, and planners — and others — for years, they have generally resulted in one-time exceptions rather than fundamental change. That could change with these new standards.

CHAPTER 30

Salt Lake City, Other Areas, Initiate Measures to Preserve Transportation Corridors

Michael Davidson

To ask why a transportation corridor should be planned and preserved is like asking why planning should exist at all. Plans for transportation corridors have become as commonplace as those for neighborhoods and downtown districts. Today, rural jurisdictions such as Sheboygan County, Wisconsin, are as likely to undertake a major corridor study as nearby urban neighbors like Milwaukee.

Corridors are the gateways to and the connectors between our towns and cities. They preserve and protect our scenic landscape, support community image, manage traffic, help communities function effectively and efficiently, and generate business for commercial enterprise. More specifically, corridors benefit local governments by providing developers with a reliable canvas on which to create environmentally appropriate and conducive developments. Corridor preservation ultimately alleviates the confusion of developers and provides for more orderly land-use management. It can help relieve local planning departments of the headaches caused by unorganized development on fragmented transportation systems. Poorly designed corridors can destroy the landscape, exacerbate congestion, create safety risks, pollute the air, repel pedestrians, and stifle business productivity.

Corridor planning is more than just an attractive transportation concept; it is now mandatory under the Intermodal Surface Transportation Efficiency Act of 1991 (ISTEA). States and regional agencies are required to include corridor preservation in their long-range transportation strategies. Future thoroughfares that are believed to be in the public interest should be identified and equipped with an established protection plan.

With the recent enactment of the Transportation Equity Act for the 21st Century (TEA-21), the basic transportation and planning requirements specified under ISTEA remain in place. Metropolitan and statewide provisions concerning fiscal constraint, planning horizon, and public involvement will continue. Freight shippers and public transit users have been added to the list of specified stakeholders. The most notable difference with the new legislation is the consolidation of 16 metropolitan and 23 statewide planning "factors" into seven general "areas." Each must be considered in both the metropolitan and statewide transportation plans. More information on TEA-21 can be found at www.fhwa.dot.gov.

In 1996, the Federal Highway Administration (FHwA) released a two-volume study on corridor preservation: *Volume I, Corridor Preservation: Case Studies and Analysis Factors in Decision-Making*, and *Volume II, Corridor Preservation: Study of Legal and Institutional Barriers*. The study addresses corridor preservation as a planning and implementation strategy for transportation programs and provides a framework that states, metropolitan planning organizations, and local agencies can follow to build an understanding of the corridor preservation process and then use for the enhancement of local and regional transportation systems.

This chapter is based partly on the FHwA study in so far as it is an examination of the latest developments in corridor planning. Examples and case studies from other sources are also used to help define corridors, determine why preservation is important, identify risks, and lay out measures that are most useful for overcoming those risks.

What Is Corridor Preservation?

For most planners, corridor preservation involves managing development, access, landscaping, and signage along major arterial roads or limited access highways. It may also involve protecting and preserving views and open space along scenic highways. But before such practices occur, the land on which future transportation corridors are to be established needs to be identified, mapped, and protected from inconsistent development. The American Association of State Highway and Transportation Officials (AASHTO)

Figure 1. Priority Checklist for Corridor Preservation

☑ **Importance of the Corridor:** Is the corridor needed to serve development patterns in the next 20 years?

☑ **Immediacy of Development:** Is the threat of development imminent? Will strategic parcels be lost if nothing is done?

☑ **Risk of Foreclosing Options:** If development does occur in the potential alignment, what corridor options will be foreclosed?

☑ **Opportunity to Prevent Loss of the Corridor:** Are planning tools available — other than outright acquisition of right of way — that can be employed to protect the corridor?

☑ **Strength of Local Government Support:** Will the affected communities do their fare share to help? Do they have the needed tools at their disposal?

Task Force on Corridor Preservation defines corridor preservation as "a concept utilizing the coordinated application of various measures to obtain control of or otherwise protect the right-of-way for a planned transportation facility."

The FHwA study identifies the two types of corridors and the fundamental planning objective:

- Proposed corridors are those yet to be designed, but which state and regional agencies have determined to be needed in anticipation of future growth and development, and that they are considering in the preparation and adoption of long-range transportation plans.

- Existing corridors, for which capacity needs to be maintained, preserved, increased, and for which development adjacent to the corridor needs to be modified, or improved in some way (e.g., by addressing access management, development densities, landscaping, or other traditional corridor planning elements).

Planners Talk Corridors

At a November 1997 Chicago-area conference, "Successful Corridor Planning: From Concept to Implementation," cosponsored by the Northwest Municipal Conference and APA's Chicago Metro Section, municipal planners discussed the obstacles encountered with corridor planning and preservation. Of most concern to conference participants were issues related to traffic flow, including safety, efficiency, and access; policy decisions about intergovernmental agreements and municipal ordinances supporting the corridor plan; aesthetic issues relating to signage, landscaping, gateway planning, and lighting; and the impacts of various land-use decisions on the corridor. For example, land-uses adjacent to a roadway corridor, which may differ in character and transportation need, are an important consideration when labeling a corridor commercial, residential, industrial, or otherwise.

A Bump in the Corridor

Planners face many challenges in preserving corridors. Daniel Mandelker, Stamper Professor of Law at Washington University in St. Louis and attorney Brian Blaesser of Robinson and Cole in Hartford — authors of Volume II of the FHwA study — list inadequate regulations, funding limitations, inadequate acquisition and condemnation powers, environmental requirements, and property rights as the legal and institutional barriers to corridor preservation facing jurisdictions today.

Mandelker and Blaesser offer several suggestions for overcoming such barriers:

• Adjusting to intergovernmental conflict is necessary because federal, state, and local government corridor preservation roles and responsibilities often conflict or overlap with one another.

• Effective corridor preservation requires local governments to adopt sophisticated development controls and procedures for administration (e.g., density transfers, transferable development rights, and development exactions).

• Local governments should be careful not to assume all of the management responsibilities.

• Local governments must be willing to cooperate with private developers on land dedications and other contributions to avoid takings challenges.

• Environmental clearances should be planned for and timed in such a way as to not jeopardize the corridor preservation measures, preferably at the mapping stage.

• Uncertainties that exist in the implementation of corridor preservation, such as responsibilities of each level of government, environmental clearances, and legal risks of takings, should be acknowledged up front so measures can be taken to minimize the consequences of these uncertainties.

• The sophistication in the design of corridor programs requires that staff, especially at the local level, are aware of the takings clause and are fluent in the use of land regulation and acquisition powers.

• Insufficiencies in the federal legislation supporting transportation programs may demand changes in program requirements and policies.

• An alternative strategy needs to be considered in the event that corridor preservation is blocked by legal constraints or the failure of governments to cooperate.

The corridor preservation programs highlighted in the study begin in advance of acquisition. This distinguishes them from standard right-of-way protection measures, which are typically taken through acquisition and regulation before the commencement of project construction, in that they occur in advance of acquisition.

To Build a Corridor

What processes shape a successful corridor planning or preservation strategy? Jurisdictions must first decide what type of corridor planning is necessary. Measures to determine this are numerous. For example, chaotic strip commercial development, problems with traffic access and management, and capacity deficiencies are all potential indicators that change is needed. For future corridors, periodic traffic projections, analyses of future systems deficiencies, population and economic projections, projected growth patterns and location, major development proposals, project approvals, and construction permits along the corridor are measures of planning and preservation needs for future corridors.

Mandelker and Blaesser divide corridor planning measures into four fundamental categories: local land-use planning and development controls, corridor mapping laws, access management, and land acquisition.

Local land-use planning and development controls. Land-use and development controls for corridor preservation are typically managed at the local level rather than by the state or federal governments. Ideally, a community's comprehensive plan and zoning ordinance will both guide corridor development and be the foundation for land-use regulation.

The transportation element of a local comprehensive plan can be key in the corridor preservation process because the plan is the formal document for identifying transportation corridors that require preservation and local development controls used for corridor preservation are based on the plan. The zoning ordinance, as the chief tool for implementing the comprehensive plan, can be used to maintain a level of land-use intensity that is compatible with corridor designation.

Montgomery County, Maryland, zones corridor lands for the least intensive use that is found in adjacent zones, but allows for interim uses in the zone that can be removed when the roadway is eventually developed.

Another land preservation technique, density transfers, is employed by local governments to protect development from obstructing corridor land. Planners in San Jose, California, used density transfers to "shift" permitted housing densities to sites outside of the corridor in order to keep the land needed for the proposed expressway free of development until the municipality could acquire the property. Lacking the funds for immediate acquisition, the city thought it imperative to work closely with developers whose projects might have threatened development of the corridor.

Density bonuses were part of a 1980s strategy to preserve the Olive Boulevard corridor in Creve Coeur, Missouri. Site consolidations were taken in exchange for the density bonuses. Planners approved specific high-traffic businesses, such as service stations and restaurants, only when they were included as part of a planned development that was three acres or larger.

Interim land uses are often allowed along corridor properties to discourage potentially long-term developments and save the land for future corridor use. The West Valley Corridor, near Salt Lake City, remained protected for more than 10 years before the corridor was completed. Local jurisdictions arranged deals with developers, allowing them to place particular — but removable — interim uses on the properties around the corridor. West Valley City even gave tax breaks to property owners who retained agricultural uses.

San Jose planners encouraged such interim uses as ground-level parking garages, storage areas, golf driving ranges, and nurseries until public funds could be acquired and corridor planning could proceed. Fortunately, this measure was not challenged by local developers. Officials claimed that the need for the corridor was strong enough to dissuade legal action. The corridor's current success as a contiguous system of roadway and light rail is largely attributed to the local government's cooperation with developers.

Overlay zoning is a technique that planners have incorporated into planning strategies for existing corridors around the country. In the 1980s, in Hilton Head, South Carolina, the aesthetic character of the resort community was threatened by development pressures. This prompted local officials to implement a corridor overlay district to protect Hilton Head's primary arterials from visual decay. The overlay district, which had statutory support from the state, was incorporated into the Hilton Head comprehensive plan. The plan encouraged viewshed protection — classifying them as natural, scenic, or rural — and set forth policies for signage and community gateways. Design review was also established as part of the comprehensive plan.

Rigorous design controls, such as those in Hilton Head, are not always necessary. Creve Coeur alleviated some of the design burdens simply by requiring parking lots to be sited behind buildings. The city implemented other land-use controls along its corridor, including the conversion of single-family residences to office space in a specific section. Standards for this area include "approximate" signage, parking in the rear, and efforts to retain the residential character of the structures.

Land-use controls in Naples, Florida, are geared toward preserving the area's two largely natural corridors rather than retrofitting sections through new sign requirements or parking changes. Preventative measures were taken to preserve the corridor's open space and historic landscapes. On developed sections, strict buffering is required to conceal walls that line the perimeter of the corridors.

When preservation is lost, retrofitting can occur to reclaim previous land. A sec-tion of the Phalen Boulevard Corridor, in St. Paul, Minnesota, is undergoing a $4.2 million restoration of wetlands and a lake on the site of a failed shopping center. The poor performance of the 200,000-square-foot mall, its status as an environmental hazard, and an ongoing neighborhood revitalization effort made the property a natural choice for restoration.

Corridor Mapping. Mapping is a valuable tool that provides visual conceptualization of corridor land development. Stakeholders, including transportation agencies, local planners, and private developers, use the maps to plan for land uses on parcels of property adjacent to the corridor.

Mapping allows for predictability of land uses and permits jurisdictions to reserve vacant parcels of property for later taking under eminent domain. Once a map is adopted, the local government has the right to prohibit development within the specified land area. These measures prevent costly repurchasing of developed land and minimize the number of developed properties that have to be moved. According to Mandelker and Blaesser, state legislation authorizing the use of mapping in corridor preservation is essential. A model state corridor mapping act has been developed by APA.

Access Management. In the context of corridor preservation, access management means protecting the capacity of existing routes and systems by controlling access rights from adjacent properties (e.g., limiting curb cuts). Although its use for the purposes of corridor preservation is relatively new, it can play a key role in managing capacity and preventative maintenance for transportation systems. If done properly, it may even alleviate the need for the construction of new roadways.

Access management programs are managed by the state. States classify highways according to their access needs and set standards for the intervals at which access will be allowed (e.g., one access point per mile). Developers and property owners are required to apply for a permit to construct an access point from their property to the roadway. Coordination between the state and local governments is essential because access management can have a major effect on local land-use planning.

Aside from corridor preservation, access management is more commonly used to meet goals of improving traffic flow and safety by removing raised medians, street widening, adding turn lanes, better traffic signal coordination, and traffic incident management.

Acquisition. Acquiring land for public ownership is important to corridor planning and preservation because it protects corridor property from development, minimizes land costs, and helps to prevent a taking of property. Land for corridors is most often obtainable through voluntary agreement with the owner. However, property occasionally is acquired through involuntary measures.

Mandelker and Blaesser suggest that corridor planners consider several factors during the land acquisition process. Among these considerations are the legal, financial, and administrative roles played by federal, state, and local governments. Corridor stakeholders need to be aware of the acquisition powers held by each level of government, as well as the limitations they bring to the process.

Land acquisition can arouse a complex, but solvable, set of problems, say Mandelker and Blaesser. For example, inadequate legal authority could be corrected if legislation favored advance acquisition in corridor programs. Poor management skills can be strengthened with guidance and training from the FHwA.

Also, funding requirements need to be established, approved, and provided by Congress with relative consistency for FHwA-approved advance acquisition programs. A state-mandated statute to support additional funding, perhaps through a special levy tax, for advance acquisition by state and local governments would arm the jurisdictions with more authority.

Corridor land acquisition is subject to intense and time-consuming environmental controls. Environmental review should be done at the corridor designation stage to shorten the lengthy environmental review process. FHwA needs to promote cooperation between agencies on issues such as environmental assessments, Clean Water Act requirements, and other federal standards.

The Tie That Binds

In Illinois, intergovernmental decision making about transportation issues is handled effectively because transportation councils have been established to facilitate successful corridor planning. The councils consist of governmental bodies that have entered into a legal partnership to address land use, transportation, environment, design, and boundary agreements for one of the six specified corridor projects in the northeastern region of the state. The councils are governed by the Intergovernmental Cooperation Act and the Local Land Resource Management Planning Act. This approach to corridor planning, which is promoted by the Northeastern Illinois Planning Commission (NICP), ensures intergovernmental cooperation in the region.

Nowhere is the relationship between governmental entities nurtured more than in suburban Lake County, Illinois, north of Chicago. The Corridor Planning Council of Central Lake County (CPC) was established to provide a forum for coordinated planning of the Route 53 extension corridor.

According to a 1996 NIPC report, the planning goals of the member jurisdictions included discussions about overloading public facilities, possible environmental damage, and "destructive" intergovernmental competition. To meet these goals effectively and efficiently, and to define CPC's role in developing the environmental impact statement (EIS), the council collaborated with the Illinois Department of Transportation (IDOT). The agreement specified the transportation alternatives to be considered for the EIS, it established the steps in the EIS process that would eventually lead to the study results for the council to review, and it committed IDOT to consider the planning and environmental standards adopted by the council members.

As a protective planning measure, and one that could provide consistency to planning and development regulations around the corridor, the CPC developed its principles of agreement. The agreement consists of 24 standards that address relevant issues like stormwater management, arterial access, open space preservation, and the management of land-use conflicts. IDOT and the Illinois State Toll Highway Authority have agreed to honor the standards, and local jurisdictions have incorporated them into development ordinances.

The Corridor Planning Council of Central Lake County was the first such transportation endeavor in the region. Its success may serve as a model for similar corridor planning projects in northeastern Illinois.

Conclusion

Although the concept of planning and preserving transportation corridors is nearly two decades old, many systems have still fallen victim to political, economic, and land-use forces that have left transportation networks in disarray. ISTEA and TEA-21 may help this by essentially forcing jurisdictions to look at transportation systems. The good news is that the resources to tackle this complex issue have increased. There is a growing consciousness among drivers who want a safer, more efficient, and attractive commute to their destinations, which may make corridor planning a higher priority.

CHAPTER 31

San Carlos Provides
Alternative Public Transit to
Reduce Traffic Congestion

Parviz Mokhtari

In the years leading up to 2001, the City of San Carlos (population 28,000) was experiencing severely clogged roadways, especially during commute hours, when gridlock and traffic delays of up to 30 minutes just to travel a few miles in and out of the city were the norm. Furthermore, traffic congestion around heavily traveled intersections, particularly near schools, made pedestrian and bicycle travel difficult and potentially unsafe.

The city's ability to implement solutions such as capacity-increasing projects and signal maintenance was limited by a funding shortfall, driven by state budget take-aways and a state policy of deferring infrastructure maintenance. Services provided by the public transportation agency (SamTrans) were very limited, operating on one fixed route with a few daily riders. With no resolution in sight, traffic congestion and unsafe roadways only worsened.

In 2001, the city's Director of Public Works Parviz Mokhtari suggested a customized shuttle service to the city's management team. He offered dramatic illustrations

of the amount of time, gas and money that parents spent to take their children to and from school, and the quantity of emissions generated by these vehicles.

"We have to change the culture of transportation," Mokhtari told the team. "It's time to start planning and designing for people and get them out of their cars. Providing convenient, reliable and community-tailored shuttle services can go a long way toward achieving that goal." The management team agreed, and the custom shuttle concept was presented to the city council, which authorized the public works director to proceed.

Residents Welcome
Shuttle Start Up

The city obtained a grant to partially fund the first pilot shuttle program with tailored routes and door-to-door services. City staff worked (and continues to work) with the San Carlos School District, SamTrans, parent-teacher associations, youth and senior residents, the chamber of commerce, and

Originally published as "San Carlos Customized Shuttle Meets Community Transportation Needs," *Western City*, Vol. LXXXI, No. 2, February 2005 © 2005 *Western City* magazine. All rights reserved. Reprinted with permission from the February 2005 issue of *Western City*, the monthly publication of the League of California Cities.

local and regional groups to provide a shuttle service that offers a practical alternative to single-occupancy vehicles. The local Youth Center enthusiastically held a brainstorming session to create a name for the shuttle, coining the name SCOOT (San Carlos Optimum Operational Transit).

In November 2002, a nine-month pilot program was created to serve stops near three San Carlos schools, the San Carlos train station, downtown, parks, library, civic area, and youth and senior centers. With partial funding from a San Mateo City/County Association of Governments grant and Measure A funds, the city contracted with a private company that provides drivers to operate four 24-passenger shuttles. Passengers can choose from four fixed routes or door-to-door service. At the end of the nine-month period, ridership was approximately 8,200 monthly rides.

Today the program has grown significantly; the demand continues to amplify the level of service needed. The shuttle service runs Monday through Friday from 6:00 A.M. to 7:00 P.M. Beginning in September 2003, the service expanded to include 10 routes during peak traffic hours and increased door-to-door reservations.

During the 2003–04 program, monthly ridership soared to between 15,000 and 19,400. Over the past two years, the ridership grew rapidly. From September 2003 to June 2004, SCOOT averaged a monthly ridership of 15,300 trips. Of those, 3,100 were door-to-door; 1,200 connected commuters with CalTrain; and 11,000 were on regular routes. Current ridership continues to hold strong at approximately 17,000 monthly trips. These data indicate that the shuttle service is fulfilling the enormous transportation need for the community.

Based on an average of 15,300 monthly riders, approximately 230,000 vehicle miles traveled have been removed from the street network each year. Furthermore, according to the San Carlos Police Department, accidents throughout San Carlos averaged 454 annually in 1999–2001 and 278 annually in 2002–04. This shows a reduction of 176 accidents (approximately 40 percent) per year after SCOOT's implementation.

Pilot Program with a Purpose

The purpose of the pilot program was to collect the necessary data and community feedback to determine the level of service needed and explore the financial options available to establish the shuttle service as a permanent program.

SCOOT has become one of the most popular services the city has provided in recent years. It has been classified locally and regionally as a unique, innovative shuttle service and trend for future transportation improvement. SCOOT is friendly, reliable, convenient and responsive.

Currently, a SCOOT Funding Task Force is considering options to implement a sustainable solution. The community and city staff are working together and passing their recommendations on to the city council. This collaborative effort has promoted and enhanced the communication and partnership between public, private and civic entities in San Carlos. The entire community is working together to create and fulfill the vision of this much-needed and used community service.

Notes: The City of San Carlos won an Award for Excellence in the Public Works, Infrastructure and Transportation category of the 2004 California Cities Helen Putnam Award for Excellence. For more information about the award program, visit www.cacities.org.

CHAPTER 32

San Diego Adopts "City of Villages" Strategy Linking Jobs, Housing, and Transit

Nancy Bragado

The last time the City of San Diego updated its general plan, charting the future of thousands of acres of then-undeveloped land was the city's primary concern. Twenty-five years later, the city is more than 90 percent developed, growth projections show a continued demand for new housing, and the city is shaping its future using a strategy based on infill and redevelopment.

"Our challenge for the new general plan was how to handle projected new growth while maintaining the qualities of San Diego that people value," explained Planning Director Gail Goldberg.

The City of Villages

After a two-year public process, the city council adopted the City of Villages strategy as the recommended course of action. The strategy calls for new growth to be targeted in mixed-use village centers in order to create lively activity hubs, provide housing, improve walkability and help support a state-of-the-art transit system. In addition to this strategy, the council adopted a slate of policies to protect the natural environment, increase housing affordability, enhance neighborhoods, improve mobility, create economic prosperity and provide for equitable development and public facilities.

The City of Villages growth strategy — and San Diego's new citywide policies — became the strategic framework element of the general plan, which provided direction to planning staff on how to update the rest of the general plan. The citywide policy areas were expanded and refined as nine elements of a new general plan. Central themes of the general plan include:

- Transit-land use connection;
- Housing;
- Community planning; and
- Infrastructure

Transit-Land Use Connection

Planning Commission Chairperson Barry J. Schultz calls "transit and land use coordination ... an integral part of the general plan and a fundamental component of a smart growth strategy."

The city's highest density residential and employment uses are to be located in village centers and corridors along the regional transit system. Equally important, lower density uses are to be located away from transit-served areas, and all parks, open spaces and residential neighborhoods are to be preserved. Additional policies further delineate where development is prohibited or limited, such as lands in the multi-habitat planning area, steep slopes and flood hazard areas.

Urban design element policies further strengthen the commitment to transit, neighborhoods and the natural environment through transit-oriented, distinctive neighborhoods and landform preservation design guidelines.

Housing

The village strategy seeks to provide opportunities for developing higher density and diverse housing types, largely through infill and redevelopment of aging commercial centers. By focusing the city's highest density housing and employment uses in transit-served areas, more opportunities are provided to improve jobs/housing balance within communities and to improve the linkages between jobs and housing citywide. However, the plan does not contain recommended density goals; actual designation of sites and implementation of the plan is deferred to the community planning program.

Community Planning

San Diego's 330 square miles are divided into more than 50 community planning areas. These areas are monitored by community planning groups comprising volunteers who serve as advisors to the planning commission and city council. The community plans provide detailed community and neighborhood-based planning recommendations that supplement the general plan's citywide focus, and are officially recognized as a part of the general plan land use element.

A drawback to the program is that community plans take several years to update, and staffing levels cannot keep pace with the need to keep community plans up-to-date. The general plan recognizes the critical role of the community planning program and seeks to help streamline the preparation of community plans so that they can be updated more frequently. Streamlining would occur in part by clearly documenting the role of the general and community plans. Rather than having each community plan function as a mini general plan covering the full range of general plan topics, community plans would focus on providing site-specific guidance to tailor the application of citywide policies.

In deference to the community planning program, no land use amendments or rezonings will take place concurrently with general plan adoption. General plan implementation will occur as community plans are updated or amended over time. Despite this linkage to the community plans, some community planning groups are opposed to the new general plan because they believe it will result in unwanted new growth in their communities.

Planning for Infrastructure

According to Council Member Toni Atkins, "For older urban communities, the primary challenge has always been to make sure that infrastructure improvements, including much needed public facilities and services, are adequately provided for in the implementation plan."

Infrastructure in the city's urban neighborhoods has not kept pace with growth. Given the city's longstanding status as a low-revenue city and a current budget crisis resulting in part from pension underfunding, the short-term outlook for making up the facilities shortfall is grim. Under these conditions, some of the neighborhood opposition to increased density is more of a logical response to funding shortfalls, rather than a NIMBY ("not in my back yard") attitude. To address this issue, the general plan proposes that new broad-based funding sources be considered and that discretionary projects provide their fair share of infrastructure and public facilities. An individual project may not be able to solve all of a community's facilities problems, but it can certainly not compound existing deficiencies.

The Regional Connection

Regional initiatives underway are adding momentum and resources to implementing San Diego's strategy. The Regional Comprehensive Plan, prepared by the San Diego Association of Governments (SANDAG), outlines a complementary smart growth strategy for the region along with a competitive grants program designed to reward smart growth planning with regional transportation funds.

SANDAG also oversees the implementation of the Regional Transit Vision, which outlines a plan to greatly improve transit service throughout the region.

The new general plan is intended to proactively address the challenges of growth and development through better linkage between transit and land use planning, preserving important open spaces, strengthening our existing communities and creating new neighborhood centers. It focuses on what residents love most about San Diego — its distinctive neighborhoods and natural environment — while addressing its most pressing infrastructure and housing challenges.

Ideally, the plan would be linked to concurrent community plan amendments that would bring the City of Villages closer to fruition. However, the incremental approach of going from the strategic framework element, to a comprehensive general plan update, to a series of community plan amendments, allows San Diego to gain faith with the public and build upon its successes over time.

CHAPTER 33

San Francisco Region, Other Areas, Use Communications System to Manage Traffic

Pete Costello

A little-known tool exists that can help untangle the perpetual traffic gridlock that threatens communities' growth and prosperity. Since July 2000 when the Federal Communications Commission (FCC) designated a dialing code to provide current travel information, 511 systems have been giving locals and visitors the scoop on traffic accidents and delays, road construction and conditions, and mass transit.

For transportation officials, 511 systems promise improvements in transportation efficiency and roadway safety and unprecedented reach for messages such as American Message Broadcast Emergency Response (AMBER) Alerts and severe weather warnings. Driver safety is enhanced with voice-activated prompts for travelers calling from their vehicles. The federal government did not set standards or financing requirements for the traffic information systems. Instead, a 511 Deployment Coalition was organized to help communities get them up and running (see "Helping create 511 systems").

511 Progress

Currently, approximately 25 percent of the nation's population has access to 511 information by phone or the Internet. In addition to the many statewide systems, regional 511 operations exist in metropolitan areas, including San Francisco, Sacramento, Cincinnati and in many Florida cities.

The public is becoming more aware of 511, although it is not as popular as the ubiquitous 411 for information or 911 for emergencies. Where 511 is established, however, users report they are pleased with the system's performance. Most of Minnesota's 511 users were satisfied with their system (93 percent in late 2002), as were southeast Florida's (96 percent as of late 2003).

Where It Works

Two of the best examples of 511 systems can be found in North Carolina and Virginia. North Carolina's statewide 511 system launched in August 2004. Its biggest test occurred almost immediately. "We went

Originally published as "The 411 on 511," *American City & County*, Vol. 120, No. 1, January 2005. Published by PRIMEDIA Business Magazines and Media Inc., Overland Park, KS. Reprinted with permission of the publisher.

through three hurricanes right after the service launched, and we were able to get information out quickly so that people could access it," says Jo Ann Oerter, 511 project manager for North Carolina's Department of Transportation (NCDOT).

In addition to updates about traffic and roadway conditions, information about weather, the ferry and rail system, and tourism is accessible through the state's 511 phone number and Web site (www.ncsmartlink. org). Because travelers can use 511, calls to NCDOT's older 800 numbers, staffed by live operators, have decreased. In most cases, callers can be re-directed to the 511 system for the information they need.

While some states and metropolitan areas operate their own systems, and others rely on vendors, North Carolina uses both NCDOT highway information and the National 511 Alliance, which operates and maintains the system. The Alliance includes Cambridge, Mass.–based SRS/Westwood One; Menlo Park, Calif.–based Tele Atlas; Minneapolis-based Meteorlogix and Miami-based PBS&J. SRS/Westwood One delivers traffic information, news, sports and weather using wireless services, in-vehicle navigation systems and voice portals. Tele Atlas provides digital maps and current traffic information, and Meteorlogix offers weather information as it affects travel. PBS&J manages the team.

Unique features of NCDOT's service include additional local incident information in the Triad Area (Winston-Salem, Greensboro and High Point); weather alerts and travel impact forecasts for specific road segments; a call overflow system and a feature that allows callers to reconnect to the system in the same place they were when the call was interrupted or a cell signal was lost.

While a few bugs were encountered during the system's setup, Oerter reports that far more problems were anticipated for bringing the new, statewide system online. Like most transportation agencies, NCDOT already offered traveler information such as

road conditions, roadway closures, construction and regional weather. Creating a 511 system required converting that existing travel information to the new dialing code as well as integrating weather, mapping and other systems to provide current travel data.

Helping Create 511 Systems

The 511 Deployment Coalition was formed in 2001 to help states and local governments create travel information systems. Its goal is to establish sustainable 511 services reaching 50 percent of the country's population and a 25 percent brand awareness by the end of 2005.

Coalition members include several Washington-based groups: the American Association of State Highway Transportation Officials, the American Public Transportation Association, Intelligent Transportation Society of America, the U.S. Department of Transportation and other public and private organizations. The group develops guidelines and educational material for those interested in creating 511 systems.

For more information on the coalition's efforts, visit www.deploy511.org. Other 511 information resources with case studies include www.its.dot.gov/511 and www.itsa.org/511.html.

North Carolina's two-year 511 contract with the National 511 Alliance totals $2.5 million, with options for three more years. The federal government funds most of the project (80 percent), and the state picks up the remainder. NCDOT made one-time payments to telephone carriers to route calls from landline and wireless customers to the 511 system prior to launching the service.

Oerter advises others looking into 511 systems to get all stakeholders in their area on board early. "Ask if any regulatory agencies need to be involved. Know the path you have to take," Oerter says.

In North Carolina's case, its Public Utilities Commission required that NCDOT be responsible for the 511 system. The agency also mandated that the state's Information Resource Management Commission would oversee the system.

From Regional to Statewide

Virginia's travel information has evolved from the "Travel Shenandoah" 800 number in 2000 to a regional 511 system in 2002 to a statewide system launching next month. Virginia's Department of Transportation (VDOT) tested 511 for travelers along a busy stretch of I-81. Now, the state is expanding 511 service statewide. "VDOT decided that 511 is the cutting edge of technology. It meets our needs for safety and incident management," says Scott Cowherd, the state's 511 travel information program manager.

Like North Carolina's system, Virginia's provides news on traffic incidents as well as weather, road conditions, transit and tourism. Virginia also offers information on roadside gasoline stations, hotels, restaurants and attractions. The system can report AMBER Alerts or homeland security warnings across the entire state or to a particular region.

Educating travelers about 511 can be challenging, as the VDOT discovered. For the I-81 application, the agency installed dozens of 511 signs on both sides of the interstate. In hosting focus groups to evaluate the test and create a program to promote the statewide rollout, though, VDOT learned that the new signs simply blended in with the existing blue highway signs. Modifications were made, and more signs are in place for the statewide launch.

Set to premier its expanded 511 systems in February, VDOT has developed a media campaign and series of public service announcements. The governor will officially launch the system at the state's capital. But the best advertising for a 511 system, according to Cowherd, is a positive user experience and accurate information. "If we don't have reliable, real-time information, we lose credibility," Cowherd says. "We feel travelers will give us two chances. If we're not right, they won't call again. Then we might as well hang it up."

System users can give feedback at the end of a 511 call or by e-mail when accessing the Web site. VDOT already has revised the statewide system based on comments made by travelers on their experiences using the field-tested I-81 operation.

Coordination and Costs

Cowherd points out that implementing a 511 system can require DOT staff to work with a few unfamiliar agencies or companies. For example, VDOT staff had to coordinate its activities with tourism information sites, transit providers and phone companies.

VDOT is evaluating all travel-related resources in the state with the goal of making 511 the main information source. Over time, the state anticipates eliminating or reducing its other information lines, primarily the 800 numbers. Existing staff likely will be used to help the remaining systems operate more efficiently.

VDOT has contracted with the National 511 Alliance to expand 511 statewide for $6.5 million over three years, which includes approximately $2 million annually for operations and maintenance. The bulk of VDOT's program has been federally funded.

Cowherd serves on a national peer-to-peer group helping other states and metropolitan areas create 511 systems. He is enthusiastic about the technology, primarily in the way transportation agencies can tailor its application. "There's no set way of doing things, so it's open," Cowherd says. "511 grows with technology."

CHAPTER 34

Santa Monica Streetscape Plan Favors People, Reduces Traffic, and Improves Public Transit

Charles Lockwood

Downtown Santa Monica is a hodge-podge. The area includes some of Southern California's most popular destinations, including the recently rejuvenated Santa Monica Pier; the two-mile-long Palisades Park; and the Third Street Promenade, a revamped and highly successful pedestrian mall. At the same time, some sections of the downtown are run-down and deserted at night and on weekends.

That picture could soon change. In late July, the Santa Monica city council approved a five-phase, $18.7 million downtown streetscape plan prepared by the ROMA Design Group of San Francisco. The plan is aimed at improving traffic and transit patterns, creating stronger pedestrian and transit linkages, and luring new shops and restaurants to the 28-block downtown core. It envisions wider sidewalks on several key streets, improved landscaping, and new street furniture and lighting.

City officials say work is scheduled to start this month on the plan's $500,000 first phase.

Inspiration

If Santa Monicans want proof that change is possible, they need only look at the Third Street Promenade.

Once a thriving main street, the old Third Street had seriously declined by the mid–1960s as shopping malls in other communities drew customers away. In 1965, in an effort to compete, the city followed the prevailing planning wisdom and converted three blocks of Third Street into a pedestrian mall.

For a while, the strategy worked. The problem was that adjacent blocks kept declining, pulling the Third Street mall down with them. The mall also had some serious design flaws, including its 600-foot-long blocks and 80-foot-wide pavement.

The final blow came with the opening in 1980 of a new enclosed shopping center, Santa Monica Place, at the south end of Third Street. The center became one of the nation's most successful downtown shopping centers, while the Third Street mall became a concrete wasteland.

Originally published as "Onward and Upward in Downtown Santa Monica," *Planning*, Vol. 63, No. 9, September 1997. Published by the American Planning Association, 122 South Michigan Avenue, Suite 1600, Chicago, IL 60603–6107. Reprinted with permission of the author.

The Promenade

In 1986, the city commissioned the ROMA Design Group to come up with a revitalization plan for the pedestrian mall. "Our design for Third Street Promenade was based on the premise that a city's public spaces — its streets, parks, plazas, and other gathering places — are the principal stages on which the life of the city is acted out," says Boris Dramov, the design principal for the project.

Following the plan, the city installed new 30-foot-wide sidewalks to encourage strolling while lessening the impact of the mall's excessive width. New sidewalk cafes soon followed. The city also planted dozens of trees and hung banners from poles. And it created a new "mixed-use zone" down the center of Third Street, a place for kiosks, newsstands, art displays, seating areas, and even topiary dinosaurs. The mixed-use zone broke up the long blocks into smaller, more welcoming activity areas.

To complement — not compete with — the popular Santa Monica Place, the 1986 plan gave priority to entertainment and food rather than retail, says former mayor Dennis Zane. At the same time, the city put zoning controls on commercial development in other areas. Among other things, the new zoning forbade the construction of new movie theaters anywhere but on Third Street.

Success came quickly. The first new occupants — several multiplex theaters and a group of moderately priced restaurants — became magnets for other new businesses, including a number of specialty shops. Thanks to a zoning incentive — an increase in floor area ratio — apartments were built atop a new restaurant and entertainment complex. Retail sales have risen every year since 1989, even during the recession years of the early 1990s. In 1992, ROMA's plan for the mall won a national urban design award from the American Institute of Architects.

This summer, the promenade had a 100 percent occupancy rate, reports Kathleen Rawson, executive director of the Bayside District Corporation, the management entity created by the city. Shops, restaurants, and movie theaters generated more than $1.3 million in local sales taxes in 1996. Some 20,000 shoppers and visitors flock to the mall on a good weekend, Rawson says.

The makeover is not without its critics. One target of their complaints is national retail chains such as Disney and Banana Republic, which moved in several years ago, displacing some of the locally owned businesses that gave the Third Street Promenade a distinctive character.

Another often-heard complaint is that Third Street caters to tourists at the expense of Santa Monicans. A particularly irksome feature, critics say, is the increasing number of noisy street performers. "What started out as a very innovative and cute feature that attracted people has gotten overloaded, almost chaotic," says Paul Rosenstein, city council member and chair of the downtown urban design plan steering committee.

Moving On

Now the city hopes to capitalize on Third Street's success and solve some of its problems at the same time. "One of the key goals of the new streetscape plan," says ROMA's Boris Dramov, "is to transfer some of Third Street Promenade's energy and crowds onto nearby streets." The hope is that lower-rent Second and Fourth streets will attract local merchants and the unusual stores and cafes that many residents and visitors look for.

The plan also seeks to create strong pedestrian activity on streets like Santa Monica Boulevard to balance the crowds that gather on the Third Street Promenade.

A second goal, Dramov says, is to restore downtown streets to their original role as public meeting places. Parades, farmers' markets, street fairs, and sidewalk sales are all part of the picture.

To improve traffic circulation and reduce congestion, the plan calls for making two one-way streets, Fifth and Broadway, two way; redirecting traffic onto other underused streets; and ensuring slow-speed vehicular access throughout the downtown. The idea, says Dramov, is to make sure that pedestrians, not drivers, get top priority on downtown streets.

In an effort to define the downtown core, the plan recommends that a richly landscaped formal gateway be created at the Fifth Street exit ramp from the Santa Monica Freeway. The plan also recommends that palms and flowering trees be planted along Ocean, Colorado, Lincoln, and Wilshire boulevards, streets that define the core.

Finally, street furniture — including specially designed transit shelters — should be installed to bolster the impression of a community-oriented space, Dramov says. For instance, benches would be placed in clusters facing away from street traffic. The plan also includes design guidelines for elements that open to and interact with the street — entries, courtyards, gardens, windows, and signs, for instance.

Getting into Gear

Phase one, which includes restriping Fifth Street and Broadway to make them two-way, and adding curbside parking on Fourth Street as a traffic calming measure, is expected to be complete by Thanksgiving. The city will use already budgeted general funds for this work, according to planning department sources.

The $5 million for phase two, which is likely to begin in mid–1998, is also budgeted. This phase involves more extensive streetscape improvements, with big changes for Santa Monica Boulevard between Ocean Avenue and Fifth Street.

"We will take a lane of traffic out of Santa Monica Boulevard, and all curbside parking will be eliminated in these four blocks," Rosenstein explains. "We will widen the sidewalks on each side by 12 feet to create a pedestrian promenade with plenty of space for sidewalk cafes. The center of the roadway will have one lane of traffic in each direction. One curbside lane will be designated for transit. The other curbside lane will be set aside for cabs, valet parking for restaurants, and loading activities."

The redesigned boulevard will lead people past the Third Street Promenade intersection, two blocks down to Ocean Avenue and Palisades Park, and then over to the Santa Monica Pier, which boasts a new Ferris wheel and roller coaster.

Uncertainties

Funding for subsequent projects could prove more difficult, particularly since last year's passage of Proposition 218, which requires California municipalities to win the approval of affected property owners before they can impose special assessments.

Nonetheless, the outlook for implementation of the downtown streetscape plan is good, given Santa Monica's excellent fiscal condition and good planning and development track record. According to the city finance department, Santa Monica is the only California municipality with an AAA bond rating.

"Most cities are so economically strapped that they will do anything to get new development," says Rosenstein. "They can't be choosy about developers or design issues. Sometimes, they're not even aware of the best thinking on urban design. So they take whatever happens."

In contrast, he says, Santa Monica has a clear vision of what it wants to be. "We have a dream of what our downtown could be like — a vibrant place where all kinds of people can live, shop, work, and recreate — and do it safely, without having to dodge traffic at every step."

CHAPTER 35

Seattle Area Uses Multimodal Transportation System to Serve Urban Centers

Clair Enlow

Destination 2030 is a transportation plan, designed to guide improvements and spending in the Seattle region over the next three decades. But it is much more.

Destination 2030 supports Vision 2020, a growth strategy adopted by the Puget Sound Regional Council in 1990. Vision 2020 called for a development pattern of urban centers connected by an efficient multimodal transportation system. Destination 2030 instructs the public and government agencies how to do it.

The region's TEA-21 funding process is now directly tied to the policies in Destination 2030, Seattle planner and architect Mark Hinshaw, FAICP, wrote in recommending the plan for the award. Through this process, Hinshaw says, the regional council directs transportation funds to designated urban and manufacturing centers and the corridors that connect them.

The APA jury liked that. "What's unusual is to think about land use and urban form as a transportation solution," says APA jury chair Bruce Knight, AICP. "The way

this plan brought that together is really unique."

The jury praised the plan for addressing an entire region in a comprehensive way, for the broad participation and collaboration of agencies, governments, and the public, and for its legislative support, financial incentives, and design guidelines. For these qualities, Destination 2030 receives APA's 2003 award for Outstanding Planning: A Plan.

A Challenging Region

The four counties of the central Puget Sound region — King, Kitsap, Pierce, and Snohomish — are closely linked, naturally and economically. They are lush and green, fed by a temperate and rainy climate. They are bounded east and west by strings of snowy peaks, and tied together by the waters of Puget Sound and a maritime history. At the same time, they're largely urbanized, centering on the cities of Seattle and Tacoma and including Everett, Bellevue, and a proliferation of smaller and newer cities.

Originally published as "Destination 2030: A Transportation Plan for the Central Puget Sound Region," *Planning*, Vol. 69, No. 3, March 2003. Reprinted with permission from *Planning*, copyright © 2003 by the American Planning Association, Suite 1600, 122 South Michigan Avenue, Chicago, IL 60603–6107.

The scenic arrangement of land and water makes transportation a technical challenge. Much of downtown Seattle is crowded onto a narrow, hilly isthmus between Elliot Bay and Lake Washington, and Interstate 5 runs through it. It would take another four lanes on this main north-south arterial to relieve rush hour traffic.

On the east-west axis, investments in more passenger ferries would add commuting choices. Tunneling is one of the ways for rapid transit to cross town. Earthquakes threaten any transportation system, and now the damaged Alaskan Way viaduct, a section of Interstate 99 that flies over the Seattle waterfront, must be replaced.

Back in 1990, the scenery was being swallowed by a monotony of lawns and cul-de-sacs stretching to the foothills of the Cascades. Throwing state, federal, and local transportation dollars after chaotic development seemed like putting the cart before the horse.

That year, the Puget Sound Council of Governments completed Vision 2020, a growth strategy for a multi-centered region that would set urban growth boundaries and concentrate development in existing cities, towns, and urban neighborhoods. Also that year the state passed the Growth Management Act. As local governments began to put together their own plans for compliance, the pattern of urban centers in Vision 2020 was largely ratified.

Realizing the Vision

The horse arrived in 2001 when the Regional Council adopted Destination 2030. "It puts meat on the bones of the vision," says King Cushman, the council's director of transportation and growth planning, who managed development of the plan.

And not a moment too soon. The four counties of the Puget Sound are well into a steep growth curve. It is leveling off in the current recession, but the population of 3.3 million is expected to grow by 1.5 million in the next three decades. The region will add

800,000 jobs and accommodate 16 million daily trips — six million more than today — by 2030.

The area has to make up for a lot of lost time, says Mary McCumber, executive director of the Regional Council.

Much of that time has been dominated recently by confrontations over whether to invest in rail or roads. Destination 2030 lays out the need for more and better roads as well as rail and other transportation options.

No more big bypasses to nowhere, says McCumber. But the lack of adequate road networks in urbanizing areas causes people to drive much greater distances than they need to. "A community is a place where you can live, work, play — and travel through," Cushman says.

The plan does not shrink from the challenge. There are guides for where and how to invest dollars. It also outlines best practices and financial incentives for the land use and channeled growth that are critical to the vision. In addition to quantifying transportation needs and costs, it lists principles of finance and options for securing reliable, long-term funding.

What Will It Cost?

The needs are staggering. Using year 2000 dollars, they add up to $105 billion. Destination 2030 would commit more than $68 billion — more than half the regional spending on transportation in the next three decades — to roads and highways. That means adding 2,000 miles of pavement.

In the first 10 years, the emphasis is on streets and county roads. But over 30 years, the amounts assigned to these and to state highways are roughly equal. The total is more than twice the amount to be spent on rail transit in the same period.

In all, Destination 2030 identifies 2,200 projects, chosen to make the most of the existing network and to add new choices for travel in the future.

High-capacity transit is high on the list.

Voters approved a plan for a regional light rail system almost a decade ago, but the project has been slowed by burgeoning cost estimates and controversies over routes, and still awaits federal funding. Despite these clouds, the start of light rail service in Tacoma is on track for this year, and the central link in Seattle is scheduled for completion in 2009.

Washington voters last fall narrowly approved a new monorail line to connect close-in western neighborhoods to each other and to downtown Seattle. Should the monorail succeed after completion in 2009, more legs will be added.

Where's the Money?

Among the most urgent needs are adequate, reliable sources or revenue. Projected revenues over 30 years now fall $57 billion short of transportation needs.

Washington voters will be asked this fall to support new options for taxing and capital spending. As the metropolitan planning organization for the region, the Puget Sound Regional Council is the gatekeeper for federal funding. It is also a clearinghouse for transportation plans specific to one mode or jurisdiction. So the council and the plan will be important in devising a proposal that voters find acceptable.

There is also hope for finding revenue through the new Regional Transit Investment District, which covers King, Pierce, and Snohomish counties.

Destination 2030 has already made a difference, says McCumber. "Now we can argue about the right things."

CHAPTER 36

Toronto, a National Model, Links Housing and Transportation with Subways and Light-Rail System

Brian Heaton

Today, the growing cost of housing and California's traditional preference for driving their own cars are contributing to long commutes, sprawl and a serious jobs-housing imbalance in some California cities. While those difficulties are a major concern, they are not unique to California. Cities in other parts of the country and Canada have successfully addressed similar problems, utilizing public transit and downtown growth strategies to improve the quality of life for their citizens.

Portland, Oregon Models
New Urbanism

In Portland, the city adopted a proactive downtown plan in 1972 that emphasized urban areas. City leaders felt that downtown should be a place where people could both live and work. A combination of good planning, increased transit options and legislation helped achieve that vision, transforming Portland into a nationwide icon of successful urban living.

That achievement was due in large part to the city setting initial goals for itself, something Portland's Planning Director Gil Kelley believed was helpful in encouraging and maintaining urban growth and reducing sprawl.

"One thing we did proactively at the policy level was to set a goal of capturing 20 percent of regional growth within city boundaries," he explained. "When we initiated that 20 years ago, we were getting just 5 percent of new growth [in the urban core]. Now, over the last 10 years, we've exceeded the goal, and we're around 25 percent."

To accomplish this, the city invested heavily in redeveloping neighborhoods near local transit lines, providing housing for all income levels and essentially making downtown Portland a pedestrian-friendly transit hub. Even more friendly is the cost: In certain areas of downtown, people can ride the light rail for free.

"Our transit agency was very aggressive with its ridership goals, doubling their rid-

Originally published as "Linking Housing and Transportation: Innovative Growth Plans Serve as Model for California Cities," *Western City*, Vol. LXXXI, No. 9, September 2005 © 2005 *Western City* magazine. All rights reserved. Reprinted with permission from the September 2005 issue of *Western City* magazine, the monthly publication of the League of California Cities.

ership every five years on the light rail system," Kelley said. "We made much of the central city a 'free-fare' zone, which helped us meet the objective of having a user-friendly system for those who choose to live downtown."

Providing more housing and public transit opportunities was just the first step in the city's plan. Portland also recognized the need for policies that made taking public transportation more appealing than driving. One solution was a maximum parking standard — a mandate that has led to less congestion on roadways and a better ride to and from work for all commuters living outside the downtown area.

"These [parking standards] were set to encourage people to take public transit, with the idea being that if parking is limited, it creates an incentive for people not to drive to their destination," explained Elaine Wilkerson, director of planning for the City of Glendale, Calif., and former director of Growth Management Services for Metro Portland (the regional government covering all 24 cities and three counties of the Portland metropolitan area).

According to Andy Cotugno, Metro Portland's planning director, the parking mandates and other programs to promote urban living and public transit are working.

"Auto ownership rates are lower and transit ridership rates are higher," he explained. "This is a reflection of both a higher level of transit service ... and the ridership response of supporting a land use pattern that is more supportive of transit."

Another important aspect of making public transit popular with people is providing amenities and housing along transit corridors. Portland emphasized mixed-use development along transit routes, enticing commuters not to drive.

"The idea was to intensify transit and services along corridors so that neighborhoods could be preserved," Wilkerson recalled. "By encouraging the use of transit and

pedestrian activity, there are a variety of benefits, including less air pollution and traffic."

Kelley agreed, noting that zoning and design rules have helped preserve that neighborhood feeling in Portland. Seventy-five percent of a building's street face must be actively used with windows and doors — all in an effort to make the pedestrian experience an enjoyable one.

Furthermore, much of Portland's desire to have a strong downtown housing community came from citizens who recalled how close-knit neighborhoods were in the past.

"People remembered and acknowledged neighborhoods that were built in the streetcar era," Kelley said. "They wanted to preserve that look and feel and replicate that sense of neighborhood around the city."

Having spent time in the San Francisco Bay Area, Portland's planning director has seen firsthand the difficulties facing California cities; in particular, how sprawl has become a problem extending from the large population centers. Although the dynamics are different for the Golden State and Oregon, he encouraged city officials in California to develop a conscious strategy regarding urban development and transportation and stick to it, much like Portland did in the 1970s.

"You have to know what you want to do and realize that urban living can be healthy and friendly," Kelley maintained. "In California, there is no clear policy that says 'build up, not out.' Embrace the notion of urbanism, and do things that make it attractive."

Toronto Puts Transit First

Sprawl is a common enemy for many locales. Some cities in the eastern region of North America have successfully made strides to prevent it.

In Canada, the City of Toronto found itself at a crossroads in the 1960s. As many smaller villages and towns were incorporated into the city during that time, officials believed a system of expressways was needed to link the central city core with the smaller outlying areas. However, the plan was halted when the transportation focus of Toronto's government switched from an auto-based system to a more balanced approach utilizing public transit, particularly subways.

The move was a successful one, spurring the city's downtown population to grow by 200,000 over the years, according to Ted Tyndorf, executive director and chief planner for the City of Toronto.

"The watershed point for Toronto was when we embarked on a process [in the 1970s] to re-urbanize our downtown core," he said. "We've found that 65 to 70 percent of residents don't use their cars to get to work. They walk, cycle or take public transit."

However, while some of the folks living on the outskirts of the city still drive, Toronto hasn't expanded its roadways. Although it's a major metropolitan city, there are only six expressway lanes available to get into Toronto. The expansion has instead come on rails, including subway and regional commuter rail lines.

That growth of public transit lines has had an impact. Officials were able to pinpoint areas of high activity along transit corridors and built higher density, mixed-use amenities areas around them. The city provided its residents everything they need to live along their commuter route, which convinced many to take the train.

"We used an approach that joined busy work centers with transit corridors," Tyndorf explained. "It's a logical way of doing things. That model is being successfully translated into areas around Toronto."

One area Toronto is currently incorporating could serve as a model for booming areas of growth in California. Toronto's waterfront is being developed with a "transit-first" mode in mind. The city is building all the public transit and infrastructure first in order to make sure residents become dependent on *it*, instead of their cars.

Tyndorf admitted the approach was risky and expensive, but very much needed, and offered a few words of wisdom for cities looking to stop sprawl.

"It's a difficult way to go because you're investing billions in infrastructure before you have the actual money," he said. "But it's the only way to make the core of the city sustainable in the long term. It's a matter of making policy decisions and sticking to them."

New Jersey Provides Incentives for Transit Villages

On the Atlantic coast, cities in New Jersey have been successful with a transit village concept. The state's Department of Transportation (DOT) and various local agencies partnered to develop the program, which has eased traffic problems.

Designed to encourage communities to be compact with both mixed-use and residential development within walking distance from transit stations, designated transit villages are given state recognition, technical assistance and higher priority for certain types of funding. The incentives have cities lining up to be a part of the program.

"In three years, I have seen a real concentrated effort for towns to want to do this," explained Monica Etz, principal planner and transit village coordinator of the New Jersey DOT. "It really seems to be catching on."

Sixteen communities are currently identified as transit villages in New Jersey. However, in order to achieve that status, those communities must meet a long list of criteria, including adopting a plan that supports pedestrian-friendly development and making a commitment to developing jobs and housing in the area.

Etz said that her department receives about 25 applications per year but approves only a handful (just two in 2004). In addition, the program has given developers confidence to build homes, slowing sprawl near those communities close to established transit lines.

"Because we don't pick a town until they have completed zoning changes and demonstrated a readiness for development, once designated, developers love it because there is certainty in the area," Etz said. "It attracts people to the area to revitalize it."

Progress in California

California cities are seeing the value in long-term growth plans that link transportation and housing. With the state anticipating 10 million additional residents by 2025, efficiency, ease of transit and the convenience of short travel times to jobs will be key factors in supporting an expanding statewide population in years to come.

Milpitas

In Milpitas, the city council is considering a plan to rezone and redevelop the midtown area near a proposed Bay Area Rapid Transit (BART) station at Capitol Avenue and Montague Expressway. If approved, the plan would allow builders to convert old industrial buildings into housing and mixed-use complexes. Although only in the planning stages, the design allows for between 5,000 to 10,000 new residences, complete with retail facilities, hotels, parking areas and parks.

Given California's soaring housing prices, new homes along a direct transit route in the area may be a welcome change of pace for weary commuters. In some instances, this would also allow drivers to keep their cars in the garage and live in an area designed to provide all their needs within walking distance or a short ride on the train.

Sacramento

California's capitol city is also recognizing the importance of linking transportation and housing. Developer Millennia Sacramento recently unveiled a plan to purchase the Union Pacific rail yard in Sacramento, and if successful, has another plan in the works to combine 10,000 housing units into an "urban village" near the site that would feature a mix of residential, commercial and office space — with public transportation as a central component.

Like the efforts in Milpitas, the Sacramento plan is still in its initial stages. However, the application marks a significant change in attitudes toward planning for mixed use and high density in conjunction with transit.

Glendale

In Southern California, cities are also looking to follow suit. Officials in Glendale are eyeing increased transit opportunities to tie into future housing developments. On June 14, 2005, 50 representatives from Glendale, Burbank and La Cañada Flintridge gathered at Glendale's Municipal Services Building to confer on mixed-use development, housing and transportation in the area over the next 30 years.

The assembled group came to one conclusion: The area's population is growing, and they need to plan for it. One new development is a proposed transportation corridor through Glendale that would connect the Pasadena Gold Line and North Hollywood Red Line, providing citizens with greater public transit mobility.

Glendale is making an effort to encourage residential development in the city's business district, and those efforts could be bolstered by the increased transportation alternatives.

"If you have residential development close to the main rail corridors, with our local transportation system we can get you to those rail corridors," said Jano Baghdanian, Glendale's traffic and transportation administrator. "We already tie into the L.A. Metro bus system. But we need something regional, reliable, clean and flexible in its scheduling. If we can provide that, then urban land-use planning will really work."

CHAPTER 37

Trenton Redesigns Its Freeways to Slow Down Traffic

Christopher Swope

Take a ride through Trenton with Gary Toth and Yosry Bekhiet, and you might conclude that these two highway engineers are the last New Jersey drivers who stick to posted speed limits. Bekhiet, behind the wheel of a state-issue Chevy Cavalier, accelerates up a ramp onto the city's downtown expressway, and then holds steady in the right lane at exactly 50 miles per hour. Toth, in the passenger seat, points out the gold dome of the state capitol as other cars fly past the white Chevy. "I drive this road at 50," Toth says, "and people pass me going 75."

State Route 29 through Trenton, like most roads in the United States, was built for speed. The engineers who designed it back in the 1950s had a hunch that motorists might race a little. So for safety's sake, they made the road a bit straighter and the lanes a tad wider than the speed limit suggested was necessary. Engineers at the time believed this to be prudent design — and many of their contemporaries would still agree with that assessment. For most of their long careers with New Jersey's Department of Transportation, this is what Toth and Bekhiet believed, too.

But lately, the two engineers have become convinced that supersizing Route 29

only made it more dangerous. Designing for the speediest drivers, they now believe, simply encouraged people to drive even faster. They note that recent accidents along a short stretch have killed six people. "The traditional engineering solution to road problems is to make the road wider, straighter and faster," Toth says. "Well, wider, straighter and faster is not always better."

Toth and Bekhiet have developed other objections to Route 29's design. The first is a matter of traffic flow. There are only a few spots where drivers can get on or off the highway. This means that Route 29 shoulders nearly all of the burden of moving cars through Trenton. When the road clogs up at rush hour or after a minor-league baseball game, drivers don't have much choice but to wait out the jam. Their second complaint is Route 29's location. It sits on an embankment along the Delaware River, completely severing downtown Trenton from its waterfront. Thousands of state employees work in a building a stone's throw from the river's edge, but their view outside is all concrete and guardrails. "The Delaware River might as well be 100 miles away," Bekhiet says.

None of the engineers' criticisms of

Originally published as "Rethinking the Urban Speedway," *Governing*, Vol. 19, No. 1, October 2005. Published by Congressional Quarterly Inc., Washington, D.C. Reprinted with permission of the publisher.

Route 29 are anything new. For 20 years, the city of Trenton has been begging the DOT to tear down this expressway. "It's the Indianapolis 500 out there," says Mayor Douglas Palmer. What is new, and is simply astonishing for anyone familiar with transportation policy to hear, is that it's the engineers themselves — finally — who are the ones saying it.

This is surprising because highway engineers have earned themselves a notorious reputation for dogmatic inflexibility. For half a century, they tended to apply a bigger-is-better formula to every road they worked on, in pursuit of a one-dimensional goal: moving as many cars as quickly and safely as possible. Along the way, DOTs ripped up neighborhoods, harmed main streets and destroyed scenic landscapes, typically foisting their plans and priorities on the public without seeking much public input. Local officials, citizen activists and even some of the engineers themselves came to call this mentality by a telling phrase: "Design and defend."

In the past five years or so, however, the priesthood of highway engineers has begun converting to a new religion. They're increasingly willing to consider road designs that slow cars down. They're learning to pay attention to pedestrians, bicyclists and other people who share the road with autos. And they're starting to listen to the public before, not after, they whip up their drawings. Design and defend is out. The new catch phrase is "context sensitivity."

Trenton's Route 29 is a good example of the new mindset. State engineers used to scoff at the city's idea of junking the expressway for a slower-speed urban boulevard. Now Toth, DOT's head of project planning, and Bekhiet, his lead engineer on this project, devote considerable energy to making it happen. The latest plans call for the new road to be meshed into a dense grid of new downtown streets. There would be lots of traffic lights, allowing pedestrians to cross between the city and the river. To be sure, the drive

through Trenton would take longer — an extra one to two minutes, according to traffic modeling. But there's an upside, too: Trenton would get its waterfront back, as well as 18 acres of freed-up land to build a neighborhood of offices and condos that favors walking over driving.

DOTs are heaving bureaucracies, and deep within them there is still resistance to this philosophy, however. The Trenton project, Toth says, is more controversial within the 4,000-person agency than outside it. "Some people say, 'What? You're ripping out a freeway for community development? Are you out of your mind?'"

But a growing number of engineers these days are buying into an utterly radical notion, one that contradicts their own training and all their career experience. The idea is this: In some circumstances, their goal should be to move fewer cars, not more of them. "I didn't think about it for my first 25 years here," says Toth, a 32-year DOT veteran. "Our mission was to build roads. Why did we build roads? Because people have to get to their jobs, to shop, go to a ballgame. But what if we can't build roads fast enough anymore?"

The Cookbook Approach

The emergence of this new attitude is linked to the completion of the Interstate Highway System. Constructing a consistent national road network in the years following World War II required states to apply rigorously uniform road designs. When that work finally wrapped up in the early 1990s, DOTs turned their attention to fixing and expanding their state highways.

Those roads run through vastly different settings from Interstates — many main streets, for example, are technically state highways. Engineers nevertheless stuck by their Interstate-era calculations, detailed in a 900-plus-page tome known to all in their profession as the "Green Book." The Green Book actually allowed a good bit of design flexibility. But engineers always read it to mean that they had to demand wide lanes, big shoulders and streetscapes optimized for driving quickly. "We had an army of literally thousands of planners, environmental analysts, designers and construction engineers who had built the Interstates for decades and who were used to this standardized approach," says Hal Kassoff, a consultant who served as Maryland's DOT chief from 1984 to 1996. "It was a collision course."

Over and over again, DOTs found themselves fighting with local governments, environmental groups, historic preservationists and community activists. The fault lines typically broke in a familiar way. Engineers wanted to widen roads, take out trees or sidewalks, and bulk up bridges, where opponents thought a simple repaving or minor bridge fix would do. Gradually DOTs began to see that they had to become more flexible if they wanted to finish projects rather than haggle over them. Scott Bradley, head of landscape architecture for the Minnesota DOT, puts it this way: "The old cookbook approach of using design guidelines and cranking it through the computer to tell us what the physical form of a road should be no longer flew."

The initial response within the highway engineering profession came to be known in the late 1990s as "context-sensitive design." No longer would engineers design roads as though only asphalt dimensions mattered. Now, they would take into account the surroundings. Is the road going through a scenic landscape? An urban neighborhood? A shopping district? Settings mattered. Process mattered, too: DOTs would ask stakeholders, typically the very people who had been holding up projects, how they wanted the roadway designed.

Suddenly, long-stalled road projects began moving again. The model that engineers everywhere pointed to was the Paris Pike in rural Kentucky. The original two-lane road ran through a historic landscape of rolling hills, stone walls and horse barns. Kentucky had long planned to widen and straighten Paris Pike into a blitzing four-lane freeway. Historic preservationists tangled the project in court for decades. Then along came context-sensitive design, and the engineers suddenly began accommodating their rivals. They routed Paris Pike to follow the hilly landscape, rather than barrel through it. Rock walls that had to be destroyed were reconstructed. Attractive guardrails were built out of timber. The end product, finished a few years ago, looks more like a 1920s parkway than a 1960s freeway.

Context-sensitive design often produced better results, but the process was still flawed. DOTs continued to view public outreach as an afterthought. Moreover, many engineers came to think of superficial treatments — brick-clad overpasses or medians planted with wildflowers — as wampum for buying off community opposition. Engineers preferred to fixate on aesthetics rather than meddle with their underlying assumptions about roadways.

A recent project in Connecticut, heralded as context-sensitive design, is an odd case in point. The state DOT built a downtown bridge in the city of Willimantic that is playfully presided over by four giant statues of frogs — an homage to the loud bullfrogs that surprised early settlers there in the 1700s. The "frog bridge" is now a popular local attraction. But don't expect to find anybody walking across it, says Norman Garrick, a University of Connecticut engineering professor. "It's still a hostile environment for pedestrians," he notes. "DOTs in most states still think that context-sensitive design has something to do with beautifying the road and aesthetic treatments. They've not come to grips with how roads that are designed like highways in the middle of cities affect the urbanity of the place."

That shortcoming is what engineers are now addressing. This is where the true revolution in thinking about highways begins. "Context-sensitive design" has evolved into "context-sensitive solutions." The difference is much more than semantics. "Design" assumed, as engineers always had, that transportation problems required some sort of construction to fix them. "Solutions" implies a broader, more objective view — one that may not result in any road construction at all. It also suggests that community stakeholders might have better ideas for how to address problems than engineers do.

Consider how highway planning has changed in New Hampshire. The last time New Hampshire came up with a long-range transportation plan a decade ago, agency engineers controlled the agenda. "It was an in-house effort," says Ansel Sanborn, the DOT's chief planner. Now, a new 25-year plan is being drafted. Rather than dictate priorities themselves, the engineers have essentially turned the public-input process over to the well-respected New Hampshire Charitable Foundation. The foundation, it is hoped, can bring to bear a broader set of community values than highway engineers ever could. "Transportation people are very interested in building transportation projects," Sanborn explains. "The Charitable Foundation is very interested in building communities."

It's a similar story next door in Vermont. By 1995, historic preservationists had grown so fed up with the state Agency of Transportation that the Preservation Trust of Vermont published an entire book on how to fight the agency's decisions. Since then, the agency has overhauled its approach. It rewrote its design standards to accommodate the small-scale village charm that characterizes Vermont. Plus, citizen advisory boards now play a large role in deciding which road projects get started first. Even Paul Bruhn, the Preservation Trust's executive director, is impressed. "We do have an agency that is much more sensitive to our concerns now."

Halting a Vicious Cycle

The new thinking is infiltrating nearly every DOT, as well as the engineering firms that states and localities hire as consultants. But nowhere has it reached the degree of complexity to which New Jersey is taking it.

That's largely because of Gary Toth, who is reshaping the bureaucracy's middle ranks with a new attitude. Toth constantly reminds his engineers that the Green Book is actually as flexible as a chili recipe — they just need to be willing to cook with different ingredients. Some 800 DOT professionals have gone through an extensive training course in context-sensitive solutions. When Toth sits down with his project managers, they question each other and brainstorm, much as doctors would in a hospital case study. "It's amazing," says David Burwell, a transportation consultant who has worked with New Jersey's DOT and several others. "There's much more of an intellectual inquiry now as to how to tackle specific issues."

Although Toth found this philosophy late in his career, he feels no remorse for the past. Engineers are problem-solvers, he likes to say. For most of his working life, engineers like him were expected to solve transportation problems within a limited set of auto-oriented parameters. But engineers, too, can roll with the changes. "Engineers can shift paradigms quickly," Toth says. "You just have to give them a different problem to solve."

Toth's new problem is an especially tricky one. His boss, Commissioner Jack Lettiere, is the nation's leading disciple of a fairly radical idea in transportation circles: that you can't build your way out of traffic congestion. This may be truer in New Jersey than in other places — but then again, New Jersey may be a national bellwether, too. Money for big road projects is scarce because New Jersey, like quite a few states, hasn't raised its gas tax in more than a decade. New Jersey also suffers, in a way, from its suburban maturity. Congested thoroughfares can't be widened without killing businesses, whose driveways and parking lots would be wiped out.

Lettiere wants Toth and his engineers to halt a vicious cycle that has spun out of control for years. In the past, DOT would see that a road was congested, and either expand it or build a new one. Then local governments, operating independently, would approve housing developments and big-box stores along those roads. Soon the roads would clog up again and the cycle would repeat itself. DOTs have always assumed they had no choice but to keep accommodating more and more cars. Lettiere now believes the exact opposite may be true. "To reduce traffic," he says, "maybe we have to reduce the number of trips on the highway."

To do that, Toth is going where no DOT has gone before. He is getting his engineers involved in local land-use planning. The goal is to make future development favor walking and driving alike. It's the ultimate test of the context-sensitive solutions mindset. Toth's "context" is much broader than usual: It's the housing developments, offices and stores located outside the state's right-of-way.

One example is Manalapan Township, in central New Jersey. Two state highways run through Manalapan: Routes 9 and 33. The first is already crammed with stores, parking lots and traffic. The second, absent intervention, will probably suffer the same fate. Recently, Manalapan's mayor asked Lettiere for help cleaning up Route 9. That fight is already lost, Lettiere responded. But Route 33 might still be saved.

So far, the planning work has focused largely on one developer's proposal to build a massive "lifestyle center" in a field of soybeans. The plan includes shopping, housing, a multiplex movie theater, a supermarket and ball fields. It's hit a wall of community opposition — largely on fears that it will clog Route 33 with traffic. DOT convened a couple of workshops to sketch out alternative ideas for how to lay out the project. The sessions brought the developer together with local transportation, planning and zoning officials, in addition to neighborhood, civic and business groups.

The daylong workshops, in March and June, produced a revised conceptual plan. The new plan emphasizes pedestrian-friendly streetscapes. It also encourages mixing land uses so that people can go from a store to a restaurant without getting in their cars. Toth is careful to note that Manalapan asked DOT to hold — and to pay for — the workshops.

Toth has a dozen other projects like this one in the pipeline. A key principle keeps emerging that breaks yet another orthodoxy of the engineering world. For years, engineers designed road networks to flow a bit like blood vessels, with smaller roads feeding into thicker ones. (In fact, the Green Book term for a major thoroughfare is *arterial*.) Toth has come to believe that engineers are putting too much pressure on these major roads. He's convinced that what would work better is something more like a grid — where drivers have lots of options for getting around, rather than one overburdened highway. "We've created a situation where everyone who wants to go out for a bagel or newspaper has to go out to the same road," Toth says.

That theory is getting a test in the borough of Flemington. Routes 202 and 31 are the main drags through town, both lined with strip malls. They carry nearly all of the traffic moving through the region, as well as local shopping traffic. For two decades, DOT had intended to build a bypass. The plan was for a four-lane separated freeway, expected to cost $150 million. DOT is too broke for that kind of a project now. And even if the agency had the coin, Toth believes that a bypass would be a waste of money. It would give drivers only one way around a traffic jam, rather than several.

Through another series of public workshops, the plan has been reworked. The bypass is gone. In its place is a two-lane boulevard that intersects with many side streets. DOT will also pay to beef up some county roads in order to further disperse traffic and ease the burden on Routes 202 and 31. In all, this costs about half as much. Mary Melfi, a Flemington councilwoman, is pleased with the change. "Everything in New Jersey is a highway," Melfi says. "DOT has always been about six-lane highways, and they're not doing it anymore. They'd rather build 14 miles of small roads than a few miles of big ones."

To be sure, New Jersey will still widen roads when it makes sense and when there's money to pay for it. "We're not going soft here," Toth says. "We're still worried about the concerns of the motoring public." But the job of designing highways couldn't be more different from when Toth started with DOT 32 years ago. Engineers don't have to be just kinder and gentler. They've got to be creative. "If you follow the book, that's not design," Toth says. "That's just following the book."

CHAPTER 38

Valencia, Other Areas, Create "New" Main Streets That Are Designed for Citizens and Their Cars

Charles Lockwood

Throughout the 1980s and 1990s, hundreds of towns — both large and small — embarked on main street revitalization programs to strengthen their communities. Now, post–World War II suburbs throughout the United States are building main streets from scratch in a bold attempt to give identity to an anonymous suburban sprawl. By doing so, they hope to gain an edge in competing with other towns for future development and increased tax revenues.

Several dozen new main streets are under construction or in the planning stages in suburbs across the country. They are *not* intended to be outdoor shopping malls masquerading as main streets. Like pre–World War II, small town main streets, they contain a full range of everyday uses and activities — including office, retail, entertainment, hotels, housing, and civic institutions such as public libraries — all integrated within a pedestrian-friendly environment.

New suburban main streets are sprouting up in virtually every kind of postwar community — from unplanned, sprawling suburbs like Schaumburg near Chicago, to new towns like Valencia outside Los Angeles, and to picture book new urbanist communities like Haile Plantation in Gainesville, Florida, and Disney's new town of Celebration, Florida. These new main streets take many forms — from streets several blocks long to tree-shaded town squares and village greens.

These developments mark the wane of an old trend and the emergence of a new movement. Since World War II, most suburban development has ignored the broader, historic role of the street as a key component in a shared public realm. Rather, development patterns have reduced the street to a pedestrian-intimidating, single-purpose traffic arterial. The last few generations of Americans rarely have had the experience of coming together on a tree-lined street to shop, to walk after dinner, or to talk with friends.

Today, the pendulum is swinging another way. More and more people want to return to the traditional main street, partic-

Originally published as "Retrofitting Suburbia," *Urban Land*, Vol. 57, No. 7, July 1998. Published by the Urban Land Institute, 1025 Thomas Jefferson Street, N.W., Suite 500 West, Washington, D.C. 20007–5201. Reprinted with permission of the publisher.

ularly as their lives become more mobile, more global, and more computerized. Despite all the talk about "going virtual," people still need to feel they belong to a community.

Why Retrofit Suburbia?

Why are a growing number of suburbs, which previously celebrated their shopping mall/automobile-dominated lifestyles, building new main streets?

The "Tin Man" Syndrome. Like the Tin Man in *The Wizard of Oz*, more and more American residents are complaining that their postwar suburban towns have no heart. They feel cast adrift, with nothing to hold onto except a steering wheel. A main street, whatever its scale or architectural style, is the heart of a community. Reston Town Center in the new town of Reston, Virginia, for example, serves not only as a downtown that brings the Reston community together but also as a regional center for residents and workers from neighboring suburban communities that lack multiuse public gathering places.

Identity. As look-alike suburbs increasingly compete for residents, jobs, conventions, and tourists, many of them are regarding the addition of new main streets as one way to create an easily recognizable — and marketable — identity and character that will attract new businesses, development, and shops, as well as generate increased sales tax revenues.

Suburban Renewal. Many 1950s and 1960s inner suburbs are declining, just as urban neighborhoods did a generation or two ago. The suburb of Park Forest outside Chicago watched its population decline by 14 percent in the 1980s and its median household income shrink by 3 percent when the nation was enjoying a 7 percent increase in median income. The 695,000-square-foot Park Forest Center regional mall has been plagued in recent years by a 70 percent vacancy rate. Now, most of the mall buildings have been bulldozed as Park Forest builds a new main street in its place to help revitalize its community.

Program Overload. Many people are turning away from overstructured, formulaic places that look alike to the diversity of traditional main streets. Big buildings, small buildings, a few ugly buildings, and some standout ones work together to make main street a real place where people can feel connected.

Changing suburban retail trends are another key factor fueling the new suburban main street trend. Medium-sized, higher-end stores like Williams Sonoma, Barnes & Noble, and Crate & Barrel no longer want to locate inside typical suburban malls. They prefer a separate identity, which means having their own building on a pedestrian-oriented main street. According to *Stores* magazine, "The revitalization of main street has caught the imagination of retailers, who see neighborhood locations as a viable means of growth…. Main street stores are answering shoppers' demands for convenience, efficiency, and something new while avoiding the sense of sameness that frequently seems to fill many suburban centers."

The Gap, Saks Fifth Avenue, Sears, Limited Stores, Express, Victoria's Secret, Bath & Body Works, and Abercrombie & Fitch are a few of the increasing number of retailers that have rediscovered the profit potential of main street. But not all retailers are appropriate for a new suburban main street, or for any main street for that matter.

"You cannot have major stores or big-box retailers on a pedestrian-oriented street," notes Kalvin Platt, chairman of the SWA Group, an international land planning and landscape architecture firm. "Their buildings and their parking lots are simply too big for the pedestrian-oriented main street scale."

Blazing the Trail: Three Pioneers

Construction of one of the first suburban main streets began in 1987. Fields Point

Development Company hired architects Andres Duany and Elizabeth Plater-Zyberk to redevelop the circa–1960 New Seabury Shopping Center in Mashpee, Massachusetts, into a three-block-long, pedestrian-oriented town center called Mashpee Commons, complete with stores, housing, a library, and a church.

In 1991, Crocker & Company completed the first phase of pedestrian-oriented, mixed-use Mizner Park in Boca Raton, Florida, on the site of the failing 420,000-square-foot Boca Raton Mall. Architects Cooper Carry & Associates created an instant community hub by designing a two-block-long village green ringed by low-rise buildings with shops and restaurants and entrances to them on the ground floors. The upper floors have offices or apartments.

In 1991, Mobil Land Development Corporation completed the first phase of Reston Town Center — the "big city" version of a traditional main street. The town center includes 530,000 square feet of office space, 200,000 square feet of stores and restaurants, an 11-screen movie theater, a 514-room Hyatt Regency Hotel, and a one-acre central plaza with a fountain. Parking structures and surface lots are located behind the buildings.

Schaumburg, Illinois: Municipality as Main Street Developer

Sometimes, a municipality — rather than a developer — is the catalyst behind a new main street. In recent decades, Schaumburg, Illinois, near Chicago's O'Hare International Airport, became one of the nation's largest, most successful edge cities. However, it had no town center, no unifying core. Then, several years ago, Schaumburg's village government purchased a run-down, half-empty retail center at Roselle and Schaumburg Roads, the community's traditional crossroads, along with several nearby parcels.

Land assemblage for this 29-acre site took several years. "Although we initiated condemnation proceedings on some proper-ties," says Mayor Al Larson, "we did not go to court. Instead, we ended up negotiating the prices, using money from the larger tax-increment financing (TIF) district to purchase and redevelop the land." After completing site assemblage in 1995, the village of Schaumburg began selling parcels to developers. "We didn't want to own the center," Mayor Larson explains. "We just wanted to create a development plan to reflect our vision for the site and the community, and then sell the parcels to developers who would build our vision."

The key was attracting strong anchors to Town Square. Larson wanted one of these to be the Schaumburg Township Library, the second busiest library in the state. He knew the library wanted to relocate, and he sold it on Town Square. A 70,000-square-foot grocery store serves as the second anchor. Together with the library, it will generate strong retail traffic for the restaurants, stores, and other businesses that will surround the central square. A nearby residential project, with more than 100 upscale townhouses and some single-family houses, will bring additional foot traffic.

Schaumburg's new Town Square, designed by Hitchcock Design Group, is rapidly taking shape. An amphitheater, a park, ponds, and waterfalls have been built in the central square. A 55-foot-tall clock tower, the traditional icon of town squares for centuries, is already standing. The grocery store is open, and the shops and professional space on the south side of the square are completed and 80 percent occupied. Parking has been placed behind the buildings, so that visitors are not confronted by an ocean of parking when they arrive. The library, which will open this September, is expected to attract an estimated 1 million patrons a year.

Village Commons: Vernon Hills, Illinois

Several postwar Chicago suburbs are following Schaumburg's lead by planning and building a wide variety of new main streets. One of these is Vernon Hills, 35 miles northwest of Chicago. Incorporated in 1958, Vernon Hills has more than 3.5 million square feet of retail space. With a population of 20,000 and rising, it has been one of the fastest-growing municipalities in the state for the last two decades. Still, the village wanted to improve its ability to compete with surrounding historic towns.

Vernon Hills is reviewing plans for the Village Commons, which will have a village green, a library, a hotel, retail space, residential uses, and a senior center. "We are trying to create some history and a sense of place," says Craig Malin, the village's assistant manager.

Part of the funding for Village Commons is coming from a $200,000 CMAQ (congestion mitigation air quality improvement) grant, which uses federal Intermodal Surface Transportation Efficiency Act (ISTEA) funds. Using CMAQ formulas, the village was able to show that reconfiguring land usage and constructing a town square would reduce automobile emissions in Vernon Hills. The Chicago Area Transportation Study, CMAQ's Chicago metropolitan planning organization, is funding this new approach to pollution reduction.

Town Center Drive: Valencia, California

In the new town of Valencia, 30 miles north of downtown Los Angeles, the Newhall Land and Farming Company is now building a half-mile-long, pedestrian-oriented main street called Town Center Drive, directly adjacent to the enclosed Valencia Town Center regional mall, which opened in 1991.

"The Valencia master plan, which was completed by planner Victor Gruen in 1965, designated this location as the community hub," explains James S. Backer, senior vice president of Newhall Land's commercial and industrial real estate division. Many industry leaders were thinking of an outdoor retail mall for this location, but Thomas L. Lee, Newhall Land's chairman and CEO, Tom Dierckman, president of Valencia Company, and Backer were main street boosters from the start.

A key component of the site plan was linking Town Center Drive with the Valencia Town Center regional mall. John Kriken, a partner with Skidmore, Owings & Merrill, LLP, had advised Newhall Land to break the traditional ring of mall parking and set aside an area for the mall's main entrance, with movie theaters, a working carousel, and fountains — all waiting to connect to Town Center Drive.

Wide sidewalks, shade trees, and benches line the new main street. The first two Town Center Drive buildings already are open and seven other buildings are under construction, including the 250-room Valencia Hyatt Hotel, an entertainment/retail complex, and office buildings, as well as several hundred apartments on the western end of the street.

Haile Village Center: Haile Plantation, Florida

In 1992, architect and developer Robert B. Kramer and his partner Matthew Kaskel began building a five-block-long main street at Haile Plantation, a master-planned community outside Gainesville, Florida. Kramer laid out Haile Village Center and designed about three-quarters of the relatively small white clapboard, tin-roofed professional buildings, most of which have apartments on the second floors.

The 50-acre project uses a network of bike paths to link Haile Village Center to the surrounding subdivisions. Popular events like a weekly farmers market help to lure residents to the new village center. More than 40 buildings already line the street. About half of the commercial property is owner occupied.

"We have the traditional mix of main street uses — plenty of shops, including a corner grocery store, a dry cleaners, a post office, a dentist, a stockbroker," says Kramer. "We didn't create a list and say 'We've got to have those people.' They came to us, so there must be a demand for our kind of main street." Future development projects include a town hall, a 100-unit apartment complex, an assisted-care facility, and a 75-unit lodge and conference center.

Roadblocks to Success

For all its benefits, the new suburban main street trend faces several roadblocks, including:

Expense. Many developers and municipalities cannot afford to fund such large, long-term development projects, particularly when they must pay today's high prices for land even as municipalities struggle with dwindling tax bases.

Site Assemblage. Like Schaumburg, most suburban cities will have to assemble their own main street sites. Will other municipalities have sufficient political support — and funds — to assemble these sites through negotiation or eminent domain?

Traffic Codes. Many jurisdictions require overly wide streets that spoil the intimate scale of pedestrian-oriented main streets and introduce high-speed traffic into their roadways.

Too Many Clones? The real estate industry's mania for formulas also threatens the success of the new suburban main street trend. Developers and municipalities are notorious for replicating successful projects, rather than creating a distinctive streetscape that reflects their area's market, history, and demographics. Others take the main street "formula" and strip it down to cut costs, leaving residents with a cheap outdoor mall. "Big developers are already jumping on the main street bandwagon," warns Plater-Zyberk, "without understanding or appreciating the many intricate components that can make or break a public realm."

Too Little Too Late? Finally, trying to create a traditional, pedestrian-oriented main street in the midst of sprawling, automobile-dominated postwar suburbia may be impossible for most communities. Without careful planning, the results can be little more than nostalgic window dressing, like the faux turn-of-the-century storefronts in a typical suburban mall.

But there is more upside than downside for this development trend. Touring developers and architects, for example, are flocking to Haile Plantation. "They come here," says Kramer, "and tell me, 'We don't have Disney's money to do something large and all at once, like Celebration.' But if you can do it in small, market-driven increments, I guess we can do this kind of main street development, too."

Equally promising, developers of some vast mixed-use complexes are making new suburban main streets a key feature in their projects. The focal point of the Winmar Company's just-completed Redmond Town Center outside Seattle is a five-block-long new main street. Built on the site of a former golf course in Redmond, Washington, this 1.375-million-square-foot, mixed-use project, designed by LMN Architects, contains retail space, office buildings, multifamily housing, restaurants, an eight-screen cinema complex, a hotel, and 40 acres of parks and open space.

Main streets also are being included in large downtown redevelopment plans. Rockville, Maryland, is in the beginning stages of replacing a failed downtown mall that physically divided its central business district with a $300 million, 1.5 million-square-foot, mixed-use development. Designed by Hellmuth, Obata & Kassabaum, the project includes a new four-block-long main street whose purpose is to unite and revitalize the downtown and create a community hub for the entire city.

"Building a main street from scratch," says Philip J. Enquist, a partner at Skidmore, Owings & Merrill LLP, "takes a total commitment from the city, the developers, and the community. Fortunately, dozens of communities are making that commitment. We are the only American generation to live without main streets. We may not have to live without them for much longer."

CHAPTER 39

Washington, DC, Protects Its Monuments and Buildings from Vehicles and Possible Acts of Terrorism

Corrina Stellitano

Cars and trucks are an American icon and the basis of the nation's transportation and commerce, but for security professionals, vehicles can represent a distressing threat. Like the Trojan horse, vehicles can carry danger to the front door — or worse yet, through the walls — directly into a facility.

Vehicle deterrence devices have increased in popularity and in sophistication in the past five years, but available products can vary in capabilities, construction and cost.

Bollards and Barriers

Devices created to keep vehicles outside a designated perimeter range from stationary concrete posts or planters to automated hydraulically-powered metal posts and steel plates that rise up against the invading vehicle.

While stationary vehicle obstructions, such as planters or concrete barricades called Jersey barriers, keep unwanted vehicles from restricted areas, they are not suitable as gates for entrances and exits. To supplement the carefully guarded perimeters of their facil-ities, security professionals need versatile, mobile access control devices — and they must be powerful enough to stop a speeding vehicle.

Bollards (or vehicle deterrents in the form of heavy-duty posts) are a balance of function and aesthetics. Even the sturdiest types, those able to repel a speeding tractor-trailer — are offered in ornamental or architecturally-consistent sleeves or finishes. Others can be painted.

Experts say bollards are less disruptive to pedestrian traffic, and are easily accepted by the public.

Bollards are available in several varieties:

• **Fixed bollards** are cost-effective ways to protect large areas permanently, and serve the same purpose as concrete planters, for example, protecting the perimeter at airports. Some decorative planters even have a bollard built in to add strength.

• **Removable bollards** are effective for creating an emergency passage. These bollards may include a mechanism to lock them in place when in use, and caps to cover the

Originally published as "Roadblocks to Disaster," *Government Security*, Vol. 2, No. 5, May 2003. Published by PRIMEDIA Business Magazines & Media Inc., Overland Park, KS. Reprinted with permission of the publisher.

holes when the bollards are removed. These devices may not fulfill U.S. State Department safety requirements because the bollard base and foundation may not reach far enough below ground. However, adding diameter will increase stopping capability.

• **Retractable or automatic bollards,** operated by hydraulic or pneumatic power units, can be lowered below ground to allow entry. Special emergency settings allow the posts to return to an upright setting in case of a security threat. These units are available with a self-contained hydraulic power unit, or more commonly, multiple bollards with internal pneumatic or hydraulic workings can be controlled by an external hydraulic power unit.

• **Manual retractable/semi-automatic bollards** are suitable for less-used entrances and exits and are more cost-effective. Manual bollards are counter-balanced, allowing ease of movement up or down, and the devices lock in either position. When semi-automatic bollards are in the upright position, a key may be inserted and turned to unlock, allowing the operator to press the bollard until it locks in the down position. Then when unlocked by key again, a compressed gas cylinder raises the bollard to an upright, locked position. The ascent may also be completed with a manual screw crank or pull system.

Many facility managers choose to pair bollards with high-security gates or barricades.

• **Crash gates** are steel rods or pickets that slide across a roadway on a track. Cantilevered versions avoid the potential difficulties of a track (which must be kept free of ice or large amounts of sand) by sliding the gate through a stanchion which borders the roadside.

• **Wedge barriers** are steel rectangles that raise a formidable edge above the surface of the road. Steel plate barriers also rise from the road to a 45-degree angle. When raised, the barrier's angle, along with the barrier's foundation pad, deflects the vehicle's force.

• **Drop arm barriers** look much like a parking lot drop arm, with crash or cable beams rising to allow vehicles to enter, but stopping an unauthorized vehicle when in the lowered position.

A similar version of the drop arm employs a one-inch steel cable to lasso any vehicle attempting to drive under a U-shaped gate, thus destroying the front of the vehicle.

• **Portable (or mobile) barriers** are praised for their speed of installation and mobility. With a swift set-up time — from 15 minutes to a few hours — portable barriers offer less strength than barriers set in concrete, but they allow perimeters to be created quickly when security issues require a larger area of safety around a facility. Portable barriers also require no excavation, thus allowing installation on existing roads or even level compacted soil.

Some portable barriers consist of a crash beam or a rising plate barrier, set on both sides with buttresses — boxes filled with a heavy substance, or 55-gallon drums filled with concrete and placed in ornamental crates. In the 55-gallon drum version, the drums can be removed, allowing the barrier to be easily moved and reinstalled. If the boxes are filled with concrete, they may become a one-time-use-only device. Water, sand and gravel may be more easily removable. A portable plate barrier on wheels can be towed into place and installed in 20 minutes.

While some of these portable solutions pass crash tests, positioning must be carefully considered, as they tend to move when hit with a vehicle. However, movement can be somewhat limited with the addition of support buttresses.

What to Consider When Purchasing

For first-time buyers, the array of vehicle access control products can be overwhelming. Security professionals working for government facilities, or businesses which

Security on the Hill

As one of Washington, D.C.'s most historic districts, Capitol Hill — referring to the area encompassing the U.S. Capitol Building, the U.S. Senate Buildings, and the Capitol Police headquarters — has a myriad of sensitive areas requiring protection.

When Clinton, Md.–based Nasatka Barriers first began helping with ongoing security upgrades in the district, the site required a variety of vehicle access control measures, recalls John Scolaro, Nasatka's international sales director.

Security measures on Capitol Hill have not only been inspired by the terrorist events of Sept. 11, 2001, but also by the shooting of two Capitol Hill officers in July 1998.

"They needed a large range of stopping abilities, depending on the location at Capitol Hill," he says. Entire roadways, parking lots, and various entrance and exits needed to be protected.

One solution requiring minimum excavation and a relatively short installation time was the steel plate barrier. "They needed something that wasn't going to affect the environment drastically, so they didn't want a lot of excavation in roadways," Scolaro says. The steel barriers' hot dip galvanized finish was also helpful in protecting against harsh conditions caused by weather and frequent construction.

Because many areas have been under construction during the last few years, changing entrances and exits in need of protection, mobile steel plate barriers were also used. The barriers-on-wheels enabled flexible perimeters, and could be moved and re-deployed in 30 minutes.

One common factor that was of less concern to the security staff at Capitol Hill was aesthetics. "They weren't really looking at the aesthetic features because they wanted people to know they were serious about unwanted vehicles not entering," Scolaro says.

Over the last several years, the extensive site has employed 60 percent of Nasatka's steel plate barrier models. Like most government entities, Capitol Hill's security professionals knew what they needed, Scolaro says.

"Really what they're looking at is which product best fits the application, and they're looking at durability," he says. "These sort of agencies do a lot of research. They know who they're looking for and they have an idea what they're looking for, but they do value our suggestions as to what product best fits their need."

often work with the government, must know the difference between crash-rated products and crash-tested products.

Crash rating describes an engineering analysis. Vehicle deterrence devices that are described as "crash tested" have actually met a vehicle in an independent test lab. While there are many commercial labs in operation, the U.S. State Department and Department of Defense only approve certain labs.

Careful consideration of each site's needs is important, suppliers say. Most will ask several key questions as they help buyers match products to security demands.

• **What type of vehicle are you trying to stop and how fast can that vehicle travel when approaching vulnerable areas of your facility?** A major measurement of a vehicle's hitting power is its kinetic energy — derived from its velocity and its weight. Upon impact, some of the vehicle's energy is converted to heat, sound and permanent deformation of the vehicle. But the barrier must absorb the remainder of this energy.

The amount of kinetic energy presented by a vehicle changes as a square of its velocity. Therefore, an armored care weighing 30 times as much as a Volkswagen and moving at 10 mph would have less hitting power than the Volkswagen moving at 60 mph. Because velocity weighs so heavily into the damaging power of a vehicle, security engineers often design entrances to force a vehicle to slow down before it reaches the barrier.

If a vehicle approaching a facility must

make a 90-degree turn, its velocity will be decreased, and the use of a less invasive barrier might be suggested. However, if the vehicle entrance is at the end of a long straightaway, barrier manufacturers may suggest their strongest-rated devices. The types of vehicles typically entering the site are also considered; a business that has tractor-trailers entering and exiting frequently will require different security measures than a site where the only visitors are cars and pedestrians.

• **How often will the entrance/exit be used?** If the barrier will operate only a few cycles per day or week, a manual option would be acceptable. Automatic barriers can open and close more than 100 times a day, but some options are slower than others.

More to Consider

Other environmental factors must also be evaluated before a final selection is made. If excavation is impossible, shallow-mount barriers would be necessary. If the area is prone to colder conditions, strip heaters would be needed to keep equipment above 32 degrees. Warning signage and signal lights are also helpful to alert visitors to the presence of barriers.

Manufacturers say vehicular access control devices work best when operating as part of a larger access control system. To this end, most can be operated by a combination of methods, including radio, remote control, card readers, keyswitch, numeric keypad, or manually on a push-button panel. Most hydraulic units will also have back-up provisions in case of power failure.

Manufacturers also suggest that bollards and barriers be kept in the closed or upright position until an approaching vehicle has been cleared for entry.

Many suggest installing additional warning systems. A velocity sensor, consisting of digital wire loops embedded in the roadway a distance away from the facility entrance or guard booth, will trigger an early warning alarm or raise barriers if a vehicle is approaching at high speeds.

Vehicle-sensing loops placed in the roadway directly in front and behind the barricade stop the raising of barricades or bollards while an authorized vehicle is in the way. The coupled loop detector suppresses accidental operation, while an emergency mode allows the safety loop to be overridden in a crisis.

An Open Door for Innovation

While many barriers are similar across the industry, manufacturers continue to produce creative variations. One company offers concrete barriers in the form of pre-cast animals; with optional water spray attachments for water park use.

Another manufactures its bollards separate from its casings. End-users can buy and install the casings now, and purchase the bollards with their decorative finishes after construction, and any changes to the architectural appearance, have been completed.

While most barriers and bollards have traditional push-button operating systems, some now include flat-screen monitors with touch-screen buttons. Operators can view graphic representations of the actions being commanded, with colors representing closed or open positions.

For areas where hydraulics and the trenching and installation of electrical wiring are impractical, one bollard model runs on a city's water supply. Approximately 60–90 psi will lift the 750-pound bollard — the only byproduct is water.

Sometimes security is needed on the water, as well. One manufacturer is perfecting a water-borne barrier. Two buoys connected with chains and a 1-inch stainless steel cable can stop a 21-ft. boat from approaching a dam or other sensitive area.

Another manufacturer has designed electromechanical versions of bollards and crash gates, as electromechanical operating systems are more suitable and safer for high-

Terror on Trial

Vehicle anti-terrorism devices become most important, perhaps, when the formidable institution of terrorism itself is being challenged.

When the federal case of the United States vs. Osama bin Laden was slated to begin in New York City's Daniel Patrick Moynahan U.S. Courthouse and the old Foley Square U.S. Courthouse in Feb. 2001, construction crews hastened to install a safe perimeter around the courthouses. Safety was of the highest priority and concern: bin Laden's alleged followers were on trial for the 1998 bombings of the U.S. embassies in Kenya and Tanzania that killed 224 people.

In the two months preceding the trial, barriers and bollards were installed, cordoning off the entire block housing the two courthouses.

Hydraulically-operated barricades, manufactured by Valencia, Calif.–based Delta Scientific Corp., blocked each end of the street.

Designed to stop a 7.5-ton truck moving at 80 mph, the thick steel plates would pop out of the ground within 1.5 seconds during an emergency. The barriers were accompanied by bulletproof guard booths.

A series of Delta bollards also guarded the front of the U.S. courthouse. The bollards were designed to destroy the front suspension, steering linkage, engine crankcase and portions of the drive train of any 15,000-pound non-armored vehicle that collided with them at 62 mph. The bollards were also intended to stop a 15-ton vehicle traveling at 44 mph, raising and lowering into the ground in one second.

Hours before the trials began each day, the bollards and barriers were raised to create a secure area. Cameras and ground surveillance contributed to the overall security precautions.

Crash Ratings

Government agencies, and the companies who contract with them, typically use products certified in approved labs.

As the State Department's crash rating system is the most widely used, manufacturers will often explain the capabilities of their products using the following ratings.

A K4-rated barrier can stop a 15,000-lb. vehicle traveling at 30 mph.

A K8-rated barrier will stop the same vehicle going 40 mph, and K12 refers to 50 mph.

Ratings of L1 through L3 describe the distance any part of the vehicle will travel past the barrier upon impact.

(For instance, L3 means that the vehicle or major components of a vehicle will travel no more than three feet after striking the barrier.)

traffic areas such as public or commercial facilities. While many hydraulic units must be housed close to the barriers they operate, an electromechanical power unit can be positioned in a closet 1,000 feet away.

While the options may seem endless, the goal remains the same. With unauthorized vehicle deterrence systems in place, security professionals are once again backed by technology in their pursuit of safety.

Research Contributors

The following people and companies were helpful in explaining the technologies described in this chapter:

David Dickinson, senior vice president, Delta Scientific Corp., Valencia, Calif. Delta Scientific manufactures vehicle barricades, parking control equipment and guard booths.

Mark Perkins, national sales manager, Automatic Control Systems, Port Washington, N.Y. The Automatic Systems Group manufactures pedestrian and vehicle access control devices, including six models of electromechanical vehicle barriers.

Scott Rosenbloom, vice-president, ARMR Services Corp., Fairfax, Va. ARMR Services Corp. manufactures crash-rated vehicle barriers and parking control equipment.

Paul Schumacher, sales manager, Petersen Manufacturing Co., Denison, Iowa. Petersen Mfg. manufactures fixed bollards and planters in a variety of shapes and sizes.

John Scolaro, international sales director, Nasatka Barrier, Clinton, Md. Nasatka Barrier specializes in vehicle access control barriers.

R. Shelton Vandiver, product manager, bollards and barriers, Norshield Security Products, Montgomery, Ala. Norshield Security Products manufactures bullet-resistant doors, windows and enclosures, and vehicle access control barriers.

CHAPTER 40

Washington, DC, Stimulates Development by Linking Its Suburbs to the Inner City with Public Mass Transit

Libby Howland

Development markets on the east side of downtown Washington are picking up steam. The opening in December of the MCI Center, the new multipurpose sports and entertainment arena, and the launching of a downtown business improvement district (BID) last summer are two examples of this trend. Mixed-use developments, destination entertainment attractions, and centralized management are the leitmotifs of the area's resurgence.

Though commercial real estate brokers may refer to the 120-block area — roughly bounded by 15th Street, Massachusetts Avenue, 2nd Street, and Constitution Avenue — as the East End, other real estate and civic interests are calling it Washington's "new downtown." Most of the office development now taking place in the District of Columbia is occurring here, where the vacancy rate for Class A space stands at around 6 percent and average Class A rents — at almost $37 per square foot — are high.

Metrorail subway access was a main reason cited by Abe Pollin, owner of the Wizards basketball team and the Capitals hockey team, for choosing a downtown Washington location for the $200 million, 1 million-square-foot state-of-the-art arena and destination retail/entertainment complex that many say already has sparked the revival of its down-at-the-heels neighborhood. The MCI Center is built over the Gallery Place — Chinatown Metro station, through which three lines pass — a situation that complicated construction — and it is near four other Metro stations.

According to Pollin, 70 percent of fans in the first weeks of the MCI Center arrived by Metro. Attendance at Wizards games was strong in the five weeks following the arena's opening but less so at Capitals games; however, Capitals games were not selling well earlier in the season when they were held at the US Airways Arena in suburban Landover, Maryland. Seating capacity is close to 20,000

Originally published as "Resurgence in Downtown Washington," *Urban Land*, Vol. 57, No. 3, March 1998. Published by the Urban Land Institute, Washington, D.C. Reprinted with permission of the publisher.

for basketball games and slightly less for hockey. Approximately 100 Wizards, Capitals, and Georgetown University Hoyas games are scheduled annually, and it is expected that another 170 concerts and other events will be booked each year.

Crews can accomplish changeovers from one sport to another or to other events in a matter of hours by taking up or installing floors that fit over the ice and rearranging the retractable seats. Also providing flexibility for quick transitions are ample equipment storage and staging areas, truck and bus access to the building interior, and an extensive backstage area that contains dressing rooms for performers, a special superstar suite, locker rooms, a fitness room, a family lounge for players' relatives, and production offices.

In some corporate circles, access to professional sports facilities increasingly is considered an amenity. The MCI Center therefore should have some influence on the market for office development in the neighborhood, and corporations should provide a primary market for the arena's luxury suite and club seat sales. The arena has 110 private suites, which are located at the 19th, 25th, and 31st rows and cost $100,000 to $175,000 a year, with minimum five-year leases. They are well appointed, with 12 theater-style seats, televisions, private restrooms, phones, wet bars, and refrigerators. Associated services include catering, underground parking, and access to a full-service business center that is still under development. Another 3,045 extrawide club seats are located between rows 20 and 31, and their ticket holders enjoy access to the Capital Club, a full-service restaurant and lounge; in-seat food service; specialty food concessions; and the business services center. The Capital Club is open to the public for private events. The arena's premium-seating food services are operated by Chicago-based Levy Restaurants.

Perhaps the most unusual aspect of the new MCI Center is its operation as a destination retail/entertainment complex. Plans call for the center to remain open from 9:00 A.M. to 11:00 P.M. daily for nonarena uses. Among the attractions are Discovery Channel's Destination: DC, the National Sports Gallery, the Velocity Grill, and Modell's Sporting Goods Team Store:

- Destination: DC, Discovery Channel's flagship store, is a 30,000-square-foot, $20 million interactive multimedia complex that opened early this month. Owned by the Bethesda, Maryland–based cable television network, the Discovery Channel store is expected to attract a million customers during its first year. Aptly tagged a cross between a museum and an entertainment center, the store features four themed floors where visitors "explore the universe" through Discovery Channel exhibits — and retail items — in paleo world (level 1), including a 42-foot cast of a Tyrannosaurus Rex skeleton; ocean planet (mezzanine); world cultures and animal habitats (level 2); and outer space (level 3). A state-of-the-art, high-definition theater is on the top level.
- Velocity Grill, a 20,000-square-foot, upscale sports-theme restaurant on three levels, can be entered from the street or from the arena's main and club concourses. It overlooks the Wizards' practice court, which also is used by local recreational basketball leagues. It features on-site video production capabilities and ubiquitous television screens and video monitors.
- The National Sports Gallery — codeveloped by Team Works-Sports Consulting Group, the American Sportscasters Association, and the MCI Center — is a 25,000-square-foot sports museum and participatory activities zone. It houses the American Sportscasters Association Hall of Fame and also showcases treasured sports memorabilia. Among the activities that can be enjoyed there are pitching to on-screen major league hitters, putting at the 18th hole of the MCI Heritage Classic in Hilton Head,

or tossing the football to onscreen receivers at rookie training camp.

• The 2,500-square-foot Modell's Sporting Goods Team Store features a full line of NBA, NHL, MLB, and NFL team apparel and merchandise, as well as 12 television monitors that show satellite transmissions of on-the-road Wizards and Capitals games and other sporting events.

Another draw for visitors is a behind-the-scenes, one-hour tour offered throughout the day for groups and individuals. Tour stops include team locker rooms; star dressing room; the television control room; the Zamboni ice resurfacing machine; a luxury suite; and *An Insider's View*— a film about the nation's capital that is shown at Destination: DC's theater.

The MCI Center features a number of other advanced technology applications. A high-speed fiber-optic network called arena Net provides tenants with Internet access, intranet capability, LAN/WAN systems, E-mail, and point-of-sales and office systems support. Seventeen interactive arena Net stations around the facility provide visitors with local tourist and MCI Center events information and also entertain them with features such as replays of great moments in sports history or digital postcards in which they appear in scenes with star athletes. A 15-ton suspended scoreboard with 12-by-16-foot video screens using LED (light-emitting diode) technology provides spectators with bright, clear images of the action on the event floor.

One clear impact that the MCI Center already has had is on development activity in Chinatown, a small area north of the arena. After years of what many consider a stagnant existence, Chinatown, with its restaurants and small shops, has become what many characterize as a boom town. Few regret the loss of some of its Chinese character as a price of transformation, although some Chinese residents and business owners fear that the area may change and drive some of them out of business as a result of high rents, huge crowds, and increasing traffic.

Downtown DC BID

Efforts to establish a downtown business improvement district began in the late 1980s, and in 1996 enabling legislation was passed. The imminent arrival of the arena provided the final push, according to Richard Bradley, the BID's executive director. Part of a burgeoning national trend, Washington's downtown BID was approved by the city last August and became operational shortly thereafter.

Directly north of the Mall, Washington's primary tourist draw, the downtown BID encompasses an area that contains 67 million square feet of office space. Fifty million square feet is in private ownership; 14 million square feet belongs to the government; and 3 million square feet is owned by tax-exempt organizations. There are 6,500 hotel rooms, and a slowly growing residential sector. All Metro subway lines serve the area.

More than a dozen new restaurants opened last year, and more are in the pipeline. Major attractions in the area include a number of theaters — National Theatre, Ford's Theatre, Shakespeare Theatre, and Warner Theatre; museums, among them the Museum of American Art, National Building Museum, National Museum of Women in the Arts, and National Portrait Gallery; a concentration of art galleries; the J. Edgar Hoover FBI Building; the Washington Convention Center; and now the MCI Center. The Washington Opera also has tentative plans to build an opera house in the new downtown area, possibly converting the vacant Woodward & Lothrop department store on F Street.

In addition, the city plans to construct a new, 2 million-square-foot, $650 million convention center on the north edge of downtown at Mount Vernon Square along New York Avenue by the year 2001. A consortium of developers has put forth a proposal to redevelop the city's current 800,000-square-foot convention center — built 15 years ago and already seen as too small to meet current demand — as an "American entertainment center" containing restaurants, retail venues, and up to 20 movie screens. The location is just three blocks away from the MCI Center.

A recently announced office project speaks to the entertainment focus of new development in the downtown district. The U.S. Mint has signed a 20-year lease with Development Resources Inc. (DRI) for a 232,000-square-foot building that DRI will develop at 801 9th Street. It is scheduled for completion at the end of next year and will occupy 140,000 square feet and lease out the remaining space. The agency is contemplating retail and entertainment uses for the first-floor space, including a historical exhibit about the U.S. Mint.

The downtown BID is a private non-profit corporation that is run by and accountable to the area's business sector. Its stated purpose is to stabilize and improve the district's environment; retain, expand, and attract businesses and investment; and create a positive identity for the downtown. The BID's organizing effort was overseen by a coalition of area property owners, business owners, and civic and cultural organizations led by Robert Gladstone, president of Quadrangle Development and of the BID planning committee, and by Robert Carr, chairman of Carr Real Estate Development Corporation and the committee's vice president. Its business plan includes six main elements:

Public Safety. Uniformed, unarmed public safety officers have begun patrolling the area as adjuncts to regular metropolitan police patrols. They monitor street activity, provide security escorts and assistance in personal emergencies, and give directions. Together with special street and sidewalk maintenance personnel, they are known as downtown SAM (safety and maintenance) personnel.

Maintenance. Downtown SAM personnel also provide street and sidewalk cleaning services, remove graffiti, maintain street furniture and signs, and provide landscaping services.

Transportation. The BID works with other organizations to improve the district's accessibility by all modes of transportation and to improve directional signage and maps and other visitor guides. Some effort will be made to persuade Metro to extend its operating hours past midnight, especially on weekends.

Marketing. The BID is undertaking a campaign to market downtown Washington to a variety of target audiences and plans to work with local businesses to support activities to bring people downtown.

Physical Improvements. The BID plans to work with the city to implement a multiyear physical improvements program involving street lights, signage, street furniture and landscaping, and visitor-attracting uses like sidewalk cafés.

Homeless Services. Downtown SAM personnel seek to provide helpful information to homeless individuals in the area and to homeless service providers. The BID helps coordinate communication among the providers and works to find support programs for the homeless, including employment in the SAM force.

The downtown BID's budget for its first full year of normalized operations is $7.7 million, distributed as follows:

Security Programs	$2,400,000
Maintenance Programs	1,340,000
Transportation Programs	270,000
Marketing	910,000
Physical Improvements	1,150,000
Homeless Programs	340,000
BID Operations, including program overhead	1,000,000
Contingency (4 percent)	290,000

Its funds come from a BID assessment on taxable commercial real properties within the BID area and from voluntary contributions and contracts for services from tax-exempt properties. First-year assessments are $50 per room for hotels and $0.12 per square foot on net rentable square footage (calculated as 90 percent of gross building area for properties for which net rentable area is not available) and on unimproved land and parking lots. The first-year budget of $7.7 million is expected to be raised from the BID assessment ($6.1 million from 51 million square feet of commercial space); an anticipated contract with the U.S. General Services Administration to sell BID services to government-owned properties in the BID area ($1.2 million); and voluntary contributions from tax-exempt properties ($400,000).

Proceeding by fits and starts, the resurgence of Washington's new downtown has been a long time in the making. With the coming of the MCI Center, the downtown appears to have chosen mixed-use development with an emphasis on entertainment to propel itself into the future.

CHAPTER 41

West Palm Beach Redesigns Its Downtown to Focus on People Rather Than Cars

Steven Lagerfeld

Shopping with Robert Gibbs is like being shown around a museum of retailing by an eccentric curator. He mutters frequently, counting under his breath and pointing vaguely at store windows. He expounds enthusiastically upon foot-candles and price-point-to-aperture ratios. He is cast into gloom by what he calls internally illuminated signs.

Gibbs has the sort of occupation Anne Tyler might invent for a character in one of her novels. He is a retail consultant who travels the country telling towns and small cities how to survive and prosper by learning the lessons of a shopping mall. Trained as a landscape architect at the University of Michigan at Ann Arbor, Gibbs worked for a dozen years as a retailing specialist in the service of strip-shopping-center and shopping-mall developers, studying, debating, and adjusting virtually everything that might affect a shopper's mood in the marketplace, from color schemes to the location of escalators. In a well-run mall, Gibbs says, even the benches are positioned so that the shopper at rest cannot help gazing at the wares offered in store windows. The overriding imperative is to lose no opportunity, no matter how small, to make a sale.

Gibbs walks down Clematis Street, the main shopping street in West Palm Beach, Florida, as if he were navigating a maze, seeming utterly distracted even as he searches intently for clues to the street's secrets. At forty he still has something of a smirking manner of the high school wise guy. But on Clematis Street he is all business.

Gibbs is impressed that most of the trash cans and newspaper vending machines have been painted the same dark green, a fashionable hue now used in many malls. Even a pair of two-by-fours supporting a tree have been painted. "A little detail you would expect in mall management," Gibbs says approvingly.

At the corner of Clematis and Dixie Highway, one of the main intersections in town, a new gym has opened, its large plate-glass windows displaying its clientele to passing pedestrians and motorists. The gym is what Gibbs calls a "generator": the traffic it draws will help attract related businesses,

Originally published as "What Main Street Can Learn from the Mall," *The Atlantic*, Vol. 276, No. 5, November 1997. Published by The Atlantic Monthly Company, Boston, MA. Reprinted with permission of the author.

such as restaurants, fast-food outlets, perhaps sporting-goods store, to the empty storefronts nearby.

The gym is also a brilliant piece of street theater, telling all who pass its windows that West Palm is young, hip, and attractive. It is not here by accident. Borrowing a page from shopping-mall management, the city's Downtown Development Authority and the City Center Partnership, an allied local non-profit organization, have used loans and other incentives to manipulate the "tenant mix." They worked for four years to lure the gym to this important location. The DDA is a significant advantage to West Palm Beach, as is the energetic mayor, Nancy M. Graham. The city has attracted several plum projects in recent years, including a massive new county courthouse. In 1992 the city council approved a $12 million bond issue to renovate the downtown district. Other money was appropriated to convert Clematis from a one-way into a two-way street and to install new sidewalks, lights, and palm trees.

Half a block east of the gym, at 331 Clematis, Provident Jewelry and Loan offers more evidence of the city's ability to shape the street. A pawnshop that once lent a vaguely disreputable air to the neighborhood, Provident has been transformed with the aid of loans from the City Center Partnership. With a fresh coat of paint, a dapper awning, and a prim new sign that doesn't shout "pawnshop," it has become an upright citizen and an asset to Clematis Street. The Imperial Gallery, a frame shop, and The Last Resort, a Generation X clothing store, both opened up with loans and other help.

Elsewhere on Clematis a large old building is being carved up into smaller stores. To lend their operations a bit of local flavor, well-managed malls often create tiny low-rent spaces called "incubators" and recruit local entrepreneurs to set up shop; some of them will thrive and open bigger stores. West Palm Beach is doing the same thing.

There are reasons to be hopeful about West Palm Beach, and about other towns and cities that are willing to borrow intelligently from the lessons of the mall. For the first time in decades strong trends in the national retail market seem to be working in their favor. A reaction is setting in against the monotony and homogeneity of the shopping mall. People are spending less time in malls — an average of only an hour and a half to two hours a month this year, according to one source, as compared with three and a half hours a month in 1990 — and few new malls are being built. Only four new regional malls (800,000 square feet or larger) opened in the United States last year, as compared with twenty-seven in 1989.

Part of the explanation for this change is simply that suburban markets have become saturated, and part is that strip shopping centers, "big-box" retailers, and "power centers" that bring high-volume discounters together in one location are drawing customers away from the malls. But mall fatigue is a potent factor. In focus groups people tell Gibbs that they are tired of shopping in malls filled with the same stores that they can find everywhere else in the country. Many say they want to shop in downtowns, in quaint, one-of-a-kind stores. Gibbs does not have a monopoly on this intelligence. Retailers are already responding. Nordstrom has recently agreed to open a store in downtown Norfolk, Virginia. Even major discount retailers like Caldor and Kmart are feeling the lure of downtown markets. Kmart plans to open a store in Manhattan next year, in the historic Herald Square shopping district. "Signs of an urban boom can be found almost everywhere," the trade publication *Shopping Centers Today* reported last fall.

Gibbs came to West Palm Beach, a city of more than 70,000, two years ago, to work on a new master plan for the city with Andres Duany and Elizabeth Plater-Zyberk, the Miami-based pioneers of the New Urbanism. This small but influential movement among architects and urban planners proposes to revive nineteenth-century town-planning principles, using denser development and gridded street systems, among other things, as an antidote to suburban sprawl. Duany and Plater-Zyberk's greatest success so far has been the much-publicized new town of Seaside, a resort community in the Florida panhandle. But Gibbs's enthusiasm for the New Urbanist cause and for downtowns in general doesn't stop him from working for the occasional shopping-mall company that seeks his services. And his own office, with its small staff, is located not in a gritty city but in the genteel town of Birmingham, Michigan, an affluent Detroit suburb.

What Gibbs contributes to complex cooperative projects like the one in West Palm Beach is a commercial sensibility unlike anything possessed by the urban planners and architects who usually design downtown-renewal efforts. Addressing audiences of such specialists, Gibbs takes a puckish delight in shocking them all with his view on conventional urban planning. He shows them slides of a generic "success" in street design and then points out, feature by feature, how the design actually hurts the town's businesses.

The shade trees and planter boxes? Lovely, he says, but they block shoppers' view of shop windows and signs. Those handsome groupings of benches and tables? They seem inviting until Gibbs points out that they often attract teenagers and other loiterers, who scare off shoppers. The elegant Victorian streetlamps, the expensive trash cans, and the distinctive granite paving stones — "so beautiful that people will stare at them as they walk by the storefronts," Gibbs says — are little more than money down the drain. Their costs must be amortized over many years, but long before they have been paid off (and before the town can afford to replace them) they will be old-fashioned, marking the entire street as out of date and out of step.

Gibbs sometimes clinches an argument by showing his audience slides of some of the world's most opulent shopping streets, including Palm Beach's Worth Avenue, which happens to be located about a mile (and a world) away from Clematis Street. The Worth Avenue slide reveals a pleasant but extremely plain street. It is lined with a row of palms and simple light poles. Its sidewalks, conspicuously, are mere concrete.

As Gibbs and I traverse Clematis Street over the course of two days, he pauses time and again to consider the textured sidewalk paving blocks that have been installed since his last visit. There is no question that they are attractive. But are they too porous to keep clean? Too fancy?

This is not the kind of question that planners and architects often ask themselves. They tend to see streets and sidewalks strictly as a civic realm, a social environment where people meet and interact, and they tend to favor the sorts of attractive sidewalks and streetscapes that seem to promote sociability. If they are not greatly concerned about the impact of their work on the welfare of haberdashers and stationers, that is not surprising. They belong to professions that are often at war with commercial interests.

Gibbs sees the street first as a commercial space. Nourish commerce, his implicit credo goes, and the people will come. A dirty street, a sidewalk spotted with old chewing gum and grime, is a turnoff for shoppers. And if people won't come downtown to shop, there simply won't be a civic realm.

Fear of crime is one of the things that keeps them away, and grimy sidewalks are one of many signs that hint at disorder, in Gibbs's view. Standing outside the gym at the corner of Clematis and Dixie Highway, he discourses at length on an untidy collection of benches, tables, and chairs outside a café across the highway. This is civic space only in theory. In fact it poses a threat to civic existence. "Those benches make it look like this is a very difficult place to walk," he says, putting himself in the shoes of the average (that is, female) shopper. "You've got to squeeze between those benches. And if a teenager or some street person happens to be there, you would have to touch them, because you're so close together. That is like a sign saying DON'T ENTER."

Ironically, one of the forces working in favor of downtowns today is the erosion of the shopping malls' image as a safe haven from crime. Only a few years ago, Gibbs reminds me, it was rare to see uniformed security officers in malls, because the mere sight of a uniform was thought to be unsettling to shoppers. Today uniforms guards seem reassuring, and they can be seen in malls everywhere. Even janitors are equipped with thick, military-style belts and walkie-talkies. Parking lots are patrolled by security vehicles that proclaim their presence with roof-mounted flashing lights. The Palm Beach Mall, just a few miles from Clematis Street, is so notorious locally as a dangerous place that all pretenses have been abandoned: the parking lot is studded with tall observation towers, making it resemble nothing so much as a prison yard.

Towns, Gibbs insists, must follow the malls' example in dealing with the public's fears. That means ensuring a visible police presence, removing or rearranging benches and other features that encourage loitering, and keeping the streets and sidewalks clean. Mall managers, ever inventive, are now improving the lighting in their parking lots. The norm for illumination was a footcandle or less just a few years ago, Gibbs says. Now it is closer to three footcandles. Many self-service gas stations, which must offer a reassuring prospect to lure passing motorists off the road, are now lit up like Hollywood sound stages. The lighting in West Palm Beach? Three quarters to one footcandle, Gibbs estimated.

A town's retail planning, Gibbs says, should begin where a mall's does — far from the selling floors. A simple example of mall thinking is what Gibbs calls the "no-left-turn rule": Never locate a shopping center in a place where commuters will have to make a left turn to get in. People tend to shop on their way home from work, the thinking goes, and they are less likely to stop if it involves making a turn against traffic.

This is no idle observation. At one point in his career Gibbs traveled around the country as a member of a team evaluating sites for future shopping malls. Gibbs recalls that the opinion of the traffic consultant mattered most. He vetoed so many sites that he was called The Terminator.

There is a corollary for towns and strip shopping centers: coffee shops and doughnut stores ought to be located on the workbound side of a main road, grocery stores and other services on the homebound side. "Just one left turn will kill you," Gibbs says.

Mall merchandising begins in the parking lot. Gibbs points out that at the Gardens of the Palm Beaches, an upscale mall several miles from West Palm Beach, the plantings around the building and parking lots, with their lush, tightly trimmed shrubs, seem to suggest that shoppers are arriving at a special place, and that perhaps they are special as well. It's almost like having a doorman. It's certainly a far cry from the feeling one gets in the rundown West Palm Beach parking lot where Gibbs and I parked.

Once, guiding me into a lavish urban mall called Georgetown Park in Washington, D.C., Gibbs was able to predict which way I would turn upon entering. Most casual shoppers who are not immediately bound for a specific store — which is to say most shoppers — travel counterclockwise. Nobody knows why, though it's reasonable to suppose that driving on the right-hand side of the road has something to do with it. A good mall designer will take special care to ensure that entering shoppers have a powerful unobstructed vista of storefronts to their right. Rarely will that vista run the length of the mall, however. It is a cardinal rule to keep shoppers' eyes on the merchandise at all times. Designers try to configure malls with enough twists and turns that the shopper looking ahead is constantly looking toward a wall of storefronts. Gibbs is so convinced of the importance of what he calls the "deflected view" that in laying out the main shopping street of a small new development in Novi, Michigan, he puts thirty-degree turns near its middle. Straight streets, he believes, are one of the biggest commercial handicaps in a town like West Palm Beach.

There are other rules. Clothing stores, for example, should never be located next to restaurants: for some reason the smell of food hurts clothing sales. In downtown areas clothing stores should never be located on the north side of a street: the colors of clothes displayed in a shop window with a southern exposure begin to fade within hours. Western exposures are bad for restaurants: the setting sun at dinnertime makes customers uncomfortable. Restaurants can prosper on side streets and in other less-desirable locations, because they usually do not rely heavily on drop-in business. They are destinations. Most retail stores count on drawing a lot of impulse shoppers, and thus need to be located in high-traffic areas.

Designers also know that the average shopper, strolling along at three or four feet per second, walks past a storefront in about eight seconds. That's how long a shop owner has to grab a consumer's attention with an arresting window display. Downtown merchants must live with the same eight-second rule, but they can also sell to passing motorists — and the window of opportunity for "merchandising to the car," as Gibbs puts it, is less than a second.

Sophisticated retailers use a variety of subliminal clues to attract shoppers. At Georgetown Park, Gibbs pointed out a high-priced stationery store that had created a window display featuring a small old wooden desk with a few pricey writing implements casually strewn about, including four ordinary-seeming lead pencils in a wooden box, priced at $215. The tableau, Gibbs informed me, was "lifestyling" par excellence —

focusing the shopper's attention not on the goods themselves but on attractive things associated with them. Buy these outrageously expensive pencils, the display suggested, and you will have taken one more step toward a life of tweeds and contemplation in the English countryside.

The lifestyling message was amplified by the window designer's skillful exploitation of what is called the price-point-to-aperture ratio. The appealing desk-and-pencils tableau was framed inside the window, much as a picture is positioned inside a mat in a picture frame. In retailing the size of the aperture is often used to provide shoppers with clues about what is in the store. A relatively small enclosed space suggests high quality and prices to match. This is one reason why Tiffany & Co. displays its wares to passersby in tiny vaultlike spaces. Big windows and big displays generally suggest lower prices.

The Duany and Plater-Zyberk plan for West Palm Beach calls for a revitalized downtown core and also thousands of units of new housing in the surrounding area, now a depressing jumble of empty lots, old buildings, and gas stations. The dimensions of the challenge facing the city became clear to me after I drove through the area for the first time on heavily traveled Dixie Highway: I sped through the intersection with Clematis without realizing that it was the heart of downtown West Palm Beach, not just another cross street in the area's endless grid of semi-urban sprawl.

In the past the neglect of commerce by planners and architects was compounded by an inability to cope with the automobile. The car has generally been treated as an enemy, with disastrous results for downtown commerce. During the 1960s and 1970s, for example, there was a great vogue in planning circles for banning cars from downtown streets and creating pedestrian malls. The experiment was disastrous. Many downtown malls have since been ripped up, and the streets rebuilt for automotive traffic.

Surveying a small parking lot just off Clematis, Gibbs says that a conventional urban planner would waste no time converting it into a park, with benches, trees, and perhaps a fountain. "The shoppers will be happier if they have a place to sit and watch the fountain," he says, in disdainful deadpan imitation of a hypothetical planner's argument. In Gibbs's view, the problem is that people won't stop, park their cars, and get out to visit such a park. And if they don't do that, the merchants of West Palm Beach won't have an opportunity to sell them anything.

Slowly, however, towns are coming to grips with the car. At the intersection of Clematis and El Campeon Boulevard, Gibbs can barely make himself heard over the roar of heavy machinery. Even before he and his colleagues were called in to help draw up the new master plan, city officials had decided to reroute the traffic that flows over one of the Palm Beach bridges and around the outskirts of town onto an extended and widened El Campeon, recently renamed Quadrille. The goal, virtually unheard of in late-twentieth-century America, is to pump more cars into the downtown.

For Gibbs's purposes, not just any kind of traffic will do. Just east of that intersection Clematis Street is bisected by U.S. 1— which is actually two one-way roads when it passes through West Palm Beach. Cars and trucks speed by, creating a forbidding double moat that slashes through Clematis and discourages pedestrians from walking the length of the street.

The city's new master plan calls for a radical alteration of the traffic pattern. Both branches of U.S. 1 will be converted into two-way roads, with on-street parking, one lane in each direction, and a turning lane. Instead of flowing through town as quickly as water, traffic will slow to the speed of syrup. The idea is to transform this soulless thoroughfare into a vital city street.

As Gibbs sees it, Clematis Street is fighting the same problem that a lot of other American main streets are: it doesn't have a purpose anymore. During the 1920s it connected the train station, on the west end of town, with the ferry to Palm Beach, on the east end. But after two bridges, on either side of town, began funneling traffic around Clematis, its fate was sealed. The Woolworth's, the McCrory's, and the Sears, Roebuck all continued to prosper for a while, but business inevitably followed the cars.

Historians analyzing the decline of America's towns and cities after the Second World War usually put most of the responsibility on the federal government's head. The interstate highway system and federal mortgage subsidies for single-family homes spurred suburban growth, the argument goes, and doomed the downtowns. In Gibbs's version of urban history, based on his travels, another force looms large: the highway bypass. As the number of cars on the road soared after the war, town merchants and residents sought relief from traffic-clogged streets. Their demands coincided with the interests of the state and highway departments and traffic engineers, who wanted to keep building roads and whose highest professional goal was the unimpeded flow of cars. Routing highway traffic around the outskirts of town must have seemed the obvious thing to do. The downtowns thus unwittingly initiated their own march to a commercial grave.

Retailers flock to what Gibbs and other retailing specialists call a "main-main" intersection — the place where the two most heavily traveled roads in an area meet. Historically, towns grew up around main-mains. In one town after another across the country, the opening of a new bypass created a new main-main outside town. There, beginning in the 1950s, strip shopping centers began sprouting. Then came the interstate highways, creating where they crossed state highways or other interstates a new set of main-mains still farther from the old downtowns.

It is usually at these new crossroads that one finds large regional shopping malls today.

Standing on the south side of Clematis under a hot Florida sun, Gibbs launches into an impassioned diagnosis — almost an autopsy — of a men's clothing store on the other side of the street, at No. 335. This touches on the matters that seem closest to his heart. Minutes before, he dragged me into the store almost against my will. Housed in an eight-year-old two-story building painted the color of putty, the store features a large blue umbrella awning overhung by a large internally illuminated white-plastic sign. The store's name appears in big letters of washed-out blue over the tag line MEN'S WEAR — SHOES. The sign seems to date from the 1950s or 1960s.

Inside, the store was everything I had feared — small, cramped, dark, and, in more ways than one, stuffy. Shoes and sport coats were displayed in closed glass case, and the store was dominated by a counter with cash register in the middle of the floor. The proprietor seemed to watch us suspiciously.

On the sidewalk Gibbs is almost angry. "You wouldn't have gone in there if I hadn't made you," he declares, "but he sells a lot of what you wear." He reels off a list of brand names he spotted in his expert visual frisking of the store: Corbin, Cole Haan, Allen-Edmonds, Bass, Sperry Top-Sider. These are "very fine names," Gibbs says, the kinds of brands that would interest affluent locals and tourists (not to mention visiting retail consultants and writers). But the store offers passersby barely a clue about what it has for sale.

Its most prominent signs should promote the brand names it carries, Gibbs says, to take advantage of the millions of dollars that big companies spend on advertising to shape perceptions of their products. And what would be good for this store would be good for West Palm Beach.

"People will see 'Cole Haan' and they will drive off the road," Gibbs explains.

"They will say, 'I thought this was a dumpy area. If they sell Cole Haan, they can't be that bad.'"

The store could give itself an even bigger lift, according to Gibbs, by making use of a few rudimentary lifestyling gestures. To hear him tell it, lifestyling is the late-twentieth-century equivalent of the barber pole, announcing to shoppers what's for sale. It is ubiquitous in the mall but virtually nonexistent on Clematis Street and other American main streets. Its vocabulary is easily acquired. Simply placing a canoe paddle or a bicycle in the window of the men's store, Gibbs says, would telegraph several messages to passing shoppers, including the vital (and correct) information that it is selling clothes that fit what Gibbs classifies as "the L.L. Bean look."

Down the street, at Mac Fabrics, we count seven signs with the store's name on them, and none displaying brand names. "Brands are what give you credibility," Gibbs says. If he had his way, signs advertising brand names would hang from the imitation-antique light poles that line the street.

This, obviously, is not a sentimental view of the American town. Gibbs is not proposing to restore the cozy village of the popular imagination. Nor does he think that the town will ever eradicate the malls, Wal-Marts, power centers, and other commercial innovations of American retailing. The American shopper's expectations have by now been completely conditioned by malls and national advertisers. The shopper wants, at the very least, much more choice than the traditional town ever provided.

The same people who tell Gibbs in focus groups that they are tired of malls complain that many small towns are, well, too small. Why drive half an hour to browse through only a handful of stores? Gibbs's rule of thumb is that a town needs at least 200,000 square feet of retail space, about the same amount as in a small mall, to become what retailers call a destination — a place that people are willing to travel to.

And once they get to their destination, people don't really want to stop in old-fashioned small-town stores. Americans, in their time-honored way, want a variety of often contradictory things. They may like quaint, one-of-a-kind stores that seem to sell unique merchandise, but they also want the comfort and security of national brand names on the goods they buy, and they don't want to pay a lot for them.

Mall operators and national retailers are moving quickly to give people what they want, and Gibbs's message is that towns must do so too if they wish to survive and prosper. That still leaves plenty of room for individuality. Each town must build on its unique strengths and its unique markets. What can't be escaped, however, is the need for a conscious strategy for commercial survival.

Gibbs's prescriptions for the streets of West Palm Beach and of other American towns and small cities borrow so heavily from the mall that it becomes difficult to see how, except for the absence of a roof over its streets, a place reconstructed along such lines would differ from a mall. It might be a town, but would it be a community?

When I ask him about this, Gibbs just shrugs his shoulders. He is not a philosopher-king. He does not pretend to know how to deliver an active civic life and a sense of community, but he believes that these things are impossible without a vital commercial life. That is something that he *can* help deliver.

He is not particularly worried that his prescriptions will lead to the homogenization of Main Street. The mall is a machine for shopping. In contrast, the pieces of the downtown shopping machine lie about unassembled, and in all likelihood they will never be put together in the way that they can be in a mall, with its single corporate owner. Main Street will always retain a certain redeeming randomness. But if it does not learn the ways of the shopping mall, it will not retain much economic vitality. People who care about cities, Gibbs says, should be outraged that mom-and-pop shoe-store owners renting space in a mall or a strip center enjoy the benefits of the latest thinking in retailing, while those who open for business downtown get virtually no help at all.

It is hard not to feel some trepidation about the world Robert Gibbs imagines. But it is also hard not to agree with him that commerce matters, even to the world his critics might prefer. The Greeks, after all, cherished their agora, but it was always first and foremost a place of business. It is probably true that community and civic spirit, like happiness and love, are often found when you're not looking — sometimes even when you're out shopping.

III. THE FUTURE

CHAPTER 42

The Future of Transportation

Alex Marshall

Shortly after the fall of the Soviet Union at the end of the 1980s, the political scientist Francis Fukuyama caused a sensation with an essay called "The End of History?" It postulated that, with Communism's near-demise, the struggle among rival political systems had ended with a permanent victory for democratic capitalism. All that was left to do was to refine it.

Is something similar happening with the way we get around? Has our transportation system reached "the end of history"? Will the automobile and the airplane continue to reign supreme? Or will something new come along to remake our world, as it has in the past?

The context for these questions is this: Since about 1800, revolutionary changes in our transportation systems have created new types of cities, neighborhoods, and housing, while leaving old ones to wither away, or become antiques.

If history is an indication, we are due for another revolution. The car and the highway, and the airplane and airport, have been dominant for almost a century. By comparison, canals lasted about 50 years, streetcars about the same, and railroads about a century as dominant modes of travel.

Yet some people say the automobile and

the highway are so imbedded in our landscape and lifestyles that nothing will ever challenge them. In effect, they say we have reached the end of the historical road.

"It's hard to imagine a fundamental change because the automobile system is so flexible," says urban historian Robert Fishman, author of the 1989 history of suburbia, *Bourgeois Utopias*, and a professor at the University of Michigan at Ann Arbor. "All I can imagine is a better balance with a revival of the train and transit connections that have been so shamefully neglected."

That doesn't mean that change won't come, just that we may not know it until it is upon us. Fishman recalls the scholar who, around 1900, predicted that the automobile would never go far because it couldn't match the utility of the bicycle.

Hovering over this discussion is a single word: sprawl. Our car-clogged environment is the product of our transportation system. Highways and airports produce low-density sprawl.

Decades ago, streetcars and subways made cities denser by attracting housing and businesses. Will the changes that are now being promoted — from high-speed trains to personal jet packs — have the same result, en-

Originally published as "The Future of Transportation: Will the Auto and Airplane Reign Supreme?" *Planning*, Vol. 69, No. 5, May 2003. Reprinted with permission from *Planning*, copyright © 2003 by the American Planning Association, Suite 1600, 122 Michigan Avenue, Chicago, IL 60603–6107.

couraging development around new transit hubs, or will they make sprawl even worse?

The Past as Prologue

Six words summarize the history of transportation over the last two centuries: canals, railroads, streetcars, bicycles, automobiles, and airplanes. Each mode remade the economy and the landscape. Each was generally adopted only after government got behind it financially and legally.

The canal era started in earnest in 1817, when New York State sold $7 million in bonds to pay thousands of laborers to dig a 350-mile trench from Albany to Buffalo. When the Erie Canal went into service in 1825, it opened the entire Midwest to shipping and made New York the commercial hub of the New World. Other states and cities frantically dug their own channels in an unsuccessful effort to catch up.

Spurred in part by these efforts, other cities began investing in a new technology — railroads — that gradually replaced canals. The railroad created railroad cities, like Atlanta, and converted canal cities, like Chicago, into railroad cities.

Because the first tracks were often laid along the first canals, the canal cities tended to prosper even as the waterways declined in importance. Economists call this phenomenon "path dependence" (even as they debate its significance), and it still occurs. New York City is no longer dependent on the Erie Canal, but it's because of the canal that the rail lines, highways, and airports are located in and around the city.

From 1880 to 1925, when the railroads were at their peak, thousands of miles of track stretched to every corner of the country. Urban palaces like New York's Grand Central Station were built to shuttle passengers in and out of the cities. Few riders could have imagined that within their lifetime, weeds would grow along miles and miles of abandoned track.

Although the automobile dates to the 1890s, drivers were scarce until cities, towns, and states began paving roads — in part at the urging of bicyclists. The League of American Wheelmen convinced the Department of Agriculture to create the Bureau of Public Roads, forerunner of the Federal Highway Administration.

At first, railroad companies lent their political muscle to the "good roads" effort, with the idea that better highways would get rail passengers to the stations more easily. Even so, in 1922, 80 percent of U.S. roads were dirt and gravel.

After World War I, cars and later airplanes, served by publicly funded roads and airports, began to supplant the passenger rail system and its intimate companion, the streetcar. During the war, massive railroad congestion forced some freight traffic onto trucks. Soon states and the federal government began investing more in roads and airports, and less in rail service.

As urban historian Eric Monkkonen noted in his 1988 book, *America Becomes Urban*, governments and taxpayers largely paid for this country's transportation systems. New York State built the Erie Canal. Federal and state governments gave away a fifth of the nation's total land area to the railroads.

Congress, at the urging of President Dwight Eisenhower, financed the Interstate Highway System. Cities and states built airports. Even the New York City subways, although operated by private companies at first, were built with public dollars.

Each of these transportation innovations — canals, railroads, streetcars, cars, highways, and airplanes — created new ways to live and work, and thus new types of neighborhoods and cities.

The banks of Schenectady, New York, are still lined with the ornate buildings created during the heyday of the Erie Canal. The streetcar era, which lasted from the late 19th century to World War II, led to thousands of streetcar suburbs at the fringes of

19th century cities. And of course, the highway and air travel system created the current pattern of low-density sprawl that defines our built environment.

The Next Big Thing

Given this history, with one mode regularly superseding another, it would appear that we are due for a big change in how we travel, and thus in the form of our cities and towns. "Nothing really revolutionary has occurred since the Wright brothers and the combustion engine, and that's now about 100 years old," says Elliot Sander, the director of the Rudin Center for Transportation Policy and Management at New York University.

What might the next big thing be? Among the possibilities is the nifty Segway, the "gyro-scooter" that takes off in the direction it's pointed in. Or it could be the Solotrek Helicopter Backpack, which so far exists only in prototype versions. Strap it on, and the rotating blades do the work. There's also the Airboard, which hovers four inches off the ground and costs a mere $15,000. Of all these, the Segway actually seems to be living up to some of its hype.

Maybe the revolution will come in the form of small airplanes. In his 2001 book, *Free Flight: From Airline Hell to a New Age of Travel*, writer James Fallows, who is himself a pilot, foresees a future where people use small planes as they would taxis or rental cars for short flights between the thousands of small airports that now are under capacity.

High-speed Hopes

Rail is another, more likely, option. High-speed rail networks are common in Europe and Japan, and in theory they hold great promise in parts of the U.S., particularly in the Northeast, where population density is about the same as in Germany. Both German and French trains scoot along at 200 mph. Congress has come tantalizingly close

to funding a new or improved train network, and even conservatives are getting behind it.

Meanwhile, various states and coalitions of states are aggressively lobbying to create or preserve high-speed corridors, under the assumption that being in the high-speed loop will be as important as being part of the interstate system was in the 1950s.

North Carolina is creating a "sealed corridor" for high-speed rail across the state. California and Florida have both received federal grants for high-speed programs. The nine-state Midwest Regional Rail Initiative (Illinois, Indiana, Iowa, Michigan, Minnesota, Missouri, Nebraska, Ohio, and Wisconsin) is pushing for a high-speed network, with Chicago as its hub.

On the national level, Amtrak is running what might be called its "almost high-speed" service, Acela Express, in the Northeast Corridor. But Congress, which perennially discusses reorganizing or even killing Amtrak, has yet to really get behind any national rail policy, although some members are quite passionate about it.

The Buck Rogers version of high-speed rail, a magnetic levitation train, has been around for a while, but working examples are still scarce. Demonstration models exist in Germany, Japan, and even Norfolk, Virginia, but the only real working version is in China, where Shanghai has just finished a $30 billion maglev line that reaches 250 mph and travels the 19 miles between airport and downtown in eight minutes, compared to an hour by taxi.

In theory, maglev trains, which float above the tracks on magnets, could reach a speed of up to 500 mph. And there is sign of renewed interest at home: The Federal Railroad Administration is administering a national competition for the construction of a working maglev line in the U.S.

Whether it's maglev or a Segway, the challenge in predicting radical change is that by its very nature it tends to be unforeseen.

"We're very bad at predicting those big

discontinuities," says Bruce Schaller of Schaller Consulting, a transportation firm in New York. "It's like the Internet. I remember in the early 1980s, I visited a friend at Stanford who had e-mail on the early ARPA network. I said, 'That's really cool.' But I never thought about it as something I could do."

In fact, most transportation planners are conservative in their predictions. "I would not be investing in jumbo helicopters, dirigibles, personal rapid transit systems, motorized scooters, or powered roller skates, although they sure would be fun," says Elliot Sander of the Rudin Institute.

Autophiles and Phobes

To its defenders, the automobile is irreplaceable, no matter what the predictions. If we run out of oil, they say, we can switch to hydrogen fuel cells. If gas prices skyrocket, we can buy smaller cars. If global warming increases, we can reduce emissions. And if our roads become overwhelmingly congested, we will simply build more roads.

"I don't think congestion will stop the automobile," says Jose Gomez-Ibanez, Derek Bok Professor of Urban Planning at Harvard University. "I think the solution to congestion is to spread out more. There's no doubt that we will have more mass transit in the future, but as people get richer in places like China, are they going to want to drive, and be mobile, and maybe drive SUVs? The answer is yes."

"The automobile will continue to be the dominant mode of getting around," says Mark Kuliewicz, traffic engineer for the American Automobile Association in New York. "Cars may be powered by something other than gasoline, and hopefully soon, but they'll still be there."

But auto travel is dependent on roads. And an increasing number of critics believe that the expanding highway universe — what historian Kenneth Jackson has called "the big

bang of decentralization that started in the 1920s"—has about reached its limit.

Robert Yaro, president of the Regional Plan Association in New York, argued in a speech last year at the World Economic Forum that for political, financial, and practical reasons, it is becoming increasingly difficult to build more highways. More and more citizens accept the fact that we cannot build our way out of congestion and sprawl, he said.

Yaro pointed out that highway construction has drastically slowed in the tristate New York metropolitan area. From 1951 to 1974, the region's highway system added some 54 miles a year. In the last decade, it has added only four miles per year.

The message is clear, said Yaro in an interview. "I strongly believe that we've used up the capacity of our 20th century infrastructure systems, and we're going to need a heroic and visionary (and expensive) set of new investments to create capacity for growth in the 21st century."

A key investment, he says, would be "new or significantly upgraded intercity rail systems in the half-dozen metropolitan corridors where high-speed rail makes sense." Yaro is essentially endorsing some version of the high-speed or improved rail networks described above.

Smart Roads

Most experts foresee increasing use of high-tech or "smart" technology to wrest more capacity from overloaded roads. In its more elaborate forms, smart technology includes things like imbedding highways with magnets, which would pull cars and trucks along at 100 mph and stop them when needed.

It also includes self-braking cars; geographic positioning systems that allow drivers (or their cars) to maneuver around traffic jams; and computer chips and scanners that enable governments to price highways and charge drivers for using them, with different rates for different times.

The latter, usually called congestion pricing, is the Holy Grail of transportation specialists. Although once considered politically impossible, the idea of paying for using roads may now be acceptable to a public searching for a way out of congestion — even if it means ending one of the last arenas of egalitarianism, the highway.

Highway space "is a scarce resource, and if it is scarce, we have to manage it. In a market economy, this means pricing," says Sigurd Grava, professor of urban planning at Columbia University, and author of the new book, *Urban Transportation Systems: Choices for Community.*

"This will be the first time we will manage the use of the public right or way. In the past, anyone has been able to walk, ride a horse, or use a motor vehicle without restrictions except for traffic control. But this is changing," says Grava.

By definition, congestion pricing would eliminate traffic jams on any highway or road in the country. But at what price? In a federal experiment on Interstate 15 in San Diego, drivers paid as much as $8 during peak periods for congestion-free travel on an eight-mile stretch of highway. At less busy times, prices dropped to 50 cents.

In 2000, transportation planners with the Portland, Oregon, Metro regional government modeled how congestion pricing could change the region if used on key highways. They found that citizens would buy smaller cars, drive less, and live closer to where they worked.

With evolving computer technology, drivers could be charged for using even a neighborhood street. The British have provided an example. In March, at the instigation of Mayor Ken Livingstone, London began charging drivers to enter the center city. Automatic cameras record license plates and drivers are sent a bill. The plan has already reduced local traffic by 20 percent and won over many of its initial opponents.

Managing traffic, with "smart cars" or congestion pricing, or something else, has the potential to add substantial capacity to our road network, say many experts.

"We've doubled and tripled the number of planes in the skies in the last generation, even though very few new airports have been built," notes a federal highway official who chose to remain anonymous. "We've done it through better air traffic control." She believes that we could do the same with our roads by taking advantage of available technology.

On the Ground

Whether the future simply brings better cars, or Star Trek-like transporters, cities and towns here and abroad will change as a result.

In France, the high-speed rail network is producing new commuting patterns. For example, some Paris residents commute to Tours, a medium-sized city about 150 miles to the southwest. Train time: 58 minutes.

In Atlanta, the excessive highway building of the last few decades has produced both suburban sprawl and, paradoxically, a revival of inner-city neighborhoods as suburbanites grow weary of gridlock. In New Jersey, old railroad towns are reviving because of substantial transit investments such as the new, $450 million rail transfer station in the Meadowlands.

Looking ahead, Yaro and several others see a future in which new transit lines make suburbs all over the U.S. more like the cities. Consultant Bruce Schaller notes that for the last few years, mass transit use has increased faster than highway use, something that hasn't happened in a half-century.

Cities evolve in unexpected ways. The introduction of freeways decimated many U.S. downtowns in the 1950s, something unpredicted at the time. Photos of downtown Houston in 1960, for example, reveal many surface parking lots and a few tall buildings.

Today, tall parking garages have replaced much of the surface parking and the downtown is substantially denser. Perhaps in the future, more office buildings will replace the garages and people will take commuter rail to work. In fact, the city is already building a light rail line downtown.

We could also go the other way. If auto use continues at the same level and personal jets take off as Fallows and some others predict, sprawl is likely to increase. New homes and businesses would spring up around small airports throughout the country.

An unstable mix of government subsidies, technological promise, and private profit will determine what comes next, and this will vary from place to place. Indicators like wealth will not always offer reliable clues as to what transportation systems particular societies will adopt.

Consider the humble bicycle. It's used extensively in China, which has a very low per capita income, and in Scandinavia, which has a very high per capita income. In Copenhagen, more than a third of all commuters use bicycles. The point is that wealth alone does not adequately predict transportation use. You might say that the Chinese use bicycles because they have to, the Danish because they want to.

What Planners Can Do

For the most part, U.S. urban planners work separately from transportation planners. The average state or city planning director tends to react to transportation decisions, rather than to make them. Planners have tended to focus on zoning and land-use regulation, which is often auxiliary to the real work being done by the traffic engineers.

In a better ordered world, land planners would have responsibility for transportation planning (or supervise those who do it), and urban designers would be directly involved with state and federal highway planning.

We probably haven't reached the end of history when it comes to transportation. But whatever the future, it would be a better one if we had a broader range of choices. As a country, we have tended to lurch from one extreme to another. In the 1890s, we had the most extensive rail system in the world — and one of the worst road systems.

By the 1950s, we had abandoned our widespread streetcar system. Today, we lack a decent passenger rail system but have great highways. Like the fiberoptic cable industry and the high-tech rage, transportation has proceeded in a boom-bust fashion.

When the next big thing does come along, let's not be too quick to abandon the proven modes. The past teaches not only that change comes, but that the best societies offer a range of transportation choices, including using one's own two feet.

CHAPTER 43

Cars, Their Problems, and the Future

Marcia D. Lowe

The automobile once promised a dazzling world of speed, freedom, and nearly limitless travel. With it, the average wage-earner could have more horsepower at his or her disposal than royalty had in other times. Small wonder the world enthusiastically embraced this new form of transport. Now, though, with the world fleet approaching half a billion cars, the automobile dream has turned into a nightmare of congestion and pollution, and city governments are looking for transportation alternatives.

Perhaps more than any other invention, the automobile embodies author Jacques Ellul's observation of all technologies: it makes a good servant but a bad master. Obeying the demands of the private car has dictated the design of cities and the very character of urban life. Vast roads and parking lots distort cityscapes, and sprawling suburbs devour open space around cities. When all available surface space has been surrendered to private cars, planners turn to aerial, subterranean, and other schemes: in the Japanese city of Yokohama, entrepreneurs recently opened a floating parking lot in the local bay.

Traffic congestion, now a fact of life in the world's major cities, has stretched daily rush hours to 12 hours or longer in Seoul and 14 hours in Rio de Janeiro. The Confederation of British Industry estimates that higher freight transport costs, lost employee time, and other results of congestion cost Britain $24 billion each year.

Motor vehicles are the single largest source of air pollution, casting a pall over the world's cities. Car-induced smog aggravates bronchial and lung disorders and is often deadly to asthmatics, children, and the elderly. Ozone (a gas formed as nitrogen oxides and hydrocarbons from exhaust react with sunlight), the major component of smog, is believed to reduce soybean, cotton, and other crop yields by 5 to 10 percent. Automobiles are also a major source of carbon dioxide, the greenhouse gas responsible for over half of the global warming trend, accounting for more than 13 percent of the worldwide total.

Oil's environmental downside includes more than air pollution; while accidental spills annually dump an estimated 2.9 million barrels into the sea, roughly six times more oil gets into the oceans simply through routine flushing of carrier tanks, runoff from

Originally published as "Out of the Car, Into the Future," *World Watch*, Vol. 3, No. 6, November/December 1990. Published by the Worldwatch Institute, www.worldwatch.org. Reprinted with permission of the publisher.

streets, and other everyday consequences of motor vehicle use.

The economic vulnerability of car-dependent societies becomes painfully evident in the event of an oil crisis, such as Iraq's invasion of Kuwait in August. Even in a stable market, increasing reliance on foreign oil weakens the strongest economies and places a crippling burden on developing countries mired in debt.

The enormity of these automobile-related problems defies mere technical fixes. Without alternatives to automobiles, improvements in fuel economy and pollution control are partly offset by more people driving more cars over longer distances. And these changes do nothing to ease traffic congestion. Even electric cars, which could greatly reduce fossil fuel consumption and pollution, would still contribute to traffic jams.

Moreover, no new automobile technology can fully address the social consequences of more than one quarter of a million people worldwide dying in road accidents each year, and several million more injured or permanently disabled. No new car technology will serve the majority of people who will never own automobiles. A Fiat mini-car currently sells in China for roughly $6,400 — a modest sum in some countries, but equal to about 16 years of wages for an ordinary Chinese worker. For all but the privileged elite in developing countries, more cars mean only more air pollution, more traffic congestion, and more dangerous streets.

Getting on Track

Creating a new vision of transportation, one that meets people's needs equitably and fosters a healthy environment, requires putting the automobile back into its useful place as servant. With a shift in priorities, cars can be part of a broad, balanced system in which public transport, cycling, and walking are all viable options.

Public modes of transport — buses, subways, streetcars, trolleys, trains, and even car and van pools — vary in their fuel use, the pollution they create, and the space they require, but, when carrying reasonable numbers of passengers, they all outperform the one-occupant private car on each of these counts.

For example, a commuter train carrying 80 passengers requires roughly 710 British thermal units (Btu) of energy per passenger per mile, and a trolley with 55 passengers uses around 1,050 Btu. A car pool with four people burns roughly 1,840 Btu per passenger mile, and a one-person car, some 7,380.

The emissions savings from using public transport are even more dramatic.

Rapid rail (also called the "metro," "tube," "underground," or "subway" if running in tunnels beneath the city) and light rail (trolleys) have electric engines. So, pollution emissions are measured not from the tailpipe but the power plant (most often outside the city, where air quality problems are less acute). For typical U.S. commutes, rapid rail emits 49 grams of nitrogen oxides (a precursor to acid rain) for every 100 passenger miles, compared with 69 grams for light rail, 154 grams for transit buses, and 206 grams for single-occupant automobiles. Public transport's potential for reducing hydrocarbon and carbon monoxide emissions is even greater.

Public transport also saves valuable city space. Buses and trains carry more people in each vehicle, and if they operate on their own rights-of-way (particularly in underground tunnels), can safely run at much higher speeds. An underground metro can carry 70,000 passengers past a certain point in a single lane in one hour, surface rapid rail can carry up to 50,000 people, and a trolley or a bus in a separate lane more than 30,000. A lane of private cars with four occupants, by contrast, can move only about 8,000 people per hour.

In the developing world, flexible, informal forms of public transport take up where overburdened bus and train systems leave off. These include minibuses, converted jeeps, vans, and pickups, shared taxis, and cycle rickshaws that give crucial service and ply the city's hard-to-get-to sections. These vehicles account for 64 percent of road-based public transport in Manila and 93 percent in Chiang Mai, Thailand.

The cost of providing public transport is, understandably, the overriding factor in a government's decision when picking from transportation options. However, comparing the costs of providing bus and train service to those for private automobile travel is an extremely complex task. A fair comparison must include the full costs of both systems, including their environmental impact and the social consequences. And the evaluation must consider which approach can move the most people; with public transport's higher capacities and greater affordability for the general public, governments could get more for their money.

Similarly, drivers would find public transit more attractive if they kept the full costs of automobile transport in mind. Few U.S. drivers realize that, including fuel, maintenance, insurance, depreciation, and finance charges on their cars, they pay $34 for every 100 miles of driving. On a yearly basis, it costs the average solo commuter nearly $1,700 just to get to work. By contrast, the average public transport fare is $14 per 100 miles.

Cities for People

Walking and cycling are the most common forms of individual transport. Low cost, non-polluting, space-saving, and requiring no other fuel than a person's most recent meal, these options are the most appropriate for short trips. In addition to the economic and environmental benefits brought by fostering cycling and walking, quality of life improves in a city that welcomes people, not just cars. Yet non-motorized transport is often ignored by urban planners.

There are several ways to remake cities as places for people, and most concern keeping motor traffic from dominating city space. Pedestrians and cyclists need safe, continuous routes to their destinations, which calls for separate lanes and paths in some situations but more often merely requires trucks and cars to share city streets with other types of traffic.

Where the road is shared, motor traffic needs to be slowed. In Europe, cities have used several techniques, known as "traffic calming," to turn streets into safe places for people who live, work, and shop nearby. The Dutch have changed the physical layout of their residential streets, transforming them into a *woonerf*, or "living yard." In the *woonerf*, cars are forced to negotiate slowly around carefully placed trees and other landscaping. Since motor traffic cannot monopolize the entire breadth of the street, much of the space is made more open to walking, cycling, and children's play.

West German cities use speed limits to slow down cars. Limiting speed on thousands of urban streets nationwide to 19 miles per hour over the past five years has reduced accidents and noise and exhaust levels. As with traffic calming, this method is most effective when applied to entire zones rather than single streets.

One of the most potent ways to make streets more amenable to pedestrians and cyclists is to restrict car parking downtown. Car commuters are forced to choose options other than driving, which reduces the number of cars on the street. Whereas many cities in the United States, West Germany, and the United Kingdom require employers and developers to provide parking spaces, Geneva prohibits car parking at workplaces in the central city, motivating commuters to use the city's excellent public transport.

Creating an automobile-free pedestrian zone is another way to make the heart of a car-crazed city livable again. Nearly all major European cities have devoted at least part of their centers to people on foot. Munich's impressive 900,000-square-foot pedestrian zone owes much of its success to easy access via convenient public transport services. Third World cities with heavy concentrations of foot traffic and street vendors could enhance safety and improve traffic conditions with pedestrian zones. After pedestrian streets were established in Lima, Peru, the number of street traders and shoppers on foot increased, and traffic flow through the center improved dramatically.

The Road Not Taken

Automobile dependence is most deeply ingrained in cities that have tried to use road building to combat traffic congestion. Los Angeles, Phoenix, Miami, and many other U.S. cities have gone this route. The result is a treadmill effect in which new roads fill to capacity as soon as they are completed. To break this cycle, the very shape of cities has to change to reduce the imperative for driving.

Although all major cities struggle with traffic congestion to some degree, those with the least sprawl are best able to promote alternatives to driving. Australian researchers Peter Newman and Jeffrey Kenworthy of Murdoch University in Perth studied 32 cities worldwide and found that low urban densities (measured by the number of people and jobs per acre of land) and auto dependence generally go hand-in-hand. Phoenix, for example, where 93 percent of workers commute by private car, is less than one-sixth as dense as Stockholm, where only 34 percent get to work by car. In Perth, Australia, 12 percent of workers commute by public transport, while in Munich, which is roughly 6 times as dense, 42 percent of workers use public transport.

Strong land-use policies to increase urban densities, then, are crucial in fostering viable alternatives to automobile dependence. Although the term "high density" evokes images of towering apartment buildings and little space, dense developments are pleasant and livable if planned well. According to a study done for the United States Environmental Protection Agency, a compact development can mix two- to six-story apartments and townhouses with clustered single-family homes, and still leave 30 percent of the developed area for open space and parks. In a typical low-density sprawl community, the study says, only 9 percent of the land is devoted to open space.

More than simply increasing density, land-use policies should create a mix of different types of development. Zoning can foster mixing of homes with commercial uses instead of making them separate and thus creating long commutes. University of California researcher Robert Cervero points out that in much of the world there is no longer a strong case for separating homes from industrial and commercial areas. Whereas the original purpose was to prevent nuisances from smokestacks and slaughterhouses, "Today the 'nuisance' facing most suburban areas seems ... more one of traffic congestion," says Cervero.

Economic benefits flow from a city's commitment to public transport and developing careful land-use planning. In direct terms, a recent study in Melbourne demonstrated that locating a new household in the central city instead of on the outskirts saves thousands of dollars in infrastructure, municipal services, commuting, and other costs.

Leaving the Auto Behind

In early 1990, President Bush unveiled a new U.S. National Transportation Strategy meant to guide the nation for the next 30 years. Unfortunately, this strategy is really just a tired collection of policies that would keep the automobile in its favored place by reducing funding for public transport, failing to revise tax policies that encourage automobile commuting, and only vaguely mentioning the importance of cycling and walking. Unwittingly, the plan shows the world exactly how not to construct a transportation strategy. What conventional transport policies of this sort fail to acknowledge is that eventually, auto-centered societies could collapse under their own overwhelming burden of congestion, pollution, and oil dependence. If cities around the world are to break out of the current transportation mess, a policy overhaul will be needed.

The surest way to lessen overdependence on cars is to force drivers to bear more of the true costs of driving. So long as automobile owners are showered with inducements, such as free parking and government-subsidized roads, they will stay in their cars, leaving trains, buses, and bike paths empty. This is a vicious cycle, since planners are unlikely to invest in transport alternatives when existing systems are underutilized.

The first step is to bring to light the hidden costs of driving, such as air pollution, municipal services, and road construction and repair. Perhaps least-recognized of these public expenses are items such as police, fire, and ambulance services required for an automobile-centered system. According to an analysis of the salaries and personnel time of the Pasadena Police Department in California, 40 percent of department costs are from accidents, theft, traffic control, and other automobile-related items. Extending this finding to the entire United States suggests that local governments spend at least $60 billion on automobiles. Employer-provided free parking (a tax-free fringe benefit) represents another huge subsidy to drivers, variously estimated to be worth an additional $12 to $50 billion a year.

A gasoline tax on the scale of $1 to $2 per gallon, which is now common in Europe, would make drivers pay more of the costs they impose on society. It also makes sense to levy a sizable tax on new cars, as well as raising the annual registration fees. Another approach is to follow the new German policy of taxing cars based on their emissions: the more they pollute, the more they pay. Given the gross imbalance of many cities' transport systems, it makes sense to dedicate some of the revenues from auto user fees and taxes to the development of cycling and pedestrian facilities and public transport. Without sizable and sustained government funding, the needed alternative transport infrastructure will be slow in coming.

If driving became more expensive, people would begin to demand alternatives. This would help counter the large and powerful road lobbies made up of oil companies, car makers, highway builders, and other interests that pressure governments to favor the automobile.

Effective land-use planning is the other key to a viable new transportation system. Here, cooperative approaches may make the most sense. Municipalities can, for example, share the cost of expanding transport services by striking deals with private land developers who benefit from enhanced access to their projects. Joint development schemes can be planned at new subway stations, helping to defray costs.

Several studies suggest that there is a threshold level of urban density — 12 to 16 people per acre — below which reliance on the automobile soars. This density level, about that found in Copenhagen today, is the minimum that urban planners should aim for.

Zoning and financial incentives can be used to cluster homes, jobs, and services along public transport corridors. Ideally, these policies would be implemented in conjunction with comprehensive and integrated regional development plans so that one community does not simply push its transport problems off on another. The aim should be to make inner cities comfortable and convenient so that people will want to live there.

The time for action on the world's urban transport crises has clearly arrived. Indeed, in many nations the costs of additional automobile ownership are already outweighing the benefits. If cities are to achieve the dream of clean, efficient, reliable transportation once promised by the automobile, they will have to steer instead toward more sustainable alternatives.

Editor's Note: Although some of the facts in this chapter are slightly dated, it was selected for inclusion in this volume since those problems associated with the automobile mentioned over a decade ago still persist. For this reason the contents of this piece are relevant today, even more than when originally written.

CHAPTER 44

Roadways of the Future

Ronald Adams *and*
Terry Brewer

Just as steam engines replaced the water wheel and electric trams took the place of horse trams, so the twentieth-century car-and-highway transportation system is due to be replaced by something dramatically different in the twenty-first century.

Since the halcyon days of its introduction, the automobile has produced half the world's carbon dioxide and hollowed out cities in the United States, and it is now doing the same in cities all over the developing world as their inhabitants rush to embrace industrialization and its mistakes. The car-and-highway system has proved to be a disastrously inefficient land-use choice for high-density urban transport in the United States.

Henry Ford's common-man cars and highways to support them were achievements of the last century. However, the ability of ordinary Americans simply to go where they need to is being vitiated by the sheer volume of vehicles in the system. We can't build enough highways where they're needed to accommodate the traffic that's already there, much less provide for what's coming.

We've reached a stage of almost constant traffic jams in urbanized areas. In a megalopolis, popular destinations add more and more traffic to the system. We simply have no more room for new roads or highways within the present system's architecture. To survive the onslaught of more and more cars, our system must *double* the capacity of urban roadways, and do so without taking up any new real estate.

Dangers of Mixed-Use Highways

One irrational feature of today's jerry-built highway system is the unholy mix of vehicles crowding onto roads and highways — from oversized cars to huge trucks mixed in with buses and vans. Today's Commuter Joe feels he must drive the biggest SUV and duke it out with monster double-bottom trucks on the trip to work. But an 18-wheeler can still squash even the biggest SUV when a truck driver pulls one shift too many and dozes at the wheel.

Since England first ran massive steam-powered trains, we have known that dinky horse-drawn vehicles could not safely share the same right-of-way with them. Mammoths shouldn't mix with mice on the road. But the U.S. highway system has us locked into this unsafe condition.

Originally published as "Changing Lanes: Watch What's Coming on Tomorrow's Roads," *The Futurist*, Vol. 36, No. 4, July/August 2002. Published by the World Future Society, Bethesda, MD. Reprinted with permission of the publisher.

While traffic balloons beyond the system's ability to cope, oil-consuming nations can no longer rely on a free-flowing supply. Now is the time to redirect energy policy away from oil and toward clean, *electrified* transportation using a different, more sophisticated roadway system.

> **Figure 1. U.S. Highways Data Box**
>
> - 132 million cars drove 1.6 trillion miles in 1999.
> - 75 million light trucks drove 900 billion miles.
> - 7.8 million commercial trucks drove 200 billion miles.
> - 4.2 million motorcycles drove 10.6 billion miles.
> - 729,000 buses (all types) drove 7.7 billion miles.
> - 30% increase in vehicle-miles of travel 1989–1999.
> - Automobiles' share of vehicle-miles of travel fell from 67% to 58% while SUVs and light trucks rose to 33% from 1989 to 1999.
>
> Source: U.S. Department of Transportation Federal Highway Administration.

Super-Productive Lanes

The only way to increase *capacity* in urbanized areas is to maximize vehicle payload and roadway productivity.

A correct mix of Intelligent Vehicle Highway Systems (IVHS) elements and the more arcane dualmode guideways — two new transportation architectures — plus wayside electric power can produce cost-effective, safe, high-density rights-of-way. And it can be done without using additional urban space by allowing certain kinds of vehicles to run in super-productive rights-of-way shoehorned into existing roadways or even above them.

By making vehicles and highways more efficient in terms of both transporting people and cargo and consuming energy, we can move toward a more secure future. Reducing petroleum imports as we phase out the carbon-fuel economy in favor of electricity means slowing global warming as we build a new post-petroleum civilization.

Why Intelligent Systems Aren't Smart Enough

In Intelligent Vehicle Highway Systems (IVHS), the road and the car work together to do the driving. Touted by the professional highway community since the 1980s, IVHS has important features for new roadway system architectures.

Unfortunately, industry pushed a bit too aggressively into the arena of IVHS, hoping to supply a huge assortment of high-tech systems for existing vehicles and an aging

American highway system without addressing the system's critical problems.

Original supporters of guideway systems were shoved aside in the hustle and bustle of IVHS development in favor of keeping the old U.S. interstate highway system as is. Motorola and Detroit's smart-vehicle products stole the show from guideway innovators whose more mechanical, architectural solutions offered higher highway capacities and greater right-of-way productivity.

For example, the highway technology establishment is still prepared to spend big bucks solving "non-recurring" delays like warning drivers of an overturned truck ahead. But that information is available on the car radio or with on-board software — and is much cheaper.

Today's real problems are *recurring* delays at "chokepoints" in urban areas. These delays are as predictable as sunrise, occurring at bridges, tunnels, and merge points along everyone's daily route every day as narrated by local news anchors in every city, morning and evening.

Another highly touted advantage of smart car/smart highway systems is the promise of hands-free driving, allowing commuters to read or munch doughnuts. But you can do that on the 7:10 A.M. train to Grand Central and save the state billions of dollars.

The most appealing aspect of IVHS is "close-interval operations." This allows vehicles to follow one another on an automated highway with only a hair's breadth of space between them — and thus can increase lane capacity by an order of magnitude.

Robotic Trucks Deliver the Goods

One attractive application for IVHS is robotic-truck operations on guideways eventually moving in close-interval mode. This novel use for robotic trucks provides an exclusive lane — width and height appropriately reduced — between guiderails for driverless "trucks." With fully computerized controls, a standard 20-foot shipping container placed on a wheeled carriage or with bogies attached can roll goods night and day. The achievement of close-interval mode within an IVHS environment will dramatically improve city-to-city trucking.

Robotic trucks will run adjacent to and pick up power from a contact rail on the highway's median barrier. When the robo-unit leaves the contact rail, it switches to its own on-board battery power. The robo-unit exits to a designated overpass using an ascending off-ramp and maneuvers itself into an exclusive queue on the elevated crossing roadway. There it waits, out of traffic and with no engine noise or pollution, for an assigned human trucker to board and drive the unit to its final destination. The driver steers and brakes as in an ordinary truck. The "robotic transporter" is driven along ordinary streets to a nearby loading dock. There, after a quick turnaround to empty and reload, the wheeled container is ready to run another hard day's night without a drink, a shave, or a nap.

Two Proposed Systems for Right-of-Way Use

It has been said that insufficient right-of-way space is endemic to older American cities and other cities all over the world because they were designed to accommodate nineteenth-century carriages, not modern vehicular traffic. Therefore, common wisdom says enough space can never be found in the present system for today's magnitude of human and goods movement.

With two proposed systems — Metropolitan Personal Transporter Systems (MPTS) and Occupancy-Rated Vehicle Architecture (ORVA) — both the existing highway system and any ordinary urban street or rear property zone can be exploited to offer virtually inexhaustible right-of-way space for significantly increased productivity.

The key to increasing commuter traffic flow is to maximize the numbers of people moving in and through the system — that is, passengers per square foot of right-of-way per unit of time. Replacing the Long Island (commuter) Railroad, for example, would require an estimated 40 lanes of interstate highway. The challenge is to achieve this level of right-of-way productivity while maintaining the mobility we associate with private passenger cars.

The typical street — the basic capillary of transportation circulation — has changed little since Iron Age and Graeco-Roman cities were first built and traffic proceeded on foot, by ox, or by two-wheeled horse-drawn chariot. The space allocated for vehicles today is based on two standing and two moving vehicles, or four "lanes."

Ancient and medieval roadways were suitable for cumbersome, horse-drawn carriages or omnibuses, but there were few of them on the road. In Europe, one-lane roads connecting towns and cities were the rule for centuries. By the last half of the twentieth century, America's limited access highways offered multiple lanes in each direction with on/off ramps to facilitate armies of traffic moving in two directions.

But the inherent problem of the loner in a touring car occupying as much street space as a truck has constrained the productivity of the multi-lane highway system enough to produce virtual megalopolitan gridlock.

Transportation Links

Intelligent Transportation Systems, www.its.dot.gov/home.htm: A U.S. Department of Transportation agency that applies information technologies and advances in electronics to the transportation network. These technologies include the latest in computers, electronics, communications, and safety systems.

Intelligent Vehicle Initiative, www.its.dot.gov/ivi/ivi.htm: A Transportation Department initiative formed to accelerate the development and availability of advanced safety and information systems applied to all types of vehicles. Its primary goal is to help drivers operate vehicles more safely and effectively.

National Transportation Library, ntl.bts.gov: Administered by the Transportation Department's Bureau of Transportation Statistics, the agency serves as a repository of transportation-related information from public, academic, and private organizations.

National Highway Traffic Safety Administration: www.nhtsa.dot.gov: Responsible for reducing deaths, injuries, and economic losses resulting from motor-vehicle crashes by setting and enforcing safety performance standards for motor vehicles and motor-vehicle equipment.

Office of Transportation Technologies, U.S. Department of Energy: www.ott.doe.gov: Dedicated to helping reduce U.S. dependence on foreign oil by developing advanced transportation and alternative fuel vehicle technologies.

Innovative Transportation Technologies: faculty.washington.edu/jbs/itrans: Managed by Jerry Schneider of the University of Washington, this site offers a comprehensive collection of information on unconventional transportation technologies and links to projects around the world. Includes a matrix comparing the ideas and reporting project status.

The Metropolitan Personal Transporter System

We can launch a Metropolitan Personal Transporter System simply by designating the smallest conventional vehicle widely available in the United States, the subcompact econobox, as our system-compatible vehicle. Using the econobox, which is driven almost universally in Europe and other environmentally conscious places, means significantly lower fuel requirements.

Once the econobox vehicles are modified (at low cost), they will operate in new and revolutionary "guidelanes" that exploit existing rights-of-way on modern highways *above* conventional traffic. At present, to prevent large vehicles from striking and rolling over the median barrier, buses and trucks are prohibited from using ordinary inside lanes that are exclusively reserved for passenger cars. Constructing an elevated guidelane above these lanes exploits air space and adds an additional lane in each direction without taking up new real estate. This proposal will also significantly reduce the small car's vulnerability to accidents with larger vehicles.

Furthermore, with a metered onramp, there will be no need for a big engine under the hood of our econobox since there will be no need to outrun oncoming 18-wheelers to enter on the highway. The MPTS transformation only requires modest adaptation of available products and equipment. There will be no need to break concrete, invent new passenger cars, or reroute traffic.

The innovative MPTS guidelane facility provides an aerial lane within a 5-foot by 6-foot right-of-way — as compared with the 12-foot by 14-foot space of the conventional highway lane. Since only a single class of vehicle is allowed to operate in the guidelane, there is no weight disparity to jeopardize the safety of the occupants of the econobox on its guidelane, as there is on today's open road.

Introducing Metropolitan Personal Transporter System on a six-lane highway increases the total facility's capacity by 25%. The number of cars per hour moving on the guidelane would be about the same as an ordinary car lane, about 2,000 vehicles per hour. Adding incremental capacity to existing facilities and adding different guideway modes will increase productivity while substantially reducing accidents.

Accepting the econobox with its (preferably hybrid) internal combustion engine as our original equipment is likely to speed public acceptance and investor interest, as well as reduce costs and system start-up time. Later, of course, with the installation of wayside power in the right-of-way, gasoline engines will be replaced completely as vehicles are retrofit for electric propulsion.

Occupancy-Rated Vehicle Architecture

An even smaller vehicle than the econobox can achieve urban right-of-way productivity on a par with rapid transit. Occupancy-Rated Vehicle Architecture is a proposed vehicle/system architecture for *solo* travelers in a guidelane high above and safe from street traffic. At its heart is an individual driving (or even pedaling) to work in an authentic micro-car, commuter capsule, or "bubble vehicle" roughly one-fourth the size of an econobox and weighing just a few hundred pounds.

The space that a driver actually uses is but a fraction of the area the typical car or SUV occupies as it moves along street and highway. Likewise, parking ties up available street space, often all day. This means a conventional vehicle's payload simply does not correlate efficiently with its size or with the amount of highway and street area used, and represents an astonishing misappropriation

of high-value urban space. To understand the futility of current traffic capacity measurement and associated "traffic correctives," we must realize that these conventional means and measurements will not solve the basic inefficiency of our car-highway system.

The problem today is the ridiculously low lane productivity as seen by comparing the payload (number of occupants — sometimes only one — delivered to a destination) to the cross-sectional area taken up by the vehicle. The conventional highway lane delivers 10 solo drivers per square foot of right-of-way per hour, while MPTS delivers 100 solo drivers and ORVA delivers 200 solo drivers.

Once the benefits of putting econoboxes on these proposed mini-highway guidelane systems are clear, investors and users should be convinced there are ready alternatives. These are far superior to what is being offered by conventional highway planners and automakers, particularly as commuters face the prospect of tens of thousands more cars crowding the ultimately limited traditional highway networks.

Where the Metropolitan Personal Transporter System would deliver a sixfold improvement — up to 60 passengers per square foot per hour, Occupancy-Rated Vehicle Architecture would deliver as much as a 15-fold improvement — 100 to 150 commuters per square foot per hour. These astounding upgrades in right-of-way productivity would be accompanied by even more compelling fuel economies and emissions reductions than MPTS.

All of these systems — robotic trucks, personal transporters, and individual microvehicles — could be combined in a commuter dualmode system. While robotic trucks would be automated, the others would operate manually and at lower cost.

Personal Transport Goes to Extremes

On the lighter side, there can be a transporter in which the commuter's individual

Highway Congestion in Metropolitan Areas

Being stuck in traffic has far-reaching impacts:

- It wastes people's time, increases the time to transport goods, and causes missed meetings and appointments.
- It increases fuel consumption because of increased acceleration, deceleration, and idling.
- Greater fuel consumption leads to higher emissions of greenhouse gases and may raise the level of other air pollutants.

The Texas Transportation Institute (TTI) studied 68 U.S. metropolitan areas in order to estimate congestion and its impacts. Between 1982 and 1997, congestion (measured by average annual delay per eligible driver) increased throughout the United States. Overall, average annual delay per driver almost tripled during the 15-year period, rising from 16 hours per driver in 1982 to 45 hours in 1997 — as high as 54 hours per driver in metropolitan areas with a population of more than 3 million. More recent data from TTI show congestion continued to increase between 1997 and 1999.

Source: Bureau of Transportation Statistics, www.bts.gov.

transportation space is only a third of the size of the tiny ORVA transporter. Right-of-way use would be so efficient that it would substantially reduce the need for large rights-of-way as in multilane highways. We can travel through right-of-way facilities that resemble the structure of today's industrial air conditioning and ventilation ducts using a "MAG-Luge."

In this mode, commuters travel feet first, head raised, body supine. The human/ vehicle is buoyed by magnetic levitation, propelled by electric linear induction motors, and protected and augmented by pneumatic pressure management within the tube type construction.

Of course, people who are less physically fit may not be attracted to the MAG-Luge mode of travel. But former skateboarders, rock-and-roll Harley bikers, fitness buffs, and sportsters will be happy to use it.

Message from the Future

Even if these hypothetical architectures became commonplace in North America, global carbon dioxide levels and temperatures will continue to rise for a half century more *after* we put our house in order. Therefore, according to current climate science, we can expect our grandchildren to witness the flooding of coastal zones and the disappearance of the world's islands as glacial deposits melt and anthropogenic warming continues.

Stuck in a car-and-highway system unfriendly to alteration or update, we can still apply innovative thinking and accomplish a (quiet) revolution to save our cities and our planet and break the impasse created by obsolescent infrastructure and old ideas.

The impact of the car-and-highway mode on human society and the biosphere makes it mandatory that the system be transformed to fit the new epoch. Ideally, a new era will allow us to cut ties to global corporations concerned with the bottom line and government institutions mired in fixed paradigms and political pork. Instead, unaffiliated inventors and innovators should rethink the architecture of land transport in the tradition of trailblazing innovation.

CHAPTER 45

Highways of the Future

William Murphy

Fuel shortages, traffic congestion, deteriorating roads, and vehicular air pollution: A convergence of factors may usher the United States into a transportation crisis. This chapter proposes infrastructure changes to help traffic flow more smoothly and safely. These changes, by providing safe, less congested corridors for narrower vehicles, will be an incentive to own smaller vehicles, offering a real solution to traffic congestion and other concerns.

Legislation is needed to allow states to build, with federal matching funds, narrow urban freeways to carry urban commuter traffic. These "small-vehicle commuter lanes" (SVCLs) will only accept vehicles 67 inches wide or less. A bill is before Congress to fund dedicated truck lanes to separate trucks from other traffic. This article suggests dedicated small-vehicle lanes as a more efficient alternative.

The SVCL Concept

The Federal Aid Highway Act of 1956 required that the interstate highway system be built to carry military traffic. It also required a body of uniform specifications for building the interstate system. The uniform standard lane width is 12 feet, allowing a reduction to 11 feet in some instances. The requirements for uniformity and for military compatibility have meant that our interstate system has no narrow lanes built specifically for cars. This article challenges the concept that all urban highways must be sized to carry military traffic or other large vehicles.

The concept of narrow lanes for narrow cars is not new. Garrison and Pitstick (1991) proposed a way to analyze the benefits of lanes suitable for 4-foot-wide "lean vehicles." However, I propose designing the lanes for readily available subcompact cars. I also propose using radio frequency identifier (RFID) technology and converting existing reversible lanes into SVCLs.

The RFID uses a small electronic transmitter, called a tag, to send date to a receiver. RFIDs are used on some toll roads, charging a toll to a vehicle while it is traveling at freeway speeds. On an SVCL, only vehicles with RFID tags (including buses and emergency vehicles) would be able to legally enter the SVCL.

Traffic-Related Problems

The SVCL may be the most practical near-term mitigation to many traffic-related

Originally published as "Using Narrow Freeway Lanes to Mitigate Transportation-Related Problems," *Public Works Management & Policy*, Vol. 9, No. 3, January 2005, pp. 190–195. Copyright © 2005 by Sage Publications. Published by Sage Publications, Thousand Oaks, CA. Reprinted by permission of Sage Publications, Inc.

problems. Traffic congestion may cost travelers almost $70 billion. There is also a huge environmental cost due to these travel delays. There were 5.7 *billion* gallons of fuel wasted in 2001 due to congestion (Lomax & Schrank, 2003, p. 17). The SVCL will ease this problem by allowing more traffic lanes to be built in a given right-of-way width.

Also, studies have shown that our roads are not being adequately maintained and that the funding for roadway maintenance is not expanding rapidly enough to keep pace with road deterioration. Thirty-two percent of our major roads are in poor or mediocre condition (U.S. House of Representatives, 2004, see "National Infrastructure Needs").

It is evident that the cost of maintaining and building our highway infrastructure is outpacing the revenues available to pay for this work. The proposals in this article offer the promise of reduced costs for maintaining and building this infrastructure.

Lastly, there is a growing consensus that we must do something to reduce our importation and consumption of oil. A *Wall Street Journal* article stated:

The Big Three auto makers, the United Auto Workers union and environmental activists are negotiating to try to come up with a joint proposal for what they have come to conclude is the most realistic way to improve the fuel economy of the U.S. automotive fleet: a big package of federal subsidies designed to seed a consumer market for vehicles that go further on a gallon of gas.

For the auto industry, an intensifying political battle over the fuel consumption of sport-utility vehicles has become a public-relations nightmare. For the union, the specter of a shift toward newer, more-efficient vehicles raises worries about job losses for its members.

For environmentalists, the realization is setting in that a severe toughening of the federal government's fuel-economy rule is a political nonstarter. Therefore, some of them are concluding, the only way to get substan-

tial improvement in the fuel economy of the U.S. fleet is to spur market demand for more-efficient vehicles (Ball, 2003).

The SVCL will spur market demand for more-efficient vehicles. Furthermore, by reducing fuel consumption, the SVCL also reduces pollution, including generation of carbon dioxide. We should note that transportation-related emissions make up about one third of all U.S. carbon dioxide emissions (U.S. Department of Energy, 2003).

Infrastructure Change Is a More Efficient Solution

Changing infrastructure to the SVCL system is a more efficient way to mitigate traffic problems. Consider:

The SVCL will, at once, mitigate congestion, funding, and environmental concerns. Traditional measures attempt to solve these problems separately. For example, corporate average fleet efficiency (CAFÉ) standards will not add additional lanes to aid congestion, and building additional 12-foot lanes will not address fuel economy issues. The SVCL addresses each of these issues.

The traditional response to fuel economy concerns increases the CAFÉ standards. However, more stringent CAFÉ standards have met resistance due to safety and economic concerns.

Safety

Higher CAFÉ standards may cause safety concerns. A higher CAFÉ standard generally means smaller cars. A National Highway Traffic Safety Administration (NHTSA) study shows an increasing number of fatalities for occupants of small cars (Summers, Prasad, Hollowell, & Kuchar, 2001). This safety versus fuel economy conflict has stalled almost all progress in increasing CAFÉ standards. Indeed, in 1990, Senate Bill 279, which would have increased CAFÉ standards, was labeled "The highway fatality bill" by opponents (U.S. Congress Office of Technology Assessment, 1991). This bill never became law.

We should not expect small-vehicle ownership to increase until we protect small-car owners from collisions with larger vehicles. The SVCL protects small cars by separating them from large vehicles in commuter traffic.

Economics

Also, automakers and the United Auto Workers union complain about more stringent CAFÉ standards, affecting the economic strength of U.S. carmakers (Power, 2003). Relying on increasingly stringent CAFÉ standards forces automakers to make huge capital investments before a market for the product is assured. It is more reasonable to let the market develop first (i.e., consumer demand for efficient cars) and let capital investment follow. If we want to reduce fuel consumption, we should change market demand. The SVCL does this.

Also, current attempts to regulate fuel economy and vehicle emission require that authorities continually monitor vehicle manufacturers. The SVCL requires no monitoring to achieve its mitigation effects. Once the SVCLs are built, the market for smaller, more efficient cars is the monitoring factor.

Furthermore, infrastructure costs will be reduced because lighter vehicles cause less wear and tear on the roads.

SVCL Design

I propose federal legislation allowing states to build, with federal monies, uniform narrow lanes 8.5 or 9 feet wide for vehicles 67 inches wide or less. The most efficient design for the SVCL is probably using reversible lanes. These lanes are in urban areas where commuter traffic is heaviest. These lanes also require a distinct urban start point and end point as do SVCLs.

One design feature in these proposals that may require further research is the portion of the lane width devoted to lateral clearance between the vehicle and the lane edge or stripe. This clearance is needed on each side of the vehicle for normal tracking. Obviously, 12-foot lanes offer plenty of clearance, even for the average truck. It has been stated that at speeds greater than 35 miles per hour (mph), a 2-foot clearance is needed on each side of the car for normal tracking (Woods & Ross, 1983). However, this rule is not always followed. Buses and trucks can generally be 8.5 feet wide without a permit and thus have less than a 2-foot clearance on each side, even on 12-foot-wide roads.

The SVC lanes I propose offer less than 2 feet of lateral clearance (a 67-inch-wide car on an 8.5-foot lane has 17.5 inches of clearance on each side or 20.5 inches of clearance on a 9-foot lane). However, there is reason to believe that small vehicles can operate safely with less than 2 feet of clearance on each side.

The American Association of State Highway and Transportation Officials and the Federal Highway Administration will allow 11-foot-wide lanes in some instances, and 11-foot-wide freeway lanes exist in many states, including Washington, Georgia, and Texas (Curran, 1995). Eight-and-a-half-foot-wide trucks and buses operating on these lanes have less than 1.5 foot of lateral clearance on each side of the vehicle. Thus, it is not unprecedented to expect vehicles to operate with less than 2 feet of lateral clearance.

European nations are also experimenting with narrowed lanes. Highway A-27 in the Netherlands has narrow rush-hour lanes that open only during morning and afternoon rush hours. The third lane is realized by dividing the preexisting two lanes and an emergency lane. The rush-hour lane (left-hand lane) is only 2.7 meters wide (approximately 8.86 feet), and rush-hour speed is restricted to 70 kilometers (km)/hour (hr) on all lanes. The non-rush hour speed is 100 km/hr for the two lanes. Trucks are allowed in the right-hand lane only (Schrijnen, 2001). Because these lanes do not use RFID technology to classify traffic, a SVCL in which traffic is classified seems very workable.

Given current fiscal constraints, the SVCL is more likely to be tested and proved if it can be done by converting existing freeways. But this retrofit process, although relatively inexpensive, will present its own design problems. For example, the risk of an accident caused by a large vehicle mistakenly entering an SVCL is a great concern. An SVCL designed from the ground up can easily detect an oversize vehicle using RFID technology and divert the vehicle onto specially designed exit ramps. However, it may not be possible to retrofit a separate oversize vehicle exit (to direct oversize traffic away from the SVCL) for an existing freeway ramp. Therefore, retrofit projects require an innovative method for handling errant oversize traffic.

The solution to this problem should be coupled with the solution to another problem — buses. Buses can possibly use the SVCL but cannot use SVCL 8.5-foot-wide lanes.

My solution allows certain lanes to be 11 feet wide. These lanes will carry buses and errant oversize vehicles. Vehicles without tags are identified by the smart traffic systems, photographed, and guided to the 11-foot lanes. Repeat offenders could be ticketed.

Buses and other large (prequalified) vehicles travel in the two outside lanes. However, many existing reversible lanes have entrances and exits to and/or from both outer lanes. The Seattle, Washington, I-5 reversible lanes, for example, run north and/or south and have ramps to and/or from both the east and west outer lanes. To convert these reversible lanes it would require bus-lane adjustment areas where a bus entering the east lane gets to the west lane if its exit is on the west lane, and vice versa.

In bus-lane adjustment areas all lanes are 11 feet wide, allowing buses to shift from lane to lane. Thus, reversible SVCLs begin-

ning and/or ending in a city center would have all lanes in the city center area 11 feet wide to allow buses to shift to their exit lanes either as they are leaving the city, looking ahead to position themselves for the correct exit, or when the lanes are reversed, as they are entering the city and preparing to take the correct exit.

Complementary Infrastructure Changes

Parking and Ferry Systems

The idea of creating parking spaces for small cars is also not new (see Garrison & Pitstick, 1991). What is needed is a way to initiate the conversion of parking spaces. I propose that the process be initiated in government-owned parking structures. Federal, state, and city parking structures could be converted to be compatible with the SVCL. Also, ferry systems could haul more vehicles if they were SVCL compatible.

Expanding the Use of Technology

RFID technology can expand to control traffic in myriad ways. RFID receivers could be altered to allow entrance of large vehicles other than buses, but only at certain hours. The primary purpose of the SVCL is to ease congestion during rush hour. During non-rush hour there may be extra space on the SVCLs. The system could be programmed to allow delivery vehicles onto the SVCL oversize lane at certain times. The delivery vehicles and drivers would be prequalified, through special training, to use the SVCL before receiving an RFID tag. This would benefit congestion relief by encouraging deliveries at non-rush hour times.

Conclusion

The SVCL has the potential to mitigate many of today's traffic-related problems. It offers several advantages for our transportation system: The division of traffic by size gives a degree of safety to small cars and will allow maintenance to be treated differently in the heavy versus light vehicle lanes, along with the financial savings due to building lanes to less robust standards. The advantages include moving more traffic within the existing right of way. The environmental advantages flow directly from the traffic and infrastructure efficiencies.

But the primary advantage of this proposal over other traffic mitigation proposals is that the SVCL is a free-market methodology. There is no continuous intervention or monitoring required by government bodies. Once the infrastructure is built, the free market carries the load.

Two or three demonstration projects are probably the only way to test the viability of the SVCL. If people like the idea of exchanging large cars and traffic jams for small cars, of safer traffic flow (the safety of like-sized traffic), and of more traffic lanes, this proposal will work. But the viability of the SVCL can only be tested by the car-buying public. Thus, demonstration projects are really the only way to test whether the public will fully embrace the SVCL.

REFERENCES

Ball, J. (2003, May 16). Divergent interests seek fuel-economy compromise. *The Wall Street Journal*, p. A2.

Curran, J. E. (1995). *Use of shoulders and narrow lanes to increase freeway capacity* (National Cooperative Highway Research Program Rep. No. 369). Washington, DC: Transportation Research Board.

Garrison, W. L., & Pitstick, M. E. (1991). *Restructuring the automobile/highway system for lean vehicles: The scaled precedence activity network (SPAN) approach*. Berkeley: University of California, Berkeley. Institute of Transportation Studies.

Lomax, T., & Schrank, D. (2003). *2003 urban mobility study* (news release). College Station: Texas A&M University, Texas Transportation Institute. Retrieved from www.mobility.tamu.edu/ems

Power, S. (2003, December 22). Rules regulating gasoline mileage face an overhaul. *The Wall Street Journal*, p. A1.

Schrijnen, L. M. (2001). Innovations in the better use of motorways in the Netherlands. *Traffic Engineering and Control, 42*, 78–79.

Summers, S. M., Prasad, A., Hollowell, W. T., & Kuchar, A. C. (2001). *NHTSA's research program for vehicle aggressivity and fleet compatibility* (National Highway Traffic Safety Administration Paper No. 249). Retrieved from http://www-nrd.nhtsa.dot.gov/departments/nrd-11/aggressivity/ag.html

U.S. Congress Office of Technology Assessment. (1991). *Improving automobile fuel economy: New standards, new approaches* (OTA-E-504). Washington, DC: Government Printing Office.

U.S. Department of Energy. (2003, June 27). *Energy information administration page* (news release). Retrieved from www.eia.doe.gov/neic/press/press216

U.S. House of Representatives. (2004, March 31). *Executive Summary, HR 3550*. Retrieved from Committee on Transportation and Infrastructure page, www.house.gov/transportation

Woods, D. L., & Ross, H. E. (1983). *Potential impact of the microvehicle on roadway facilities* (Transportation Research Circular 264). Washington, DC: Transportation Research Board.

CHAPTER 46

Cars of the Future

Glen Hiemstra

Imagine the following scene, circa 2020. You have taken manual control of your car, just for the fun of it, until you enter the Interstate Guideway. There you relinquish control to the autodriver, which takes your car up to high speed within inches of cars to the front and rear.

You survey the countryside. As you pass a billboard advertising a new sensor-equipped running shoe, you ask the car to contact the Web for more information. A Web page appears on the virtual heads-up display on the windshield. Using verbal prompts, you explore the information and call the vendor on your cell phone to place an order for the shoe.

As the trip continues, "augmented reality" advertising screens appear on the windshield, triggered by various landmarks that the car sensors see. One is for an amusement park 30 miles ahead. This virtual display knows the car is in autodriver mode and fills the entire front windshield with a virtual ride on the park's most popular roller coaster. The ad concludes with the offer of a special admission price for the next month, if ordered now.

An audible warning interrupts the trip. There is Guideway maintenance ahead. Your car asks whether you wish to view the slowdown. The Guideway, like most roads, is lined with thousands of cameras, each the size of a pinhead. You ask to see the slowdown and decide to take an alternate route.

You ask the car to identify good alternatives, and, after a few moments searching the Web, the car says the best alternative commences at Exit 94, which will take you to a manual-drive road. As the car approaches the exit, it smoothly moves right and you take control. A directional arrow appears superimposed on the road ahead, and you follow the blinking arrow off the exit and onto the side road.

Fill 'er Up

While on the manual drive road, you decide to recharge your fuel cell. You ask the car for stations close by. You see no signs, but a virtual screen appears that lists three stations within a two-mile radius. You ask for comparison prices and select the station you prefer.

A virtual image of the station appears far in the distance. As you drive toward it, the image morphs into a blinking arrow pointing right. After turning the corner you see the actual station, and the virtual arrow changes

Originally published as "Driving in 2020: Commuting Meets Computing," *The Futurist*, Vol. 34, No. 5, September/October 2000. Published by the World Future Society, Bethesda, MD. Reprinted with permission of the publisher.

into an ad for the "Slurpel" drink served in the station quick mart.

Meanwhile, in the back seat, one of your children has been using her mediatronic paper with its wireless Internet connection to call up videos of her favorite musician. This signal is detected by a sensor on a land-based sign for Suny Records, which sends a small box message into the corner of the mediatronic paper asking politely whether she would like to see the video from the hottest Suny recording artist.

After recharging, you reenter the Guideway and almost immediately come to a toll plaza. It is not really a plaza but a marked strip of road with readers built into the pavement, which scan the bar code on the car. You have paid for this bar code, which allows for 30 trips on this Guideway.

The Guideway has been built by a private-public partnership involving several companies. Participating companies purchase rights to sponsor the road and to display a certain amount of real signs as well as the augmented-reality advertising. Using credit-card databases, the companies develop profiles of road users and adjust their mediatronic and other outdoor displays to offer products and services of interest to drivers with these profiles.

A New Era for Autos

Does this scene seem real, or does it read more like a bad science-fiction movie? In fact, it is an entirely plausible scenario of transport and advertising in 2020, based on current technological trends.

There was a time when many believed that the days of the auto were numbered because of rising energy prices, a looming shortage of petroleum, and environmental concerns. It is far more plausible, however, that we are at the beginning of the second automobile era.

This second era will be ushered in by "hybrids," vehicles that combine a small in-ternal combustion engine with an electric generator. The gasoline engine drives the generator and adds additional boost when needed, but the car drives primarily on electricity. A new model from Toyota, the Prius, gets more than 65 miles per gallon and generates only about 10% of the tailpipe emissions of conventional cars. The car never needs to be plugged in and can drive 850 miles without refueling.

The Battelle Institute forecasts that such hybrid cars will be a top-10 consumer product by about 2006. (However, many in the auto industry remain skeptical because past success with energy-efficient cars proved to be transitory.)

Following the hybrids by a few years will be cars driven by fuel cells. Fuel cells generate electricity through a chemical reaction between hydrogen and oxygen. They produce little waste except water. Practical fuel-cell technology could be available to the market as early as 2010.

With this development, the internal combustion engine can be completely eliminated, and we could see a shift in the auto paradigm more sudden than most imagine. Hybrids and fuel-cell cars will extend the auto-based lifestyle far into the future.

Cars Will Get Smarter

But such a future is not assured by energy efficient and environmentally friendly cars only; it will also be created by high-tech, intelligent cars suitable for a highly technological world and an intelligent transportation system.

It has been frequently observed that the average car today has more computing power than the Apollo spacecraft. In fact, a 2000 model car is likely to have dozens of built-in computers that monitor transmission functions, fuel use, braking, air-bag deployment, and virtually all other functions. Yet, compared with the cars to come, today's car is a Model-T.

Computing power and speed continue to double on a nearly annual cycle, according to the well-known Moore's Law. This will continue for at least the next 10 years. Inexpensive computers will approach the intelligence of the human brain, as measured by density and speed, by the year 2020. Computer chips costing pennies will become integral parts of every manufactured item, including — and especially — automobiles.

The car itself will become intelligent. Built-in sensors will view the road in front, in the back, and on the side, and they will produce a 3-D view for the operator. These sensors will establish safe zones around the car and apply accelerator and brakes to maintain the zone.

Other computers will be tied to the Internet and to the Global Positioning System, enabling the car to know where it is at all times. By 2025, the car will be fully capable of driving itself, and it most certainly will do so on Interstate Guideways and perhaps on city streets as well.

Cars May "Morph" into Trains

The same kinds of technologies will be applied to trains and mass transit, yet their use as personal transportation is unlikely to grow much over the next 25 years. In the late 1990s, transit accounted for about 3% of work-related trips in the United States, despite many years of concerted policy effort to increase that number.

In cities with concentrated work centers and good systems, mass transit provides as much as 40% of work-related trips. Still, the shift to environmentally friendly automobiles will keep mass transit marginal.

In a certain sense, we might actually witness the morphing of autos into quasi-trains. Intelligent, self-driving cars on a guideway, moving at high speeds and within inches of each other, form a kind of train. But this train is flexible, private, and personal, all of which Americans prefer.

Flying Cars: Pie in the Sky?

Yes, the Jetsons may have had it right all along: Personal transportation may one day take to the skies. Small, private flying vehicles suitable for short-haul personal transportation are in the experimental stages.

One such vehicle, the Skycar, is being developed by Moller International. This flying machine features four redundant engines and complete computer control of flight. If you can drive a car, you will be able to fly this vehicle.

Purported to get 15 miles to a gallon of fuel at 350 miles per hour, the Skycar would be safe to fly because of the redundancy of the engines, any one of which could keep the vehicle aloft. Plans are to sell the Skycar for about the cost of a luxury automobile.

These scenarios, which indeed read like science fiction, are if anything likely to be far too modest compared with the real possibilities.

Even as I typed this article on my laptop, the person sitting next to me on the plane struck up a conversation. An IBM salesman, he told me he made his first big sale in the early 1970s, of a $1.5-million computing system, to a municipal government. The system he sold them, he explained, had about half the capacity of the $1,200 machine sitting on my lap.

Glossary

Aerial Tramway — Unpowered passenger vehicle suspended from a system of aerial cables and propelled by separate cables attached to the vehicle suspension system. The cable system is powered by engines or motors at a central location, not on board the vehicle.

Automated Guideway Transit — Guided transit vehicle operating singly or multi-car trains with a fully automated system (no crew on transit units). Service may be on a fixed schedule or in response to a passenger-activated call button. Automated guideway transit includes personal rapid transit, group rapid transit and peoplemover systems.

Bus — Rubber-tired vehicle operating on fixed routes and schedules on roadways. Buses are powered by diesel, gasoline, battery or alternative fuel engines contained within the vehicle.

Commuter Rail — Urban passenger train service for local short-distance travel operating between a central city and adjacent suburbs. Service must be operated on a regular basis by or under contract with a transit operator for the purpose of transporting passengers within urbanized areas, or between urbanized areas and outlying areas. Such rail service, using either locomotive-hauled or self-propelled railroad passenger cars, is generally characterized by multi-trip tickets, specific station-to-station fares, railroad employment practices and usually only one or two stations in the central business district. It does not include heavy rail rapid transit or light rail/street car transit service. Intercity rail service is excluded, except for that portion of such service that is operated by or

under contract with a public transit agency for predominantly commuter services. Predominantly commuter services means that for any given trip segment (i.e., distance between any two stations), over 50 percent of the average daily ridership travels on the train at least three times a week. Only the predominantly commuter service portion of the intercity route is eligible for inclusion when determining commuter rail route miles.

Ferryboat — Vessel carrying passengers and/or vehicles over a body of water. The vessel is generally a steam or diesel-powered conventional ferry vessel.

Heavy Rail — High-speed, passenger rail cars operating singly or in trains of two or more cars on fixed rails in separate rights-of-way from which all other vehicular and foot traffic are excluded.

Inclined Plane — Special tramway type of vehicle operating up and down slopes on rails via a cable mechanism so that passenger seats remain horizontal while the undercarriage (truck) is angled parallel to the slope.

Light Rail — Lightweight passenger rail cars operating singly (or in short, usually two-car, trains) on fixed rails in right-of-way that is not separated from other traffic for much of the way. Light rail vehicles are driven electrically with power being drawn from an overhead electric line via a trolley or a pantograph.

Monorail — Guided transit vehicle operating on or suspended from a single rail, beam, or tube. Monorail vehicles usually operate in trains.

Source: Federal Transit Administration, *Glossary of Transit Terms*, December 2005. Published by the U.S. Department of Transportation, Washington, DC. (Website: http://www.fta.dot.gov/)

U.S. Periodicals Focusing on Urban Transportation

1. *Public Transportation Fact Book.* American Public Transportation Association, Washington, DC: 2004. Annual. 111 pages.

Provides aggregate data for the United States and Canada on transit finances and operating statistics by mode, transit vehicle characteristics, and deliveries, as well as legislative and industry historical information.

2. *ITE Journal.* Washington, DC: Institute of Transportation Engineers. Monthly. Abstracts available online at: http://www.ite.org/itejournal/index.asp

Traffic and transportation engineering with and emphasis on U.S. urban and suburban environments.

3. *Journal of Advanced Transportation.* Calgary, Alberta: Institute for Transportation. Three issues per year. Abstracts available online at: http://www.advanced-transport.com/

State of the art developments in mass transportation technologies and operational innovations.

4. *Journal of Public Transportation.* Tampa: University of South Florida, Center for Urban Transportation Research. Electronic resource accessed June 2004; available at: http://www.nctr.usf.edu/jpt/journal.htm

This quarterly, international journal presents original research and case studies relating to public transportation and policy issues. There is a special emphasis on innovative solutions to transportation problems. Many full-text issues are freely available online.

5. *Journal of Transportation Engineering.* New York: American Society of Civil Engineers. Bi-monthly. Abstracts available online at: http://scitation.aip.org/teo/

Includes technical and professional papers of the ASCE Urban Transportation Division.

6. *Journal of Urban Planning and Development.* New York: American Society of Civil Engineers. Bi-monthly. Abstracts available online at: http://scitation.aip.org/upo/

Application of civil engineering to area-wide transportation, urban development, and planning of public works and utilities.

7. *Urban Transportation Monitor.* Fairfax Station, VA: Lawley Publications. Available online through subscription at: http://www.urban-transportation-monitor.com/

This bi-weekly publication presents current news on all modes of urban transportation and includes regular readership surveys, and a section on new publications.

Source: Bureau of Transportation Statistics, *National Transportation Library* (virtual library), December 2005. Published by the Research and Innovative Technology Administration, U.S. Department of Transportation, Washington, DC. (Website: http://ntl.bts.gov/)

U.S. Research Centers and Libraries Focusing on Urban Transportation

Institute of Transportation Engineers
Technical Information Center
1099 – 14th Street, NW
Suite 300 West
Washington, DC 20005
Telephone: (202) 289-0222
FAX: (202) 289-7722
Website: http://www.ite.org/

Institute of Transportation Studies
Harmer E. Davis Transportation Library
University of California
412 McLaughlin Hall
MC 1720
Berkeley, CA 94720
Telephone: (510) 642-3604
FAX: (510) 642-9180
Website: http://www.lib.berkeley.edu/ITSL

**John A. Volpe National Transportation
  Systems Center**
Technical Information Center
Research and Innovative Technology
Administration
U.S. Department of Transportation
Kendall Square
55 Broadway
Cambridge, MA 02142
Telephone: (617) 494-2000
FAX: (617) 494-3005
Website: http://www.volpe.dot.gov/

National Transportation Library
Bureau of Transportation Statistics
Research and Innovative Technology
Administration
U.S. Department of Transportation
400 – 7th Street, SW
Suite 7412
Washington, DC 20590
Telephone: (800) 853-1351 (Toll Free)
FAX: (202) 366-3197
Website: http://ntl.bts.gov/

Technological Solutions for Transportation
Intelligent Transportation Society
of America
1100 – 17th Street, NW
Suite 1200
Washington, DC 20036
Telephone: (202) 484-4847
FAX: (202) 484-3483
Website: http://www.itsa.org/

Transportation Library
Northwestern University Library
Northwestern University
1970 Campus Drive
Evanston, IL 60208
Telephone: (847) 491-7658
FAX: (847) 491-8306
Website: http://www.library.northwestern.edu/
transportation/

Source: Science Reference Services, *Science Tracer Bullets Online/Urban Transportation* (research guide), December 2005. Published by the Science, Technology, & Business Division, Library of Congress, Washington, DC. (Website: http://www.loc.gov/)

Transportation Research Board
Management and Inquiry Services
Transportation Research Information Services
National Research Council
Keck Center of the National Academies

500 Fifth Street, NW
Washington, DC 20001
Telephone: (202) 334-2990
FAX: (202) 334-2527
Website: http://www4.trb.org/trb/tris/nsf

Regional Resource Directory

Local government organizations, special districts, and other public agencies that are included in the case studies in this volume are listed below in alphabetical order by city, county, or agency name.

Alberta Infrastructure and Transportation Ministry
Office of the Minister
Twin Atria Building
4999 – 98th Avenue
Edmonton, Alberta T6B 2X3
Canada
Telephone: (780) 427-2731
FAX: (780) 466-3166
Website: http://www.trans.gov.ab.ca/

Austin
(See City of Austin)

BART
(See Bay Area Rapid Transit District)

Bay Area Rapid Transit District (BART)
Office of the General Manager
Administration Building
300 Lakeside Drive
23rd Floor
Oakland, CA 94612
Telephone: (510) 464-6065
FAX: (510) 464-6009
Website: http://www.bart.gov/

Beaverton
(See City of Beaverton)

Bethesda
(See Montgomery County and Washington Metropolitan Area Transit Authority

Boston
(See City of Boston)

Boston Metropolitan Area
(See Metropolitan Area Planning Council)

Boulder
(See City of Boulder)

Central Florida Regional Transportation Authority
Office of the Chief Executive Officer
455 N. Garland Avenue
Orlando, FL 32801
Telephone: (407) 841-5969
FAX: (407) 843-0747
Website: http://www.golynx.com/

Central North American Trade Corridor Association (CNATCA)
Office of the President
1906 South Broadway
Minot, ND 58702
Telephone: (701) 852-7191
FAX: (701) 839-6375
Website: http://tradecorridor.net/

Chicago
(See City of Chicago)

Cincinnati
(See City of Cincinnati)

City and County of Denver
Office of the Mayor
City and County Building
1437 Bannock Street
Room 350
Denver, CO 80202
Telephone: (720) 864-9000

FAX: (720) 865-9040
Website: http://www.co.denver.co.us/

City and County of San Francisco
Office of the Mayor
City Hall
1 Dr. Carlton B. Goodlett Place
Room 200
San Francisco, CA 94102
Telephone: (415) 554-6141
FAX: (415) 554-6160
Website: http://www.sfgov.org/

City of Austin
Office of the City Manager
City Hall
301 West 2nd Street
3rd Floor
Austin, TX 78701
Telephone: (512) 974-2200
FAX: (512) 974-2833
Website: http://www.ci.austin.tx.us/

City of Beaverton
Office of the Mayor
City Hall
4755 SW Griffith Drive
Beaverton, OR 97005
Telephone: (503) 526-2497
FAX: (503) 526-2479
Website: http://www.beavertonoregon.gov/

City of Boston
Office of the Mayor
1 City Hall Plaza
Boston, MA 02201
Telephone: (617) 635-4500
FAX: (617) 635-3496
Website: http://www.cityofboston.gov/

City of Boulder
Office of the City Manager
Municipal Building
1777 Broadway, 2nd Floor
Boulder, CO 80306
Telephone: (303) 441-3090
FAX: (303) 441-4478
Website: http://www.ci.boulder.co.us/

City of Chicago
Office of the Mayor
City Hall
121 North LaSalle Street
Room 507
Chicago, IL 60602

Telephone: (312) 744-6670
FAX: (312) 744-8045
Website: http://www.egoc.cityofchicago.org/

City of Cincinnati
Office of the City Manager
City Hall
801 Plum Street
Room 152
Cincinnati, OH 45202
Telephone: (513) 352-3243
FAX: (513) 352-6284
Website: http://www.cincinnati-oh.gov/

City of Duxbury
(See Metropolitan Area Planning Council)

City of Hayward
Office of the City Manager
City Hall
4th Floor
777 "B" Street
Hayward, CA 94541
Telephone: (510) 583-4305
FAX: (510) 583-3601
Website: http://www.ci.hayward.ca.us/

City of Houston
Office of the Mayor
City Hall Annex
900 Bagby Street
Houston, TX 77002
Telephone: (713) 247-2200
FAX: (713) 247-2710
Website: http://www.cityofhouston.gov/

City of Kansas City
Office of the City Manager
City Hall
414 East 12 Street
29th Floor
Kansas City, MO 64106
Telephone: (816) 513-1408
FAX: (816) 513-1363
Website: http://www.kcmo.org/

City of Los Angeles
Office of the City Administrative Officer
City Hall
200 North Main Street
Suite 1500
Los Angeles, CA 90012
Telephone: (213) 485-2886
FAX: (213) 978-0656
Website: http://www.lacity.org/

City of Madison
Office of the Mayor
City Hall
210 Martin Luther King Jr. Boulevard
Room 403
Madison, WI 53703
Telephone: (608) 266-4611
FAX: (608) 267-8671
Website: http://www.ci.madison.wi.us/

City of Minneapolis
Office of the Mayor
City Hall
350 South 5th Street
Room 331
Minneapolis, MN 55415
Telephone: (612) 673-2100
FAX: (612) 673-2305
Website: http://www.ci.minneapolis.mn.us/

City of Mountain View
Office of the City Manager
City Hall
500 Castro Street
Mountain View, CA 94041
Telephone: (650) 903-6301
FAX: (650) 962-0384
Website: http://www.ci.mtnview.ca.us/

City of Nagano
(See Nagano City)

City of New Bedford
Office of the Mayor
City Hall
133 William Street
New Bedford, MA 02740
Telephone: (508) 979-1410
FAX: (508) 991-6189
Website: http://www.ci.new-bedford.ma.us/

City of New York
(See New York City)

City of Oakland
Office of the City Administrator
City Hall
One City Hall Plaza
3rd Floor
Oakland, CA 94612
Telephone: (510) 238-3301
FAX: (510) 238-2223
Website: http://www.oaklandnet.com/

City of Orlando
Office of the Chief Administrative Officer

City Hall
400 South Orange Avenue
3rd Floor
Orlando, FL 32802
Telephone: (407) 246-2226
FAX: (407) 246-3342
Website: http://www.cityoforlando.net/

City of Palo Alto
Office of the City Manager
City Hall
250 Hamilton Avenue
7th Floor
Palo Alto, CA 94301
Telephone: (650) 329-2392
FAX: (650) 325-5025
Website: http://www.cityofpaloalto.org/

City of Petaluma
Office of the City Manager
City Hall
11 English Street
Petaluma, CA 94952
Telephone: (707) 778-4345
FAX: (707) 778-4419
Website: http://cityofpetaluma.net/

City of Portland
Office of the Chief Administrative Officer
City Hall
1221 SW 4th Avenue
Room 110
Portland, OR 97204
Telephone: (503) 823-4000
FAX: (503) 823-5384
Website: http://www.portlandonline.com/

City of St. Louis
Office of the Mayor
City Hall
1200 Market Street
St. Louis, MO 63103
Telephone: (314) 622-3201
FAX: (314) 622-4061
Website: http://stlouis.missouri.org/

City of Salt Lake
(See Salt Lake City)

City of San Carlos
Office of the City Manager
City Hall
600 Elm Street
San Carlos, CA 94070
Telephone: (650) 802-4228

FAX: (650) 595-6728
Website: http://www.ci.san-carlos.ca.us/

City of San Diego
Office of the City Manager
City Hall
202 "C" Street
Room MS9A
San Diego, CA 92101
Telephone: (619) 236-6363
FAX: (619) 236-6067
Website: http://www.sandiego.gov/

City of San Francisco
(See City and County of San Francisco)

City of Santa Monica
Office of the City Manager
City Hall
1685 Main Street
Room 209
Santa Monica, CA 90401
Telephone: (310) 458-8301
FAX: (310) 458-1621
Website: http://pen.ci.santa-monica.ca.us/

City of Seattle
Office of the Mayor
City Hall
600 – 4th Avenue
12th Floor
Seattle, WA 98104
Telephone: (206) 684-4000
FAX: (206) 684-5360
Website: http://www.ci.seattle.wa.us/

City of Toronto
Office of the Chief Administrative Officer
City Hall
100 Queen Street West
11 Floor East Tower
Toronto, Ontario M5H 2N2
Canada
Telephone: (416) 397-5707
FAX: (416) 395-6440
Website: http://www.city.toronto.on.ca/

City of Trenton
Office of the Mayor
City Hall
319 East State Street
Trenton, NJ 08608
Telephone: (609) 989-3030
FAX: (609) 989-4260
Website: http://www.ci.trenton.nj.us/

City of West Palm Beach
Office of the Mayor
City Hall
200 – 2nd Street
West Palm Beach, FL 33401
Telephone: (561) 822-1400
FAX: (561) 659-8026
Website: http://www.cityofwpb.com/

County of Dane
(See Dane County)

County of Hamilton
(See Hamilton County)

County of Los Angeles
Office of the Chief Administrative Officer
Kenneth Hahn Hall of Administration
500 West Temple Street
Room 713
Los Angeles, CA 90012
Telephone: (213) 974-1101
FAX: (213) 687-7130
Website: http://lacounty.info/

County of Montgomery
(See Montgomery County)

County of St. Louis
(See St. Louis County)

County of San Francisco
(See City and County of San Francisco)

Dane County
Office of the County Executive
City County Building
210 Martin Luther King Jr. Boulevard
Room 421
Madison, WI 53703
Telephone: (608) 266-4114
FAX: (608) 266-2643
Website: http://www.countyofdane.com/

Denver
(See City and County of Denver)

Denver Regional Transportation District
(See Regional Transportation District —
Denver)

Department of Transportation
State of New Jersey
Office of the Commissioner
Administrative Offices
1035 Parkway Avenue
Trenton, NJ 08625

Telephone: (609) 530-3536
FAX: (609) 530-3841
Website: http://www.state.nj/transportation/

District of Columbia
(See Washington, DC)

Duxbury
(See Metropolitan Area Planning Council)

Florida Power & Light Company
Office of the Director of Fleet Management
P.O. Box 025576
Miami, FL 33102
Telephone: (800) 432-6554
FAX: (561) 691-3092
Website: http://www.fpl.com/

Georgetown University
Office of the President
204 Healy Hall
37th and "O" Streets, NW
Washington, DC 20057
Telephone: (202) 687-4134
FAX: (202) 687-6660
Website: http://www.georgetown.edu/

Greater London Authority
Office of the Mayor
City Hall
The Queen's Walk
London SE1 2AA
United Kingdom
Telephone: 020-7983-4100
FAX: 020-7983-4057
Website: http://www.london.gov.uk/

Hamilton County
Office of the County Administrator
138 East Court Street
Room 603
Cincinnati, OH 45202
Telephone: (513) 946-4400
FAX: (513) 946-4444
Website: http://www.hamiltoncountyohio.
  gov/

Hayward
(See City of Hayward)

Houston
(See City of Houston)

Kansas City
(See City of Kansas City)

London
(See Greater London Authority
  and Transport for London)

Los Angeles
(See City of Los Angeles
  and County of Los Angeles)

LYMMO (Bus Rapid Transit)
(See Central Florida Regional
  Transportation Authority)

Madison
(See City of Madison)

**Madison Area Metropolitan
  Planning Organization**
Office of the Transportation Planning
  Manager
121 S. Pinckney Street
Suite 400
Madison, WI 53703
Telephone: (608) 266-4336
FAX: (608) 261-9967
Website: http://www.madisonareampo.org/

METRO, Portland Area
Office of the Chief Operating Officer
600 NE Grand Avenue
Portland, OR 97232
Telephone: (503) 797-1541
FAX: (503) 797-1793
Website: http://www.metro-region.org/

Metropolitan Area Express (MAX)
(See Tri-County Metropolitan
  Transportation District)

Metropolitan Area Planning Council
(Serving the Greater Boston Metropolitan
  Area)
Office of the Executive Director
60 Temple Place
Boston, MA 02111
Telephone: (617) 451-2770
FAX: (617) 482-7185
Website: http://www.mapc.org/

**Metropolitan Bay Transportation
  Authority (MBTA)**
Office of the General Manager
45 High Street
9th Floor
Boston, MA 02110
Telephone: (617) 222-5000

FAX: (617) 222-3340
Website: http://www.mbta.com/

Metropolitan Council
Office of the Executive Director
Mears Park Center
230 East 5th Street
St. Paul, MN 55101
Telephone: (651) 602-1000
FAX: (651) 602-1358
Website: http://www.metrocouncil.org/

Metropolitan Rail Authority (METRA)
Office of the Executive Director
Administration Building
547 W. Jackson Boulevard
13th Floor
Chicago, IL 60661
Telephone: (312) 322-6777
FAX: (312) 322-6511
Website: http://metrail.com/

Minneapolis
(See City of Minneapolis)

Montgomery County
Office of the County Executive
Executive Office Building
101 Monroe Street
Rockville, MD 20850
Telephone: (240) 777-2500
FAX: (240) 777-2517
Website: http://www.montgomerycountymd.
  gov/

Mountain View
(See City of Mountain View)

Nagano City
Office of the Chairman
City Hall
1613 Midori-cho
Nagano City 380-8512
Japan
Telephone: 81-(0)26-226-4911
FAX: 81-(0)26-224-5100
Website: http://www.city.nagano.nagano.
  jp/english/index-e.htm

New Bedford
(See City of New Bedford)

New Jersey Department of Transportation
(See Department of Transportation, State of
  New Jersey)

New Jersey Port Authority
(See Port Authority of New York
  & New Jersey)

New York City
Office of the Mayor
City Hall
31 Chambers Street
New York, NY 10007
Telephone: (212) 788-3000
FAX: (212) 788-2460
Website: http://www.nyc.gov/

New York Port Authority
(See Port Authority of New York
  & New Jersey)

Oakland
(See City of Oakland)

Oakland Transit District
(See Bay Area Rapid Transit District)

Orlando
(See City of Orlando)

Palo Alto
(See City of Palo Alto)

Petaluma
(See City of Petaluma)

Port Authority of New York & New Jersey
Office of the Executive Director
225 Park Avenue South
18th Floor
New York, NY 10003
Telephone: (212) 435-7000
FAX: (212) 435-7827
Website: http://www.panynj.gov/

Portland
(See City of Portland and METRO, Portland
  Area)

Puget Sound Regional Council
Office of the Executive Director
1011 Western Avenue
Suite 500
Seattle, WA 98104
Telephone: (206) 464-7090
FAX: (206) 587-4825
Website: http://www.psrc.org/

Rapid Transit — San Francisco Bay Area
(See Bay Area Rapid Transit District —
  BART)

**Regional Transportation District —
  Denver**
Office of the Executive Manager
1600 Blake Street
Denver, CO 80202
Telephone: (303) 628-9000
FAX: (303) 299-2312
Website: http://www.rtd-denver.com/

St. Louis
(See City of St. Louis)

St. Louis County
Office of the County Executive
Administration Building
41 South Central Avenue
9th Floor
Clayton, MO 63105
Telephone: (314) 615-7016
FAX: (314) 427-0384
Website: http://www.co.st-louis.mo.us/

Salt Lake City
Office of the Mayor
City Hall
451 South State Street
Salt Lake City, UT 84111
Telephone: (801) 535-7704
FAX: (801) 535-7681
Website: http://www.ci.slc.ut.us/

San Carlos
(See City of San Carlos)

San Diego
(See City of San Diego)

San Francisco
(See City and County of San Francisco)

Santa Monica
(See City of Santa Monica)

Seattle
(See City of Seattle)

**STAR (Suburban Transit Access Route)
  Line**
(See METRA)

Toronto
(See City of Toronto)

Transport for London
Office of the Commissioner
Empress State Building
Lillie Street
23rd Floor
London SW6 1TR
United Kingdom
Telephone: 020-7222-5600
FAX: 020-7649-9121
Website: http://www.tfl.gov.uk/

Trenton
(See City of Trenton)

**Tri-County Metropolitan Transportation
  District**
Office of the General Manager
TriMet Administrative Offices
4012 SE 17th Avenue
Portland, OR 97202
Telephone: (503) 962-7505
FAX: (503) 962-6451
Website: http://www.trimet.org/

Valencia
(See County of Los Angeles)

Washington, DC
District Municipal Government
Office of the City Administrator
John A. Wilson Building
1350 Pennsylvania Avenue, NW
Suite 301 and 302
Washington, DC 20004
Telephone: (202) 727-6053
FAX: (202) 727-9878
Website: http://www.dc.gov/

**Washington Metropolitan Area Transit
  Authority (WMATA)**
Office of the General Manager/CEO
Administrative Offices
600 Fifth Street, NW
Washington, DC 20001
Telephone: (202) 962-1234
FAX: (202) 962-2722
Website: http://www.wmata.com/

West Palm Beach
(See City of West Palm Beach)

National Resource Directory

Major national professional associations and research organizations serving public officials, as well as concerned professionals and citizens, are listed below in alphabetical order. Many of these organizations focus on various issues related to both public and private transportation.

Alliance for a New Transportation Charter
1100 – 17th Street, NW
10th Floor
Washington, DC 20036
Telephone: (202) 466-2636
FAX: (202) 466-2247
Website: http://www.antc.net/

Alliance for National Renewal
c/o National Civic League
1319 "F" Street, NW
Suite 204
Washington, DC 20004
Telephone: (202) 783-2961
FAX: (202) 347-2161
Website: http://www.ncl.org/anr/

American Association for State Highway & Transportation Officials
444 North Capitol Street, NW
Suite 249
Washington, DC 20001
Telephone: (202) 624-5800
FAX: (202) 624-5806
Website: http://transportation.org/

American Economic Development Council
9801 West Higgins Road
Suite 540
Rosemont, IL 60018
Telephone: (847) 692-9944
FAX: (847) 696-2990
Website: http://www.aedc.org/

American Planning Association
122 South Michigan Avenue
Suite 1600
Chicago, IL 60603
Telephone: (312) 431-9100
FAX: (312) 431-9985
Website: http://www.planning.org/

American Public Transportation Association
1666 "K" Street, NW
Washington, DC 20006
Telephone: (202) 496-4800
FAX: (202) 496-4321
Website: http://www.apta.com/

American Public Works Association
2345 Grand Boulevard
Suite 500
Kansas City, MO 64108
Telephone: (816) 472-6100
FAX: (816) 472-1610
Website: http://www.apwa.net/

American Real Estate and Urban Economics Association
Kelley School of Business
Indiana University
1309 East Tenth Street
Suite 738
Bloomington, IN 47405
Telephone: (812) 855-7794
FAX: (812) 855-8697
Website: http://www.areuea.org/

**American Society for Public
  Administration**
1120 "G" Street, NW
Suite 700
Washington, DC 20005
Telephone: (202) 393-7878
FAX: (202) 638-4952
Website: http://www.aspanet.org/

American Society of Civil Engineers
1801 Alexander Bell Drive
Reston, VA 20191
Telephone: (703) 295-6300
FAX: (703) 295-6222
Website: http://www.asce.org/

Association for Commuter Transportation
1401 Peachtree Street
Suite 440
Atlanta, GA 30309
Telephone: (678) 916-4940
FAX: (678) 244-4151
Website: http://tmi.cob.fsu.edu/act/

**Association of Metropolitan Planning
  Organizations**
1730 Rhode Island Avenue, NW
Suite 608
Washington, DC 20036
Telephone: (202) 296-7051
FAX: (202) 296-7054
Website: http://www.ampo.org/

Best Workplaces for Commuters
c/o U.S. Environmental Protection Agency
1200 Pennsylvania Avenue, NW
Room 64061
Washington, DC 20460
Telephone: (888) 856-3131 (Toll Free)
FAX: (202) 343-2803
Website: http://www.commuterchoice.gov/

**Brownfields and Land Revitalization
  Technology Support Center**
c/o U.S. Environmental Protection Agency
1200 Pennsylvania Avenue, NW
Washington, DC 20460
Telephone: (877) 838-7220 (Toll Free)
FAX: None Listed
Website: http://www.brownfieldstsc.org/

**Building Officials and Code
  Administrators International**
4051 Flossmoor Road
County Club Hills, IL 60478

Telephone: (708) 799-2300
FAX: (708) 799-4981
Website: http://www.bocai.org/

**Center for Compatible Economic
  Development**
7 East Market Street
Suite 210
Leesburg, VA 20176
Telephone: (703) 779-1728
FAX: (703) 779-1746
Website: http://www.cced.org/

Center for Neighborhood Technology
2125 West North Avenue
Chicago, IL 60647
Telephone: (773) 278-4800
FAX: (773) 278-3840
Website: http://www.cnt.org/

Center for Transportation Excellence
4000 Albemarle Street, NW
Suite 303
Washington, DC 20016
Telephone: (202) 244-2405
FAX: (202) 318-1429
Website: http://www.cfte.org/

Committee for Economic Development
477 Madison Avenue
New York, NY 10022
Telephone: (212) 688-2063
FAX: (212) 758-9068
Website: http://www.ced.org/

Community Association Institute
225 Reinekers Lane
Suite 300
Alexandria, VA 22314
Telephone: (703) 548-8600
FAX: (703) 684-1581
Website: http://www.caionline.org/

Community Development
(See Office of Community Development)

**Community Development Society
  International**
1123 North Water Street
Milwaukee, WI 53202
Telephone: (414) 276-7106
FAX: (414) 276-7704
Website: http://www.comm-dev.org/

**Community Transportation Association
  of America**

1341 "G" Street, NW
10th Floor
Washington, DC 20005
Telephone: (202) 628-1480
FAX: (202) 737-9197
Website: http://www.ctaa.org/

Congress for New Urbanism
The Marquette Building
140 South Dearborn Avenue
Suite 310
Chicago, IL 60603
Telephone: (312) 551-7300
FAX: (312) 346-3323
Website: http://www.cnu.org/

**Council for Urban Economic
Development**
1730 "K" Street, NW
Suite 700
Washington, DC 20006
Telephone: (202) 223-4735
FAX: (202) 223-4745
Website: http://www.cued.org/

**Council of University Transportation
Centers**
c/o American Road & Transportation
Builders Association
1219 – 28th Street, NW
Washington, DC 20007
Telephone: (202) 289-4434 (Ext. 106)
FAX: (202) 289-4435
Website: http://cutc.tamu.edu/

Department of Transportation
(See U.S. Department of Transportation)

**Downtown Development and Research
Center**
215 Park Avenue South
New York, NY 10003
Telephone: (212) 228-0246
FAX: (212) 228-0376
Website: http://www.DowntownDevelopment.
com

Environmental Protection Agency
(See U.S. Environmental Protection Agency)

Federal Highway Administration
c/o U.S. Department of Transportation
400 Seventh Street, NW
Washington, DC 20590
Telephone: (202) 366-0660

FAX: (202) 366-9981
Website: http://ops.fhwa.dot.gov/

Federal Transit Administration
c/o U.S. Department of Transportation
400 Seventh Street, NW
Washington, DC 20590
Telephone: (202) 366-4033
FAX: (202) 296-9445
Website: http://www.fta.dot.gov/

Housing and Urban Development
(See U.S. Department of Housing and
Urban Development)

Institute of Transportation Engineers
1099 – 14th Street, NW
Suite 300 West
Washington, DC 20005
Telephone: (202) 289-0222
FAX: (202) 289-7722
Website: http://www.ite.org/

**Intelligent Transportation Society
of America**
1100 – 17th Street, NW
Suite 1200
Washington, DC 20036
Telephone: (202) 484-4847
FAX: (202) 484-3483
Website: http://www.itsa.org/

**International City/County Management
Association**
777 North Capitol Street, NE
Suite 500
Washington, DC 20002
Telephone: (202) 289-4262
FAX: (202) 962-3500
Website: http://www.icma.org/

**International Conference of Building
Officials**
5360 South Workman Mill Road
Whittier, CA 90601
Telephone: (310) 699-0541
FAX: (310) 699-3853
Website: http://www.icbo.org/

International Downtown Association
190 – 17th Street, NW
Suite 210
Washington, DC 20006
Telephone: (202) 293-4505
FAX: (202) 293-4509
Website: http://www.ida-downtown.org/

International Transportation Management Association
P.O. Box 924146
Houston, TX 77292
Telephone: (713) 747-4909
FAX: (713) 747-5330
Website: http://itma-houston.org/

Joint Center for Sustainable Communities
(See National Association of Counties)

Local Government Commission
1414 "K" Street
Suite 250
Sacramento, CA 95814
Telephone: (916) 448-1198
FAX: (916) 448-8246
Website: http://www.lgc.org/

Main Street Center
(See National Main Street Center)

National Association of Counties
Joint Center for Sustainable Communities
440 First Street, NW
Washington, DC 20001
Telephone: (202) 393-6226
FAX: (202) 393-2630
Website: http://www.naco.org/

National Association for Environmental Management
1612 "K" Street, NW
Suite 1102
Washington, DC 20006
Telephone: (202) 986-6616
FAX: (202) 530-4408
Website: http://www.naem.org/

National Association of Development Organizations
444 North Capitol Street, NW
Washington, DC 20001
Telephone: (202) 624-7806
FAX: (202) 624-8813
Website: http://www.nado.org/

National Association of Housing and Redevelopment Officials
630 Eye Street, NW
Washington, DC 20001
Telephone: (202) 289-3500
FAX: (202) 289-8181
Website: http://www.nahro.org/

National Association of Regional Councils
1666 Connecticut Avenue, NW
Suite 300
Washington, DC 20009
Telephone: (202) 986-1032
FAX: (202) 986-1038
Website: http://www.narc.org/

National Association of State Development Agencies
730 First Street, NE
Suite 710
Washington, DC 20002
Telephone: (202) 898-1302
FAX: (202) 898-1312
Website: http://www.ids.net/nasda/

National Association of Towns and Townships
444 North Capitol Street, NW
Suite 294
Washington, DC 20001
Telephone: (202) 624-3500
FAX: (202) 624-3554
Website: http://www.natat.org/

National Center for the Revitalization of Central Cities
College of Urban and Public Affairs
University of New Orleans
New Orleans, LA 70148
Telephone: (504) 280-6519
FAX: (504) 280-6272
Website: http://www.uno.edu/-cupa/ncrcc

National Civic League
1445 Market Street
Suite 300
Denver, CO 80202
Telephone: (303) 571-4343
FAX: (303) 571-4404
Website: http://www.ncl.org/

National Community Development Association
522 – 21st Street, NW
Washington, DC 20006
Telephone: (202) 293-7587
FAX: (202) 887-5546
Website: http://www.ncdaonline.org/

National Congress for Community Economic Development
1030 – 15th Street, NW

Washington, DC 20005
Telephone: (202) 289-9020
FAX: (202) 289-7051
Website: http://www.ncced.org/

**National Council for Urban
    Economic Development**
1730 "K" Street, NW
Washington, DC 20006
Telephone: (202) 223-4735
FAX: (202) 223-4745
Website: http://www.cued.org/

National League of Cities
1301 Pennsylvania Avenue, NW
Washington, DC 20004
Telephone: (202) 626-3000
FAX: (202) 626-3043
Website: http://www.nlc.org/

National Main Street Center
c/o National Trust for Historic Preservation
1785 Massachusetts Avenue, NW
Washington, DC 20036
Telephone: (202) 588-6219
FAX: (202) 588-6050
Website: http://www.nthp.org/

**National Trust for Historic
    Preservation**
(See National Main Street Center)

New Urbanism
(See Congress of New Urbanism)

Office of Community Development
U.S. Department of Agriculture
Whitten Building
Washington, DC 20250
Telephone: (202) 720-3621
FAX: (202) 720-5043
Website:
http://www.ocdweb.sc.egov.usda.gov/

Partners for Livable Communities
1429 – 21st Street, NW
Washington, DC 20036
Telephone: (202) 887-5990
FAX: (202) 466-4845
Website: http://www.livable.com/

Partnership for Regional Livability
2125 W. North Avenue
Chicago, IL 60647
Telephone: (773) 278-4800 (Ext. 135)

FAX: (773) 278-3840
Website: http://www.pfrl.org/

Trust for Historic Preservation
(See National Main Street Center)

United States Conference of Mayors
1620 Eye Street, NW
Washington, DC 20006
Telephone: (202) 293-7330
FAX: (202) 293-2352
Website: http://www.usmayors.org/

U.S. Department of Agriculture
(See Office of Community Development)

**U.S. Department of Housing and
    Urban Development**
451 – 7th Street, NW
Washington, DC 20410
Telephone: (202) 708-1112
FAX: (202) 401-0416
Website: http://www.hud.gov/

U.S. Department of Transportation
(Also See Federal Highway Administration
    and Federal Transit Administration)

U.S. Department of Transportation
(ISTEA & TEA 21 Program Information)
400 Seventh Street, NW
Washington, DC 20590
Telephone: (202) 366-2332
FAX: (202) 366-9634
Website: http://www.dot.gov/

U.S. Environmental Protection Agency
Ariel Rios Building
1200 Pennsylvania Avenue, NW
Washington, DC 20460
Telephone: (202) 272-0167
FAX: None Listed.
Website: http://www.epa.gov/

**Urban and Regional Information
    Systems Association**
1460 Renaissance Drive
Suite 305
Park Ridge, IL 60068
Telephone: (847) 824-6300
FAX: (847) 824-6363
Website: http://www.uli.org/

The Urban Institute
2100 "M" Street, NW
Washington, DC 20037

Telephone: (202) 833-7200
FAX: (202) 331-9747
Website: http://www.urban.org/

Urban Land Institute
1015 Thomas Jefferson Street, NW

Suite 500 West
Washington, DC 20007
Telephone: (202) 624-7000
FAX: (202) 624-7140
Website: http://www.uli.org/

About the Editor
and Contributors

Editor

Roger L. Kemp has been a city manager on both the West and East Coasts for more than two decades. Dr. Kemp has also been an adjunct professor over the years at the University of California, Rutgers University, Golden Gate University, and the University of Connecticut. He holds a B.S. degree in business administration, both M.P.A. and M.B.A. degrees, and a Ph.D. degree in public administration, and is a graduate of the Program for Senior Executives in State and Local Government, John F. Kennedy School of Government, Harvard University. He has written and edited numerous articles and books on various topics related to America's cities during his career.

Contributors

Affiliations are as of the times the articles were written.

Ronald Adams, Technology-Assessment Consultant, New York, New York.

Craig Amundsen, Principal of Urban Design, URS Architects, Minneapolis, Minnesota.

Jonathan Barnett, FAIA, FAICP, Professor of City and Regional Planning and Director of the Urban Design Program, The University of Pennsylvania, Philadelphia, Pennsylvania; and Principal, Wallace Roberts & Todd, LLC, Philadelphia, Pennsylvania.

Nancy Bragado, Acting General Plan Program Manager, Planning Department, City of San Diego, San Diego, California.

Terry Brewer, Freelance Writer and Independent Management Consultant, New York, New York.

Pam Broviak, Senior Technical Editor, *Public Works*, Hanley Wood, Washington, DC.

Dan Burden, Executive Director, Walkable Communities, Inc., Orlando, Florida.

Zia Burleigh, Transportation Project Manager, International City/Council Management Association, Washington, DC.

Committee on Intelligent Transport, World Road Association (PIARC), Cedex, France.

Pete Costello, Project Manager, PBS&J, Orlando, Florida.

Roger Courtenay, Principal, EDAW, Alexandria, Virginia.

Michael Davidson, Research Associate, Research Department, American Planning Association, Chicago, Illinois.

Patrick DeCorla-Souza, Team Leader, Office of Policy, Federal Highway Administration, Washington, DC.

Rosalyn P. Doggett, Senior Development Specialist, Washington Metropolitan Area Transit Authority, Washington, DC.

John W. Dorsett, Principal, Walker Parking Consultants, Indianapolis, Indiana.

Robert T. Dunphy, Senior Director for Transportation, Urban Land Institute, Washington, DC.

Clair Enlow, Freelance Writer and Columnist, *Seattle Daily Journal of Commerce*, Seattle, Washington.

John Fernandez, Director of Information Services, Department of Community Planning and Development, City of Boulder, Boulder, CO.

Lawrence D. Frank, Assistant Professor of City Planning, Georgia Institute of Technology, Atlanta, Georgia.

Pamela Freese, Ph.D. Candidate in Urban Planning and Public Policy, University of Illinois at Chicago, Chicago, Illinois.

Rob Gurwitt, Staff Correspondent, *Governing*, Congressional Quarterly Inc., Washington, DC.

Brian Heaton, Communications Specialist, League of California Cities, Sacramento, California.

Glen Hiemstra, Professional Speaker, Writer, and Consultant, Kirkland, Washington.

Libby Howland, Freelance Editor and Writer, Tacoma Park, Maryland.

Sean Kilcarr, Senior Editor, *Fleet Owner*, PRIMEDIA Business Magazines & Media, Overland Park, Kansas.

Steven Kleinrock, Design Principal, Einhorn, Yaffee, and Prescott, Washington, DC.

Ruth Eckdish Knack, Executive Director, Planning, Bay Area Rapid Transit District, Oakland, California (1995, 1997); and Executive Editor, *Planning*, American Planning Association, Chicago, Illinois.

Steven Lagerfeld, Deputy Editor, *The Wilson Quarterly*, Woodrow Wilson International Center, Washington, DC.

Terry J. Lassar, Communications Consultant, Portland, Oregon.

Charles Lockwood, Freelance Writer, Topanga, California.

Marcia D. Lowe, Senior Researcher, Worldwatch Institute, Washington, DC.

Alex Marshall, Freelance Writer and Senior Fellow, Regional Plan Association, New York, NY.

Bruce D. McDowell, Director of Government Policy Research, U.S. Advisory Commission on Intergovernmental Relations, Washington, DC.

Alvin R. McNeal, Manager of Property Planning and Development, Washington Metropolitan Area Transit Authority, Washington, DC.

Jim Miara, Freelance Writer, Needham, Massachusetts.

Adam Millard-Ball, Principal, Nelson/Nygaard Consulting Associates, San Francisco, California.

Parviz Mokhtari, Director, Department of Public Works, City of San Carlos, San Carlos, California.

William Murphy, Graduate Student in Civil Engineering, University of Washington, Seattle, Washington.

Sam Newberg, Research Analyst, Maxfield Research, Minneapolis, Minnesota.

Elaine Robbins, former Executive Editor of *Texas Parks and Wildlife*, is a Freelance Writer and Editor, Austin, Texas.

Corrina Stellitano, Freelance Writer, Mobile, Alabama.

Christopher Swope, Staff Writer, *Governing*, Congressional Quarterly Inc., Washington, DC.

Laura Thompson, Planner, Bay Trail Project, Association of Bay Area Governments, Oakland, California.

Emanuel Tobier, Senior Fellow, Taub Urban Research Center, New York University, New York, New York.

Jeffrey Tumlin, Principal, Nelson/Nygaard Consulting Associates, San Francisco, California.

Ernesto M. Vasquez, Vice President and Managing Partner, McLarand Vasquez Emsiek & Partners, Oakland and Irvine, California.

Jay H. Walder, Managing Director, Finance and Planning, Transport for London, London, England, United Kingdom.

Janet Ward, Associate Publisher and Editor, *American City & County*, Intertec Publishing Corporation, Atlanta, Georgia.

Index